INTERNETWORK MOBILITY
The CDPD Approach

**Prentice Hall Series in
Computer Networking and Distributed Systems**
Radia Perlman, editor

Kaufman, Perlman, and Speciner	*Network Security:* *Private Communications in a Public World*
Taylor, Waung, and Banan	*Internetwork Mobility:* *The CDPD Approach*

INTERNETWORK MOBILITY
The CDPD Approach

Mark S. Taylor
William Waung
Mohsen Banan

To join a Prentice Hall PTR internet mailing list, point to:
http://www.prenhall.com/register

Prentice Hall PTR
Upper Saddle River, NJ 07458
http://www.prenhall.com

Library of Congress Cataloging-in-Publication Data

Taylor, Mark S.
    Internetwork mobility : the CDPD approach / Mark S. Taylor
  William Waung, Mohsen Banan.
        p.   cm. -- (Prentice Hall series in computer networking and distributed systems)
    Includes bibliographical references and index.
    ISBN 0-13-209693-5
    1. CDPD (Standard) 2. Wide area networks (Computer networks)
  3. Internetworking (Telecommunication) 4. Mobile communication
  systems   I. Waung, William. II. Banan, Mohsen. III. Title
  IV. Series.
  TK5103.48.T38 1996
  004.6'7--dc20   96-29175
                                      CIP

Acquisitions editor: Mary Franz
Editorial/production supervision: Craig Little
Manufacturing manager: Alexis R. Heydt
Cover design: Anthony Gemmellaro
Cover illustration: Thomas Post
Cover design director: Jerry Votta
Page layout/formatting: Bear Mountain Type

© 1997 Prentice Hall P T R
Prentice-Hall, Inc.
A Simon & Schuster Company
Upper Saddle River, NJ 07458

The publisher offers discounts on this book when ordered in bulk quantities. For more information, contact:

  Corporate Sales Department / Prentice Hall P T R
  1 Lake Street
  Upper Saddle River, New Jersey 07458
  Phone: 800-382-3419
  FAX: 201-236-7141
  E-mail: corpsales@prenhall.com

Printed in the United States of America

10 9 8 7 6 5 4 3 2 1

ISBN 0-13-209693-5

Prentice-Hall International (UK) Limited, *London*
Prentice-Hall of Australia Pty. Limited, *Sydney*
Prentice-Hall of Canada, Inc., *Toronto*
Prentice-Hall Hispanoamericana S.A., *Mexico*
Prentice-Hall of India Private Limited, *New Delhi*
Prentice-Hall of Japan, Inc., *Tokyo*
Simon & Schuster Asia Pte. Ltd., *Singapore*
Editora Prentice-Hall do Brasil, Ltda., *Rio de Janeiro*

Contents

List of Figures

Preface

This book discusses user mobility in a *wide area network* (*WAN*) environment. In this discussion, a mobile data device is one which can receive WAN services from essentially any location without requiring any special actions by the user of the device. User mobility is described in the context of the *Cellular Digital Packet Data* (*CDPD*) standard, in whose development we actively participated.

Two trends provide a backdrop for this subject matter. The first of these is the rapid growth of the Internet.[1] Both in terms of numbers of users and traffic, this growth has been nothing short of phenomenal. What was once strictly the domain of computer scientists, engineers, and university students has now become headline news. Censorship of the World Wide Web is now discussed by politicians and URLs[2] are commonly displayed in advertisements.

The popularity of the Internet reflects a change in the media of choice for people wishing to communicate. Electronic mail (email) allows the thoughtfulness of a letter while providing the potential immediacy of the telephone. Complex ideas can be conveyed in an organized manner, then further developed by the receiving party. Several rounds of a discussion can take place in a matter of minutes, quickly resolving issues that might be difficult to present orally. The CDPD specification itself was rapidly developed by remote parties largely via email discussion.

The second trend is that of mobile communications. The cellular industry is experiencing explosive growth, with over 32 million subscribers in North America at year-end 1995. The paging industry has also experienced rapid growth; the advent of new two-way messaging services is likely to extend that growth in the face of competition from low cost (to the subscriber) mobile cellular handsets.

The next step in this evolution of communications is that of mobile data communications. Mobile data usage is expected to grow from its original 200,000 subscribers in 1990, past its 1.1

---

1. In this book we use the convention of ("big I") "Internet," meaning the worldwide interconnection of networks. We use ("little i") "internet" to mean either an internetwork (collection of networks) or a protocol suite (typified by TCP/IP).
2. A *URL* or *Universal Resource Location* is an address used to access information on the World Wide Web.

million subscribers in mid 1995, to roughly 5.2 million subscribers in 2000.[3] Several technology developments, aimed at mobile data communications, are in various stages of progress or completion.

The Mobile IP Task Force of the IETF[4] has been addressing the requirements for mobility in data communications. Their charter is to define the protocols necessary for a correspondent to send and receive data anywhere. The media to be used is unspecified. Presumably, a person in the future will be able to find an Internet "socket" in the wall of a hotel room as easily as they currently find electrical outlets. However, many "real world" considerations, such as usage accounting, remain unaddressed by this group.

The RAM and Ardis mobile data services, supported by RadioMail, provide gateway connections between proprietary radio technology and the Internet or other wide area networks. However, the need to port applications to nonstandard proprietary mobile devices and APIs limits the generality and user adoption of these service offerings.

Rather than using gateways between proprietary radio technology and the Internet, CDPD defines an open standard that allows mobile devices to be as directly accessible as any other IP host. Standard APIs allow the immediate use of current data applications, such as email, on mobile devices. We have done this many times.

This book is intended to complement the CDPD specification but not replace it. Our emphasis is on the data networking aspects of CDPD and its solution to the mobility challenges. CDPD is a data network which happens to have an RF-based data link resembling a low-speed Ethernet. The fixed end of the radio link, called the *Mobile Data Base Station,* or *MDBS,* is little more than a LAN hub from a data networking perspective.

This book is clearly focused on CDPD as the pre-eminent wide area mobile data solution. We don't apologize for our bias—we were highly involved in the creation of CDPD. However, no system or technology lasts forever; one of our design goals was that CDPD be readily amenable to evolution. CDPD is much more than an airlink—it is an architecture that supports host mobility over a wide area.

The chapters that follow describe the CDPD solution to the challenges of mobility in wide area networks. A discussion of mobility (of which wirelessness is a special case) is followed by a summary of cellular technology, an overview of CDPD, a description of CDPD architecture and how it supports mobility, a description of security and other support services provided by CDPD (and needed by *any* public mobile data network!), a survey of other (noncellular) mobile systems, and finally, a discussion of future directions in mobility in the wide area environment. For readers unfamiliar with data networking concepts, a primer on this subject precedes the first chapter.

The target audience for this book is any individual interested in mobile data communications or, more specifically, the rationale behind the design of CDPD. The discussion of technical issues

---

3. Source: Economic and Management Consultants, Inc., estimate [EMCI95].
4. Internet Engineering Task Force

avoids the jargon and abstractions necessary and typical in technical specifications. Because we are not radio engineers, we focus on the system and networking aspects of CDPD, rather than the radio technologies, which are better described elsewhere. Our goal is to explain mobility and CDPD in plain English. Please let us know whether we have succeeded at our goal. Our current email addresses are mark.taylor@airdata.com, wwaung@direct.ca and mohsen@neda.com.

Bellevue, Washington
June 11, 1996

Acknowledgments

We would like to take this opportunity to recognize the other members of the original CDPD specification team: Jim Baichtal, Chris Bennett, Bob Brenner, Jock Embry, Bob Lukas, Pete McConnell and Larry Thomas. Honorable mention for their "unofficial," yet crucial, participation should also go to David Chan, Steve Gardner, Tom Hiller, Tojo and Otto. In the second edition—formally known as Release 1.1—the team was joined by Nick Alfano, George Bumiller, Randy Chapman, Claude Desroches, Keith Knightson, Ken Lee, and Gary Roshak.

The original 1992-93 CDPD specification development effort was funded by seven of the largest North American cellular service providers: Ameritech, Bell Atlantic, GTE, McCaw, Nynex, Pactel, and Southwest Bell. But every high-risk project depends on financial support, which is unconditional in the short term. McCaw Cellular Communications (now AT&T Wireless Services) filled that need; it is unlikely that CDPD would have been created without the active and enthusiastic support of Nick Kauser and Rob Mechaley at McCaw.

We should also mention those people instrumental in the production of this book—Radia Perlman, Mary Franz, Noreen Regina, Craig Little, and our reviewers: Jock Embry, Jim Grams, Bill Haymond, Tom Hiller, David Holmes, Pattabhamiran Krishna, Pete McConnell, Mark McDonald, Radia Perlman, and Carrie Schnelker, who provided many helpful suggestions (unfortunately we must accept full responsibility for any and all inaccuracies and remaining bad jokes!). Many of the figures were created by Betty Taylor of OTTO, Inc. Other figures were adapted from the CDPD specifications, courtesy of the CDPD Forum, Inc.

Most important to us is the support we receive from our wives and families every day. It is to them, and all of the other "CDPD widows and widowers," that this book is dedicated.

Preliminaries

> *Basically, one always gets into trouble trying to define these things*
> *too precisely because they aren't really clean concepts.*
>
> —Radia Perlman, 1996.

This chapter introduces some of the standard data networking terminology and concepts used throughout this book. Those readers already familiar with data networking technology could begin with Chapter 1, which is the *real* first chapter, with no loss of continuity.

Familiarity with the concepts presented in this chapter is important to understanding the issues of mobility and is assumed in the chapters that follow. Topics discussed in this overview include the communications channel, protocols, connection-oriented and connectionless protocols, the OSI reference model and it layers, protocol data units, and networking entities.

This chapter is presented as a survey and is no substitute for the real thing—it is necessarily brief. Many fine texts, such as [STAL93], [PERL92], and [TANN95], are devoted to teaching data networking and cover this subject much more rigorously. Of course, true expertise comes only with study of actual standards documents.

P.1 Basic Data Communication Model

Communication is the conveyance of a *message* from one entity, called the *source* or *transmitter*, to another, called the *destination* or *receiver*, via a *channel*[1] of some sort. A simple example of such a *communication system* is conversation; people commonly exchange verbal messages, with the channel consisting of waves of compressed air molecules at frequencies that are audible to the human ear.[2] This is depicted in Figure P.1.

---

1. "Channel" is one of those words whose meaning varies with the context and the level of "source" and "destination." It could consist of a physical medium or a logical data path.
2. Of course, many messages are conveyed more or less explicitly in the form of body language, in which the channel is the visual medium of electromagnetic radiation, commonly known as reflected light. Difficulties arise when these visual messages conflict with the verbal messages they accompany.

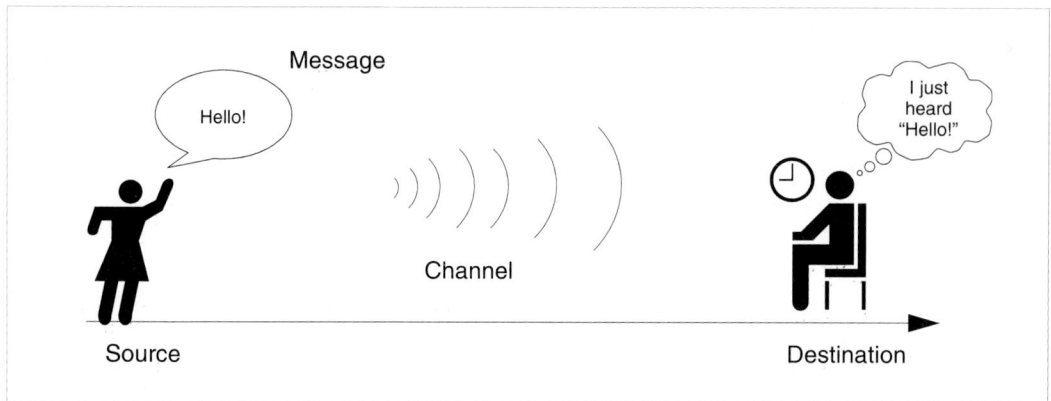

Figure P.1 Basic Communication Model

The conveyance of a message could be followed by a reciprocal *response* message from the original destination (now a source) to the original source (now a destination) to complete one cycle in a *dialogue* between *corresponding entities*. Depending on the application or need for the information exchange, either atomic one-way *transactions* or a two-way dialogue could be appropriate.

The only way that a message source can be certain that the destination properly received the message is by some kind of *acknowledgment* response from the destination. Conversing people might say "I understand" or nod their head in response to a statement made by their peer. This acknowledged form of dialogue is the basis of reliable communication—somehow the source must get feedback that the destination correctly received the message.[3]

P.2 Variations on a Theme

The conveyance of a message could be *direct* between the corresponding entities or it could be *indirect*, with one or more intermediaries participating in the message transport. The presence or absence of an intermediary depends on the definition of the source and destination entities and the

---

3. Correct message reception is one thing, agreement with the message content is another thing entirely. Cultural variances in acknowledgment responses have often led to difficulties in international relationships between people.

channel used to communicate; data communication between entities at one level might be considered to be direct and at another level to be indirect.

Considering the directness or indirectness of the communicating entities simply depends on the relevance of any intermediaries to the discussion. In Figure P.2, the translator is important but should not really be a factor in the communication between the source and destination. Perhaps in a twist on the old parents' saying, a good translator is heard but not seen.

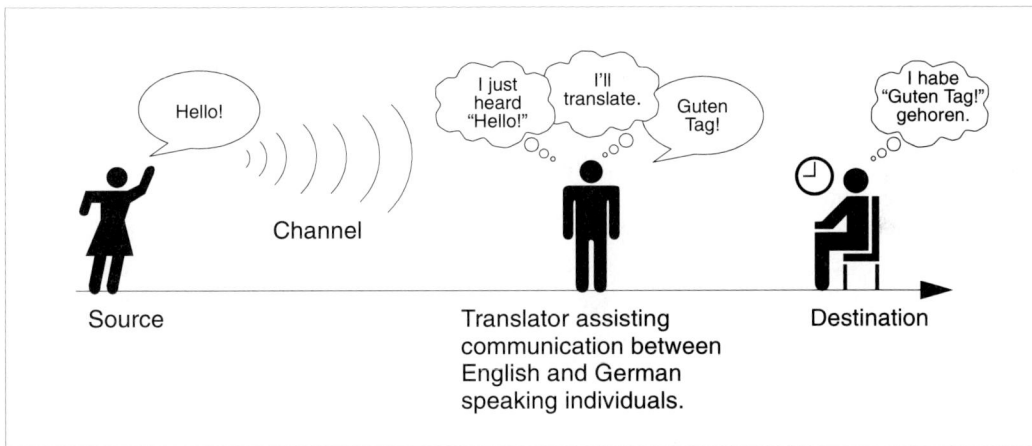

Figure P.2   Indirect Message Conveyance

Communication can be from a source to a single destination, known as *point-to-point* or *unicast*, or to multiple destinations, known as *point-to-multipoint* or *multicast*. A special case of multicast is the conveyance of a message from a source to every possible destination, which is referred to as *broadcast*; the broadcast can be local or global in scope.

The primary difference between multicast and broadcast is that multicast communication is targeted at specific destinations, regardless of location, while broadcast communication is targeted at all possible destinations within the range (location) of the source. Multicast and broadcast communications are typically one-way, "best effort" modes of communication, which are unacknowledged.[4]

---

4. The primary reason for using broadcast and/or multicast communications is to gain channel efficiency by communicating with multiple entities via a single common message. However, the complexity of matching acknowledgments with intended message recipients at the source quickly overrides any efficiencies gained in a reliable multicast scenario. Depending on the number of channels, the number of members in the multicast group, etc., a set of unicast messages might be equally efficient for reliable communications. It really depends on where you want to handle reliability—in the networking technology transporting the message or in the application itself. We'll talk more about reliability later.

Communication can also be described in terms of the relative timeframes of the corresponding entities. Depending on the definitions of source, destination, and channel, the communication could be asynchronous, synchronous, or isochronous.

In *asynchronous* communication, there is a minimal assumed timing relationship between the source and destination. In such a typically *byte-oriented* system, each character or byte is transmitted and received individually as a message. Asynchronous protocols were predominant in the early days of data communications because of limited processing capability and low quality transmission infrastructure.

In *synchronous* communication, the relative bit timing of the source and destination is similar, allowing transmission and reception of relatively large groups of bits in a single message; the source and destination must be "in sync." This *bit-oriented* mode of communication can be much more efficient than asynchronous communications but places requirements on the source (processing), channel (quality), and destination (more processing). Synchronous data communications are predominant today.

Isochronous communication is the extreme case of synchronous communication—source and destination are "in sync" in the absolute sense of real time, allowing continual transmission of bits. An everyday example of isochronous communication is a telephone conversation; if such a conversation occurs across a large distance (such as transatlantic), the delays introduced can be disconcerting because the isochronicity that people are accustomed to has been negatively impacted. Effective isochronous communication depends on both transmission delays, which are inconsequential to the corresponding entities and a consistent high quality transmission.

P.3 The Communications Channel

A communication channel can be *simplex*, in which only one party can transmit, *full-duplex*, in which both correspondents can transmit and receive simultaneously, or *half-duplex*, in which the correspondents alternate between transmitting and receiving states (such as conversing adults). Even though the channel might be capable of supporting full-duplex communication, if the corresponding entities are not capable of transmitting and receiving simultaneously, the communications system will be half-duplex (as in the example of the conversing adults).

Communication between two entities can be considered either in-band or out-of-band, depending on context. *In-band* communication is communication that occurs via the primary channel between the communicating entities. *Out-of-band* communication occurs via an alternative channel, which is not considered to be the primary channel between the entities.

Which channel is primary and which is an alternate depends on context and the existence of an alternative channel. In the case of a conversation between two people, the primary channel could consist of verbal communication while the alternate channel consists of visual body language. Of course, if emotions rise, these two channels might reverse roles, with body language becoming the primary channel!

P.4 Channel Characteristics

A communications channel may be described in terms of its characteristic properties. These *channel characteristics* include *bandwidth* (how much information can be conveyed across the channel in a unit of time, commonly expressed in bits per second or *bps*[5]), *quality* (how reliably can the information be correctly conveyed across the channel, commonly in terms of bit error rate or *BER*[6]), and whether the channel is *dedicated* (to a single source) or *shared* (by multiple sources).

Obviously, a higher bandwidth is usually a good thing in a channel because it allows more information to be conveyed per unit of time. High bandwidths mean that more users can share the channel, depending on their means of accessing it. High bandwidths also allow more demanding applications (such as graphics) to be supported for each user of the channel.

The capability of a channel to be shared depends of course on the medium used. A shared channel could be likened to a school classroom, where multiple students might attempt to simultaneously catch the teacher's attention by raising their hand; the teacher must then arbitrate between these conflicting requests, allowing only one student to speak at a time.

Reliability of communication is obviously important. A low quality channel is prone to distorting the messages it conveys; a high quality channel preserves the integrity of the messages it conveys. Depending on the quality of the channel in use between communicating entities, the probability of the destination correctly receiving the message from the source might be either very high or very low. If the message is received incorrectly, it needs to be retransmitted.

If the probability of receiving a message correctly across a channel is too low, the system (source, channel, message, destination) must include mechanisms that overcome the errors introduced by the low quality channel. Otherwise, no useful communication is possible over that channel. These mechanisms are embodied in the communication protocols employed by the corresponding entities.

The *effective bandwidth* describes what an application experiences and depends on the *quality of service (QOS)* provided by the channel. For example, modems scale back their transmission

---

5. Channel bandwidth is most often expressed in thousands of bits or kilobits per second (kbps) and in millions of bits or megabits per second (Mbps).
6. Channel quality is also measured in terms of block error rate (BLER) and sometimes packet error rate (PER).

speed based largely on their perception of channel quality in order to optimally use the transmission medium.

In general, shared and reliable channels are more resource efficient than those that enjoy neither of these characteristics. Shared channels enjoy greater efficiency than dedicated ones because most data communication is bursty in nature, with long idle periods punctuated by brief message transmissions. Reliable channels are more efficient than unreliable ones because retransmissions are not required as often (because there are fewer transmission-induced errors).

P.5 Communication Protocols

Protocols specify the rules for communicating over a channel, much as one person politely waiting for another to finish before they speak. Protocols coupled with channel characteristics determine the net efficiency of communications over the channel.

Protocols can improve the effective channel quality. An example is an *ARQ (automatic repeat request)* protocol in which a source automatically retransmits a message if it fails to receive an acknowledgment from the destination within some predefined time period following the original transmission of the message. The destination knows whether to acknowledge the message based on some *error detection* capability, which is typically based on redundant information added to the message, such as a *parity code* or *cyclic redundancy check (CRC)*.

Figure P.3 depicts a message ("Pick-up at 1:30 p.m.") being transmitted from a source to a destination via "packets," which contain four characters at a time. Additional redundant information in each packet allows the destination to know whether or not it has received that packet correctly. Once the destination is satisfied that it has correctly received a packet, it sends an acknowledgment ("ack") message to the original packet source. When the source receives the acknowledgment, it may transmit the next packet in sequence. In an ARQ arrangement, failure to receive an acknowledgment within a specific time period causes the source to retransmit the packet that was not acknowledged. Only a single transmitted packet remains outstanding (i.e., unacknowledged) at a time.

Error detection and recovery mechanisms can be much more sophisticated than this simple ARQ scheme. One way to enhance the effective channel performance is to allow multiple packets to be outstanding at a time. Individual packets are assigned a sequence number that reflect their order in a sequence of packets flowing from a specific source to a specific destination, which the allows them to be separately acknowledged or retransmitted in the event of a failure.

This type of *windowing* scheme is commonly used when significant delays are involved in the end-to-end data transmission or when the channel has a relatively high quality. When an individual packet is not received correctly, the destination could request retransmission of either the individual bad packet, called *selective packet rejection*, or that packet plus all succeeding packets. Which of these modes is employed depends on the nature of the communication and the medium used.

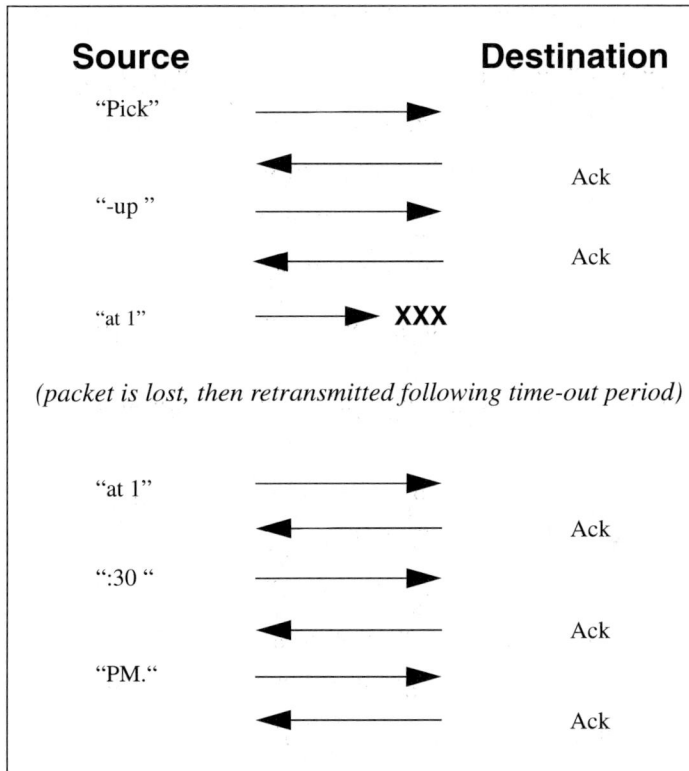

Figure P.3   ARQ Message Acknowledgment

Figure P.4 depicts such a windowing scheme applied to the packet-based transmission example from above, but with each packet individually numbered in sequence. In this example, up to three packets may be outstanding at a time and the destination must notify the host of the next expected packet number, implicitly acknowledging all preceding packets. Unless a *time-out* occurs at the source, it will continue to transmit packets until the *window size* of three outstanding unacknowledged packets is reached. The destination periodically acknowledges all received packets.

Source		Destination
(1) "Pick"	⟶	
(2) "-up "	⟶	
	⟵	Ack (1)
(3) "at 1"	⟶	
(4) ":30 "	⟶	
	⟵	Ack (3)
(5) "PM. "	⟶	
XXX	⟵	Ack (5)

(acknowledgment is lost, packets are retransmitted following time-out period)

(4) ":30 "	⟶	
(5) "PM. "	⟶	
	⟵	Ack (5)

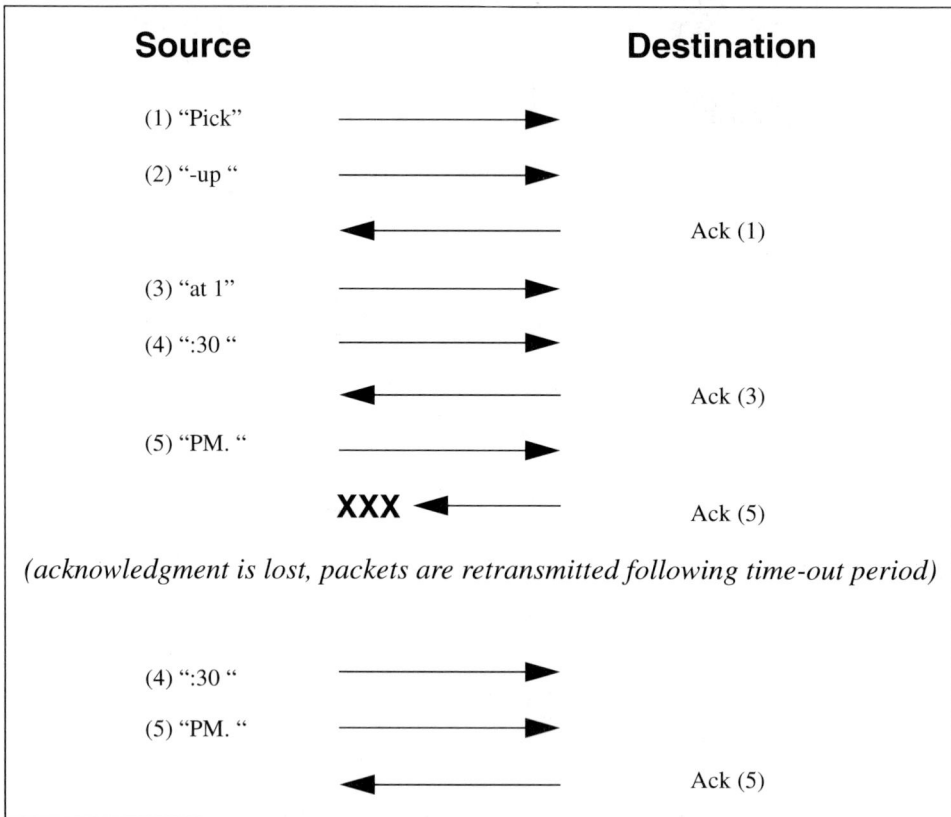

Figure P.4   Windowing-Based Message Acknowledgment

If sufficient redundant information is added to a message, it could enable the receiver of the message to not only detect an error but also correct it. Although this requires some additional processing by the destination, it could obviate the need for retransmission. This error correction capability is generally desirable in channels that are expensive, prone to distortion, or suffer from long latency in the dialogue cycle.

P.6 Connection-Oriented and Connectionless Protocols

Protocols can be either connection-oriented or connectionless in nature. In *connection-oriented* protocols, corresponding entities maintain state information about the dialogue in which they are engaged. This connection state information supports error, sequence and flow control between the corresponding entities. The windowing scheme presented earlier is an example of a connection-oriented protocol.

Error control refers to a combination of error detection (and correction) and acknowledgment sufficient to compensate for any unreliability inherent to the channel. *Sequence control* refers to the ability for each entity to reconstruct a received series of messages in the proper order in which they were intended to be received; this is essential to being able to transmit large files across dynamically-routed mesh networks. *Flow control* refers to the ability for both parties in a dialogue to avoid overrunning their peer with too many messages.

Connection-oriented protocols operate in three phases. The first phase is the *connection setup* phase, during which the corresponding entities establish the connection and negotiate the parameters defining the connection. The second phase is the *data transfer* phase, during which the corresponding entities exchange messages under the auspices of the connection. Finally, the *connection release* phase is when the correspondents "tear down" the connection because it is no longer needed.

An everyday example of a connection-oriented protocol is a telephone call. The call *originator* must first "dial" the destination phone number. The telephony infrastructure must setup the end-to-end circuit, then "power ring" the call *terminator*. From this point on, the connection is in place until one of the parties hangs up. Once the called party answers the phone, another level of connection (between people) must be established before real messages can be exchanged.

Connectionless protocols differ markedly from connection-oriented protocols in that they do not provide the capability for error, sequence and flow control; nor do they have any connection state maintenance requirement. Each message is considered to be independent of all others in a connectionless protocol. Whether or not, or when, a given message is received correctly has no bearing on other messages; somehow the destination must sort things out and make sense of it all. Connectionless protocols are always in the data transfer phase, with no explicit setup or release phases, as in connection-oriented protocols.

P.7 The OSI Reference Model

The *Open Systems Interconnect (OSI) reference model* is commonly used to describe, in an abstract manner, the functions involved in data communication. This model, originally conceived in the International Organization for Standardization (ISO), defines data communications functions in terms of layers.

In the OSI reference model, each *layer* is responsible for certain basic functions, such as getting data from one device to another or from one application on a computer to another. The functions at each layer both depend and build on the functions—called *services*— provided by the layers below it. Communication between peer entities at a given layer is done via one or more protocols; this communication is invoked via the *interface* with the layer below.

The OSI reference model is depicted in Table P.1. Successful communication between two applications depends on successful functions at all seven layers. In terms of implementation, it is possible for some layers to be trivial; in the end what is required depends on the needs of the applications (and people) engaged in communication.

Table P.1   OSI Reference Model

	Layer	Title
Higher Layers	7	Application
	6	Presentation
	5	Session
Lower Layers	4	Transport
	3	Network
	2	Data Link
	1	Physical

We must emphasize that the definition of a layered data communication architecture is only an abstraction. The intent of this definition is to unambiguously describe the functions involved in data communication in a way that allows different systems to be compared. The OSI reference model definition is intended to neither imply nor constrain the implementation of any communication system.

Although various companies and standards bodies have created different layered communications models, the OSI reference model remains the universally-accepted common denominator for abstract definition. Other models define the layer functions somewhat differently and often have fewer than seven layers. In some cases, constituent protocols were specified before the abstract models defining the end-to-end communication.

We will now review the functions of the OSI layers and some of the primary protocols at each layer.[7]

---

7. The protocols at each layer come from one of essentially three sources: the ISO, the "Internet world," or proprietary sources, such as Novell. The political and philosophical differences between these sources run deep. None of these sources of protocol definitions is without flaw. We will try to maintain a balanced presentation, while acknowledging that the current dominating influence (at least in North America) is what we refer to as the "Internet world."

P.7.1 Layer 1 - The Physical Layer

The *physical layer* functions include all physical aspects of communicating between two directly-connected physical entities. Typically, these physical properties include electromechanical characteristics of the medium, or link, between the communicating physical entities such as connectors, voltages, transmission frequencies, etc. This layer summarizes the physics that underlie the communication path.

The essential service provided by the physical layer consists of an unstructured *bit stream*, which can be used by higher layers to provide the basis for higher layer communication services. An example of a physical layer is the ink on paper used by this book to convey information. Another example is the radio frequencies used in a wireless communications system.

P.7.2 Layer 2 - The Data Link Layer

The *data link layer* accepts the unstructured bit stream provided by the physical layer and provides reliable transfer of data between two directly-connected Layer 2 entities. "Directly-connected" means that the Layer 2 entities' communication path does not require another Layer 2 entity. However, this does not imply a dedicated path; in the case of Ethernet, many Layer 2 entities can be sharing a common (physical) medium such as a coaxial cable or a 10BASE-T hub.

Layer 2 functionality is limited in its scope to deliver messages over a local area. It could be likened to an intra-office correspondence between co-workers; there is a need for reliability but addressing is relatively simple. *Local area networks (LANs)* operate at Layer 2.

The data link layer is itself conceptually subdivided into two sublayers—medium access control and logical link control—which more specifically define the primary aspects of data link layer functionality. However, this conceptual partitioning is somewhat arbitrary and subject to debate.

P.7.2.1 The MAC Sublayer

The *medium access control (MAC) sublayer* is closely associated with the physical layer and defines the means by which the physical channel (medium) may be accessed. It coordinates the attempts to seize a shared channel by multiple MAC entities, much as a school teacher must arbitrate between pupils' conflicting desires to speak. The MAC layer commonly provides a limited form of error control, especially for any header information that defines the MAC-level destination and higher-layer access mechanism.

Ethernet (defined by the Institute of Electrical and Electronics Engineers (IEEE) standard 802.3) is a prime example of a shared medium with a defined MAC sublayer functionality. The shared medium in Ethernet has traditionally consisted of a coaxial cable into which multiple entities were "tapped," as depicted in Figure P.5. Although this topology still applies conceptually, a hub and spoke medium is now typically used, where as the earlier coaxial cable has been physically collapsed into a *hub* device.

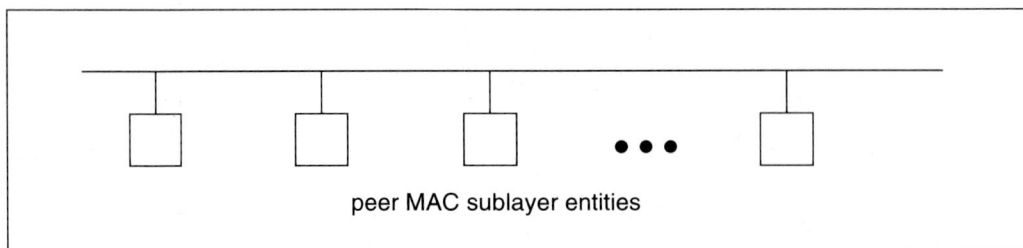

Figure P.5 Ethernet MAC System

As a *contention* medium, Ethernet defines how devices *sense* a channel for its availability, wait when it is busy, *seize* the channel when it becomes available, and *back-off* for a random length of time following a *collision* with another simultaneously transmitting device. On a shared channel, such as Ethernet, only a single entity can transmit at a time or messages will be garbled.

Not all shared channels involve contention. A prime example of a *contentionless* shared medium is *token ring (IEEE 802.5)*, in which control of the channel is rotated between the devices sharing the channel in a deterministic round-robin manner. Conceptually, control of the channel is given to the entity currently possessing a "token." If the device has nothing to transmit, it passes the token to the next device attached to the topological "ring," depicted in Figure P.6.

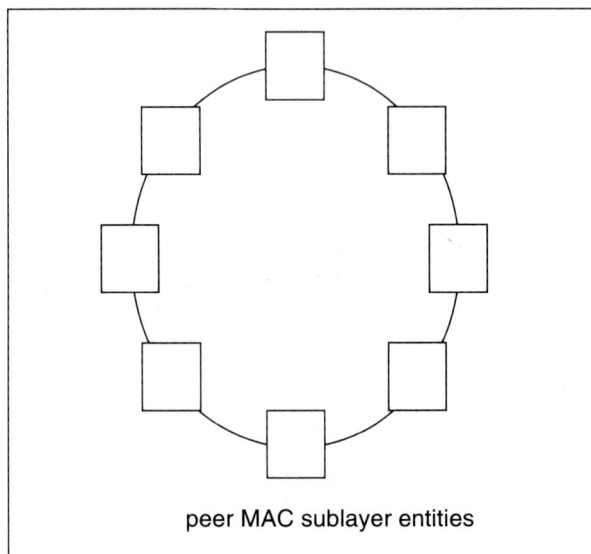

Figure P.6 Token Ring MAC System

IEEE-defined MAC sublayer addresses are six bytes long and permanently assigned to each device, typically called a *network interface card* or *NIC. The* IEEE administers the assignment of these addresses in blocks to manufacturers to assure the global uniqueness that the MAC sublayer protocols rely on for "plug-and-play" network setup. Each manufacturer must assure individual device identifier uniqueness within their assigned block.

P.7.2.2 The LLC Sublayer

The *logical link control (LLC) sublayer* is responsible for reliable transfer of messages—called *frames* or, more formally, *link protocol data units (LPDUs)*—between two directly-connected Layer 2 entities. Functions needed to support this reliable transfer include *framing* (indicating where a Layer 2 message begins and ends), sequence control, error control, and flow control.

The degree to which sequence, error, and flow control are provided by the LLC sublayer is determined by whether the link protocol is connection-oriented or connectionless. A connectionless link protocol provides little if any support for these functions. A connection-oriented link might use a windowing technique for these functions, in which frames are individually numbered and acknowledged by their sequence number, with only a few such frames outstanding at any time.

The connection-oriented functions of sequencing, error, and flow control provide a foundation for services provided by higher layers. As mentioned earlier, not all layer or sublayer functions are explicitly designed or implemented in any given system. Provision of these functions depends on the services required by higher layers.

If the connection-oriented functions of the LLC sublayer are not implemented, they must be performed by higher layers for reliable end-to-end communication. If these functions are provided by several layers, they might be somewhat redundant and add unnecessary overhead (inefficiency) to the system. In the worst case, redundant provision of these functions at multiple layers could serve cross purposes and actually degrade overall system performance.

An example of a connectionless LLC protocol is *frame relay*, which defines point-to-point links with *switches* connecting individual links in a mesh topology. In a frame relay network, endpoints are connected by a series of links and switches. Because frame relay is defined in terms of the links between *frame relay access devices* (*FRADs*) and switches, and between switches themselves, it is an LLC protocol.

Connectionless Layer 2 protocols are best suited for high quality transmission media. With high quality transmission media, errors are rarely introduced in the transmission between network layer entities, and the discovery of and recovery from errors is most efficiently handled by the communicating hosts. In this case, it is better to move the packets quickly across the traversed subnetworks from source to destination rather than checking for errors at Layer 2.

Frame relay is derived from the *X.25* protocol, which spans Layers 2 and 3. X.25 is a connection-oriented packet-switching technology that defines how neighboring *packet switches* exchange data with one another in a reliable manner from end-to-end. Frame relay simply removes the connection-oriented functions of error and sequence control; however, *congestion control* functions are provided in frame relay, to prevent the total traffic seen at any point in the network from overwhelming it.

Connection-oriented Layer 2 protocols are best suited for low quality transmission media, where it is more efficient and cost-effective to discover and recover from errors as they occur on each hop than to rely on the communicating hosts to perform error recovery functions. With ever-increasing quality of transmission facilities and decreasing costs of computation capability at hosts, the need for connection-oriented network layer protocols is diminishing. However, X.25 remains popular outside of North America, where it has been tariffed at levels that encourage its use.

End-to-end communications may be via shared or dedicated facilities or *circuits*. Shared facilities involve the use of *packet switching* technology to carry messages from end-to-end; messages are subdivided as necessary into packets, which share physical and logical channels with packets from various sources to various destinations. Packet switching is almost universally used in data communications because it is more efficient for the bursty nature of data traffic.

On the other hand, some applications require dedicated facilities from end-to-end because they are isochronous (e.g., voice) or bandwidth-intensive (e.g., large file transfer). This mode of end-to-end circuit dedication is called *circuit switched* communication. Because the facilities are dedicated to a single user, this tends to be much more expensive than the packet switched mode of communication. But some applications need it—it is an economic trade-off.

Dedicated circuits are a rather extreme form of connection-oriented protocol, requiring the same setup and tear-down phases prior to and following communication. If the circuit setup and tear-down is statically arranged (i.e., out-of-band), it is referred to as a *permanent virtual circuit* or *PVC*. If the circuit is dynamically setup and torn down in-band, it is referred to as a *switched virtual circuit* or *SVC*.

P.7.3 Layer 3 - The Network Layer

The *network layer* defines the functions necessary to support data communication between indirectly-connected entities. It provides the capability of forwarding messages from one Layer 3 entity to another until the final destination is reached.

The network layer introduces another layer of abstraction to the data communications model. It moves messages—called *packets* or, more formally, *network protocol data units* (*NPDUs*)—between communicating Layer 3 entities—called *end systems*, *nodes,* or *hosts*. Network layer functions include route determination or *routing* and *forwarding* of packets to their final destinations.

In order to forward a packet to its destination host, routing information must be provided to the *intermediate systems (ISs)* or *routers* responsible for forwarding packets to their respective destinations. This routing information includes the *address* of the destination, which is contained in each packet. The next *hop* to be traversed by the packet is determined primarily by this destination address. We will talk more about addressing and routing in Chapter 1.

This packet forwarding and routing is accomplished independent of both the media and transmission types used at any step along the way. The unimportance of local topology to the network layer is demonstrated by the common use of "cloud diagrams" to depict networks, as in Figure P.7. Since the network layer is concerned with getting packets across many local networks, called *subnetworks*, its title would be more accurate if it were the "Internetwork Layer."

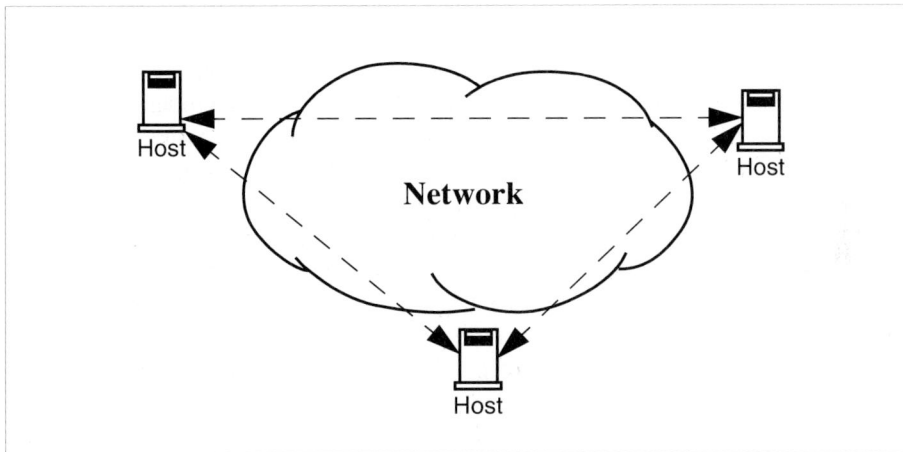

Figure P.7   Network Layer "Cloud" Diagram

The network layer functionality is global in scope: delivery of messages over a wide area. It could be likened to the postal system, in which correspondence is passed from location to location until it eventually reaches the destination address on the envelope.[8] The network layer is the domain of *wide area networks* (*WANs*).

In order for routers to know how (i.e., on which link) to forward packets, they must have some knowledge of network topology. This knowledge may be complete or partial, and is dynamically created and maintained via *routing protocols*, used by routers to share their knowledge of network topology with each other. Routing is essentially the reduction of global internetwork topology to local "hop-by-hop" routing decisions made independently by each router.

As with Layer 2, Layer 3 protocols may be connection-oriented or connectionless. A connection-oriented Layer 3 protocol, such as *X.25*, operates more statically. The basic idea is that an end-to-end route (X.25 virtual connection) is established from the originating *data terminal equipment (DTE)* to *data communications equipment (DCE)*, from DCE to DCE through the network, then from the last DCE to the terminating DTE; this is the call setup. Packets are then transmitted via this prearranged route, with all packets following the same path through the network. Finally, the route is torn down (release) and packets cease flowing.

---

8. Given the postal system, this is clearly an example of a connectionless protocol.

X.25 operation is like a phone call because it *is* a phone call. X.25 Layer 3 operation assumes that a reliable connection-oriented service is provided by Layer 2 (also defined by the X.25 standard), although it does provide flow control via sequence numbers.

Connectionless Layer 3 protocols, such as the ever popular *internet protocol (IP)(RFC*[9] *791 and 792)* and its ISO counterpart *connectionless network protocol (CLNP) (ISO 8473*[10]*)*, route packets dynamically. There is no prearranged path that is followed by subsequent packets flowing from one host to another. Instead, each packet is individually routed through a routing mesh; there is no reason to believe that sequential packets flowing between hosts will follow the same path. So, sequence errors may be introduced at Layer 3, which must be corrected by a higher layer entity.

Connectionless data packets are commonly referred to as *datagrams* and the service provided by connectionless Layer 3 protocols is referred to as *datagram service*. Stateless datagram service is simpler for Layer 3 entities than connection-oriented network layer services. Because there is no state information to maintain, dynamic routing protocols can be used. If a router fails during the dialogue between two communicating hosts, neighboring routers will discover this via the routing protocols and find alternate routes that bypass the failed router.

There seems to be a fair amount of ambiguity between the network layer and the LLC sublayer. Both can provide connection-oriented or connectionless services to higher layers. To a large extent, if Layer 3 is explicitly implemented, there is no need for an LLC sublayer. The primary difference is in scope—LLC addresses and protocols are oriented toward a more local environment, whereas network layer addresses and protocols are global in scope.

Excellent references to routing and forwarding of data packets can be found in [PERL92] and [STEN95].

P.7.4 Layer 4 - The Transport Layer

The *transport layer* is concerned with getting Layer 4 messages—called *segments* or, more formally, *transport protocol data units (TPDUs)* —from source to destination in a reliable manner. The perspective of Layer 4 is of end-to-end communications rather than the hop-by-hop perspective of Layer 3. Layer 4 assumes that packets can be moved from network entity to network entity, eventually getting to the final destination host. How this is accomplished is of no concern to Layer 4 functionality.

Like other layers, transport layer protocols can be either connection-oriented or connectionless, depending on the services required by higher layers. A common implementation of Layers 3 and 4 involves a connection-oriented transport layer protocol running over a connectionless network layer protocol, such as the ubiquitous TCP/IP[11] protocol suite. In this instance, the communicating

---

9. Internet standards are defined by means of so-called "Requests for Comment" or *RFCs*, which are numbered sequentially.
10. ISO standard number 8473.
11. Transport Control Protocol over the Internet Protocol.

hosts maintain state information on communications with each other to determine when and what to send. This state information defines the connection between the communicating Layer 4 entities.

The general idea here is that two communicating hosts need not be concerned with the topology of the internetwork that lies between them. They only need to know the state of their pair-wise communication. If part of the intervening internetwork "cloud" suffers a failure, the Layer 3 entities (routers) will deal with it and recover dynamically. Aside from potential retransmission of any lost segments, the hosts' Layer 4 entries do not have to be at all concerned with routing and recovery activities at Layer 3.

In the IP protocol suite, the primary connectionless Layer 4 protocol is the *User Datagram Protocol* (UDP)(RFC 768), which is carried by IP. The primary connection-oriented protocol is the *Transmission Control Protocol* (TCP)(RFC 793). The ISO world defines five classes of transport layer protocol, beginning with Class 0 (TP-0) and range up to Class 4 (TP-4)(ISO 8073), and are described in [STAL93].

P.7.5 Layer 5 - The Session Layer

The *session layer* provides a control structure for communication between applications on hosts. The communication at Layer 5 is called a *session*, which defines the relative timing of communications between the hosts' applications. This includes synchronization of the dialogue between the communicating applications and managing the information flow between them.

Remember, layers define communication functions, not implementations. It is unlikely that a session layer would be explicitly implemented as a stand-alone program, although its functions would be implemented somewhere. Session layer functions depend on the reliability of communications between the endpoints, and session layer functions must therefore be implemented above Layer 4.

P.7.6 Layer 6 - The Presentation Layer

The *presentation layer* performs any necessary data transformations or formatting required for system-independent encoding between corresponding end applications. Functions provided by the presentation layer could include data compression, encryption, and byte reordering. Common data formatting is important because it allows the same application file to be accessed by the application running on different computer platforms. This book is itself the product of an application running on different platforms, with common files being modified via these different platforms.

Abstract Syntax Notation (ASN.1) is commonly used to specify data values in a way that allows processors to communicate independent of their varying native integer sizes, bit orderings (big or little endian), character sets, etc. ASN.1 is a transfer syntax, a presentation layer formatting, which appears frequently in the CDPD specification for unambiguous definition of network management, accounting, limited size messaging, and other functions.

An example of ASN.1 encoding from an accounting Traffic Matrix Segment in the CDPD specification is the following:

```
TrafficType ::= INTEGER {
    registration (0),
    deregistration (1),
    ip(2),
    clnp(3)
    }
```

P.7.7 Layer 7 - The Application Layer

The *application layer* provides the services that directly support an application running on a host. These services are directly accessible by an application via common well-known *application program interfaces (APIs)*, which can actually occur at many layers. Examples of Layer 7 services include *FTP (file transfer protocol)*, Telnet, and *SNMP (simple network management protocol)*. Most network management activities are based on the services provided by Layer 7 application entities, which in turn rely on lower layer services to be able to perform their functions.

P.8 Protocols, Primitives, Services

In general, a *Layer (N)* entity provides services to higher Layer (N+1) entities and relies on the services provided by the Layer (N-1) and below entities supporting it. Layer (N) services consist primarily of transferring messages from one Layer (N+1) entity to another; both the source and destination Layer (N+1) entities rely on their underlying Layer (N) entities to accomplish this task.

A Layer (N) entity requests services of a local Layer (N-1) entity via *primitives* directed at a Layer (N-1) *service access point (SAP)*. If the primitives are explicitly implemented, they can be thought of as function calls.

Protocols refer to relationships and messages between peer entities at a given layer. A Layer (N) entity communicates with another Layer (N) entity via a protocol. A protocol message is actually invoked by means of a service request primitive, called *(N)—PRIMITIVE_NAME.request*, to its underlying Layer (N-1) entity, where "PRIMITIVE_NAME" is the name of the operation being invoked by the primitive. The peer Layer (N) entity receives the Layer (N) protocol message via a service indication primitive, called *(N)-PRIMITIVE_NAME.indication,* from its underlying Layer (N-1) entity.

In a connection-oriented protocol, the peer Layer (N) entity responds via a response primitive, called *(N)-PRIMITIVE_NAME.response*— to its underlying Layer (N-1) entity. The original Layer (N) entity receives the Layer (N) protocol response from its underlying Layer (N-1) entity via a *(N)-PRIMITIVE_NAME.confirm* primitive. This primitive flow, supporting the Layer (N) protocol, is displayed in Figure P.8.

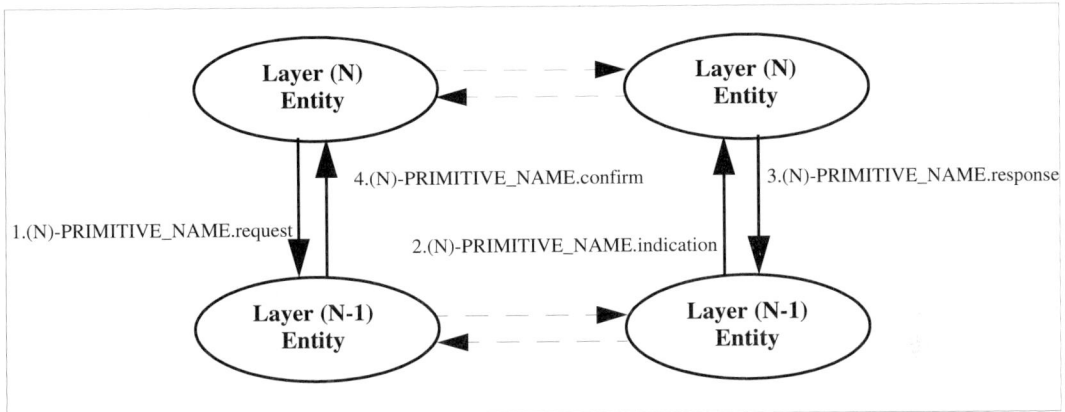

Figure P.8   Layer (N) Protocol Primitives

P.9 Protocol and Service Data Units

Protocol data units or *PDUs* are the messages passed between entities at a given layer. Layer 2 PDUs are called LPDUs or frames; Layer 3 PDUs are called NPDUs or packets; Layer 4 PDUs are called TPDUs or segments.

In general, a PDU—regardless of the protocol layer—consists of *header*[12] and *data* fields. The header field contains the information necessary to get the PDU to the peer entity and typically includes the source and destination addresses appropriate for that layer as well as error sequence and flow control information. The data field contains the information carried by the Layer (N) protocol in support of Layer (N+1); it is formally referred to as the Layer (N) *service data unit* or *SDU*.

Conceptually, when a Layer (N+1) PDU is passed via primitive to Layer (N) as a Layer (N) SDU, a Layer (N) header is prepended to create a Layer (N) PDU. Sometimes, part of the "header" is actually appended at the end, usually for error correction purposes. The Layer (N) PDU is then passed via primitive to Layer (N-1) as a Layer (N-1) SDU where a Layer (N-1) header is added. This process continues as data units are passed down the OSI reference model "stack." This is depicted in Figure P.9.

Similarly, when a Layer (N-1) SDU is passed up to Layer (N), the Layer (N-1) header is removed from the Layer (N-1) PDU. Likewise, the Layer (N) PDU header is stripped to provide the

---

12. Formally called *Protocol Control Information* or *PCI*.

Layer (N) SDU for Layer (N+1). This process continues as data units are passed up from layer to layer in the OSI reference model. Eventually, as shown in Figure P.9, the original data element has been recreated at the application layer of the destination.

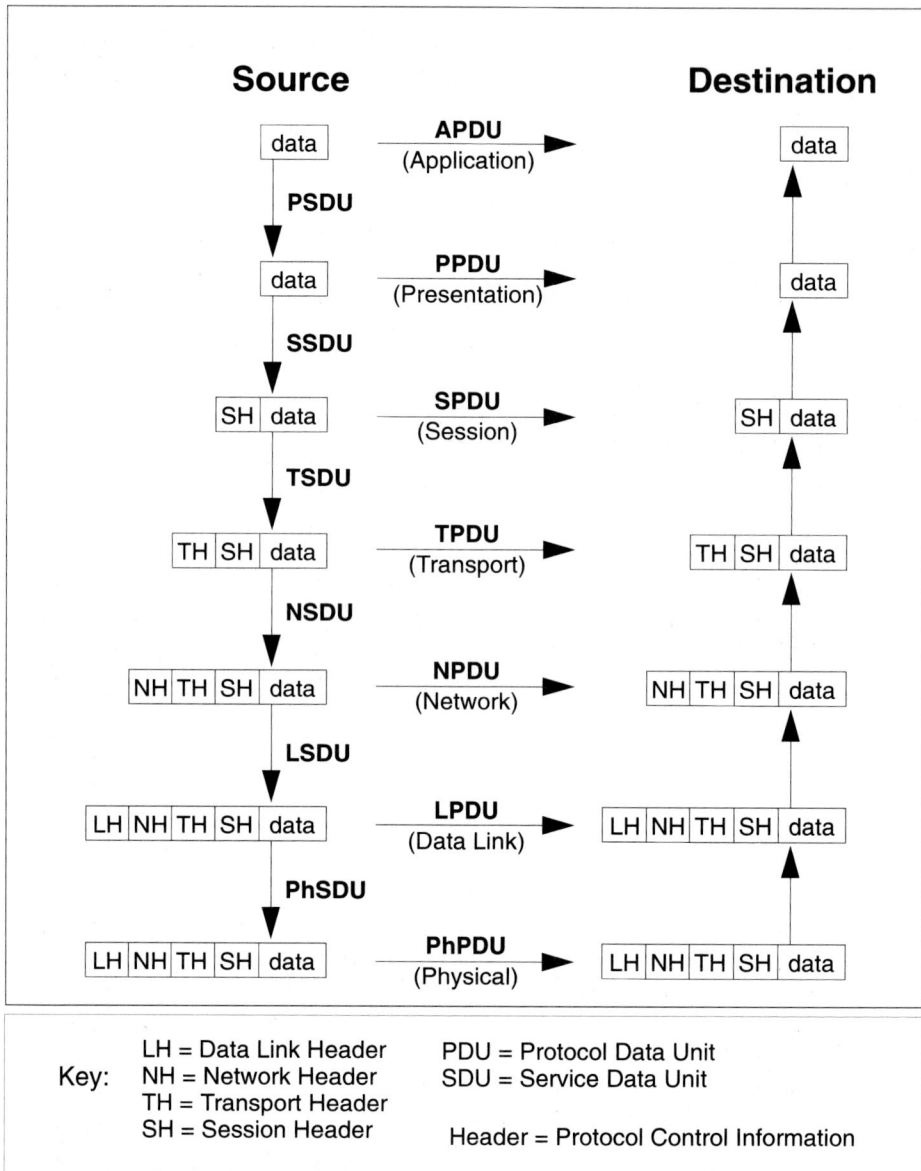

Figure P.9 Protocol and Service Data Units

P.10 Mobile Data Communications Entities

At each layer of the OSI reference model there are protocol entities communicating with each other. They are the sources and destinations of PDUs at that layer. Because this book is about mobility in WANs, the entities of greatest interest are Layer 3 entities, commonly called hosts, nodes or end systems. Layer 3 PDUs, commonly called packets, are exchanged between hosts via Layer 3 entities commonly called routers.

Adding the capability of mobility to a wide area data network creates a need for defining additional entities, as depicted in Figure P.10.

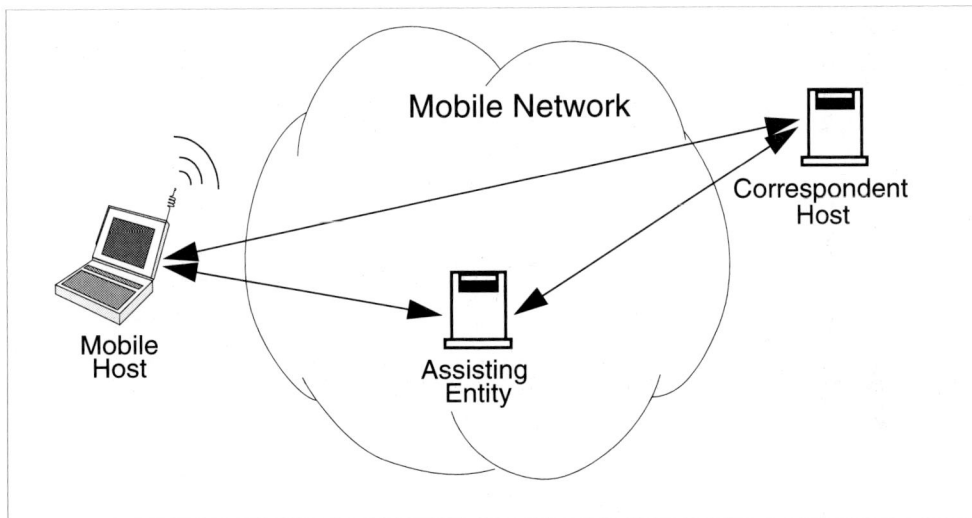

Figure P.10   Roles in Mobility and Message Flow

A *mobile host* or *mobile* is a host that can receive network services regardless of its location. The extent to which this host enjoys transparent location-independence is a key concern. Different systems use different terminology for the mobile; CDPD adopts ISO terminology by calling it a *Mobile End System (M-ES)*. The mobile is an *occasionally-connected* entity, which means it may or may not be connected at any given moment to a subnet somewhere in the mobile WAN.

The second role necessary in any communications is the opposite side of the correspondence. In this book, we refer to this as the *correspondent host* or *correspondent*. The correspondent is the location of the opposite side of a mobile's application association; it could be the ultimate source of data destined for the mobile or another entity such as a store-and-forward device. The correspondent could itself be mobile or fixed in location, but this is generally not material to our analysis. CDPD refers to the correspondent as the *Fixed End System (F-ES)* when it is fixed in location.

In circuit-switched systems, there will be a maximum of one correspondent per mobile host. However, in the packet-switched systems of greatest interest to us, there can always be multiple correspondents per mobile host.

Associated with the mobile communications is the *assisting entity* or *assistant*. The assistant is an enabler of mobility. It could be a network store-and-forward device or mobility-supporting intermediate system (router). Most likely, it consists of multiple entities in a mobile network infrastructure that collectively support host mobility. In CDPD this role is largely filled by a combination of the *Mobile Serving Function* and the *Mobile Home Function*; the Mobile IP Task Force calls this combination the *foreign agent* and the *mobile router* or *home agent*.

As we shall see, the essential problem of mobility is getting data *to* the mobile. Thus, the mobile will generally be the destination host in any mobile system scenario of interest. Consistent with this, we will adopt a system-centric viewpoint by defining the flow of data traffic to a mobile as moving in the *forward* direction (i.e., mobile network to mobile host). Likewise, the flow of data traffic from a mobile is said to move in the *reverse* direction (i.e., mobile host to mobile network). This terminology is consistent with the cellular industry, which is the origin of CDPD, and is displayed in Figure P.11.

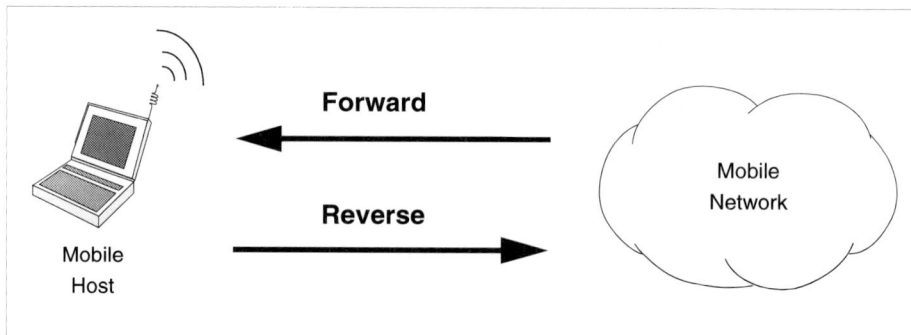

Figure P.11   Directions of Mobile Transmission

P.11 Summary

This chapter has presented a brief survey of data networking terminology and concepts used throughout the remainder of this book. We strongly encourage readers who are new to this terminology to peruse the many fine texts on this subject, some of which have been referenced in this chapter. Given the terminology presented in this chapter, we will now begin discussing mobility.

1

Introduction to Mobility

*If a host moves from one network to another, its IP address must
change.*
         —Douglas E. Comer, *Internetworking with TCP/IP*, Volume 1, 1991

This chapter introduces some of the key concepts of mobility, setting the stage for later
detailed discussion of mobile WAN systems. Although the emphasis of this book is CDPD, this
chapter presents a more generalized and abstract view of mobility.

Previous books on the subject of mobile data communications have covered wirelessness[1]
more than mobility. Our intent is to begin from a data networking perspective, independent of
medium-specific considerations, then consider the effects of media on networking technology.
Indeed, one of the primary conclusions of this book is that mobility is most naturally handled in
the network layer (Layer 3), so any discussion of mobility should begin there.

1.1 What is Mobility?

Mobility means different things to different people. Some people are quite happy being able
to get around town. Others view the world in terms of time distance—four hours from Chicago to
San Francisco by airline, perhaps. Obviously, range of motion is an important aspect of mobility.

Another factor in mobility is ease of access. What might be considered mobile in one context
is quite immobile in another. Certainly the pioneers crossing the North American continent in
ox-drawn wagons covered the same distance as the airliner from Chicago to San Francisco, but
today, we would hardly consider these pioneers to have had much mobility.

A more pertinent example of mobility is the ever decreasing size of cellular telephones. What
was once considered a "mobile phone" had to be transported in a vehicle. A major step forward was
the "transportable" phone, which freed the user from their vehicle but weighed in at about twenty

---

1. "Wirelessness" refers to the use of a wireless media, most typically *radio frequency (RF)*
systems.

pounds, still huge by today's standards. With the advent of "brick" phones in the mid-1980s came the era of "portable" phones. The diminishing size and weight of handsets has greatly increased the mobility of cellular subscribers.

In this book on mobile data communications, we define *mobility* as *the ability to send and receive communications anytime, anywhere.* Mobility means that both source and destination devices, applications and people are free of the constraints imposed by physical location. Access to an Ethernet port, for example, need not limit one's ability to send and receive data in a mobile WAN environment any more than access to a landline phone currently limits one's ability to place a voice call in an area covered by cellular service.

1.2 Basic Approaches to Mobility

The issues of mobility in a WAN environment can be discussed in the context of a modern day "road warrior," whom we shall call Gary.[2] Gary is never totally alone in his travels—as in real life, he cannot survive on the road for long without active support from his administrative assistant, whom we shall call Pat.[3] If you had to communicate with Gary, who (as always) is on the road, how could you accomplish this?

1.2.1 Approach 1: Application Awareness

One way to communicate with Gary is to contact him at his hotel or wherever he may be. If he had provided you with a copy of his itinerary and none of his plans changed (certainly an ideal case!), you could call or send facsimiles to Gary at the location specified in the itinerary.

Of course, Gary would have had to anticipate your need to contact him, or he would likely have not provided you a copy of his itinerary. In the absence of clairvoyance, Gary or Pat would have to provide copies of his itinerary to all people who might ever have a need to contact Gary while he is traveling—all of the time! Even people he might not really want to hear from.

Obviously, there are serious logistical problems with this approach to mobile communications. On top of the logistics and overhead of broadcasting Gary's itinerary to the world, there are issues of privacy and the undesirability of always being accessible. It is just possible that Gary would prefer to not be interrupted for an unrelated issue while in the midst of a serious contract negotiation.

---

2. Gary is a true road warrior we know who regularly logs over 300 nights on the road per year. Someone who really needs free airline mileage awards.
3. Pat is a good name for an administrative assistant example because it avoids all sexist stereotyping.

An equivalent situation in mobile data communications would be a mobile host having to directly notify each of its applications' peers about its current location or *address*, as depicted in Figure 1.1. Any peer application not receiving this location update would be unable to communicate with or engage in a session with the mobile host. This would be like trying to call someone at their office phone number when they are really at home, at a different number (address).

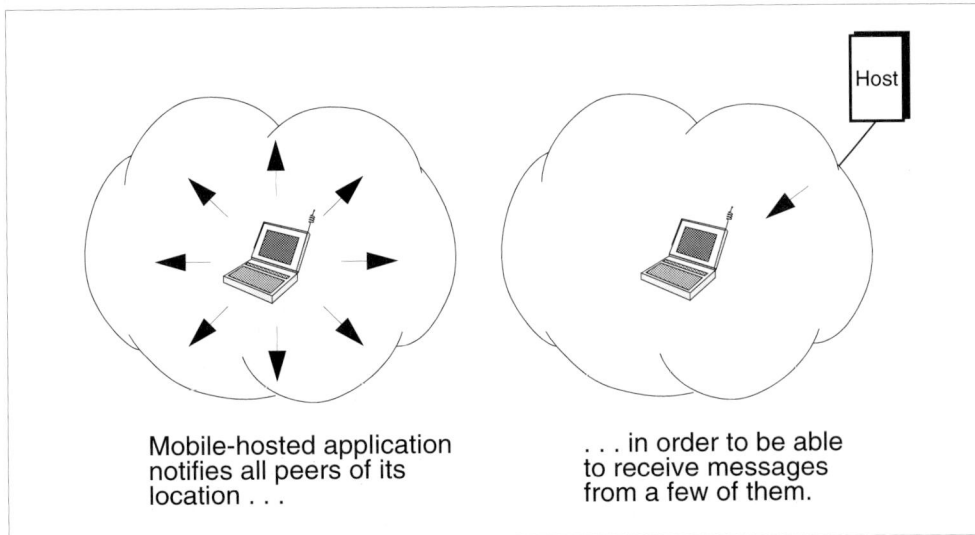

Figure 1.1   The Application Awareness Approach to Mobility

The primary advantage of this *Application Awareness* approach to mobility is that the network infrastructure does not, itself, need to be involved in or even aware of the mobility.[4] Mobility management and network access are entirely within the scope and control of end users and applications. The mobile host and application must provide location and routing information to each of the application's peers. Each peer then cooperates by connecting with the mobile application according to the new routing rules.

The primary disadvantage of this scheme is that by eliminating network involvement, end users and applications must perform routing tasks typically handled by other entities. This approach requires custom (i.e., nonstandard) applications to furnish mobility awareness and support. These applications on both the mobile and peer sides would then differ from those that operate in an immobile world. However, success of a mobile data technology depends to a large extent on the ease of application attachment to the mobile network.

---

4. For now, we shall not consider real-world concerns like charging for services, etc.

This disadvantage is exacerbated in that end applications would have to collect and maintain evolving routing information for hosts that might be mobile. This is highly inefficient and goes against the grain of a functionally-layered network architecture. Application layer entities should not be concerned with network layer issues such as routing and addressing.

A variation of the Application Awareness approach was previously used in the cellular phone environment for "roaming" subscribers. Prior to "roaming" into another service provider's territory, a cellular subscriber would have to prearrange for service in that area with their home service provider.[5] In this case, the end user was involved in what is essentially a routing issue in order to be able to receive calls on their cellular handset.

Perhaps for these reasons, there are no good implementations of the Application Awareness approach to mobile data communications. This approach is only feasible in vertical applications running in closed networks in which protocol layers are not functionally separated.

1.2.2 Approach 2: Directory Lookup

Another way to contact Gary the Road Warrior is via Pat, his administrative assistant. If Gary always notifies Pat about his location (by itinerary and verbal updates), you could first call Pat's office to get current phone or facsimile numbers for Gary. Armed with this information, you could then contact Gary directly.

This approach is more flexible than only using a previously furnished itinerary, which is subject to change. However, if Gary has been less than diligent in his location updates, Pat may not really know where Gary is. Furthermore, anyone wishing to contact Gary must first go through Pat, which means they must know how to reach Pat; and Pat must always be available.

Although this approach is logistically feasible, Pat may not always know whom to give Gary's location information. It is possible that Gary uses Pat as much for call screening as for support of his mobility. But at least you would know to always contact Gary by first calling Pat.

This *Directory Lookup* approach is similar to the use of the *Domain Name System (DNS)* to determine addresses used for routing in the conventional Internet. In the World Wide Web, sites are typically accessed via *Universal Resource Locator (URL)* identifiers and not via Internet addresses. These human-recognizable names are used by Web browser software to interrogate one or more DNS servers, which respond with an Internet address reflecting the Web site's network location. The IP address returned by the DNS query is used to route subsequent Web page accesses (i.e., data packets).

The DNS system provides this ubiquitous name-to-address translation function via a highly distributed and replicated database of translation information. The degree of replication of this database provides dependable and rapid worldwide address translation. However, this replication also makes the *synchronization* of updates throughout the database somewhat slow. This is the price of success.

---

5. Fortunately, this prearrangement has been replaced by inter-carrier "roaming agreements" and business relationships that allow cellular subscribers to simply use their handset while in another carrier's region without any special pre-arrangements.

The DNS mechanism works well because Web sites typically do not change network access points (i.e., addresses) very often. The relatively static domain name to IP address translation information can be safely propagated and cached without fear of rapid obsolescence. Unfortunately, this is not the case for mobile hosts, whose locations change far too quickly for efficient DNS tracking.

Unlike current DNS queries, mobile host location queries would have to be done (almost) every time peer applications wanted to correspond with the mobile host, as depicted in Figure 1.2. Although some caching of location information could be done—as in DNS—this information is extremely time sensitive. If the destination host is in motion, the location information could quickly become obsolete. Thus, the overhead of determining a route (address) for a mobile host would have to be incurred prior to sending every packet.

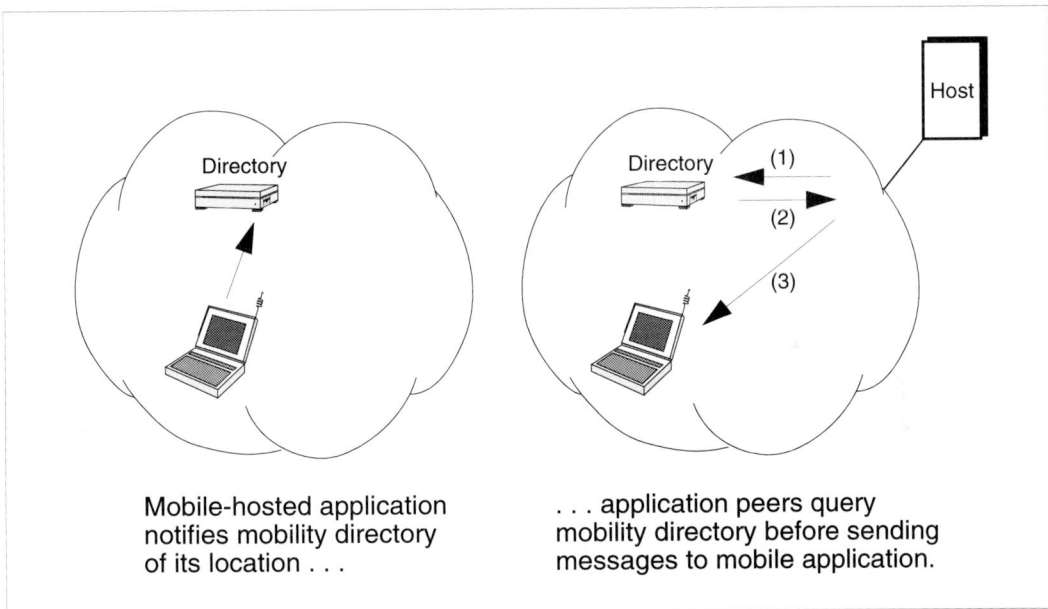

Figure 1.2 The Directory Lookup Approach to Mobility

To avoid this overhead with the Directory Lookup approach to mobility, the mobile host cannot move to a different network attachment point, while one of its applications is engaged in a session with a remote peer. Doing so would break the connection, forcing the session and application to end prematurely in a highly disruptive manner.

To prevent this disruption in a Directory Lookup scheme, the mobile host must restrict its movement whenever connections are active. While this might be acceptable for mobile host-originated application associations, it is clearly deficient for application associations originated by application peers of the mobile.

The Directory Lookup approach enjoys the advantage that any peer application wishing to contact the mobile host need only query a central repository of location information. Likewise, the mobile host need only notify the central directory service of its location. There is no need to contact each and every one of the potential peer applications that might have a need to communicate with that mobile host.

However, the Directory Lookup approach to mobility still involves application participation. Applications must understand mobility enough to maintain associations between the mobile host and the directory lookup procedures. If the mobility directory is implemented in a standardized manner *a la* DNS, the lookup can be a natural part of any application. However, if it is not standardized, applications would need to be modified specifically for mobile hosts.

For all of these reasons, CDPD does not use the Directory Lookup approach to mobility. The CDPD network is required to support mobile devices that change their point of access frequently. Within a metropolitan area, a moving host may traverse multiple points of network attachment in a few minutes. This type of movement requires extremely frequent mobile directory updates.

Furthermore, as we have seen, the Directory Lookup approach to mobility is ineffective for any session, lasting longer than a few seconds involving a moving host. Since an application connecting with a mobile host cannot rely on routing information obtained from the mobility directory more than a few seconds ago, it must reacquire routing information for every new association. This is a change to the current DNS mechanism as well as inefficient from a system perspective. For all of these reasons, this approach is inappropriate for a mobile data network such as CDPD.

1.2.3 Approach 3: Mailbox Service

A third way to contact Gary the Road Warrior is to use a messaging service of some kind, such as voice mail. With this approach, all of Gary's associates would call the number on his business card to leave messages for him. At a later time, Gary could retrieve his messages from the answering service and return calls.

Unfortunately, this approach does not allow any live discussions between Gary and his peers. Unless Gary happens to check his messages frequently or happens to return calls at just the right moment, he will simply end up leaving a message himself. Although many business relationships can proceed via exchange of voice mail messages, the unavailability of live communication will eventually become a problem. This approach is often intentionally used to screen unwanted phone calls.

This *Mailbox Service* approach to mobility is similar to email repository services such as RadioMail®. This approach allows the users of mobile hosts to retrieve their email whenever they are in an area of mobile connectivity. However, this approach prohibits interactive activities such as on-line database queries.

This Mailbox Service approach benefits from peer applications no longer having to involve themselves in the mobility tracking process. Each peer application wishing to communicate with the mobile host simply sends information to the designated message repository for the mobile user. In this way, the peer application is no different than any standard electronic messaging application.

In order to use the Mailbox Server approach to mobility, a peer application must send a message to the mailbox and await a response, as depicted in Figure 1.3. The mobile host will only become aware of the message by interrogating the mailbox or by the mailbox broadcasting notifications to the mobile host, wherever it is. As we shall see, this dilemma has been addressed by CDPD with the *Status Notification Service* (SNS) support for applications like messaging.

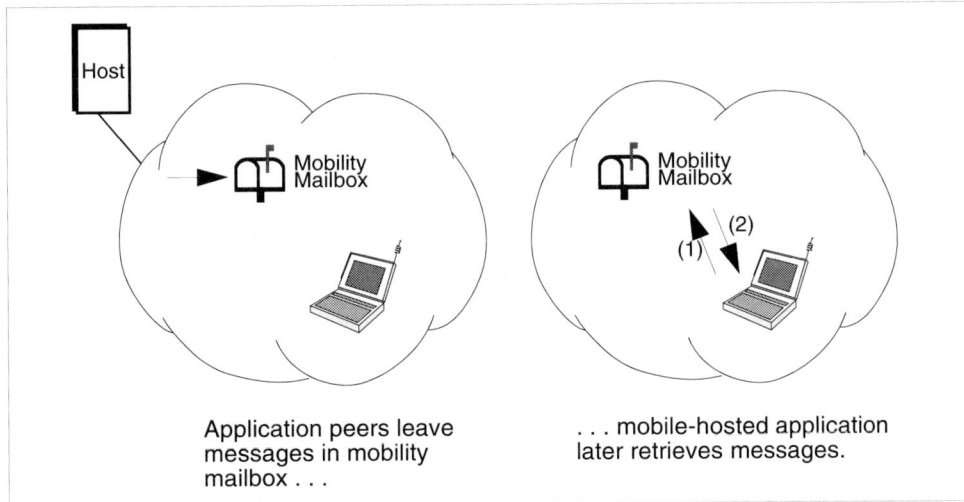

Figure 1.3　The Mailbox Service Approach to Mobility

The Mailbox Service approach does not provide real-time communications and is thus inappropriate for interactive applications. It also requires mobile network-specific protocols between the mobile host and the network infrastructure. Both the network and application are impacted by and must be modified for mobility. In that sense, it could be considered to be the worst of both worlds.

1.2.4　Approach 4: Administrative Redirection

Another approach to contacting Gary the Road Warrior is for your calls and facsimiles to be forwarded to his current location. You don't even have to know that this is happening. Packages and mail can also be redirected to someone on the move like Gary—Pat simply repackages them for overnight delivery to Gary's anticipated future location.

This approach greatly simplifies communicating with Gary. All you need to know is his "anchor" location—his home office, where a combination of modern telephony and Pat support Gary's mobility. As long as Gary notifies Pat of his anticipated next day's whereabouts and keeps his phone forwarded (or, better yet, uses a mobile phone), no one else need be aware of Gary's absence from the office.[6]

---

6. Variations of this scheme have been used by many creative people to further develop their golf games.

This *Administrative Redirection* approach to mobility can be applied in a data networking context by associating the mobile host with a "home" location. This network address and its corresponding domain name, URL, etc., would be the communication coordinates used by applications corresponding with the mobile host. All of these coordinates could be advertised in the conventional ways—via routing information protocols, DNS servers, etc.

Whenever corresponding entities wish to communicate with a mobile host, they would send packets to the home address associated with the mobile host, as depicted in Figure 1.4. These data packets would be redirected by a mobility-aware home server or agent, much as Pat would repackage and forward written correspondence to Gary. In this way, peer applications (and people) could remain blissfully unaware of the mobility and location of the host (person) they are corresponding with.

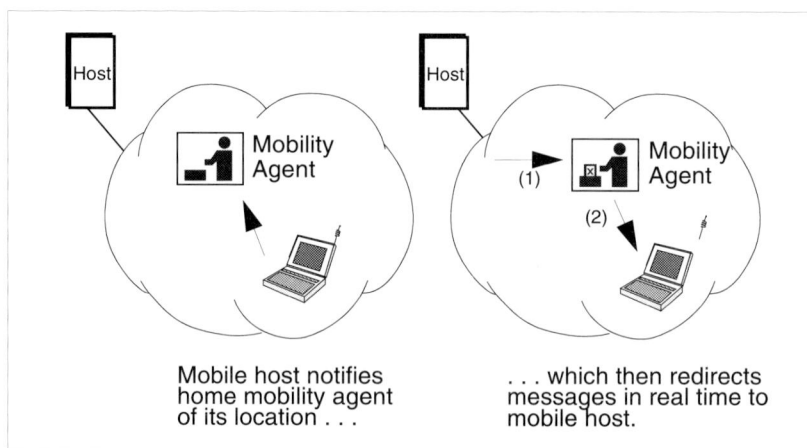

Figure 1.4   The Administrative Redirection Approach to Mobility

The primary advantage of the Administrative Redirection approach to mobility is that it supports direct interactive communication between a mobile host and peer applications in a transparent manner. The data connection or association is achieved without the peer applications being aware of mobility and routing management issues. This greatly eases application attachment, which in turn encourages mobile network acceptance and adoption.

Obviously this approach requires some work on the part of the network to maintain transparency of mobility at the application level. The home mobility server must always know where the mobile host is, then redirect data packets to that location. Standard techniques available for this redirection include readdressing the original packets or encapsulation of the packets within new packets with updated destination addresses. In any case, new protocols and procedures must be established for the network infrastructure to support transparent mobility.

The Administrative Redirection approach to mobility has been adopted by both the CDPD and the Mobile IP Task Force specifications, as well as Novell in its proprietary Mobile IPX protocols. This approach can be implemented via one of several mobility management schemes, described in section 1.6.

1.3 Aspects of Mobile Communications

There are two aspects to mobile communications: mobile network access and mobility management, which are depicted in Figure 1.5. In this book we will address both of these aspects in the context of mobile data communications, as well as other issues that, although less centric to mobility, are important to any "real world" business.

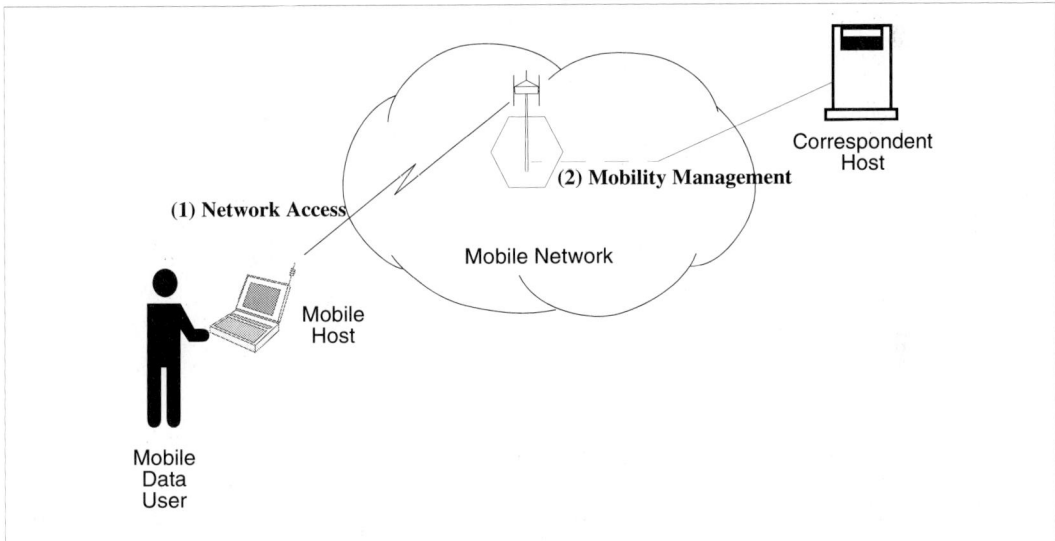

Figure 1.5   Two Basic Aspects of Mobile Communications

1.3.1 Mobile Network Access

The first aspect of mobility is accessing or connecting to the communications network. This *network access* is medium-specific and might involve using a pay phone, plugging a 10BASE-T jack into a wall socket or powering-up a wireless device within an appropriate coverage area. We discuss network access for CDPD systems in Chapter 5.

Because mobile network access is a big issue, previous books on mobile data communications have tended to focus on it. But "getting connected" is only half of the battle.

1.3.2 Mobility Management

The second aspect of mobile communications is the ability to efficiently send and receive communications from wherever you are, once you have accessed the network. This is called *mobility management* or *location management*. Somehow, the rest of the world must be able to reach you wherever you are. This is the essential challenge of mobile communications, and the manner in which this challenge is addressed has broad implications on mobile data applications.

1.4 The Essential Challenge of Mobility Management

If we ignore (for now) the physical issues involved in data transmission and network access, it is clear that sending messages from a mobile entity is not a challenge from a data networking perspective. If a mobile device has data to send, it does so and, neglecting medium-specific issues, the data can be forwarded in the usual way to its destination. [IOAN93] states that "routing traffic from the mobile [device] is considered a trivial problem; if the destination is an ordinary host in the network, normal routing procedures should be followed."

However, being able to receive data at a mobile entity is a significant challenge from a data networking perspective. *The essential problem of mobility management is efficiently getting data to a mobile entity, which can be anywhere[7] or nowhere.* The mobile is essentially nowhere if it is powered down or out of range of the system; this is an important situation to consider in any mobile system.

1.4.1 Knowing Where the Mobile is

The first part of getting data to a mobile device is knowing where the mobile is. Of the previously described basic approaches to mobility, only the Mailbox Service approach did not require prior knowledge about the mobile's location by another entity. So any interactive data communications application will require some assisting entity in the mobile network to know where the mobile is before engaging in the communication.

There are two basic strategies that a data sender can employ to know the location of the intended mobile recipient. The sender (or, alternatively, the system) must either continuously *track* the location of the mobile device or *search for* the mobile immediately prior to sending it data. Which of these mobile device location strategies should be used depends to a large extent on the nature of the intended communication.

---

7. By definition, if a mobile device can receive data (service) anywhere, that service must be available everywhere. Here, "anywhere" is a geographic concept. Ubiquitous provision of service would thus seem to encourage wireless media for mobile services.

There is a tradeoff between ease of tracking and ease of searching in a mobile environment; the efficiencies realized by these techniques are mutually exclusive. One of the primary conclusions of [IOAN93] is that a system can only be optimized for tracking or searching, but not both. A mobile system could support both strategies but only be optimized for one of them.

If the nature of the intended communication is brief and bursty with potentially multiple sources sending data asynchronously to a mobile host, continuous tracking of the mobile device is more efficient than trying to locate the mobile in real time [IOAN93]. Continuous tracking generally requires the mobile device to actively participate in the tracking process by notifying the system of its initial location and any subsequent changes in its location.

This continuous tracking technique is how systems such as Mobile IP and CDPD operate. It is also similar to conventional routing protocols, such as RIP[8], OSPF[9], etc., which allow routers to automatically adapt their routing tables based on changes in network connectivity, although at a much slower rate.

If the nature of the intended communication is relatively lengthy and typically involves a single peer at a time, greater efficiencies can be realized by searching for the mobile device immediately prior to sending it data [IOAN93]. The relative overhead per communication event is small and the system can be greatly simplified by not requiring a continuous tracking mechanism for mobiles.

Searching for a mobile device generally involves some kind of paging operation by the system immediately prior to sending it data. This is how circuit-switched systems, such as cellular voice or circuit-switched data operate. With relatively lengthy sessions involving the mobile host, this is often the best option. The search can be optimized to a degree by beginning where the mobile was last observed.

If the network itself cannot perform this searching function, the corresponding entity must locate the mobile, perhaps via a "mobility agent." Such an agent would look for the mobile device and report its location to the corresponding agent. Of course, all of this must happen quickly to be of much use.

Regardless of whether a mobile system is optimized for tracking or searching, it is essential to maintain an information base of mobile locations and to be able to quickly propagate that information whenever needed. The approach used will, of course, depend on the tracking vs. searching system design decision. This location information base is analogous to routing table information in conventional networks.

1.4.2 Routing Data to the Mobile

The second part of getting data to a mobile device is routing the data to the mobile host. This consists of determining the route to be followed by the data in its journey to the mobile, then actually forwarding the data along that route. Both of these steps are identical to packet routing and forwarding in conventional connectionless data networks, and depend on readily available and accurate mobile location information.

---

8. Routing Interchange Protocol.
9. Open Shortest-Path First.

1.5 Mobility Management is a Network Layer Function

It should be clear from our discussion thus far that mobility management consists largely of routing data packets (NPDUs) to hosts that change location and network access frequently, relative to conventional hosts.[10] By definition, routing is a network layer function and thus mobility management should also be a network layer function. Efficient support for mobility must be designed into the network layer for any mobile WAN.

As observed by [IOAN93], "The problem of Mobile Internetworking [can be] posed as follows: how to provide seamless and transparent network connectivity to mobile networked computers (or other communicating devices) as they change location, networking interfaces, or even service providers. We term this work 'Mobile Internetworking' because it enables *mobile* entities to communicate within an *internetwork*, i.e., a network of networks, and not just a local, connected network."

1.5.1 Network Layer Addresses

Data packets are routed across conventional internetworks via their destination host network layer addresses. The ability to route packets toward their final destination is based on the fact that network layer addresses are typically composed of a network-identifying part and a host-identifying part. The network-identifying part of the address specifies on which network the host may be found. The host-identifying part of the address specifies which host on the network is desired.

Figure 1.6 depicts an IP address, which is four bytes long. The network-identifying part is called the *netid* and the host-identifying part is called the *hostid*. Originally the separation between these fields was required to be at one of the three byte boundaries; three corresponding classes of network address space were defined. Now with IP version 4 (IPv4), the boundary between netid and hostid is identified via a bit mask, allowing complete flexibility for IP address space allocation

Because of the rapid adoption of IP-based technology and the Internet, IP address space had become a precious resource by the early 1990s. Four bytes sounds like a lot of addresses, but typically host address assignments are relatively sparse, based on organizational and network boundaries.[11] Partly as a result of the address space limitation and also because of the protocols defined, the IP addresses are typically manually administered and statically assigned to hosts. IPv6 (the "next generation") [BRAD96] has extended the size of IP addresses to 16 bytes, largely to alleviate these concerns about address space availability.

---

10. While conventional hosts might be relocated over a period of weeks or (more typically) months, a mobile host would relocate over a period of minutes or possibly seconds.

11. For example, a so-called Class C IP address block is the smallest contiguous block assignment that can be made to an organization. The Class C block defines a three-byte netid and a single-byte hostid, enough for 255 hosts. (All zeros in the hostid field means the network address rather than a host address). If a network administrator only had a dozen hosts to actually assign addresses to, they would only use 12 out of the 255 host addresses available to them. This is not an uncommon situation.

netID	hostID

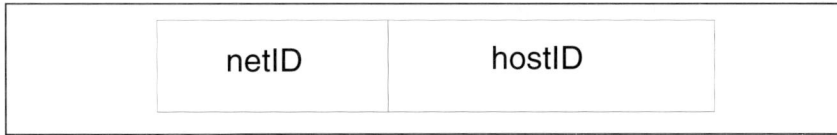

Figure 1.6   IP Network Address

1.5.2 Network Topology Changes

The assignments of network layer addresses to hosts is based on the topology (state of connectivity) of the network. Routing information (contained in the routers of the network) can be considered to be a form of distributed database, where a partial view of the network topology information is contained in each router. Each router must be capable of selecting the "next hop" for each packet based on its ultimate network layer destination address.

Figure 1.7 depicts routing in conventional data networks. A data packet is forwarded from its source, located somewhere in the rest of the world, to its destination host, Host 1. Table 1.1 depicts the corresponding entries in the routing tables at Routers W, X, Y, and Z, which participate in the packet forwarding. The null entry in the "next hop" field for Router X indicates that Host 1 is local to Router X.

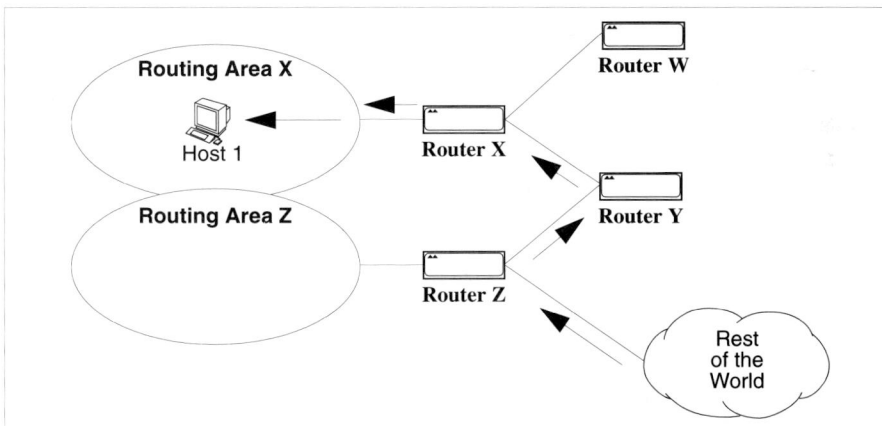

Figure 1.7   Conventional Data Network Routing

Table 1.1   Routing Table Entries for Host 1

Router X		Routers W & Y		Router Z	
Host Address	Next Hop	Host Address	Next Hop	Host Address	Next Hop
X.1	—	X.1	X	X.1	Y

Over time, this distributed routing database evolves to reflect changing WAN connectivity. As links and nodes come and go, the routing tables must reflect these changes. This routing table adaptation can either be manually administered (called "static routes") or automatic (i.e., based on router protocols such as RIP and OSPF) [PERL92]. Automatic routing table updates support changing network environments due to configuration changes and failures.

1.5.2.1 Novell IPX

Novell's proprietary IPX protocol uses ten-byte network layer addresses in a creative fashion to support a plug-and-play network configuration capability. The first four bytes of the address represent the network and are called "network." The last six bytes are called "node" and identify the host ("node" in Novell terminology). This field is identical to the device's permanent six-byte MAC sublayer identifier.

In IPX there is no requirement for network administrators to explicitly configure each node address, only each router's network value. Plug-and-play capability—certainly a factor in mobility—is supported in that a host only needs to determine its "network" value by querying a local router when the host is joined to a network. The node must then notify each of its application peers of its new "permanent" address, which it has self-configured.

This self-configuration by IPX significantly reduces the effort required to move devices from one location to another and prevents node address conflicts. It also eliminates the need for a protocol, such as ARP,[12] to provide the network layer to data link layer address mapping for local routing.

1.5.3 Routing Table Updates

Rapid *convergence* of router protocols (i.e., adaptation of the routing information database to changing network state) is a primary concern in WANs. Routing protocols must converge more quickly than network topology changes occur or the internetwork operation will break down from the congestion caused by misdirected packets. In fact, one of the biggest drawbacks to the popular RIP protocol is its slow convergence in large-scale internetworks.

Conventional data network routing table updates must be done frequently enough to prevent congestion in the event of a link or router failure or network reconfiguration. [IOAN93] observes

---

12. The Address Resolution Protocol in the IP world.

that "if the links go up and down faster than the [routing] protocols can converge, routing may not be possible even though the physical paths exist."

The need for rapid convergence is amplified in mobile environments, where the movement of hosts creates and destroys links (to those hosts) dynamically and presumably more frequently than failures occur. Routing information needs to be rapidly shared amongst mobility routers to ensure consistency between their routing tables and the represented physical network topology.

[KRIS95] notes that "conventional routing protocols were not designed for networks where the topological connectivity is subject to frequent, unpredictable change." Although current routing information protocols support adaptive routing updates to reflect network and host connectivity changes, these protocols are designed for infrequent updates and failures, and thus inadequate to support mobility.

1.6 Mobility Management Schemes

According to [IOAN93], network layer-based mobility management schemes can be categorized as falling into one of three basic types, as summarized in the following subsections.

1.6.1 Permanent Address Scheme (PAS)

The first mobility management scheme is called the *Permanent Address assignment Scheme (PAS)* [IOAN93]. In *PAS,* the mobile host network layer address remains constant, with the routing system adapting itself to changes in the host's location.

To support PAS, each router in the mobile internetwork must maintain a *host route* (routing table entry consisting of the host address and the "next hop" for that host's current location) for each mobile host in the internetwork. As each mobile host moves throughout the internetwork, all routers must update their routing tables accordingly.

Figure 1.8 depicts a mobile host, Mobile 2, changing its point of access to the mobile internetwork from Area X to Area Z. Accommodating this change in PAS network topology entails changes to the routing tables in Router X, Router Y, and Router Z; these routing tables are displayed immediately prior to the movement of Mobile 2 in Table 1.2 and immediately following the movement of Mobile 2 in Table 1.3. Because Router W has Router X as the "next hop" for both Area X and Area Z, its routing table remains unchanged by the movement of Mobile 2.

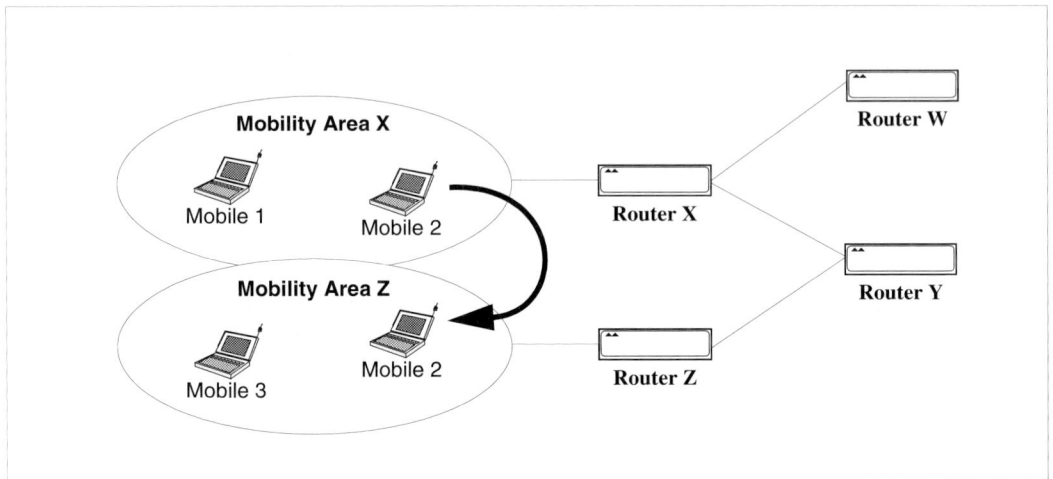

Figure 1.8   Permanent Address Scheme (PAS)

Table 1.2   PAS Routing Tables prior to Mobile 2 Movement

Router W		Router X		Router Y		Router Z	
Mob. Host	Next Hop	Mob. Host	Next Hop	Mob. Host	Next Hop	Mob. Host	Next Hop
1	X	1	-	1	X	1	Y
2	X	2	-	2	X	2	Y
3	X	3	Y	3	Z	3	-

Table 1.3   PAS Routing Tables following Mobile 2 Movement

Router W		Router X		Router Y		Router Z	
Mob. Host	Next Hop	Mob. Host	Next Hop	Mob. Host	Next Hop	Mob. Host	Next Hop
1	X	1	-	1	X	1	Y
2	X	2	Y	2	Z	2	-
3	X	3	Y	3	Z	3	-

PAS is problematic because it requires every router in the mobile internetwork to have a current host route entry for every mobile host—which might number in the millions. This simple scheme clearly does not scale well and is thus inappropriate for large mobile networks. Too bad—it's easy for the mobile hosts and transparent to their correspondents.

1.6.2 Temporary Address Scheme (TAS)

The second basic mobility management scheme is called the *Temporary Address assignment Scheme (TAS)* [IOAN93], which is the logical opposite of PAS. In *TAS* a mobile host adopts a network layer address consistent with its current subnet location. When the host moves, its network layer address changes to reflect its new location.

In TAS, the onus of work supporting mobility is placed on the mobile host and its applications rather than the network infrastructure. TAS is a form of the Application Awareness approach to mobility.

Figure 1.9 depicts a mobile host, Mobile X.1, moving from Area X to Area Z; in the process its temporary address changes from X.1 to Z.2. Because this new address reflects its new location in Area Z, packets addressed to Mobile Z.2 will be forwarded to it via conventional routing. The routing tables for Routers W, X, Y, and Z are depicted before the move in Table 1.4 and following the move in Table 1.5. In all routing tables, the entry for host X.1 has been deleted and a new entry for host Z.2 has been created

Unfortunately, peer applications will not be able to create associations with the mobile host for a while because its network layer address changed. Until peer applications know to use the Z.2 address rather than the X.1 address, the mobile host will be unable to receive packets.

Obviously, TAS is trivial for routers to support—they don't need to do anything special.[13] However, maintenance of accurate DNS name server information is extremely difficult with TAS.[14]   Also, mechanisms are required to ensure global network address uniqueness.[15]

Changing network addresses impacts TCP and other transport layer protocols that assume permanent[16] network layer addresses. Under TAS, sessions would have to be torn down whenever a host move required a change of address. This is the same problem created by the Directory Lookup approach, discussed earlier, and conflicts with our desire for transparent mobility.

---

13. One way to implement TAS in a way that is transparent to routers is to have mobile hosts assign their own temporary address, possibly based on the router's (subnet's) netid and their own permanent hostid (which must be globally unique). This is similar to Novell's IPX networking, which greatly reduces the administrative overhead of operating and maintaining a network.
14. The Domain Name System, or DNS, provides mapping between host names, which rarely change, and host addresses, which change whenever hosts are moved to new subnets in conventional networks.
15. Network addresses must be globally unique in order to prevent data intended for one recipient to be mistakenly forwarded to the wrong host.
16. "Permanent" is a relative term, which usually implies human administration! A configuration can be considered to be "permanent" whenever human intervention is required to change it.

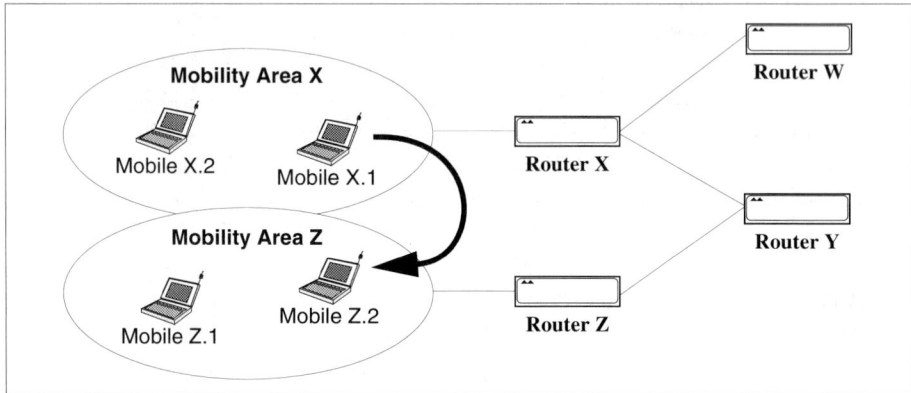

Figure 1.9   Temporary Address Scheme (TAS)

Table 1.4   TAS Routing Tables prior to Mobile X.1 Movement

Router W		Router X		Router Y		Router Z	
Mob. Host	Next Hop	Mob. Host	Next Hop	Mob. Host	Next Hop	Mob. Host	Next Hop
X.1	X	X.1	-	X.1	X	X.1	Y
X.2	X	X.2	-	X.2	X	X.2	Y
Z.1	X	Z.1	Y	Z.1	Z	Z.1	-

Table 1.5   TAS Routing Tables following Mobile Z.2[a] Movement

Router W		Router X		Router Y		Router Z	
Mob. Host	Next Hop	Mob. Host	Next Hop	Mob. Host	Next Hop	Mob. Host	Next Hop
X.2	X	X.2	-	X.2	X	X.2	Y
Z.1	X	Z.1	Y	Z.1	Z	Z.1	-
Z.2	X	Z.2	Y	Z.12	Z	Z.2	-

1.6.3 Embedded Network Scheme (ENS)

The third basic scheme for mobility management is called the *Embedded Network Scheme (ENS)* [IOAN93]. *ENS* embeds a virtual network of mobile hosts and support infrastructure (mobility routers and other assistant entities) in the midst of a larger internetwork. These mobility routers serve to provide mobility in the virtual network; other elements in the data network infrastructure, such as routers, can remain ignorant about host mobility.

Figure 1.10 depicts a mobile host, Mobile X.1, moving from Area X to Area Z. Only the routing tables for the "special" mobility aware routers, Routers X* and Z*, have been changed to reflect this change in network topology. The routing tables for all routers are depicted in Table 1.4 prior to the mobile's movement and Table 1.3 following the mobile's movement.

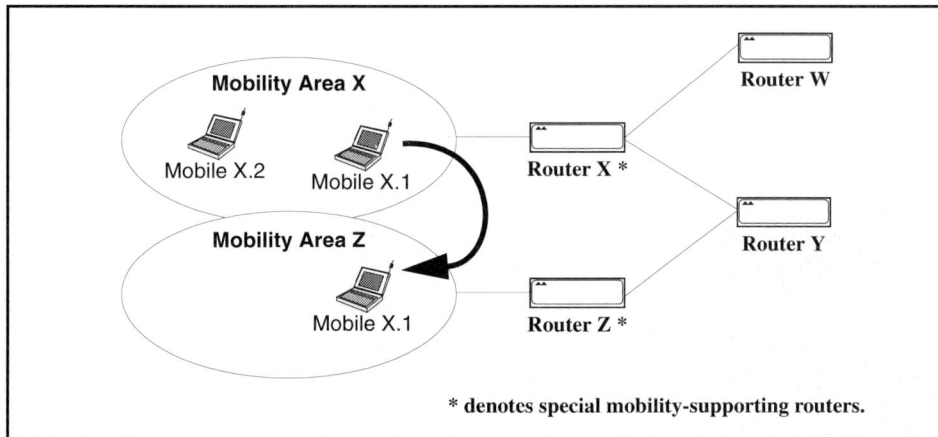

Figure 1.10   Embedded Network Scheme (ENS)

Table 1.6   ENS Routing Tables prior to Mobile X.1 Movement

Router W		Router X*		Router Y		Router Z*	
Mob. Host	Next Hop	Mob. Host	Next Hop	Mob. Host	Next Hop	Mob. Host	Next Hop
X.1	X*	X.1	-	X.1	X*	X.1	Y
X.2	X*	X.2	-	X.2	X*	X.2	Y
Z.1	X*	Z.1	Y	Z.1	Z*	Z.1	-

Table 1.7   ENS Routing Tables following Mobile X.1 Movement

Router W		Router X*		Router Y		Router Z*	
Mob. Host	Next Hop	Mob. Host	Next Hop	Mob. Host	Next Hop	Mob. Host	Next Hop
X.1	X*	X.1	[Y]	X.1	X*	X.1	-
X.2	X*	X.2	-	X.2	X*	X.2	Y
Z.1	X*	Z.1	Y	Z.1	Z*	Z.1	-

By decoupling mobility management from the conventional routing mechanisms, ENS provides a more efficient means of routing to mobile hosts and supports constant network addresses. ENS typically involves either data packet encapsulation or the use of secondary temporary addresses by the "special" routers in order to provide mobility. ENS embodies the Administrative Redirection approach to mobility in its transparency to the rest of the world.

CDPD services are provided via an ENS-type of mobility management; this mobility is transparent to existing routers and hosts. The Mobile IP definition and Novell's Mobile IPX are also implementations of the ENS concept. The primary difference between these systems is in the way that the assisting entities are defined.

1.6.3.1 ENS Variations

In CDPD and Mobile IP, two cooperating assisting entities provide mobility management. One of them—the Mobile Home Function (MHF) in CDPD, the mobility router in Mobile IP—serves as the public local router for packets destined to the mobile host. The second assistant—the Mobile Serving Function (MSF) in CDPD, the foreign agent in Mobile IP—receives packets that have been redirected by the first assistant and forwards them on to the mobile via the local data link.

Packet *encapsulation* or *tunneling* is used by CDPD and Mobile IP to redirect packets from the first to the second assisting entity, as depicted in Figure 1.11. The details of this mobility management scheme is presented in Chapter 4 (for CDPD) and Chapter 10 (for Mobile IP).

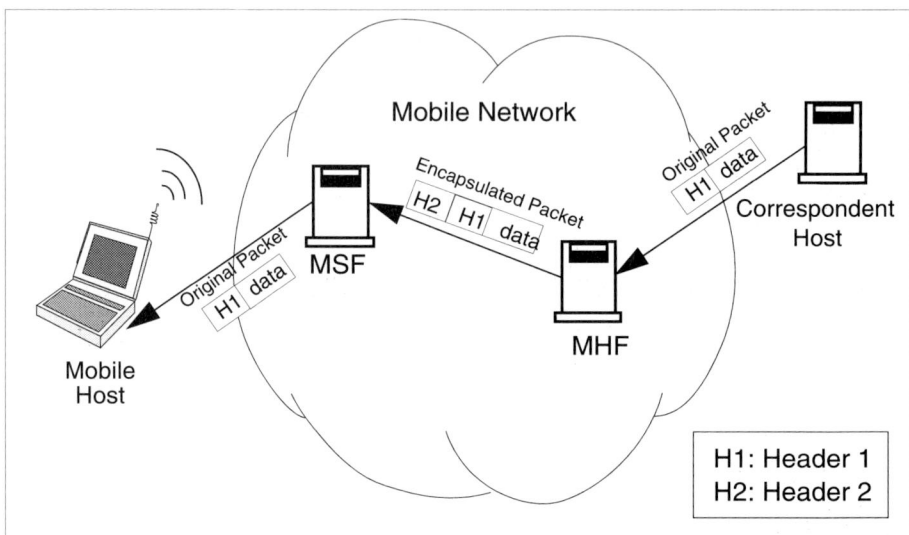

Figure 1.11   Packet Encapsulation in CDPD

Novell's Mobile IPX differs in that it uses a single assisting entity, called the home router, to forward packets to a mobile node (host). The home router advertises an "internal" network number that the mobile adopts as its network number field in a so-called "permanent" address; the node number field for this permanent address is sequentially assigned by the home router to registering mobiles.

Whenever a mobile relocates, it determines its location-dependent (physical) IPX address in the usual way (by prepending a local router's network number to its hardwired MAC identifier, as we discussed in Section 1.5.1). The mobile then notifies its home router of its new location. All the home router has to do is maintain a table of the mobile's permanent address as related to its physical address mappings.

Whenever an IPX packet destined for the mobile's permanent address arrives at the home router (based on standard IPX packet routing), the home router replaces that destination address (the mobile's permanent address) with the mobile's current physical address and then redirects the packet onward as depicted in Figure 1.12. The mobile then internally replaces the substituted physical address with its permanent address to avoid confusion by higher layers and applications. This destination address substitution may be contrasted with the packet encapsulation technique used by CDPD and Mobile IP.

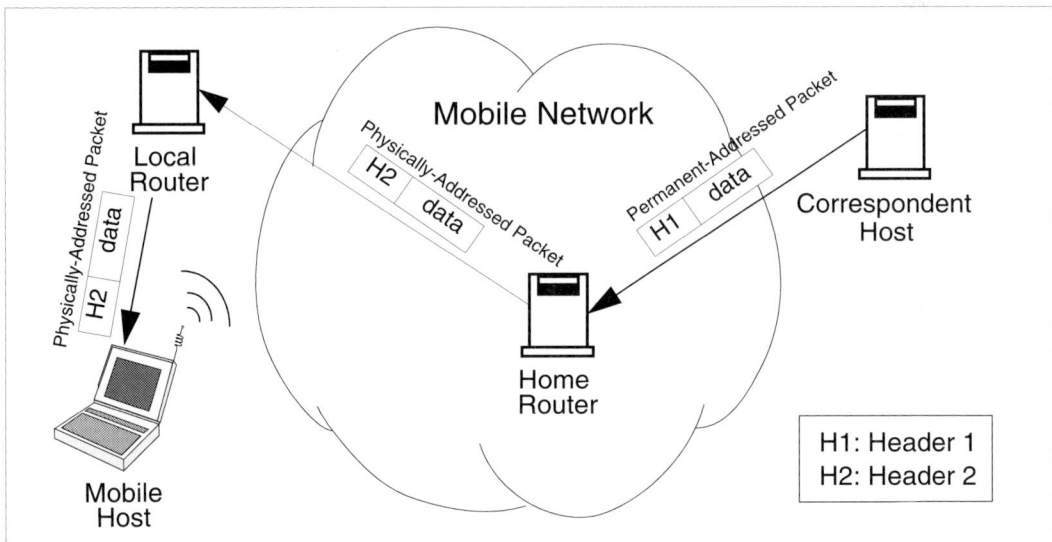

Figure 1.12   Address Substitution in Mobile IPX

1.7 Steps in the Mobility Management Process

Three steps are involved in accessing and using mobile data networks. These steps are necessary for mobility management and are analogous to the phases of a connection-oriented protocol. The details of each step depend largely on whether the system uses a tracking or searching mobility management strategy as described in Section 1.4.1.

1.7.1 Registration

At some point, the mobile host must announce itself to the system ("Here I am!") before it can receive services. This announcement, or *registration,* serves several purposes, including establishment of a *SubNet Point of Attachment* or *SNPA* (i.e., the local address where the mobile can be accessed), obtaining network connectivity via the local mobility-supporting router, authentication of its identity, authorization for use, encryption key exchange, link layer parameter negotiation, etc. The mobile registers to a single mobility area at a time.

If the system employs a tracking-based mobility management strategy, the mobile will register once and thereafter remain virtually connected to the system, even if it neither sends nor receives data. If the system employs a search-based mobility management strategy, the mobile will register each time it wants to transmit data, or in response to a system page (because another entity wants to send it data).

Registration includes but is not limited to mobile network access. After performing the actions necessary to access the mobile network, the mobile host must then initiate the mobility management process.

1.7.2 Usage

Once the mobile host has registered to the system, it may use the resources of the system to access the rest of the world. At this point, the mobile host must behave and serve its applications much the same as a conventional host. Mobile network usage could last a long time or for only the duration of a brief data communication. During this interval, the mobile host is accessed (i.e., data packets are sent to it) via the mobility router to which it is registered.

1.7.3 De-registration

Following its use of the system, the mobile host leaves its subnet point of attachment. The *de-registration* serves the purpose of freeing-up network resources (such as identifiers, memory blocks, routing table entries, etc.) that would otherwise be allocated to a quiescent mobile. A mobile host might deregister because it no longer requires mobile access or because it has moved out of the mobility area to which it was registered.

1.8 A Simple Taxonomy of Mobility

Mobility can exist in many forms. To assist in analyzing different mobile systems, we offer a simple taxonomy of mobility. In this taxonomy, levels of mobility depend on the degree of location-independence and in-motion capability provided by the mobile system.

We should point out that mobility is just one dimension of a mobile data system. As pictured in Figure 1.13, the medium in use and the protocols supported are additional dimensions to consider. Depending on the situation and desired application, different mobility solutions are more or less appropriate.

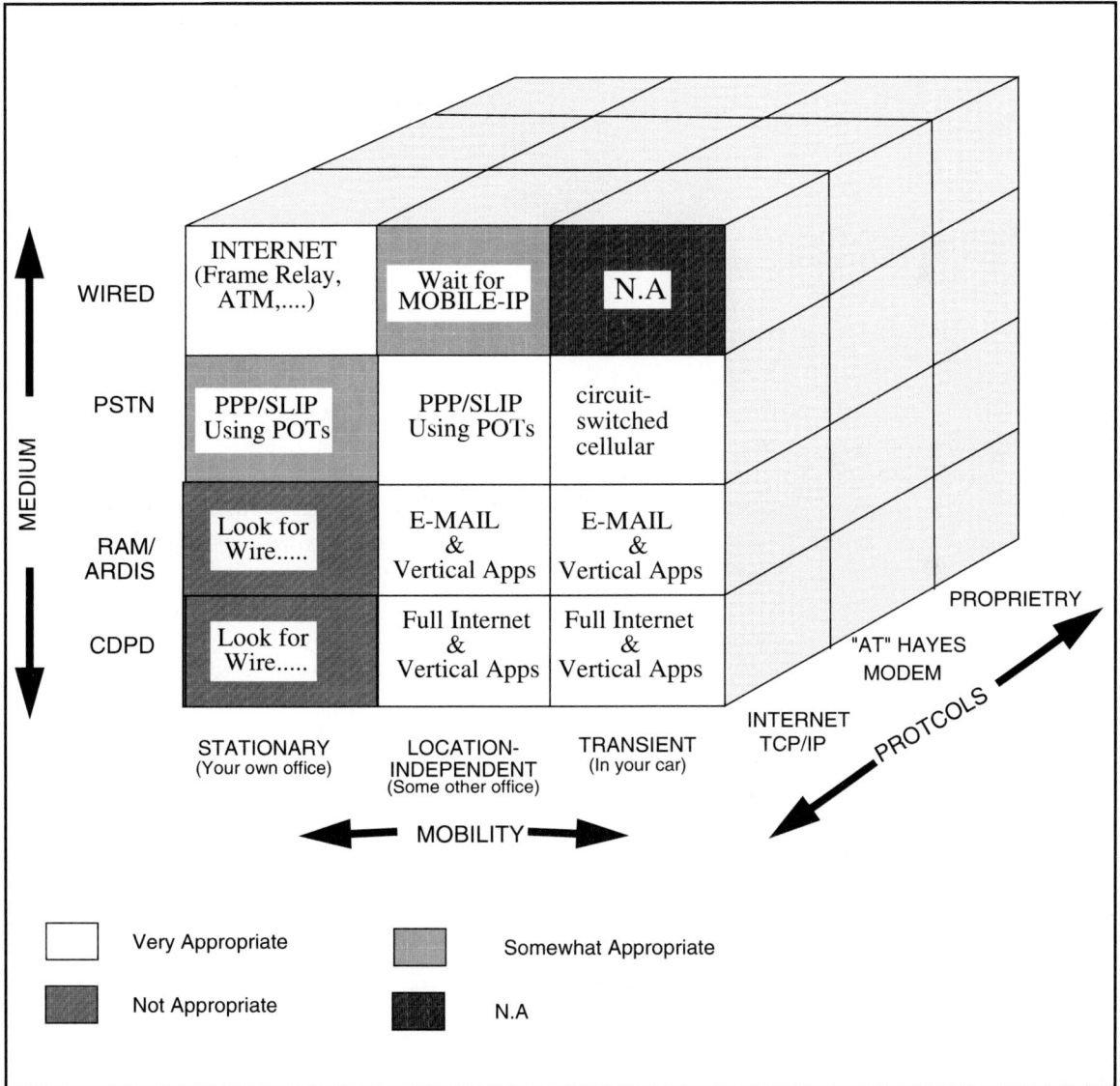

Figure 1.13   The Mobility Cube

As mentioned earlier, transparency is a key aspect of mobile systems. If a peer application needs to know about the mobility of a host, then the benefit of that mobility is limited. In particular, systems requiring effort to port applications to them, while supporting mobility, are limited by the lack of mobile transparency.

Typically, these systems require gateways to "spoof" protocols on one side of their networks and use proprietary protocols to convey data over radio channels. The horizontal market acceptance of these systems has been somewhat limited by obstacles such as nonstandard APIs and mobile devices.

In many cases, these systems have been designed from the bottom up, with an initial design focus on the Physical layer, which is typically RF-based. Early mobile systems were developed from an RF perspective and customized to minimize radio traffic, using techniques such as canned messages and proprietary protocols at all layers. This effort to optimize the Physical layer resulted in systems with physical (RF) protocols visible to applications. These systems are poor examples of protocol layering.

1.8.1 Type 0 Mobility: Stationarity

Type 0 Mobility describes systems that do not support mobility. Network entities are limited to essentially fixed locations for communication with others. This is the level of mobility provided by conventional data networking technology.

In conventional networks, the network layer address indicates the topological location of the host. The *netid* part of the address identifies the subnet on which a host can be found and is used by routers to forward a packet to its destination. Once the packet reaches the "last router," which connects the destination subnet to the rest of the world, the *hostid* part of the address is used to identify the destination host on that subnet.[17] In general, the network address (netid + hostid) defines the host's location relative to well known places in the internetwork.

Typically, human intervention is required to configure and administer network addresses of hosts in Type 0 systems. In these systems, moving a host from one location (subnet) to another amounts to creating a new entity (i.e., network address). [RICH95] states that "the static addresses of traditional network architectures bind a computer to a specific LAN or subnet. Current versions of IP, for example, assume that an IP node has a fixed point of connection to its network."

Type 0 systems are location-dependent and are thus not mobile. Examples of Type 0 systems include not only traditional networks, but also wireless LANs and campus networks such as Metricom Ricochet. The limitations to mobility in such systems are often due to technology not being scalable to the magnitude required for ubiquitous mobile operations. In any case, the mobility is limited to the subnet or immediate (LAN) medium containing the host.

---

17. Actually, a protocol such as Address Resolution Protocol (ARP) is used to resolve the hostid to a Layer 2 identifier in use by that host on the subnet. This mechanism is described in [PERL92] and [STEV94].

1.8.2 Type 1 Mobility: Location Independence

Type 1 Mobility describes systems in which hosts enjoy mobility regardless of location. An example of a Type 1 system is Mobile IP.[18] Mobile IP is a very recent mobile technology development that is media-independent. Regardless of the underlying physical and MAC layers, Mobile IP provides the capability for two mobile hosts to directly communicate regardless of location. CDPD's mobility management paradigm is based on that of Mobile IP, which is discussed in Chapter 10.

1.8.3 Type 2 Mobility: Transience

Type 2 Mobility describes systems in which in-motion operation is supported in a transparent and location-independent fashion. Type 2 mobility is the ultimate form of anywhere, anytime communications capability. An example of such a system is CDPD, which was originally conceived of as a cellular overlay. In this system, the efficiency of mobility management (and radio resource management) is optimized to support active moving hosts, which are capable of automobile speeds. As we have seen, support for in-motion mobile hosts places strong operational requirements on the network. Other examples of Type 2 systems include RAM and Ardis, which are described in Chapter 9.

1.9 Range of Mobility

In order to describe mobility in WAN environments, we need a terminology describing range of motion. Mobility consists of receiving service anywhere; movement to another region should result in receiving service in the new region. Although the application running on the mobile host should be oblivious to the regional boundaries (transparency of service), the mobile host itself will likely need to be aware of the boundary crossing and actively participate in it.

The region types we define are a hybrid of conventional data network and cellular terminology; this reflects our need to define mobility in both (network) topological and geographic terms. Since WANs are hierarchical in nature, so are these regional definitions. This is depicted in Figure 1.14.

---

18. We make no distinction between systems that *could be* deployed everywhere and those that *are* deployed everywhere. Rather than discuss the current state of deployment, which is itself a moving target, we assume that a system capable of global deployment is globally deployed; this makes it location-independent.

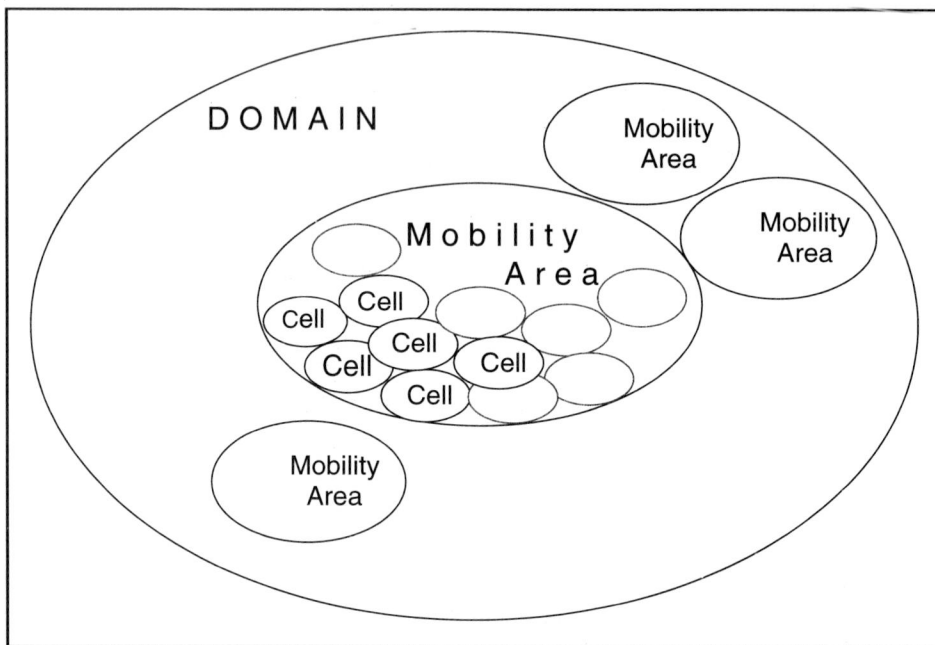

Figure 1.14   Range of Mobility

1.9.1 Channel

A *channel* is the means by which a mobile host receives service; it is the subnet used by the mobile to access the network. The channel is both a physical medium and a logical location (i.e., network access point) of the mobile host. In many cases, such as CDPD, the channel is shared by multiple mobile hosts. In other cases, the channel may be dedicated to a single mobile host.

1.9.2 Cell

A *cell* is defined by the geographical area covered by a channel. This means that a mobile host could potentially continue to receive service from the channel even while moving about the cell.

A cell can be either large or small, depending on the system and the situation; medium-specific physical limitations and capacity constraints determine the size of a cell. In a wireless system, a cell is defined by the RF coverage area of a single channel. Depending on the mobile system, the cell might be identical to the mobility area; in this case, geography and network topology would be essentially identical.

Multiple channels could cover a single cell. This would be akin to multiple Ethernet LANs being available to office workers in a building; which Ethernet is used is based on the need for logical interconnectivity (e.g., a group of users who work together a lot) or traffic (load balancing).[19]

Sometimes, depending on the medium used, cells overlap. In such a situation, a mobile could receive service from any number of channels. This could be significant from the standpoint of mobility management if the channels covering the mobile's geographic location are based in different network topological locations. An example of this is the A-side and B-side systems in the cellular industry.

In some systems, the mobile hosts in a cell can directly communicate with one another in a peer-to-peer fashion. In other systems, the mobile hosts in a cell must communicate with one another via some kind of hub. The requirement for a hub is typically due to the limitations of the physical medium in use.

1.9.3 Mobility Area

A region controlled (from a mobility perspective) by a single mobility-supporting router is called a *mobility area*; this is analogous to a routing area in conventional data networks [PERL92]. The mobility router is responsible for accepting network layer packets destined for mobile hosts in its area of control (its mobility area) and forwarding those packets to their destinations.

From a WAN perspective, the mobility router is directly connected to all of the mobile hosts in its mobility area; this is a network layer topological concept. The mobility router is the last entity to handle the NPDUs (in their Layer 3 form) before the destination host; any intervening entity operates at a strictly lower layer. The mobility router is an assisting entity in any mobility scenario.

A mobility area will generally consist of one or more cells. Each cell is contained entirely within a single mobility area.

1.9.4 Administrative Domain

An *administrative domain* in a mobile network is the same as in a conventional data network: a region under the control of a single authority. This is important from the standpoint of accounting, directory services, security, and authorization. The administrative domain is the highest-level region for mobility.

An administrative domain is under the jurisdiction of a single authoritative body; this body either accepts or rejects a mobile entity requesting services in the domain. The idea is that someone

---

19. Another strategy for configuring LANs is based on building geography (e.g., all PCs in one area of a floor are connected to the same LAN). With hub-based LAN architectures, a given LAN tap could be connected to any one of the (logical) LANs hosted by the hub.

has to pay for and run a network (or subnetwork); the collection of subnets under control of one organization is an administrative domain. An administrative domain is a logical concept and is sometimes referred to as an *autonomous system.*

An administrative domain will generally consist of one or more mobility areas. Each mobility area is contained in its entirety within a single administrative domain.

1.10 Mobility Is Not Wirelessness

Our discussion thus far has introduced many issues of mobility that are independent of the medium used to access a network. This is not an original idea—groups such as the Mobile IP Task Force have worked on mobility for some time without any media-specific considerations.

From this, it is obvious that *mobility is not equivalent to wirelessness.* Mobility is the ability to communicate anytime, anywhere; this is a topological capability—always being able to "connect with" another party. Ideally, this *connectivity* can be maintained regardless of the location or motion of the mobile entity. This location independence should be available over an area that is physically too large for any single medium, such as an Ethernet cable or an RF channel.

A *wireless* host is a communications end-point[20] that is physically untethered by a communications link or cable; this is a capability of the physical medium in use. Obviously, wirelessness enables greater mobility than is possible with wired media, especially in-motion correspondence.

Mobility management is closely associated in wireless systems with *radio resource management.* Radio resource management is typically concerned with assuring proper (effective and efficient) use of the RF medium and is part of accessing the mobile network. In cellular-type systems such as CDPD, radio resource management could actually be considered to be a highly granular form of mobility management. However, in this book, we shall be very specific about mobility management as a Layer 3 activity.

However, *WAN mobility does not require a wireless medium.* We can easily conceive of ubiquitous Internet taps sometime in the future that would support mobility but not require wireless access. A user of such a system could take a portable computer from place to place, connecting via readily available universal network taps, to send and receive data; this would comprise a mobile capability that doesn't involve any wireless technology.

Conversely, *a wireless capability in a host does not imply mobility.* There are a number of wireless LANs and campus networks that, although free from the physical constraints of cables, cannot be considered to be WANs because of their limited range of operation. Many telemetry

---

20. We are being purposefully vague here because the host could be a device, an application, or other entity, depending on context.

applications, such as building security systems or utility meters, entail wirelessness but not mobility.

1.10.1 Wireless Considerations

Wireless systems are limited by constraints such as the availability of radio frequencies, licensing from the Federal Communications Commission (FCC) and other regulatory authorities, [21] and the expense associated with whatever technology is used to transport data "over the air." Radio Frequency spectrum is depicted in Figure 1.15.

The easiest to use (and therefore least expensive) radio spectrum has already been assigned to commercial broadcast applications such as television and radio; much of the previously-allocated spectrum is reserved for government use. Higher radio frequencies are available, but require more complex (more expensive) technology and suffer from greater attenuation (and thus, limited range). As we shall see, cost and coverage are key issues for wireless systems.

Some radio spectrum is freely available for use without requiring FCC licensing. This unregulated spectrum is typified by the 902-928 MHz region, commonly referred to as the *ISM (Industrial, Scientific, and Medical) band*. The ISM band is used for applications such as garage door openers, remote controls, home security systems, microwave ovens, etc. Effective use of this unregulated spectrum for data communications requires the use of jam-proof radio technology such as spread spectrum (which is not an inexpensive technology).

The U.S. government has now reassigned and held public auctions for radio spectrum to be used for two-way *Personal Communications Systems (PCS)*. This newly available spectrum will encourage further advances in the use of wireless technology for data communications. As a result, we can expect continued growth in (wireless) mobile data applications.

Other factors currently limit the ubiquity of wireless data communications, including power control and signal propagation. Power control is a significant issue because the wireless host can operate only as long as its battery will allow. Although battery technology continues to make great strides, battery life is still a critical design factor for wireless systems. Techniques such as sleep mode operation have been designed as key system functions that support wireless hosts by extending their battery life.

Signal propagation is always a factor in wireless systems because an RF signal at a given frequency and power level can be reliably received within a limited range of the transmitter. Increasing power levels tends to extend the range of wireless communication, limited by the battery capabilities of the wireless host. Having smaller RF *coverage areas* helps reduce wireless host battery requirements but increases the network deployment costs because of an increased number of *base stations* providing landline connectivity.

---

21. The FCC is the governmental body that allocates RF frequencies for various applications and industries in the United States. The World Administrative Radio Conference (WARC) is responsible for coordinating frequency assignments internationally.

All of these considerations are important to the design and deployment of wireless systems. However, they have little to do with mobility.

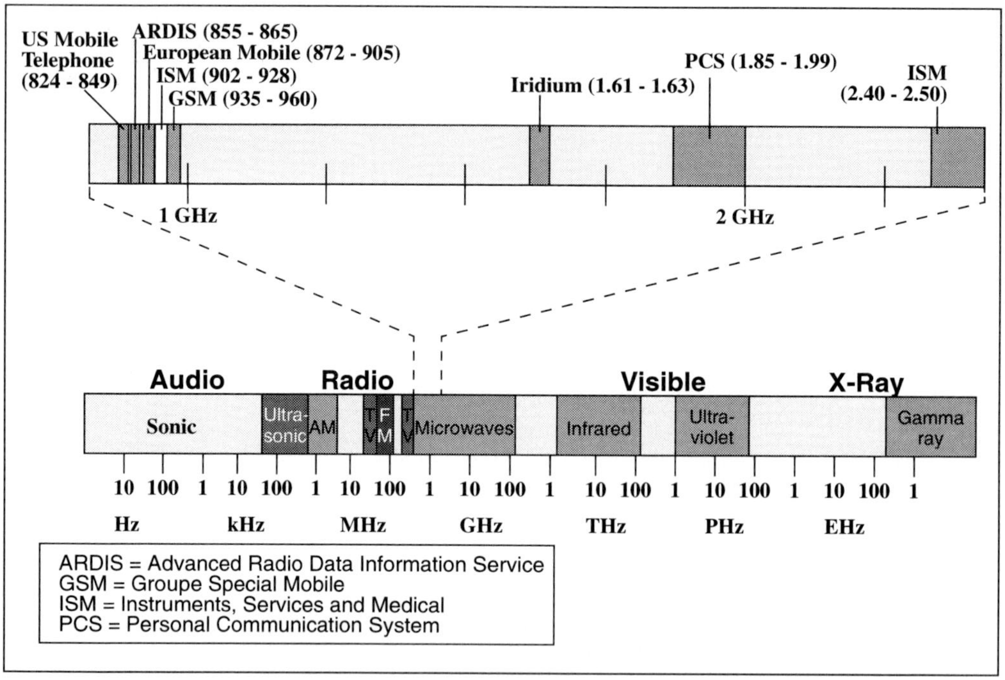

Figure 1.15   Radio Frequency Spectrum

1.11 Challenges of Mobility

The capability for mobility introduces a number of challenges to conventional wide area data networking. One measure of a mobile system's usefulness in the real world is the extent to which that system addresses these challenges.

1.11.1 Geography vs. Network Topology

The first challenge of mobility is the mapping of geographic coordinates to network addresses. Data networking is inherently topological in nature: two hosts are either (directly or indirectly) connected or they are not. Physical location of the hosts is immaterial, except for the physical limitations of the medium in use.

A network address, including a netid and a hostid, indicates the topological connectivity of a host (i.e., the subnet defined by the netid) but not its geographic location. Moving a host to a new geographic location might or might not require a change in network address, depending on whether the topological (network) connectivity has changed.

However, mobility is inherently a geographic capability—being able to be anywhere, anytime. Since the essential problem of mobility is being able to receive communications anywhere and the routing of data to a host is via network address (netid), there needs to be a mapping of some sort between the geographic location of the mobile host and the network connectivity. This mapping can be either explicit or implicit, but it must be done to get data packets to a mobile host.

Because the geographical to topological mapping is loose and dependent on the system's technology and architecture, movement in the geographic sense may or may not be reflected in the topological sense. Either the system can provide this geographic to topological location mapping or corresponding entities must do this mapping themselves. This is the heart of mobility management.

1.11.2 Part-Time Destinations

Another challenge of mobility is the part-time connectivity of mobile entities. This is an issue for any networked host that is frequently unavailable.

Accessing an *occasionally connected* host is an issue because it requires effort above and beyond what is normally required in conventional networks. Data networking paradigms today assume the essentially continuous availability of networked hosts to receive correspondence. If a host is unavailable, current applications must either continuously page for the intended recipient or have the temporarily disconnected host poll each of its potential application servers as soon as it rejoins the network.

In conventional networks and LANs, polling is not a problem because there is generally plenty of bandwidth to accommodate this overhead. However, in mobile WANs, which could support millions of users, accessing part-time destinations (which could be anywhere) is an issue! If each mobile host had to poll each of its application servers (across a wide area) the result would be a system that does not scale well.

Another aspect of part-time destinations is the fact that connectivity is a network layer concern, while correspondence between entities is typically at the application layer. Thus, there needs to be an efficient mechanism for bridging between applications layer entities' desire to correspond and network layer connectivity. The CDPD approach to this is called Status Notification Service and is described in Chapter 8.

What is needed in a mobile WAN environment is the capability for efficient storing and forwarding of data in a manner that is transparent to corresponding application entities. This might involve storing and forwarding of messages (application layer PDUs) rather than packets (network layer PDUs).

For example, if two systems need to exchange data but are never operating at the same time, an intermediary system of some kind is needed to facilitate the data exchange. The intermediary store-and-forward entity would first receive the data (e.g., email) from the source when both are operating. The intermediary would then forward the data on to the destination system when they are both operating.

1.11.3 Moving Targets

Another challenge of mobility is getting data to a potentially moving target. Given a geographic to topological address mapping capability and an efficient store and forward capability, there remains a need for efficient routing of the data to a host that frequently changes location. Routing tables need to be updated more frequently than a mobile host changes its cell location. This challenge is exacerbated in transient (i.e., Type 2) entities which can be in motion at the time a correspondent is communicating with it.

Some systems address this moving target challenge by having the current assisting entity notify its predecessor. This solution can be effective, but suffers from the creation of a potentially long trail of assistants that forward messages from one to another until eventually reaching the current one. This is not unlike the method used by the postal service[22] or cellular voice systems.

1.11.4 Application Transparency

Another challenge of mobility is *transparency*. Neither an application on a mobile host nor the peer with which it is communicating should be directly impacted by location independence. The application should operate and—to the human using it—look and feel the same as it would in a non-mobile context. Transparency requires standard *Application Program Interfaces* or *APIs* to provide the normal "look and feel" to applications and the humans using them; as we shall see, lack of standard APIs has limited the adoption of some otherwise appropriate mobile data systems.

The mobility of the host should also be transparent to the rest of the world with which it is communicating. Any entity wishing to communicate with a mobile entity should be able to do so regardless of the target's mobility.

The "hourglass" of protocols of Figure 1.16 depicts one way that transparency is naturally provided in internetworking environments. By having a common Layer 3 protocol—typically IP—many applications can be supported independently of the many subnetwork technologies and media available.

---

22. Commonly referred to by "techies" as "Snail Mail." In this case, "service" is a loose terminology.

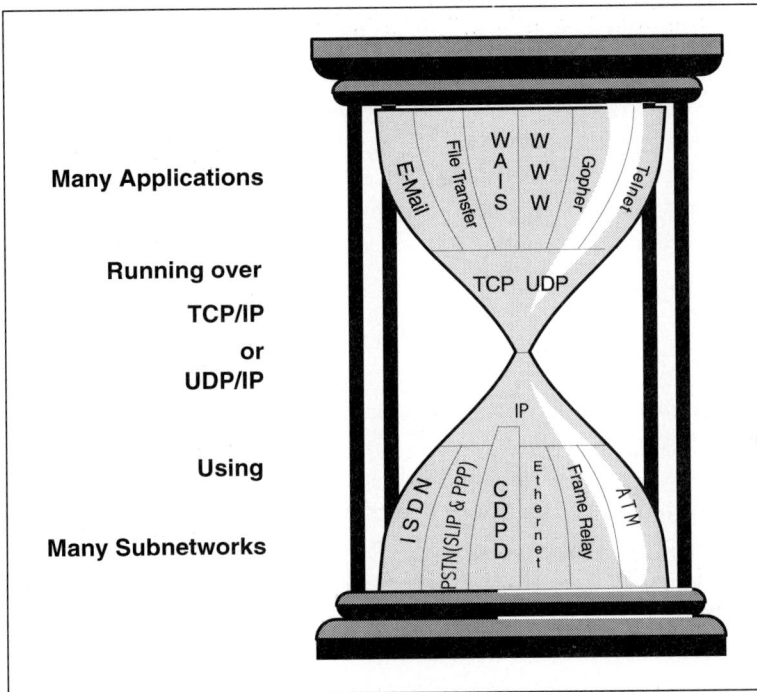

Figure 1.16   The Protocol Hour-Glass

The conventional world of data networking is based on a paradigm of routing data packets on the basis of their destination network address. This paradigm should be unaffected by the mobility of the destination. Whether the host is "at home" or "on the road," the peer attempting to communicate with it should not have to do anything special beyond what normally would be done to communicate with another host. As we shall see, this has many implications in areas such as directory services, routing, security and accounting.

Transparency of mobility has further implications. Since many applications require connection-oriented transport layer services, Type 2 Mobility data systems must maintain end-to-end transport connections even while the mobile host is in motion. This implies that host network addresses must not change to support mobility, otherwise transport and higher layers are impacted.

Finally, [IOAN93] says that: "An issue that cannot be handled in lower level protocols, is that of coping with intermittent operation, disconnected operation, or operation during which network characteristics such as bandwidth and latency change significantly. Even if the network layer hides the addressing aspect of mobility from higher levels, applications may want to be 'mobile-smart,' and function differently as the service provided by the network link changes (for example, by increasing the granularity of communication)."

1.11.5 Name-to-Address Mapping

Another challenge of mobility is support for DNS-type directory services. The primary function provided by the *Domain Name System (DNS)* is the translation between host network layer addresses and more user-friendly names. These services allow applications such as email to use names such as "joe@BigCompany.com"[23] as destinations rather than the more human error-inducing addresses such as "joe@123.45.6.789." If changing geographic coordinates implies changes to network addresses, clearly DNS services cannot work in their current format. This again seems to imply the need for "permanent" network addresses of some kind for mobile hosts.

1.11.6 Security

There has been much recent discussion about security in WAN environments. The focus of this discussion is the use of firewalls of various kinds [KAUF95] to prevent unauthorized access to networks from the outside. The assumption is that an attack will come from outside of the local subnet; unfortunately, a high percentage of security "incidents" involve people inside the subnet (e.g., disgruntled employees).

However, mobility of hosts creates new opportunities for compromised network security because the physical security of a subnet is no longer provided. Each time a mobile host establishes a new subnet point of attachment (SNPA), it must authenticate itself to the subnet it is attaching itself to. (Authentication is the process of verifying a host's identity and is essential to detection and prevention of clone devices.)

Typically, authentication involves the use of a password of some kind. Protection of this password, as well as the identity and data of a mobile from potential "eavesdroppers," requires the use of encryption techniques. This (encryption and security in general) raises the costs of providing mobile data services in terms of network and processing overhead, royalties (for the security technology), key management, etc. All of this needs to be embedded within a mobile system, not a later add-on.

Security issues in mobile data networks are discussed in Chapter 6.

1.11.7 Scale

Mobility in WANs raises concerns of scalability to higher levels than ever before. In a mobile WAN environment one could expect millions of hosts and routers.

However, many current routing update protocols (e.g., RIP) fail with a much smaller number of hosts. The need to exchange mobile routing information across the network more frequently

---

23. This is an invalid Internet addess.

adds significantly to network overhead. The larger the network grows (e.g., larger routing tables), the longer it takes to propogate routing information. Also, the amount of computation required by each router (to determine the next hop for a packet) increases with network size.

Additional concerns for authentication and accounting for system usage exacerbate the scalability concern. In a mobile WAN, where mobile hosts can suddenly appear anywhere, rapid access to authentication data is essential. However, replication of the data to enable rapid access raises concerns in areas such as distributed database consistency, etc.

1.12 Summary

In this chapter, we have provided an overview of mobility in the WAN environment and issues that result from mobility. For the most part, these issues are due to inherent conflicts between conventional WAN technology and mobile systems. Mobility directly challenges many of the underlying assumptions of the conventional WAN world, most notably the relative stationarity of host location. Historically, mobile systems arose from the connection-oriented paradigm of telephony. The following chapter describes cellular systems, the archetype of the mobile world.

2 *Introduction to Cellular Systems*

> *Mobile telephony will break out of today's constraints, but not with today's technology. The story of analog cellular radio will be written in vivid hindsight as one of the classic technological miscues of modern history, on a par with, say, the zeppelin airship. The trend it represents is real, but the instrumentality is fatally flawed.*
> —G. Calhoun, *Digital Cellular Radio*, 1988.

In this chapter, we introduce cellular technology, the most pervasive mobile communications technology. Although cellular systems have historically been voice-oriented, much of the underlying technology provides a model for mobile data systems such as CDPD. As we shall see, the application (voice) has driven the design of cellular systems in a way that is less than optimal for data applications.

This chapter presents topics such as cellular radio transmission, cellular capacity, the North American *Advanced Mobile Phone System* (*AMPS*), voice and data services, digital cellular, and the emerging *Personal Communications Services* (*PCS*). Other cellular-based systems that are not "common carrier" systems (e.g., two-way paging) are described in Chapter 9. Although it provides an overview of cellular technology and the cellular industry, this chapter is by no means a complete portrayal—several references such as [CALH88], [LEE-89], [LEE-93], and [PAHL95] provide a much more complete presentation of this fascinating technology.

2.1 The Ubiquity of Cellular

Rapid and accelerating growth of the cellular telephone industry over its first 12 years has resulted in extensive coverage of populated areas by cellular services. Cellular is now the dominant two-way mobile communications technology, with more than eighteen thousand cell sites covering over 95 percent of the U.S. population and serving over 33 million *subscribers*—a 13 percent market penetration—at year-end 1995, as depicted in Table 2.1.[1]

Table 2.1   Growth of AMPS Subscriber Base[a]

Year	AMPS Subscribers (Thousands)	1-Year Annual Growth	Compounded Annual Growth
1984	92	—	—
1985	340	270%	270%
1986	681	100%	172%
1987	1,230	81%	137%
1988	2,000	63%	116%
1989	3,500	75%	107%
1990	5,300	51%	97%
1991	7,600	43%	88%
1992	11,000	45%	82%
1993	16,000	45%	77%
1994	24,000	51%	75%
1995	33,800	40%	71%

[a]Source: Cellular Telecommunications Industry Association

This extensive coverage provided by cellular voice services would seem to make cellular the ideal medium for providing ubiquitous wireless data services. Unfortunately, the cellular industry's voice heritage impacts its ability to support data applications. Cellular's circuit-switched orientation and radio channel characteristics conflict somewhat with the needs of data applications.

Cellular systems have followed the traditional *circuit-switched* channel model of telephony. In this model, the end-to-end circuit, including the cellular channel, is dedicated to a single user or

---

1. Similar growth and subscription rates are becoming the norm in other countries as well. According to the International Telecommunications Union, in late 1995 there were over 55 million cellular telephone subscribers, as compared with 648 million wired telephone lines. Cellular subscriber penetration rates at year-end 1994 for a few representative countries were as follows: Sweden 14.7%, Norway 13.2%, Finland 12.8%, Denmark 9.8%, U.S. 8.8%, Singapore 8.7%, Iceland 8.3%, Hong Kong 7.7%, Kuwait 6.6%, and Canada 6.5%.

application before they can transmit on the channel. The channel remains dedicated to the user or application for the duration of the transmission, until it is explicitly released.

A single dedicated channel per user may be suitable for voice applications albeit somewhat inefficient from a channel perspective. However, a dedicated channel per data user is extremely inefficient and thus prohibitively expensive, unless the data application involves bulk transport of large quantities of data[2] or the application is of a high-performance mission-critical nature.[3] In support of the circuit-switched nature of cellular, billing systems have been oriented toward billable units of time on the order of minutes of airtime, rather than quantities that better match the activities of data users.[4]

The characteristics of the radio channel used by cellular systems have also challenged data applications attempting to use the cellular channels. As we shall see, these radio characteristics are further exacerbated by call control messages that are transmitted in-band while the call (data transmission) is in progress.

2.2 Radio Channels

Cellular channels are *radio frequency (RF)* channels. In an RF-based system, any receiver within range of a transmitter (i.e., within its *coverage area*) can tune to the frequency in use by the transmitter and, with the proper demodulation and decoding, capture the information transmitted.

However, two or more nearby transmitters simultaneously using a common *frequency* or *channel*[5] will *interfere* with one another, unless perfectly synchronized in both timing and content. A receiver within range of both transmitters will most likely receive a garbled message, which is undecipherable.

This potential for interference limits the capacity of any RF-based system. Like any other system employing a shared medium, such as an Ethernet LAN, only a single device can transmit at a time. The greater the number of devices sharing the physical channel, the less often each can transmit. The only difference between an RF-based system and a LAN is the scope of the

---

2. Examples include file transfer, database download, etc., which benefit from committed bandwidth.
3. Examples include emergency public service, etc., which require guaranteed bandwidth availability.
4. Things are changing. In recent years sub-minute billing rate plans have been made available and are gaining popularity as a means of attracting customers. Unfortunately, data transmissions rarely need more than fractions of seconds of dedicated bandwidth.
5. The term "channel" is inherently ambiguous. We will attempt to always precede the word "channel" with an adjective that clarifies the context—such as "physical" or "logical"—unless the meaning is clear.

shared medium; the RF-based system is not as physically bound, thus the opportunity for interference is greater.

This RF capacity constraint increased the expense to users of early mobile phone systems such as *Mobile Telephone System (MTS)* and *Improved Mobile Telephone System (IMTS)*. These systems typically broadcast all channels from a single antenna location. Within a city covered by one of these systems, the number of simultaneous users was limited by the number of RF channels available to the system; each RF channel could be used by only one transmitter at a time.

2.3 The Cellular Concept

RF bandwidth has always been the primary constraint in wireless systems; there is never too much. Efficiently using this precious resource involves what is called *frequency reuse*, in which a radio channel is allowed to be simultaneously used by multiple transmitters as long as they are sufficiently separated to avoid interference. The essential idea of cellular radio is to transmit at power levels sufficiently low so as to not interfere with the nearest location at which the same channel is *reused*.

In this way a physical (RF) channel can be used more than once in a given city. The greater the *reuse distance*, the lower the probability of interference. Likewise, the lower the power levels used in cells sharing a common channel, the lower the probability of interference.[6] Thus, a combination of power control and frequency planning is used in cellular systems to prevent interference.

The unit area of RF coverage for cellular is called a *cell*.[7] In each cell, a *base station* transmits from a fixed *cell site* location, which is often centrally located in the cell, to *mobile stations* or *subscriber units*. The base station and mobiles are allowed to use a subset of the RF channels available to the system. These channels cannot be reused in any potentially interfering cells.

Base stations are supported by and interconnected to each other and the *public switched telephone network (PSTN)* via *mobile switching centers (MSCs)*, as depicted in Figure 2.1. The operation of AMPS systems has historically been based on intelligent MSCs controlling the opera-

---

6. In the world of radio (like much of life), there are no absolute rules, only probabilities! RF signal strength doesn't adhere to strict boundaries, it just sort of dwindles away. Certain geographic features, such as bodies of water, allow RF transmission to carry over greater distances than is sometimes desired (i.e., beyond cell boundaries). Variable conditions, such as mist, can also greatly (adversely) affect RF signal propagation.
7. Cells are commonly depicted as being hexagonal in shape. Hexagons barely approximate actual cellular radio coverage areas, which are actually circular under ideal conditions with an omnidirectional transmitter in the center. However, the hexagons are effective for the purpose of tiling a system-wide coverage map without gaps or overlaps. That is why they are used as an industry icon.

tions of the base and mobile stations. Cellular mobility management is handled by *home location registers (HLRs)* and *visiting location registers (VLRs)*, described in Section 2.7.7.

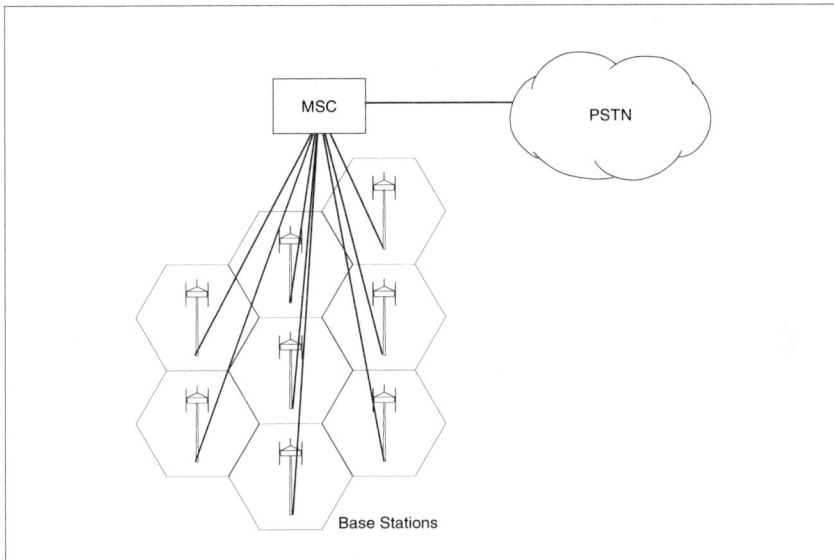

Figure 2.1   *AMPS* Architecture

Cellular system capacity or *spectrum efficiency* can be most easily and inexpensively increased by subdividing cells into smaller cells[8] or by sectorizing the cells. Sectorization consists of dividing an *omnidirectional* (360 degree) view from the cell site into non-overlapping slices called *sectors*, which when combined provide the same coverage but are considered to be separate cells.[9] This trend has continued with the creation of *microcells*, which are aimed at increasing capacity in areas of dense user populations.[10] While cells typically range in size from two to twenty kilometers in diameter, microcells range from about one hundred meters to a kilometer in diameter.

The capacity gain provided by cellular systems is offset somewhat by loss of *trunking efficiency*, which is the queueing efficiency resulting from a large number of customers receiving

---

8. Subdividing cells by creating new cells is expensive. AMPS cell sites cost approximately $1M on average, including support infrastructure, real estate, etc.; the embedded base of 18K or so base stations represents an investment of approximately $18 billion.
9. In terms of RF channel assignments, etc. Unless there is a reason to specify "sector," we'll use the word "cell" to refer to either an omnidirectional cell or a sector.
10. Early microcells were aimed primarily at filling RF coverage "holes"; current microcells are aimed largely at filling capacity "holes," reflecting the successful penetration of cellular into the marketplace. Small cells are ideal for low power (i.e., portable) mobiles.

service from a set of servers rather than proportionally assigning each customer to one of the servers.[11] If a disproportionate number of mobile stations are simultaneously located in a single cell, a cellular system might actually end up supporting fewer users than a wide area radio system. Because relatively few of the users who are aggregated in the cell can receive service (due to the fact that only a subset of channels is available in the cell), the cellular system could appear ineffective. If the cell can only support m channels, the (m+1)st simultaneous user could be *blocked* from receiving service.[12]

So there is a trade-off: an *n-cell frequency reuse* scheme, in which RF channels can be "reused" every n cells, provides better channel quality the larger the value of n (due to reduced opportunities for interference).[13] However, an n-cell frequency reuse scheme allows only 1/n of the total number of channels to be available in each cell, which greatly increases the probability of blocking for a user trying to access the system. Sectorization is actually more reuse efficient in that a smaller number of cells are needed in the reuse pattern, each providing a larger fraction of the total frequency spectrum. Typical values for n are 7 for *sectored* cells (typically partitioned into three sectors, as in Figure 2.2) or 12 for *omnidirectional* (non-sectorized) cells.

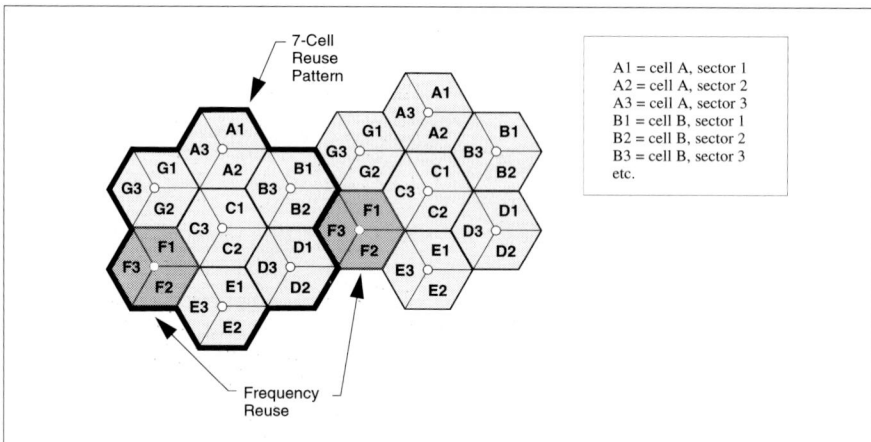

Figure 2.2   Frequency Reuse

11. This queueing theoretic result is due to the variances in arrival and service distributions, as discussed in [KLEI75]. This result is also reflected in the "banker's paradox," in which a single line for all of the tellers works more efficiently than having a separate line for each teller.
12. This is a common occurrence at airports or large trade shows that is combatted by installation of microcells to help meet the demand for service.
13. A larger value of n implies a greater reuse distance, since a larger cluster of cells would share the full set of channels, with each channel used in only one of the cluster's cells.

Frequency planning—the assignment of channels to cells—can be static or dynamic. A static assignment of channels to cells and sectors is referred to as *fixed channel allocation* or *FCA*. FCA has historically been used by cellular service providers in their frequency plans and results in each cell having a fixed capacity for serving mobiles. The maximum number of simultaneously-transmitting mobile stations is equal to the number of channels statically assigned to the cell.

A more recent technique for channel assignment is called *dynamic channel assignment* or *DCA*. With DCA there is no fixed association of channels to cells. Each of the channels available to a cluster of cells could be used in any cell or sector within the cluster as needed. DCA eliminates the need for up-front frequency planning and provides the ultimate flexibility for capacity. However, DCA requires processing and signalling to coordinate dynamic channel assignments and avoid interference. It is really frequency planning on the fly.

2.4 Cell Handoff

One of the goals of a cellular system is for a user to remain "in touch," even as they move through the system. When a user moves from the coverage area defining one cell into that of another, the system must provide the capability for that user to remain "in touch," even while breaking the connection with one base station and establishing another connection with another base station. This operation is called a *handoff*. Smaller cells mean more frequent handoffs, which requires greater system resources to support and coordinate. Handoff is really a localized form of mobility.[14]

Cellular handoff is done in one of two ways, as shown in Figure 2.3. *Hard handoff* is when the airlink connection between the mobile and its initially-serving base station are momentarily severed before reconnecting with a new base station. This is the method traditionally used in existing cellular systems, because it requires the least processing by the network providing service. However, it causes a momentary interruption in reception that is sometimes noticeable to the humans engaged in the call being handed off.

The second handoff mode is called *soft handoff*, in which two base stations are briefly simultaneously connected via the airlink with a mobile during the handoff. As soon as the mobile's RF link with the new base station is acceptable, the initially-serving base station disengages from the mobile. Diversity techniques are employed at both ends of the radio link to ensure a smooth handoff, which is largely undetectable to the humans affected.

---

14. Handoff is a function of radio resource management, which is closely related to mobility management. If a user never moved, there would be no need for mobility management and minimal need for radio resource management.

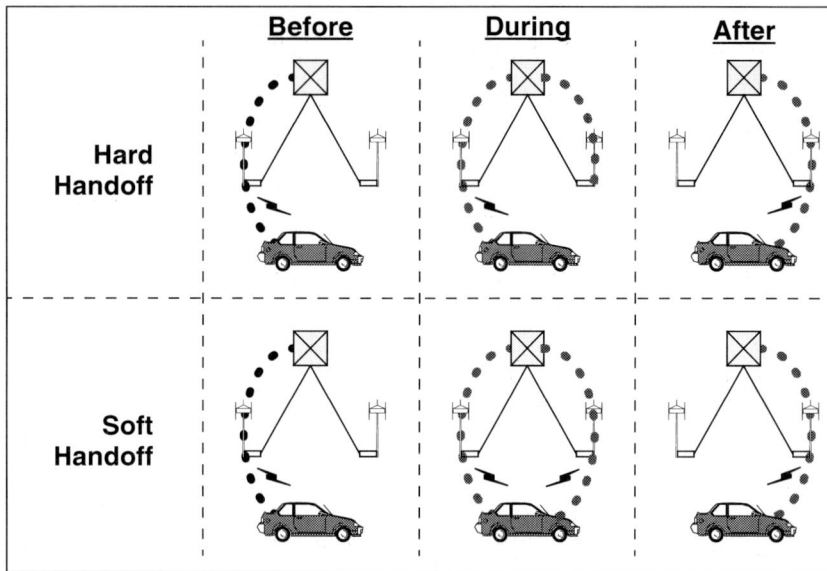

Figure 2.3   Cell Handoff Strategies

Handoffs can be further categorized as being either controlled or assisted by the network or the mobile. A network-controlled handoff is referred to as a *base-controlled handoff,* or *BCHO.*[15] *Mobile-controlled handoff,* or *MCHO,* is less commonly used in voice systems, although it is used in CDPD because of the burst mode of transmission employed by CDPD mobiles. Second generation cellular voice systems take advantage of greater intelligence in mobile stations and time-division techniques to perform *mobile-assisted handoff,* or *MAHO,* in which the mobile participates but does not control the handoff.

Whichever technique is employed, the handoff process is complex. A decision algorithm is used to determine when the handoff should occur, based on factors such as the received power level and signal quality (bit error rate or supervisory tone). Once predetermined threshold values have been exceeded, indicating that the edge of cell coverage has been reached, another decision must be made—where should the mobile next receive service?

The target cell for the handoff is determined by RF measures designed to minimize interference coupled with capacity considerations such as the need for load balancing, availability of idle channels, etc.[16] All of the decisions for a handoff must be made quickly, because the subscriber

---

15. BCHO handoffs are usually controlled by the MSC, not the base station.
16. This is important because a mobile requiring a handoff to a cell without any available channels will be dropped. This type of service disruption is to be avoided at all costs. It is considered better to refuse new calls originating in a cell than to drop calls because there are no channels to handoff to. So, service might be denied to new originating calls in order to preserve one or two available channels for handoffs. With DCA this is becoming less of an issue.

could be traveling at highway speeds. This need for rapid handoff decision making is accentuated by the ever decreasing cell sizes used in urban areas. The requirement for rapid handoffs can only be met with a sufficient level of processing and signalling capability.

The ability of a network to support cell handoffs can be a capacity constraint. Therefore, it is important to avoid unnecessary and undesirable handoffs. The system (network plus mobiles) must distinguish between an actual movement from one cell's coverage area to another and a mobile simply moving to a fringe area, where the RF reception is poor. Smart algorithms involving timers, power control and hysteresis[17] have been developed to reduce the number of unnecessary handoffs.

2.5 Cellular Channel Quality

One of the physical measures of RF channel quality is the *carrier-to-interference* or *C/I ratio.*[18] The larger the C/I ratio, the better the channel quality.

C/I ratios of 17 dB are ideally used to determine the edge of coverage for a cell. If the measured C/I falls below this level, the mobile should be in the coverage region of another cell and a cell handoff should be performed. The interior of the cell should provide C/I ratios that exceed 17 dB, unless the mobile is located in an RF coverage "hole."

There are two kinds of RF interference possible: co-channel and adjacent channel. Either of these forms of interference can occur if the cellular frequency reuse scheme is inadequate (i.e., the "n" in n-cell reuse is too small for the geography available and power level in use).

Co-channel interference results when two transmitters within range of a common receiver use the same channel (frequency) simultaneously. The receiver will receive a combination of the two signals and will be unable to make any sense of the combined signal.[19] In this case, the two channels can be said to have interfered with one another.

---

17. Hysteresis is the mechanism that requires a high threshold value to be exceeded before a handoff decision is made. The current channel continues to be used until it has degraded enough that other channels are significantly better for the mobile. In this way, unnecessary and undesirable handoffs are avoided. Hysteresis could describe the process of crowning a new boxing champion; the challenger ("the contendah") must defeat the reigning champion soundly, not just barely, to be declared the new champ.
18. Pronounced "C-to-I ratio." C/I ratios relate the desired carrier signal (C) to an interfering signal (S). They are valued in terms of decibels (dB) determined by $10 \log (C / I)$.
19. An exception to this is so-called "FM capture," in which the stronger received signal "captures" the receiver and is properly decoded despite the presence of the interfering signal.

Adjacent channel interference occurs when two transmitters within range of a common receiver use adjacent channels (i.e., neighboring frequencies) simultaneously. Because the physical characteristics of the RF channel causes some spill-over of the signal into neighboring frequencies, adjacent channel transmissions could interfere with one another.

Because of the interference caused by the simultaneous transmission on co-channels or adjacent channels within a cell, only one can transmit at a time. The earliest mobile phone systems used the same channel for the network and the mobile devices. This *half-duplex* mode of operation greatly hindered the efficiency of these early mobile RF systems.

Current cellular systems are *full-duplex*. This is accomplished by using different physical channels in the *forward channel* direction (i.e., network to mobile) and the *reverse channel* direction (i.e., mobile to network). The channels used in each direction are sufficiently separated in the frequency domain (they are separated by 45 MHz in current AMPS systems) so as to prevent interference. Of course, full-duplex operation means that the mobile and the base station must each have two RF transceivers (i.e., one transmitter, one receiver) simultaneously engaged.[20]

Even if no other transmitters are causing interference, a received RF signal can be garbled due to a phenomenon known as *multipath* or *Rayleigh fading*. This form of self-interference occurs when multiple out-of-phase copies of the same signal destructively interfere with one another due to reflections of the signal off of natural or man-made surfaces.[21] Multipath fading can occur when the mobile is stationary or in motion.

2.6 Power Control

An important part of radio resource management is controlling the power levels used by transmitters. This *power control* is important, because even in the best conditions the received power level is inversely proportional to the distance from the transmitter. Without power control, nearby mobiles could overwhelm transmissions from distant mobiles at the base station transceivers.

The domination by a nearby transmitter can prevent distant transmitter signals from ever being detected at the receiver. Even more pernicious is the so-called *near-far* or *hidden terminal problem*. This occurs when one transmitter is much closer to a receiver than another transmitter. If the nearby transmitter signal is captured successfully by the receiver, the receiver might acknowledge the successful reception of the signal. The distant transmitter might then incorrectly conclude that its signal was successfully received. Undetected errors are quite undesirable.

---

20. As we shall see, in time-division digital systems, the mobile can get by with a single transceiver, which rapidly switches between transmitting and receiving modes.
21. Buildings and mountains do a good job of this. So do walls, windows, and even flourescent lights!

A base station must prevent nearby mobiles from transmitting with power levels that overwhelm other mobiles in the cell. The *received signal strength (RSS)* at the base station should be approximately the same for all mobiles in the cell. Often, power control algorithms are based on the so-called *reciprocity* of RF signals (i.e., the RSS in one direction is the same as in the other direction if both transmitters are at the same power level).[22] Of course, the base station can always direct individual mobiles to use another power level. Power control is especially important at cell boundaries, to reduce the number of unnecessary handoffs and avoid interference.

2.7 Advanced Mobile Phone System (AMPS)

The *Advanced Mobile Phone System* is one of the earliest commercial cellular systems. *AMPS* technology is currently deployed throughout North America and AMPS-derivative systems are deployed in many worldwide cellular markets.[23]

AMPS was invented at Bell Labs and initially deployed in the U.S. in the early 1980s. Ownership of the local cellular service operations was transferred from AT&T to the regional Bell operating companies (RBOCs) at the time of AT&T's divestiture in January, 1984. Other landline telephone service providers, such as GTE, were unaffected by the divestiture and retained their own cellular operations.

To promote the consumer benefits of competition (i.e., low cost), government authorities mandated a duopoly structure for the fledgling cellular industry. This duopoly structure for cellular services has been largely imitated by other nations and has resulted in fierce competition between the service providers in many of the 734 markets defined by the FCC.

At the beginning of the cellular industry, local telephone companies (including the RBOCs) were automatically granted one of the two licenses in each of the markets in which they provided wireline service. This is the so-called "B" license, which can be remembered by the initial of the word "Bell".

The second license for each market was initially drawn by lottery and later auctioned. Initially, few investors perceived their value—after all, who could compete against the local telephone

---

22. In reciprocity-based power control, the base station transmits a continuous signal, which includes information about the power level it is using. The mobile measures the strength of the received signal and takes the ratio of that measurement to the indicated transmit power level at the base station. This ratio indicates the *path loss* of a signal between the mobile and the base station and allows the mobile to determine the transmit power level it should use.

23. Similar first-generation analog cellular systems include Total Access Communication System (TACS) in the U.K., Italy, Spain, Austria, and Ireland; Nordic Mobile Telephone (NMT) in the Scandinavian countries; C-450 in Germany and Portugal; Radiocom 2000 in France; Nippon Telephone and Telegraph (NTT) in Japan; and JTACS/NTACS in Japan. These systems have varying voice and control channels and signaling standards.

company? Some entrepreneurs[24] quickly recognized the potential of these licenses and obtained as many as possible by buying out other license holders. The early days of cellular are reminiscent of the gold rush days, with pioneers rushing to buy controlling interests from lottery winners. Thus, the "A" side, which can be remembered as "A" for "Alternate," was born.

Early deployments and business deals in the cellular arena were based more on intuition than analysis. An early market analysis, conducted at Bell Labs in the late 1960s concluded that the entire nationwide cellular market would peak at about 900 thousand users. Despite analyses of this nature, pioneers were willing to bet that cellular service would prove to be popular.

Over time, as the value of cellular licenses were more widely recognized, prices were driven to extreme levels. It became the accepted custom to value licenses on the basis of (potential subscriber) population or "POPS." The price of a cellular market is now evaluated in terms of "dollars per POPS" normalized value, with high water marks in the hundreds of dollars per POPS.

Cellular markets are defined by *cellular geographic statistical areas* or *CGSAs*. Of the 734 CGSAs comprising the U.S., 306 are in metropolitan areas and are called *metropolitan statistical areas* or *MSAs*. The remaining 428 are called *rural service areas* or *RSAs*. MSAs are valued more highly because of their greater density of potential subscribers.

The following subsections describe AMPS, the most widely used cellular technology.

2.7.1 AMPS Channels

The frequencies allocated to AMPS by the FCC range between 824 to 849 MHz in reverse channels (mobile to base) and 869 to 894 MHz in forward channels (base to mobile). As displayed in Table 2.2, they are not contiguous blocks because the initial 40 MHz allocation by the FCC was later extended by 10 MHz when the service's popularity became evident. There are now a total of 416 channels available in each direction, numbered from 1 to 1024 with gaps in the numbering where frequencies are not allocated.

Table 2.2 AMPS Frequency Allocations

Carrier Side	Reverse Direction	Forward Direction
A (initial)	825-835 MHz	870-880 MHz
A (extended)	845-846.5, 824-825 MHz	890-891.5, 869-870 MHz
B (initial)	835-845 MHz	880-890 MHz
B (extended)	846.5-849 MHz	891.5-894 MHz

---

24. Most notable among these was Craig McCaw, founder of McCaw Cellular Communications.

Each physical channel is 30 kHz wide and is dedicated to a single mobile station for the duration of the call while the mobile is in the current cell. Each call uses a dedicated forward channel paired with a dedicated reverse channel at a 45 MHz offset. Some of the channel pairs (21 of them) are used for control purposes in the AMPS environment. Analog *frequency modulation (FM)* with 8 kHz deviation is used in the *traffic channels*, which convey voice conversations. Binary *frequency shift keying (FSK)* at 10 kbps—a digital modulation technique—is used in the *control channels* used for signalling.

AMPS is an analog FM system, with all of the associated ramifications of such a system. AMPS channels are insecure—anyone with a channel scanner can listen to unsuspecting AMPS users.[25] AMPS channels can suffer from interference, which sounds like static to a user; analog signals suffering from multipath fading cannot be corrected. Finally, AMPS radio resource management is based on signal strength and *supervisory audio tones (SAT)*.

2.7.2 Roaming

Since no cellular service provider covers the entire country, carriers must provide service to one another's customers in order for those customers to be able to receive service whenever they are outside of their home area. This capability to receive service while in another service provider's domain is called *roaming*. Intercarrier business agreements and network to network interoperation (messaging) are essential to support roaming.

The IS-41 standard has provided the technical solution to roaming between networks implemented by different equipment manufacturers. Prior to IS-41, all signalling between systems was proprietary in nature and the roaming capability had to be manually administered. In early years, intercarrier business relationships sometimes abused the customers' need for roaming with service providers sometimes surprising subscribers with larger than expected roaming charges. This has cost the cellular industry much in terms of reputation and customer relations.

Despite these early business foibles and technical incompatibilities, the cellular industry is rapidly moving toward universal service, with more reasonable roaming agreements in place between service providers. Service providers who are extremely competitive with one another in some markets must simultaneously be extremely cooperative with one another in other markets.[26] This is becoming more important as reduced-size mobile stations encourage wider roaming.

---

25. This is illegal.
26. The nature of the cellular industry is further fragmented into direct market to market relationships by the fact that many A-side licenses are owned by partnerships of service providers. Often these partners are competitors in different markets. Thus, even within a cellular service provider, it is necessary to functionally separate operations by regions or markets.

2.7.3 AMPS Cellular Operation

AMPS cellular operation consists of call origination and call termination procedures, supported by radio resource management and mobility management functions. It is important to remember that AMPS was designed as a voice-only system, which impacts how these processes are handled. Data transmission on AMPS systems is based on this circuit-switched mode of operation and is described in Section 2.8.

When an AMPS mobile station powers up, it searches through up to 21 predefined control channels. These control channels are physically no different than AMPS traffic channels, except for how they are used—for control purposes only. Each cell utilizes a forward control channel to continuously broadcast information needed by the mobile station for registration. This information includes the *system identification* or *SID* of the MSC, which allows the mobile to know whether it is roaming.

An AMPS mobile station finds the best forward control channel it can receive (in terms of received signal strength) and announces itself, or *registers,* to the serving network via the matching reverse control channel. From that point on, the mobile remains in a passive state tuned to the control channel it selected. When the channel quality degrades (radio resource management determines this), a call event occurs or the mobile crosses a boundary between *location areas,*[27] the mobile again signals the network. This receive-only mode reduces the traffic on the reverse control channel, a shared resource.

In communicating with the network, the mobile provides two identifiers for registration, call control and validation. The first of these identifiers is the *mobile identification number* or *MIN*, which is the programmed handset phone number used to call the subscriber. This programmed identifier is associated with the subscriber and is stored in erasable non-volatile memory in the handset.

The second identifier is the *electronic serial number* or *ESN*, which is a manufactured characteristic of the mobile unit. This identifier is (in theory) permanent and associated with the physical equipment. It is 32 bits in length, with the first 8 bits identifying the manufacturer.

Both the MIN and the ESN are transmitted unencrypted by both the mobile and the network. Simple scanning receivers can be used to capture these values, which has provided many opportunities for fraudulent use of cellular services. Recently, the cellular industry has instituted a subscriber-entered personal identification number or PIN as an escalation in the war on cellular fraud. But this measure has proven to be only a temporary complexification for the "bad guys," and in early 1996 cellular service providers began deploying authentication mechanisms.

---

27. A *location area* consists of a group of cells (or clusters), which conveys a page for a mobile station. Paging is done on the basis of location areas; presumably one of the location areas is where the mobile station is currently situated.

2.7.4 AMPS Mobile Call Origination

The mobile *originates* a call (following its owner's depression of the "send" button) via the reverse control channel in the cell the mobile is currently located in. The mobile "knows" which control channel to use by information broadcast by the network on its selected forward control (paging) channel.

Access to the reverse control channel is by a CSMA-type[28] scheme. The mobile simply transmits its request (which includes information about the subscriber such as the MIN and ESN) and "listens" on the forward channel for its subsequent channel assignment. The base station forwards the request to the MSC.

After validating the mobile (i.e., does the subscriber pay their bill and do we have a business/ roaming agreement with the subscriber's home service provider?) via the HLR and the VLR, the MSC selects a traffic channel pair for the mobile. If no channels are available, the MSC simply rejects the request (which results in the mobile producing the annoying "fast busy" audible signal).

If the MSC grants a channel for the subscriber, it must then connect the call through to the destination. This is done via standard telephony procedures—the MSC simply appears to be a private branch exchange (PBX)[29] to the PSTN. The channel grant message is relayed to the mobile via the forward control channel.

The mobile then tunes its transmitter and receiver to the assigned traffic channel pair for the duration of the call. Call and power control from this point forward are handled in-band on the AMPS traffic channel assigned to the mobile.

2.7.5 AMPS Mobile Call Termination

When an AMPS mobile is not engaged in a call, it monitors the forward control (paging) channel. A call attempt directed at the mobile (i.e., to the MIN assigned to the mobile) is received by the mobile as a page on the control channel. The page is repeated several seconds later, in case the mobile was temporarily in an RF "hole" or otherwise unable to receive the first page. The time interval between pages is short to minimize the ringing delay experienced by the originator of the call.

The mobile responds to the page via the reverse control channel and awaits the traffic channel assignment. The mobile response is also repeated, in case the initial response collided with another mobile on the reverse control channel or suffered from bad RF conditions.

---

28. *Carrier Sense Multiple Access* is a common MAC protocol, used in Ethernet LANs. It is described in the Preliminaries chapter.
29. A PBX is a small typically privately-owned switch, which provides many of the advanced voice features available in businesses. It interfaces to public telephone switches via special protocols.

When the mobile receives the traffic channel assignment from the network (the MSC via the base station), it proceeds to that channel and produces an audible ringing tone for the subscriber. From this point forward, all further signalling between the system and the mobile is conducted in-band.

2.7.6 AMPS Radio Resource Management (RRM)

AMPS channels are controlled by the MSC. The traffic channel assignment process was described in the preceding subsections. However, there are other aspects of *Radio Resource Management (RRM)*, including power control and handoff.

Power control is handled by monitoring the received signal strength of the reverse channel at the base station, which in turn passes this and other channel quality information to the MSC. The MSC evaluates this data, including a trend analysis, to determine whether the mobile should increase or reduce its power level or be handed-off to another cell. AMPS defines eight power levels in 4 dB steps. This power level control is a means of controlling the local access point to the network for a mobile station.

Cell handoff is handled in a BCHO manner, as discussed in Section 2.4. The system controls handoffs by transmitting the SAT in-band on the forward channel. This tone is filtered by the mobile—it is outside the range of the audible channel—before reaching the subscriber's ear, and is reflected back to the system in-band on the reverse channel.

The base station filters the reflected SAT and evaluates the quality of the reflected tone. The base station forwards SAT quality information on to the MSC. Based on RSS and SAT data, the MSC determines whether or not to initiate cell handoff procedures.

Cell handoff procedures include having neighboring cells' base stations monitor the mobile's reverse channel and evaluate the received signal strength. If another base station "hears" the mobile better than the current base station, the mobile is instructed to move to a new channel pair via a "blank and burst" message transmitted in-band by the base station. The mobile then tunes its RF transceivers to the channel pair instructed. All of these steps are orchestrated by the MSC.

The *"blank and burst"* message [30] sounds like static to the ear of the subscriber and is momentarily disruptive to the conversation taking place. It is also highly destructive to any data transfer that could be occurring at that point in time via modems on the cellular channel. This is one of the reasons that cellular has historically been a harsh environment for mobile data users.

Intelligent algorithms are used to prevent unnecessary and premature handoffs, especially for non-moving mobiles, mobiles located in poor in-cell coverage areas, mobiles traveling along the border between cells and situations in which no cellular channels are available beyond the cell's boundary.

---

30. The "blank and burst" refers to the blanking of the audio (voice) carriage in favor of a brief burst of data, including the modem training, between the subscriber's handset and the cellular network.

2.7.7 AMPS Mobility Management

Mobility management in AMPS networks appears to be based on the engineering assumption that most calls are originated by the mobile and seems optimized for mobiles that are usually in their home area.

Intelligent paging algorithms are employed by AMPS to reduce the collective forward bandwidth required for a page. The paging algorithm starts by paging in only a small area, based on where the mobile usually receives service (the home area), or perhaps where the mobile was last registered (i.e., the location area).[31] When a mobile receives a page, it responds and proceeds to the assigned traffic channel pair.

AMPS mobility management has been greatly enhanced by IS-41, which defines the standard for interoperation between networks. Mobility management is handled by databases known as the *home location register* or *HLR* and the *visiting location register* or *VLR*.

The purpose of the HLR is to track the network (i.e., the VLR) currently serving each of its mobiles. The HLR also contains profile information about each of the mobiles (e.g., is the mobile allowed to originate an international call, etc.). This database logically unites data describing both the subscriber and the subscriber's equipment into a single service profile. Because this "permanent" information is critical to serving customers, the HLR function is typically supported by multiple distributed fault-tolerant computers.

The purpose of the VLR is to track all mobile stations currently receiving service in the local MSC coverage area. The VLR contains the downloaded service profile of each roaming mobile as well as other information necessary for calls terminating at the mobile station. Because the VLR function is so closely aligned with an operating MSC, it is typically collocated with or part of that MSC. Since the information it contains is of a temporary nature, fault-tolerance is less critical than for the HLR.

Because base stations periodically broadcast the SID and location area identifiers on the forward control channel, the mobile station knows immediately when it has roamed into another system or location area. An option in IS-41, known as *autonomous registration*, allows the mobile to register to the host MSC. This registration is forwarded by the MSC to the VLR. Another IS-41 message is then used by the VLR to notify the HLR that it is currently hosting the mobile.

The HLR passes necessary service profile information to the VLR in another IS-41 message, enabling the host system to provide service to the mobile station. Information such as whether or not the mobile is allowed to originate international calls is contained in this service profile. Since the HLR now knows the location of the mobile, more efficient paging can be used for

---

31. The trade-off of a gradually expanding paging "radius" is increased ringing delay experienced by the originator of the call attempt. If it has been a while since the mobile last registered, the last location area used by the mobile is probably obsolete.

mobile-terminated calls. The HLR also notifies any other VLR which had been previously hosting the mobile to deregister the mobile.

A mobile-terminated call attempt is always initially directed to the mobile station's HLR by the gateway MSC first contacted from the PSTN. The HLR is responsible for contacting the current serving system, obtaining a temporary local directory number (TLDN) from the serving system, and transferring the call to that number. The serving system is responsible for the connection between the TLDN and the roaming mobile station.

IS-41 supports uninterrupted voice services while the mobile station moves between MSCs. This is equivalent to maintaining a session between a mobile data device and another host while the mobile host is in motion between areas. Because trunk connections are used to carry the voice traffic, the concatenated trunk length could grow as the mobile moves about while the conversation is active (i.e., the mobile "grows a tail"). This is usually not a significant problem, because most conversations are only a few minutes in duration and even fast-moving vehicles cover only so much ground in a typical call period.

HLRs and VLRs are not affected by cell handoffs, only by wider-scale mobility (between MSCs). Mobiles re-register every time they cross boundaries separating location areas. These location areas are clusters of cells large enough to minimize the number of re-registration messages (on the contended reverse control channel), while also minimizing the number of paging channels involved in a page.

2.8 Data Transmission via AMPS

The native AMPS environment is harsh for data transmission. RF modulation and coding techniques, such as vocoders, ADPCM [32] trunking compression, and FM pre-emphasis—which are optimized for voice transmission—distort data and disallow the use of standard (landline) modems on cellular channels. Cell handoffs, channel reassignments and power level change commands are all transmitted in-band by the system, further distorting the data channel. Finally, static, signal fading and interference make cellular a noisy channel for data applications. Standard landline modems typically react by either losing data or hanging up.

Despite these challenges, the ubiquity of AMPS analog cellular coverage and demand for wireless data services have motivated development of technology supporting cellular-based data services. Today, circuit-switched cellular data is the most widely used mobile data service.

Special modem technology has been developed by Paradyne (Enhanced Throughput Cellular or ETC), Microcom (MNP10), Motorola (EC2) and others to optimize the capabilities of AMPS channels for data transmission. These enhanced cellular data protocols allow approximately 9 kbps

---

32. Analog to Digital Pulse Code Modulation.

under normal RF conditions, with 14.4 kbps becoming increasingly available. Data compression further increases the effective throughput enjoyed by cellular data users.

Modem pools supporting these new protocols are now being deployed by cellular service providers. These modem pools provide a gateway function bridging the specialized cellular modem protocols and standard landline modem protocols. A special code is added to the dialed digit string at the mobile, which alerts the cellular switch to connect the call to the modem pool rather than simply placing a call. The gateways allow continued interoperability of AMPS with conventional modems.

The modem pool concept has been extended with backbone packet services offered by AT&T, MCI, Sprint and others. Typical of these offerings is MCI's Xstream Air Network, depicted in Figure 2.4, an X.25-based backbone supporting cellular modem-based data applications. Access to Xstream is via third party cellular service providers. Special 800-number access is available from anywhere to the MCI cellular modem pool, which supports both MNP10 and ETC protocols.

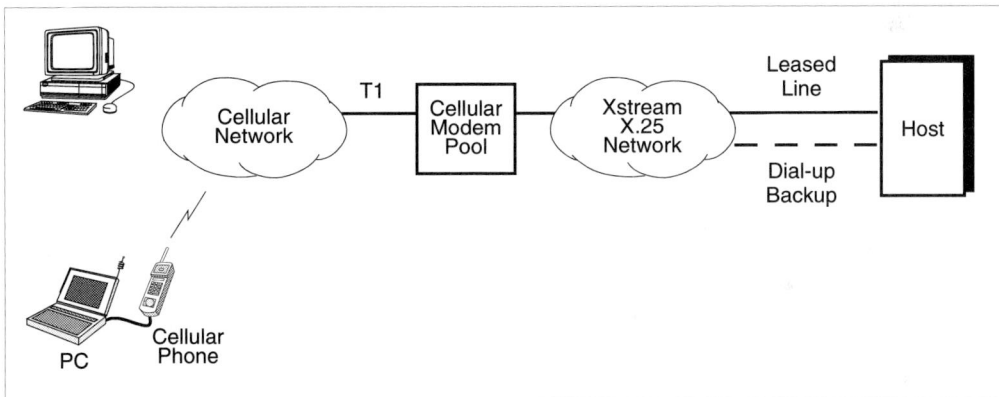

Figure 2.4   MCI's Xstream Air Network

Another data solution for the cellular airlink is a single-sided protocol such as Air True by Air Communications, Inc. This protocol only requires support at the transmitting side (presumably the mobile) of the airlink to effectively counter the debilitating effects of the cellular environment. It recognizes network event (call control) messages for cell handoff, power control and channel changes for what they are rather than interpreting them as random noise. After the interrupting network event message has completed, the mobile transmitter resumes where it left off, increasing the effective bandwidth.

Channel characteristics are not the only challenge for AMPS-based data applications. Current cellular systems are voice-oriented and thus have usage accounting mechanisms, which are based on time of usage rather than actual data transmission. The time-of-usage billing schemes typically begin with a minimum usage of one minute. Cellular service providers are gradually offering sub-minute billing schemes for competitive reasons.

In 1995, Bell South Wireless, Inc., announced a wireless telemetry solution named Cellemetry, which would be licensable by, at most, one cellular service provider per market. Cellemetry operates over the AMPS control channels and thus is limited by the amount of data which can be transported by cellular registration and paging messages (32 bits) and the amount of additional traffic that can be borne on the control channel without impacting the primary purposes of these control channels—cellular registration and paging.

2.9 Digital Cellular Technologies

Digital technology offers the opportunity for improved transmission in cellular systems. This is due to powerful error detection and recovery techniques, which can be used to counter the debilitating effects of noise, fading and interference. Digital technology also provides the basis for security in the forms of encryption and authentication. Finally, digital technology requires less in the way of mobile transmit power, which increases battery life in portable mobile units.

Digital cellular technologies also offer the promise of effective data transmission via cellular services. Although their vocoders prohibit the use of conventional modems, recent extensions to standards provide low-throughput data traffic in either a circuit-switched mode or via a digital control channel. Packet-switched data services are also being developed by the proponents of digital cellular standards.

However, the primary motivations for the digital cellular standards are unrelated to data. Development of the North American digital standards was motivated by the need for increased capacity in light of the 40-plus percent compounded growth rate in AMPS penetration during the early 1990s.[33] Overseas, development of the GSM standard was motivated by the desire to unify cellular service across European national boundaries.[34]

Once the commitment to digital cellular voice standards was achieved in the various standards bodies, it was quickly recognized that digital services could include much more than mere capacity enhancement. Data applications, secure channels, and enhanced voice services, such as caller identification, are now possible with the new digital standards.

Before presenting the primary digital cellular technologies, understanding the basic differences between FDMA, TDMA, and CDMA is essential. As depicted in Figure 2.5, a *frequency division multiple access (FDMA)* system, such as AMPS, separates individual conversations in the frequency domain—different conversations use different frequencies (channels). In this depiction,

---

33. After a while, continually subdividing cells into sectors and microcells becomes prohibitively expensive and inefficient. The more cells, the more cell handoff signalling and decision-making required, etc.

34. Prior to GSM, each nation had its own analog system, which was mostly incompatible with the systems of neighboring countries. No cross-border roaming was possible with these analog systems.

the frequency domain is represented by the vertical dimension and the time domain is represented by the horizontal dimension. The numbers identify separate conversations.

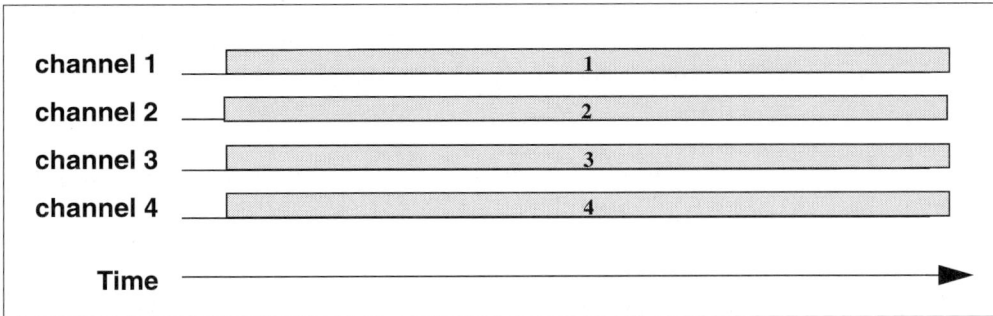

Figure 2.5 Time vs. Frequency for an FDMA System (e.g., AMPS)

Figure 2.6 shows how *time division multiple access (TDMA)* systems, such as IS-54/136, GSM, or PDC, separate conversations in both the frequency and time domains; each frequency (channel) supports multiple conversations, which use the channel during specific timeslots. Typically, there is a maximum number (3 in the example) of conversations that can be supported on each physical channel. Each conversation occupies a logical "channel." These TDMA systems are discussed in Section 2.10, Section 2.11, and Section 2.13.

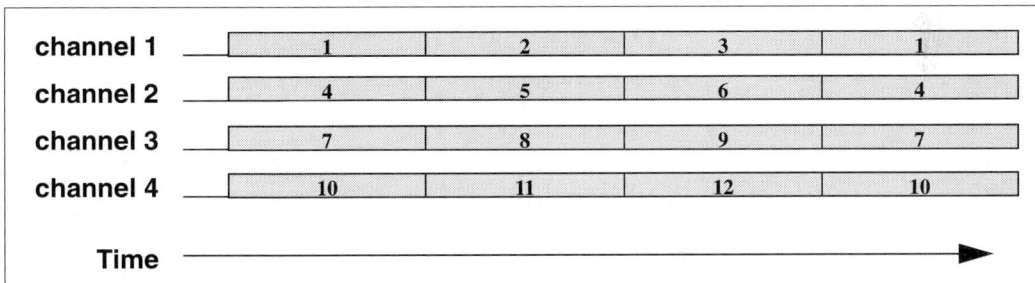

Figure 2.6 Time vs. Frequency for a TDMA System (e.g., IS-54/136)

Figure 2.7 shows how frequency-hopping *code division multiple access (CDMA)* systems, such as spread spectrum wireless LANs, separate conversations in both the frequency and time domains. By rotating conversations through frequencies (channels) on a synchronized basis, each conversation experiences a variety of channel conditions.[35] This rotation through the frequency set also tends to reduce the interference levels. These systems are discussed in Chapter 9.

35. This is because each frequency is impacted by environmental conditions, including interference, differently.

channel 1	1	2	3	4
channel 2	2	3	4	1
channel 3	3	4	1	2
channel 4	4	1	2	3

Time

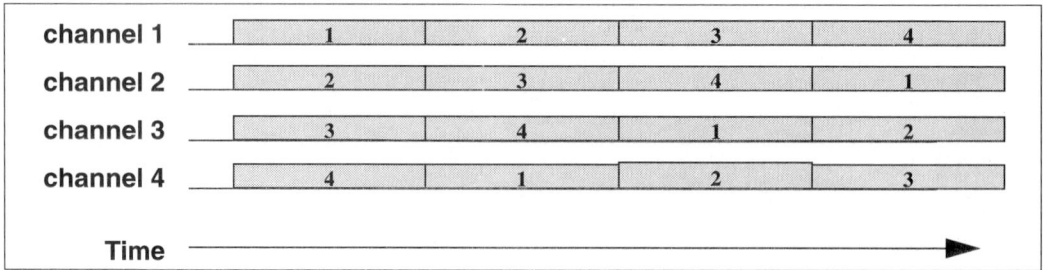

Figure 2.7   Time vs. Frequency for a FH-CDMA System

Figure 2.8 shows how *direct sequence* CDMA systems, such as IS-95, separate conversations on the basis of something entirely different than frequency or time. It's hard to show in a time versus frequency diagram, but we will discuss it in Section 2.14.

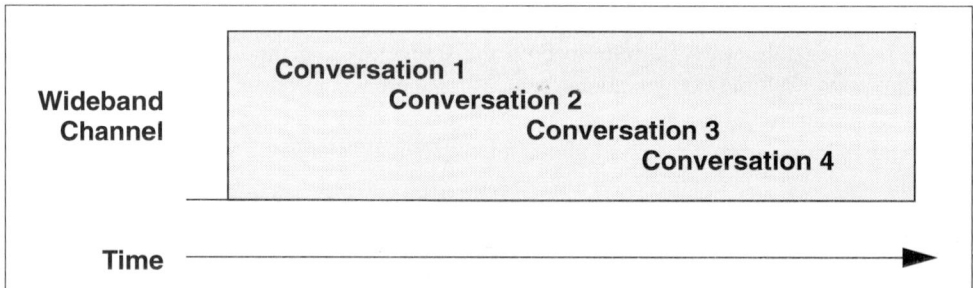

Wideband Channel

Conversation 1
Conversation 2
Conversation 3
Conversation 4

Time

Figure 2.8   Time vs. Frequency for a DS-CDMA System (e.g., IS-95)

2.10 Europe: GSM and DCS 1800

Definition of the *Groupe Special Mobile (GSM)* system began in 1982, under the auspices of the Committee of European Posts and Telecommunications. Now called *Global System for Mobile communications,*[36] the goal of this time-division-based digital cellular system was a unified pan-European system. In mid-1995, there were over 11 million customers using GSM worldwide;

---

36. The story is that early GSM industry participants in the UK rephrased GSM to mean "God Send Mobiles." Then, as the mobiles became increasingly available, GSM meant "Good Sales and Marketing." Another example of an acronym taking on a life of its own.

that number was expected to double by year-end 1996 with more than 140 service providers in 86 countries.

Prior to GSM, many independent analog systems were in use throughout Europe, with incompatible standards preventing intercountry roaming in many cases. Cellular usage was essentially regional in scope. The goal of GSM was to eliminate this fragmentation of the European cellular market. Since this was intended to be a "next generation" system, it uses digital technology with the capability of supporting data applications.

GSM was originally specified in the 900 MHz band and currently runs in that spectrum (see Table 2.3). However, in 1989 the U.K. Department of Trade and Industry allocated frequencies in the 1.8 GHz band for *Personal Communications Network (PCN)*.[37] Cellular service providers in the U.K. then selected GSM to operate in those frequencies, because it was already available. This upbanded system is referred to as *Digital Cellular System 1800 (DCS 1800)*, with deployment anticipated by 1998.

Table 2.3   GSM Frequency Allocations

	Reverse Direction	**Forward Direction**
initial allocation	890-915 MHz	935-960 MHz
extended allocation	880-890 MHz	925-935 MHz

GSM is a TDMA-based system with 8 user timeslots per frame in a 200 kHz channel. Like other TDMA systems, staggered transmit and receive timeslots allow modems to use half-duplex radios, thereby reducing their costs. The transmit/receive offset still leaves enough idle time for the mobile to participate in handovers [38] by monitoring neighbor cell channel signal strengths in a MAHO scheme, as depicted in Figure 2.9.

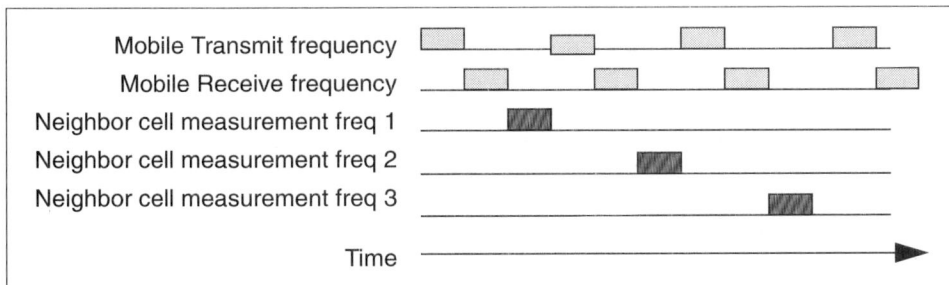

Figure 2.9   MAHO Process in TDMA Systems

37. PCN is the European equivalent to what is called PCS in North America. More on PCS later.
38. GSM calls handoffs "handovers."

The GSM system uses GMSK[39] modulation; rate ½-convolutional coding with interleaving[40] addresses Rayleigh fading. The net data rate[41] is 22.8 kbps with error correction in what is called *full-rate* mode. An additional *half-rate* mode at 11.4 kbps is also defined by using 16 timeslots (which are half as large as the full-rate timeslots) per frame.

A form of slow frequency hopping is used by GSM to help combat the multipath burst errors characteristic of cellular environments. Each base station has its own pattern for hopping from one carrier frequency to another from slot to slot, with mobiles using that base station following suit. This frequency hopping also reduces the incidence of co-channel interference between clusters of cells.

GSM, with slow frequency hopping and coding requires an approximately 9 dB C/I ratio for effective operation. If we assume a frequency reuse factor of 3 with 3-sector antennas and 8 users per 200-kHz bandwidth, we can estimate relative system capacity for GSM to be approximately

$$\textbf{[8 users / (200 kHz * 3 cells)] / [1 user / (30 kHz * 7 cells)]} \qquad \textbf{(Eq 2.1)}$$

or 2.8 times AMPS capacity [FALC95].[42]

The radio data link layer is based on a LAPD-like protocol called LAPDm. LAPDm modifications (from LAPD) include using no frame flags or bit stuffing, instead relying on a "length indicator" field, as depicted in Figure 2.10. Also, the SAPI (SAP identifier) is included in the address field, shown in Figure 2.11. LAPDm also has no CRC bits for error detection, instead relying on lower layer block and convolutional coding for error detection and correction.

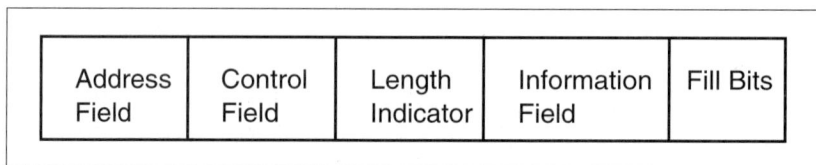

Address Field	Control Field	Length Indicator	Information Field	Fill Bits

Figure 2.10   LAPDm Frame Format

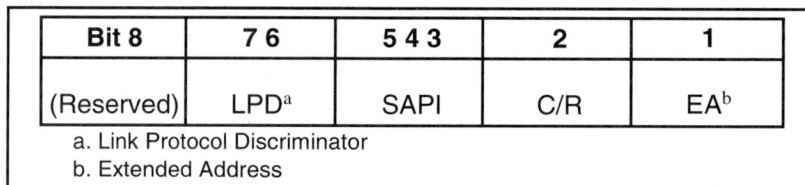

Bit 8	7 6	5 4 3	2	1
(Reserved)	LPD[a]	SAPI	C/R	EA[b]

a. Link Protocol Discriminator
b. Extended Address

Figure 2.11   LAPDm Address Field

39. Gaussian Minimum Shift Keying.
40. Interleaving is a shuffling of the bits in a transmitted packet that distributes and randomizes those bits impacted by noise and interference. This has the net effect of transforming an error burst into random bit errors, which are much easier to correct via standard techniques.
41. Digital voice is data!
42. For this comparison AMPS is assumed to require one 30-kHz band per user with an 18 dB C/I ratio and a frequency reuse factor of 7 (cells) in a 3-sectored arrangement.

GSM mobility management is provided by specific layer entities that establish, maintain, and release separate connections between the mobile station and the MSC under control of the higher connection management sublayer. These separate connections are for call control, short message service, and the call-independent supplementary services. Each mobility management connection provides services such as encryption and authentication.

GSM mobility management is based on Signalling System 7 (SS7), an international *intelligent network (IN)* telephony standard. Each mobile is identified by a *mobile station ISDN (MSISDN)* number consisting of a country code (CC), national destination code (NDC) and subscriber number (SN). The MSISDN is used by a serving MSC to interrogate the appropriate HLR prior to providing service. The serving VLR provides a mobile station roaming number (MSRN)—similar in format to the MSISDN and in function to the TLDN—for temporary use in forwarding calls to the roaming mobile.

GSM provides the capability for a base station to autonomously handle handovers between coverage areas under its control without involvement from the MSC. This process is called internal connection handoff. Following handoffs, the original MSC handling the call retains control even though the call may be going through a new serving MSC.

Synchronous and asynchronous data services have been defined at 9.6, 4.8, and 2.4 kbps for both full-rate and half-rate operation. Interfaces to V.22bis and V.32 audio modems are also defined for GSM. ISDN and Group 3 facsimile interfaces are also included in the GSM system definition. Industry experts believe that the introduction of data capabilities and interfaces to PC (formerly PCMCIA[43]) cards will spur continued exponential growth in worldwide adoption of GSM. Key to this growth is "plug and play" interfaces, which enable standard computer applications as well as vertical applications.

A connectionless packet data service called *General Packet Radio Service* (*GPRS*) is in standards development. This GSM capability will define the interworking between the cellular environment and those of X.25 and the Internet world. Two approaches are being considered—dedicated data channels (i.e., a voice channel shared by multiple data mobiles) and fast data channel setup for a single user. The data service objectives include a packet error rate of 10^{-4} with delay under one second. CCITT recommendation X.121 numbering is used for addressing mobile packet data in GSM.

A GSM-based datagram service called Short Message Service (SMS) is defined in support of email and other messaging-type applications. This service allows transmission of datagrams that are up to 160 bytes in length at 300 bps on the reverse control channel. Higher data rates are available via traffic channels, which require a call setup; the resultant 9600 bps is better suited to longer messages.

2.11 Japan: PDC

The primary Japanese digital cellular technology is entitled *Personal Digital Cellular* or *PDC* and was established as a standard in 1991 by the Ministry of Posts and Telecommunications.

---

43. Personal Computer Memory Card Industry Association.

It is a TDMA-based technology, which is replacing the analog NTT and JTACS systems, and will operate in the 800 and 1400 MHz frequency bands (Table 2.4). The motivation for PDC was similar to that of GSM—allowing roaming between different regions of the country..

Table 2.4 PDC Frequency Allocations

Reverse Direction	Forward Direction
810-826 MHz	940-956 MHz
1429-1453 MHz	1477-1501 MHz

PDC multiplexes three timeslots onto each carrier, like IS-54/136, but has 25 kHz channel spacing to facilitate migration to PDC from the analog systems. PDC uses π/4-DQPSK modulation, also like IS-54/136, with interleaving. The signalling rate is 42 kbps. Mobile-assisted handoffs are used, like in GSM and IS-54/136. With a typical frequency reuse factor of 4, the same calculation as in Section 2.10 results in a PDC relative system capacity of 6.3[44] times AMPS.

2.12 North American Digital Standards

North America has two concurrent digital cellular standards. One is based on TDMA and has been in service since 1992. The other is based on CDMA and is imminent.[45] The CDMA standard was accepted by the TIA[46] as an interim standard in 1992, but has not yet been commercially deployed.

Having two incompatible digital standards in North America is ironic, considering the fact that the countries of Europe have long since united behind the common digital standard of GSM. Unless one of the two competing North American standards proves to be clearly superior over the other or cellular service providers agree to support only one of them, roaming subscribers will likely be restricted to the common denominator of AMPS whenever the service area they are visiting supports the "other" digital standard.[47]

---

44. The calculation: [3 users / (25 kHz * 4 cells)] / [1 user / (30 kHz * 7 cells)] = 6.3.
45. Strictly speaking, the TDMA standard is a combination of FDMA (frequency division multiple access) and TDMA. Likewise, the CDMA standard is a combination of FDMA and CDMA.
46. The Telecommunications Industry Association is the North American standards body that oversees the cellular industry.
47. Given the mixture of investment, technical theology, and ego involved, it is difficult to see any of the service providers switching their technical allegiance.

Each of TDMA and CDMA has advantages and disadvantages relative to the other, which are bandied about by their respective adherents and detractors. In general it is difficult to objectively compare TDMA and CDMA systems because their underlying assumptions differ and are not easily related to one another.

Advantages of TDMA-based systems include the capability for variable bit rates (by increasing or decreasing the timeslots in use for one or more users), less stringent power control requirements (time slots reduce mobile duty cycles and thus mobiles' ability to interfere with one another), the capability for half-duplex (less expensive), radios plus the ability to monitor alternative slots and frequencies for MAHO or MCHO operation (both due to offset transmit and receive time slots).

Advantages of CDMA-based systems include theoretically higher capacity per bandwidth, the ability to withstand noise and fading (due to the spreading of the channel), and the reduced frequency planning and complexity needed (due to shared channels and soft handoffs).

A comparison of AMPS, GSM, TDMA, and CDMA transmission systems is displayed in Table 2.5. The following sections describe the two primary North American digital cellular standards.

Table 2.5   Cellular System Comparison

Characteristic	AMPS	GSM	IS-54 TDMA	IS-95 CDMA
Bit rate	N/A	270.8 kbps	48.6 kbps	1.2288 Mbps
Carrier spacing	30 kHz	200 kHz	30 kHz	1250 kHz
Channels/ carrier	1	8 (16 half-rate)	3 (6 half-rate)	85
Channels	832	1000 (2000)	2496 (4992)	12
Time slot	N/A	.577 ms	6.7 ms	N/A
Time slot efficiency	N/A	73%	80%	N/A
Modulation	FM	GMSK	$\pi/4$-DQPSK	QPSK/OQPSK
Modulation efficiency (b/s/Hz)	N/A	1.35	1.62	
Channel coding	N/A	1/2-convol.	1/2-convol.	1/2-convol.
Speech coding	N/A	13 kbps RPE-LTP	7.95 kbps VSELP	CELP

2.13 TDMA (IS-54/136)

Time Division Multiple Access or *TDMA*   was initially defined by the IS-54 standard and is now specified in the IS-13x series[48] of specifications of the EIA/TIA. Because of its heritage as the original North American digital standard and its common channel (frequency) set with AMPS, TOMA is sometimes called *digital AMPS* or *D-AMPS*.

TDMA services were initially deployed during 1992 by McCaw, Southwest Bell, Bell South, and others. Although initial customer adoption was slow, there were an estimated half million TDMA subscribers by yearend 1994. This number is expected to grow dramatically in coming years, especially with new generation vocoders (which improve the perceived voice quality). Because TDMA physical channels are the same as the physical channels of AMPS, TDMA can be easily migrated into and coexist with AMPS systems in a dual mode manner.

TDMA subdivides each of the 30 kHz AMPS channels into 3 *full-rate* TDMA channels, each of which is capable of supporting a single voice call.[49] In the future, each of these full-rate channels will be further subdividable into two *half-rate* channels, each of which—with the necessary coding and compression—could also support a voice call. Thus, TDMA could provide 3 to 6 times the capacity of AMPS traffic channels, with a corresponding gain in trunking efficiency. A similar calculation to that of previous sections yields an estimate of 3.5 to 6.3 times the capacity of an AMPS system [FALC95].

Like AMPS, some of the digital channels are designated as control channels, called *digital control channels* or *DCCH*. These control channels serve the same purpose as in AMPS—paging and call control. However, IS-136 call control messages are layered into paging slots, unlike AMPS.

Because of its time-division nature, by offsetting corresponding forward- and reverse-direction time slots, TDMA allows half-duplex phones to be used. This has the benefit of reducing cost and power consumption (i.e., battery size) of the mobile station, but with an increase in complexity due to the variable power envelope. It also allows the monitoring of control channels for out-of-band signalling during a call. Finally, the half-duplex operation allows mobiles to monitor the quality of channels used in neighboring cells in order to assist handoffs.

Originally, TDMA used parametric coding voice digitization, which is based on mathematical models of human vocal sounds. This prohibited the use of analog facsimile and modems due to the resultant distortion of modem signals (which are unlike human voice). The vocoders specified for TDMA have been upgraded with the 1995 standards revision to use A-CELP (algebraic code excited linear prediction).

TDMA traffic channels use $\pi/4$-DQPSK modulation at a 24.3-kbaud channel rate. This results in an effective 48.6 kbps data rate across the six time slots comprising one frame in the

---

48. These standards are numbered IS-130, IS-135, and IS-136.
49. A TDMA *frame* is 40 msec or 972 2-bit symbols long and consists of six timeslots. Each full-rate TDMA channel consists of two of these six timeslots.

30-kHz physical channel. TDMA standards (IS-135) specify RS-232 and AT-command set-capable mobile units that can use the system at a full-rate data speed of 9.6 kbps, which can be effectively doubled with V.42*bis* data compression. A triple-rate data speed of 28.8 uncompressed (57.6 kbps compressed) is also specified. Gateways for facsimile and landline modems can be installed at MSCs by TDMA service providers.

A capability called short messaging service (SMS) has been specified in IS-136 to use the DCCH for short messages. This two-way service can deliver messages of up to 256 characters to the display on a subscriber's phone. Similar services are also specified for CDMA and N-AMPS[50] systems.

A very recent packet data initiative has been underway under the auspices of the TDMA Forum, the trade association for TDMA technology participants. The approach favored by the committee working on packet data services uses a dynamic time slot assignment with reservation algorithm that melds directly into the existing TDMA standard to provide CDPD-type services over TDMA channels.

In this proposed standard, all of the usual capabilities are supported in addition to variable bandwidth, which is potentially very large if enough TDMA channels are momentarily available for this purpose. Also specified is an efficient MAC layer ARQ mechanism plus the capability for a mobile unit to monitor both voice and data services simultaneously [CHAN96].

2.14 CDMA (IS-95,99)

Code Division Multiple Access or *CDMA* was introduced as a cellular standard by QUAL-COMM, Inc., in 1989. Based on technology initially discovered during World War II,[51] CDMA was accepted as an alternative North American digital cellular standard (IS-95) by the TIA in 1992 and has undergone development in the standards process since then. At year-end 1995 there were still no commercially available CDMA systems.

The basic idea of spread spectrum is to rely on something other than time division or geographic attenuation of a signal to prevent co-channel interference. This makes sense because there are general tendencies of signal strength attenuation, but no absolute rules; topography, weather, foliage, presence of reflectors, etc., are all major factors determining the strength of a received signal.

---

50. Narrowband AMPS, defined by IS-88 and IS-91.
51. Frequency hopping spread spectrum patent number 2,292,387 belongs to none other than Hedy Lamarr, a screen siren for MGM in the 1940s. Who says you need an engineering degree?

There are two flavors to spread spectrum technology. One flavor is called *frequency hopping* spread spectrum and is discussed in Chapter 9. The second flavor of spread spectrum is called *direct sequence* spread spectrum, which forms the basis of the IS-95 physical layer.

CDMA addresses the two basic problems with radio systems—multipath fading and interference from others in the cellular environment. Both of these challenges are mitigated via the frequency diversity introduced by the wide bandwidth used in CDMA. No single source of interference can impact more than a subset of the spread spectrum in use. CDMA redistributes a base signal across a broad bandwidth under control of digital circuitry.

In CDMA, average interference limits system performance rather than worst-case interference as in FDMA- and TDMA-based systems. Thus, CDMA systems reuse the same frequency in neighboring cells. It's a good thing, because CDMA RF channels are large—1.25 MHz—and thus there are relatively few of them.

Cellular CDMA systems code speech in a compact 8 Kbps format and transmit a basic data rate of 9600 bps in a spread format of 1.2288 Mbps called "Mchips per second." This *spreading factor* of 128 resulting in a coding gain of 21 dB, which combats many of the vagaries of RF transmission. The spreading mechanism differs between the forward and reverse channels because the capabilities of transmitter and receiver differ on the mobile and system sides of the airlink. Different frequencies are used in forward and reverse directions also, for a limited form of frequency division duplexed or FDD operation.

CDMA uses a soft base-controlled handoff for mobiles transitioning between cells. This improves the quality of service for both voice and data applications. CDMA enjoys somewhat reduced complexity in the network—frequency planning and cell handoff processes—for somewhat increased complexity on the radio link side of the system in the form of power planning. This is an interesting approach.

Estimating the capacity of CDMA systems objectively is difficult because of the number of assumptions required.[52] QUALCOMM claims a relative capacity of 14 times AMPS capacity [VITE95]. A better estimate might be half that value.

The size of CDMA channels (1.25 MHz) will make migration to dual mode cellular operation (i.e., CDMA and AMPS) more of a quantum leap than an evolutionary process. How this will be accomplished—removing large numbers of AMPS channels from AMPS service to CDMA service—in the face of already overloaded systems will be an interesting challenge to the CDMA service providers.

Data services in CDMA systems have been specified for facsimile and asynchronous data applications. Both of these are included in the IS-99 standard and are circuit-switched in nature. A packet-switched service has been defined for CDMA systems with IS-667. Current 14.4 Kbps data rates could be augmented under a proposed Extended CDMA specification to support 76.8 Kbps data streams.

---

52. In fact, one could argue that the lack of commercial CDMA deployment at year-end 1995—following numerous delays—reflects the degree of difficulty in mapping between these assumptions and the vagaries of real-world cellular environments.

2.15 PCS: Back to the Future?

A number of trends in wireless communications are becoming evident. First among these is the imminent deployment of *Personal Communications Services (PCS)* by licensed service providers. Auctions held in 1994-96 resulted in the assignment of licenses for both narrowband PCS-based services and broadband PCS-based services in the U.S.[53] The objective of PCS is to offer so-called "next generation" digital cellular, as well as competition for local loop services. Despite its hype, PCS is simply cellular at higher frequency.

The creation of a PCS industry has been driven by a combination of demand and technological evolution. Early cellular "mobiles" were large and bulky, requiring an automobile for transport. Cellular systems were designed with this vehicular bias and were expected to serve no more than four or five million subscribers by the mid-1990s. As the size of mobile equipment has decreased to that of portable handsets, the costs of providing service has similarly decreased and cell phones have become almost a consumer staple. PCS is aimed at meeting this growing demand for ubiquitous communications.

The narrowband PCS services will be offered via 10 nationwide licenses in the 930 MHz region. The inbound and outbound channel sizes vary between 12.5 and 50 kHz, depending on the particulars of the license. The target service offering for narrowband PCS is advanced messaging (e.g., acknowledged or two-way paging). A variety of technologies are under development to provide these services. Although the bandwidth for narrowband PCS prohibits general-purpose data networking applications, there is certainly the opportunity for specialized applications, such as telemetry, credit card verification, etc. These services and technologies are discussed in Chapter 9.

The broadband PCS services will initially be offered via 3 30-MHz licenses per market in the 1850-1990 MHz region (Table 2.6). Aimed at all types of voice and data communications, PCS services will compete with cellular and other existing wireless services. Existing technologies such as CDMA, TDMA, and GSM (called PCS-1900 in this context) are targeted for broadband PCS; the additional spectrum created by PCS will also encourage enhancements of these standards to better support data services. New technologies are also likely to appear.

---

53. Motivated largely by huge budget deficits, Congress authorized the FCC to use an auction process for allocating PCS licenses in the 1993 Budget Reconciliation Act. This auction process replaced the earlier lottery for AMPS licenses, which resulted in widespread fraud (by promoters on an unsuspecting public) and abuse (stuffed ballot boxes). The A- and B-block auctions lasted 111 rounds and raised over $7 billion for the U.S. Treasury, averaging $15.50 per POPS; the most expensive market was Chicago at over $30 per POPS. The C-block auctions were held later and, despite being targeted for small businesses, raised over $10.2 billion.

Table 2.6   PCS Frequency Allocations[a]

Block (trading area type)	Reverse Direction	Forward Direction
A (MTA)	1850-1865 MHz	1930-1945 MHz
D (BTA)	1865-1870 MHz	1945-1950 MHz
B (MTA)	1870-1885 MHz	1950-1965 MHz
E (BTA)	1885-1890 MHz	1965-1970 MHz
F (BTA)	1890-1895 MHz	1970-1975 MHz
C (BTA)	1895-1910 MHz	1975-1990 MHz

a. 1910-1920 and 1920-1930 MHz bands are reserved for unlicensed asynchronous (packet-switched) and isochronous (circuit-switched) services, respectively.

The current distinction between market segments is likely to disappear with the new technologies and services. A continuum of services—paging, two-way paging, short messaging, and data at varying bandwidths—will likely replace the current paging and data segments. With existing cellular service providers and partnerships expanding their coverage area via the broadband PCS auction, the need for cooperation and interoperation between service providers is likely to become less important than it currently is in cellular.

Western Europe is expected to award up to 4 PCN licenses per country beginning in 1996, based on the DCS1800 standard, to compete with the GSM duopoly in these countries. However, the European Commission policy on PCN is vague, giving wide scope for national discretion in deciding who should obtain or bid to obtain PCN licenses. Also, licensing procedures vary between countries. The European Radiocommunications Committee (ERC) is likely to allocate 1710 to 1785 and 1805 to 1880 MHz bands for PCN use by January of 1998.

2.15.1 PCS Licensing

Like AMPS, licenses for North American PCSs are assigned on a per market basis. However, rather than considering only local markets, the FCC has also defined PCS markets that are regional in scope. These fifty-one regional markets are referred to as *Major Trading Areas* or *MTAs*. The A and B blocks of PCS licenses have been awarded on a per MTA basis.

The C- through F- blocks of PCS licenses will be awarded on the basis of the local markets, called *Basic Trading Areas* or *BTAs*. There are 491 BTAs defined in the United States, Canada, and Mexico are likely to follow suit in defining PCS licenses on the basis of MTAs and BTAs for commonality amongst North American mobile service providers.

The magnitude of the bets placed by the "winners," coupled with the fact that the "winners" have to underwrite the costs of relocating existing users of these frequencies (i.e., point-to-point microwave applications) to new frequencies, will exert great pressure on the service providers to get revenues flowing. The PCS service providers are free to use any air interface and system architecture, so long as transmit power levels, etc., are within specified ranges. The need for rapid service deployment will encourage the "winners" to use the existing digital cellular standards.

2.15.2 PCS Standards

Probably the most controversial aspect of PCS is the continuation of the digital standards battle from the cellular industry; with the addition of GSM as a contender, one could argue that the holy wars have escalated. With the possibility of one or more service providers offering nationwide service with their existing cellular licenses and the new PCS licenses, proprietary standards could also emerge. In some cases previously supported standards and licenses from their cellular markets are being dropped by service providers in favor of the standards and licenses selected by PCS partnerships in which they are involved to avoid conflicts of religion (technical standards) and geography (licenses).[54]

In any case, as in digital cellular, the multiplicity of standards will limit the capability for "roaming" in another service provider's coverage area. As always, the old standby—AMPS in the 800 MHz bands—will be the common denominator. Most portables are likely to continue to support this analog standard to prevent subscribers from being limited to "islands" of mobile services.

At this time (mid-1996), the *Joint Technical Committee (JTC)* of the TIA and the T1/T45 engineering group have approved four technical airlink standards for PCS. They are CDMA, TDMA, GSM, and a composite CDMA/TDMA/FDMA standard proposed by Omnipoint. All of the standards running in the 800-900 MHz bands have been modified in the appropriate ways to support "up-banded" operation. Each of the standards has its supporters and detractors.

2.15.3 PCS Challenges

The primary challenges for PCS service providers—once the standards decision has been made—are the relocation of current users of PCS frequencies to other frequencies and site acquisition. Relocating the current spectrum users—called "incumbents"—is projected to cost the PCS "winners" over $1 billion. Each market must be negotiated separately. According to the rules established by the FCC, the incumbents have provisions to return to the 1900 MHz frequencies if they

---

54. The FCC prohibits a single entity from operating both a cellular service and a PCS service in the same market.

are not satisfied with the new higher-frequency microwave operations. Up to ten thousand such microwave links must be relocated.

Site acquisition has always been a challenge for cellular service providers and will be for PCS service providers as well. Many of the best cell sites have already been taken by existing cellular service providers and zoning board approvals are getting harder to come by. The higher frequencies and lower power levels to be used for PCS dictate a greater number of cell sites than in conventional cellular systems.[55]

The general idea of PCS is for base stations to be located on utility poles and billboards, etc., which will greatly reduce the costs of acquiring real estate. However, this will be mitigated by the additional infrastructure equipment required. Meanwhile, the existing cellular carriers aren't exactly standing still; both in terms of additional deployment and customer penetration, they have been extremely active.

The marketing emphasis of PCS services is on small, low power mobile devices. The user is assumed to be a pedestrian, rather than an occupant of a vehicle—the design point for early cellular services. PCS cell sizes are small—less than one kilometer in diameter for small low power mobile devices. Three-dimensional coverage considerations apply, as opposed to the conventional cellular "flatland."

However, there really is no difference between PCS and cellular service. With the threat of increased competition from PCS, existing cellular service providers are increasingly offering services that are indistinguishable from PCS except for the frequencies in use. The decreasing prices paid by subscribers will force lower margins and a continuation of the mergers between service providers. It has been estimated that in the end there will be at most three nationwide service providers for combined cellular and PCS services.

2.16 Summary

This chapter has presented an overview of cellular systems. Although these systems have traditionally been voice-centric in terms of services and operation, they are now being extended to better support data applications. The most significant of these extensions is Cellular Digital Packet Data, which we introduce in the following chapter.

---

55. PCS can be expected to suffer from a 10 dB propagation penalty because of the higher frequencies. This amounts to a coverage range of about one-half of cellular and a coverage area of about one-quarter of cellular.

3 Overview of CDPD

The cost is truly trivial.

—R. Mechaley, April 22, 1992, *Wall Street Journal*,
"Cellular Carriers Announce Data Service"

This chapter presents an overview of Cellular Digital Packet Data technology—its history, objectives, services, and architecture. CDPD is an open system definition that uses digital transmission on analog cellular (AMPS) channels to provide mobile packet-switched data services. CDPD is also a system concept, with a layered architecture that supports evolution to future technologies.

Many aspects of CDPD are generic in the sense that any wide area data network that supports mobility will share these aspects—both positive and negative. Other aspects of CDPD are unique to the cellular industry, which is CDPD's heritage.

The purpose of CDPD is to provide mobile access to the services available via standard connectionless data protocols such as IP and CLNP. CDPD could be considered to be a wireless extension to the Internet that is available anywhere. As we shall see, CDPD could be easily enhanced to support other connectionless network protocols, such as IPv6.[1]

3.1 CDPD Background

During 1991, IBM and McCaw Cellular Communications, Inc.,[2] began a collaborative effort to determine the feasibility of overlaying a digital packet-switched data network on the North American AMPS analog cellular system. This joint venture resulted in a proof of concept implementation at McCaw's headquarters in Kirkland, Washington, at the end of the year. The

---

1. Formerly known as Internet Protocol next generation or IPng [BRAD96].
2. Now known as AT&T Wireless Services, Inc.

technology was named "Celluplan II" by IBM, the provider of the initial conceptual framework for the technology.[3]

3.1.1 CDPD Prototypes

The initial prototype system used a private partition of cellular channels in a single cell to demonstrate the concept of *frequency hopping*, also called *channel hopping*.[4] In this demonstration, the RF coverage exceeded that provided by AMPS because of the digital GMSK modulation and the Reed-Solomon (63,39) forward error correction coding employed.

Following the demonstration's success, plans were made for extending the scope of the project to include a field trial of a larger system. The technology was renamed "Data Over Cellular" and again renamed *Cellular Digital Packet Data* or *CDPD*. From this point forward the prototype CDPD effort was dominated by schedules that were highly aggressive and accompanied by hyperbole to match.

In order to standardize the technology and increase the geographic coverage of the eventual service, McCaw enlisted the support of other large cellular service providers. The public announcement of CDPD and its backing by eight of the largest North American wireless services providers was made in April, 1992. In May, 1992, these wireless services providers (Ameritech, Bell Atlantic, GTE, McCaw, Nynex, PacTel, Southwest Bell, and US West) staged a CDPD Technical Conference in Santa Clara.

The Santa Clara conference drew more than 600 attendees, reflecting the widespread interest in mobile data communications. Copies of a preliminary technical specification (Release 0.1) were distributed and plans for an upcoming field trial in the Bay Area were disclosed.

The early CDPD system architecture was telecommunications-oriented. A modified version of SCCP from SS7 provided the connection-oriented transport service, then considered necessary for support of mobile devices. This architecture required gateway services[5] to interconnect with the rest of the data networking world, not unlike the competing RAM and Ardis systems. The RF channel used the same GMSK modulation with Reed-Solomon (63,39) forward error correction as in the earlier demonstration system. The RF MAC sublayer was specified with both polled and contention-based modes of shared channel operation.

---

3. Many of the original system concepts, such as channel hopping, originated at Novatel; rights to this technology were subsequently transferred to IBM.
4. In frequency hopping, the logical data channel "hops" to an idle RF channel upon either a timer expiry or the incidence of a voice call coming up on the former RF channel. This is different from the "frequency hopping" employed by some spread spectrum systems.
5. The earliest specifications for CDPD included an entity called the Mobile Data Gateway, a precursor to the current Mobile Data Intermediate System. Despite its name, the actual network gateway services were to be located in entities called Network Interface Modules, one of which was to be defined for each of IP, SNA, etc.

The so-called "field trial" took place in the Bay Area during the latter half of 1992 and validated the radio resource management operation of the CDPD overlay on cellular systems. Channel hopping, cell transfer, and interference avoidance were all exhaustively tested. Suspicious police often followed rented antenna-clad Cadillacs, occupied by test personnel and equipment, slowly cruising Camino Real in the dead of night, when potential cellular voice customer impact would be minimized.

The results of the trial were sufficient to convince seven of the cellular service providers supporting the effort (Ameritech, Bell Atlantic, GTE, McCaw, Nynex, PacTel, and Southwest Bell) to continue the development of the technical specifications.

The early focus of the technical specifications effort was on the RF aspects of the system. The end result was a Reed-Solomon (63,47) forward error correction designed to increase the effective user bandwidth of the GMSK-modulated bitstream and a contention resolution scheme, similar to Ethernet, which provides both collision avoidance and collision detection. This MAC protocol is called slotted nonpersistent *Digital Sense Multiple Access* (*DSMA*) with collision detection.

3.1.2 "CDPD Lite"

Although the 1992 CDPD specification team focus was robust airlink protocols, work continued on the overall system architecture. In the fall, several members of the team concluded that the telephony-based system architecture was inappropriate for the services to be provided by CDPD.[6] During the first week of December, a five-person subteam designed an alternative architecture, informally dubbed "CDPD Lite."

The "CDPD Lite" architecture was based on existing data networking standards and on the open connectionless Layer 3 protocols (IP and CLNP) that were available. This open architecture eliminated the need for gateways and leveraged conventional network recovery mechanisms to help support transient mobility. Its mobility management scheme was based on the early work of the IETF Mobile IP task force. This architecture, elegant in its simplicity, was later adopted as the "official" CDPD architecture by the group of seven cellular service providers who continued to support the effort.

The first half of 1993 saw the completion of the Bay Area "field trial." Preliminary specification releases of the new CDPD architecture were published in March (Release 0.8) and May (Release 0.9). The first official release of the specification (CDPD System Specification Release 1.0 [CDPD93]) followed in July. All of these published releases embodied the "CDPD Lite" architecture.

---

6. At the Comdex trade show that fall in Las Vegas, the seven sponsoring cellular service providers demonstrated the CDPD prototype in a common booth. A second more-detailed release of the specification for the telephony-based system architecture was scheduled for publication immediately following the show. However, one of the cellular carriers abstained in the vote to approve the publication. A cautious voting process, in which an abstention could block action, arguably may have preserved the credibility of the cellular service providers as potential mobile data services providers.

The second half of 1993 saw the initial development of legitimate CDPD infrastructure and mobile devices. Separate efforts by McCaw and a collaboration of other cellular service providers resulted in two demonstrations of CDPD operation at the large Comdex trade show in Las Vegas in November. This rapid four month specification to demonstration timeframe reflects the benefits of the open CDPD architecture.

3.1.3 CDPD Forum

In 1994, the cellular service providers behind the CDPD specification development created the CDPD Forum to enlarge the base of support for CDPD. This trade association of service providers, infrastructure and mobile unit vendors, and software and applications developers continues to have as its objective the support and promotion of CDPD as a basis for mobile data applications.

The CDPD Forum supported the development of CDPD System Specification and Implementor Guidelines Release 1.1 [CDPD95] during 1994. This release was published in January, 1995, and includes enhancements to the radio resource management procedures, the Mobile Data Link Protocol (MDLP), accounting, and multicast capabilities, as well as protocol test specifications and implementation guidelines. The primary purpose of Release 1.1 was to finish the definition of incomplete or unclear capabilities of CDPD Release 1.0.

Release 1.1 also restructured the CDPD specification into a System Specification and Implementor Guidelines. This restructuring provided a better distinction between stable protocols (which were placed into the System Specification) and other Parts,[7] which might be less mature or more implementation-specific or otherwise unsuitable for a system standard (and which were placed into the Implementor Guidelines).[8]

In 1995, the CDPD Forum developed certification test plans for mobiles and initiated a selection process for an agency to conduct these tests. Further extensions to CDPD were contributed by Forum members and ratified by the Technical Steering Committee in the areas of circuit-switched access to CDPD services and limited size messaging. By mid-1995, the CDPD Forum had almost 100 member companies, reflecting the diverse and dynamic interests in CDPD technology. It continues to actively support the contributions of members to CDPD standards and implementor guidelines development. A standards track process has been developed that is loosely modeled after that of the IETF.

---

7. The CDPD System Specification and Implementor Guidelines are divided into "Parts," which discuss specific system aspects or protocols.
8. Unfortunately, some developers of CDPD equipment and software have mistakenly interpreted the CDPD Implementor Guidelines as just guidelines, which was not the intention of the specification team. A more formal standardization process has been established in the CDPD Forum to clarify any such misperceptions.

3.1.4 CDPD Service Providers

Separately, a Service Provider Corporation was created in 1995 to provide a forum for resolving inter-service provider concerns. This SPCo manages the activities of the CDPD *Network Information Center* (*NIC*), which include administration of CDPD network address blocks, DNS names and unique CDPD identifiers amongst the service providers.

Over the course of the year, CDPD service providers deployed services and expanded the customer base for those services. At year-end 1995, CDPD services were offered in over thirty markets, as depicted in Figure 3.1. Inter-service provider testing and interconnection was also well underway, with agreements and interoperation amongst the major service providers in place by mid-1996.

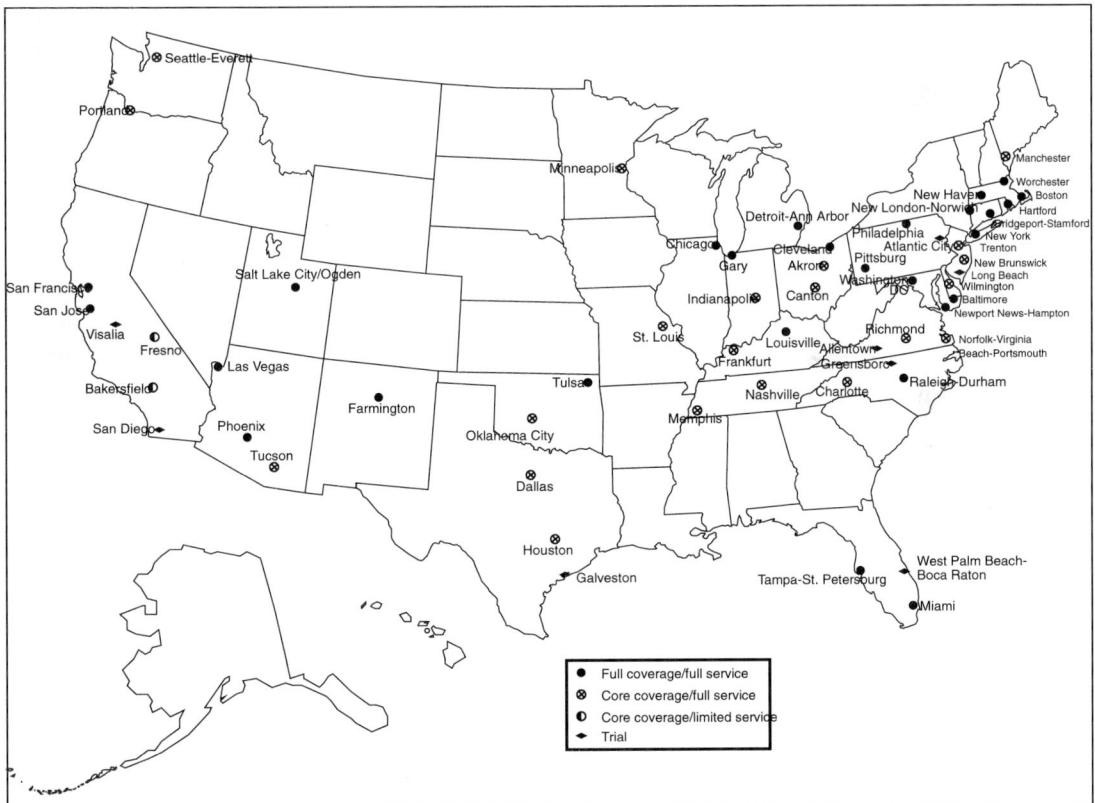

Figure 3.1   CDPD coverage at year-end 1995

Time will tell just how successful CDPD will be in terms of commercial adoption. In any case, the technology is likely to influence future mobile data systems. Both the CDMA and TDMA Forums are developing technical specifications for packet data services whose mobility management mechanisms are identical to and will interoperate with CDPD; this will allow service providers to offer CDPD services via multiple airlinks and leverage their current infrastructure investment.

3.2 Relationship of CDPD to Other Cellular Data Initiatives

When CDPD was first conceived and specified in the early 1990s, the CDMA (IS-95) and TDMA (IS-54, now IS-136) standards efforts for North American cellular voice services were well underway. In fact, TDMA digital voice services were already being deployed in a number of markets. It was a foregone conclusion that both of these competing digital voice standards would eventually support data services as well.

Unfortunately, the schism between the North American cellular service providers that support CDMA and those that support TDMA shows little sign of closing. In early 1996, the only common North American cellular standard is still the analog *AMPS* (*Advanced Mobile Phone System*) standard. The common denominator for data services likewise remains CDPD.

In the future, it is likely that both CDMA and TDMA will be deployed throughout North America, thanks in large part to the new PCS spectrum. These standards are being extended to support data services, both in circuit-switched and packet-switched modes. The packet-switched modes are based on a CDPD system design—all that is changed is the necessary radio modulation techniques and protocols, primarily at Physical and MAC Layers. So rather than replacing CDPD, these digital cellular standards will instead adopt CDPD for their base data services-providing architecture.

Another more recent adoption of CDPD architecture is embodied in the new *personal Air Communications Technology (pACT)* announced by AT&T Wireless Services and others. This two-way messaging technology modifies CDPD to use the narrowband PCS channels auctioned in 1994—another example of CDPD operating over alternative airlinks. pACT is discussed in Chapter 9.

CDPD architecture was conceived with this kind of extensibility in mind. CDPD is more than an airlink specification—it is a system architecture for mobile data services that can support multiple RF technologies. One of the more common misperceptions in the trade press has been the eventual "replacement" of CDPD by emerging standards that were based on the new RF technologies.[9]

Another initiative is that of the *Portable Computer and Communications Association* (*PCCA*), which has defined standard APIs for the mobile computing industry since 1993. Their recent STD-201 wireless modem standard is based on the commonly-used *Microsoft*

---

9. This misperception has been fed to a large extent by misleading comments from some purvey- ors of alternative technological solutions for the airlink. It seems that as technology advances, there are increasing opportunities for apples-to-oranges comparisons by "technologists" with agendas. It is our hope that this book will clarify some of the misperceptions about mobile sys- tems in general and CDPD in particular that have been promulgated over the past few years.

Network-Device Driver Interface Specification (NDIS), and will allow software developers to support wireless modes of operation to Windows applications. STD-201 complements the earlier STD-101 standard, also developed in the PCCA, which defined hardware- and network-independent extensions to the popular Hayes AT modem command set for wireless operation. CDPD is one of the primary target networks for these interface specifications.

3.3 CDPD Services and Characteristics

CDPD is an enabling technology that provides support for mobility in the WAN environment. To accomplish this, CDPD provides three kinds of services—network services, network application services, and network support services. As Figure 3.2 depicts, these services provide support for applications ranging from stationary vending machines to mobile vehicle tracking. The services also support applications ranging from telemetry (extremely low data rates) to interactive PC-based applications such as remote server access.

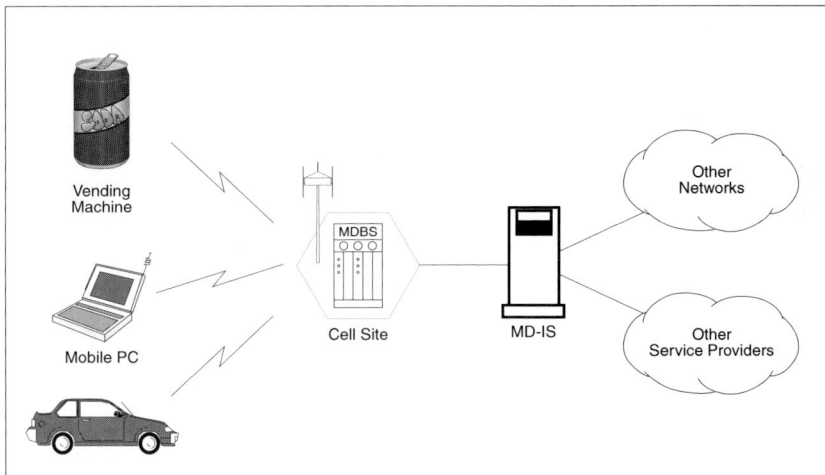

Figure 3.2   The CDPD System

3.3.1 CDPD Network Services

Network services are data transfer services—capable of moving data from one location to another. This is the basic service type offered by CDPD. It neither adds value nor content to what the user intends; it is simply data carriage to and from a mobile device.

In terms of data networking, CDPD provides support for routable connectionless peer-to-peer Layer 3 protocols, such as IP and CLNP. Other Layer 3 protocols, such as IPv6 are likely to be supported in the future as well. By definition, Layer 3 is the layer responsible for getting data from one point to another across one or more networks.

Part of basic network service is the provision of access to systems and services—both public and private—external to CDPD. These services can be data resources or networks. In most cases, a mobile user sends data to and receives data from a resource external to the CDPD network. CDPD simply provides a means of accessing that external resource and could simply be regarded as an extension of existing data communications networks that are IP- or CLNP-based.

Basic CDPD network services are summarized in this overview chapter and described in more detail in Chapter 4 (mobility management) and Chapter 5 (network access).

3.3.2 CDPD Network Support Services

Network support services are the services necessary to support the operation of a mobile data network. Network support services include things such as network management, usage accounting and security, which are necessary to operate any network. CDPD network support services also include things such as mobility management and radio resource management, which are necessary for mobile wireless WANs.[10]

In theory, an end-user of the system could use the network services while perfectly oblivious to the existence of the network support services (at least as long as these services are running correctly, save accounting!). In many cases, the support services could be considered to add "intelligence" to the system; an example is the fault recovery actions taken by network management when an exceptional condition arises.

CDPD network support services are described in Chapter 6 (security) and Chapter 7 (other support services).

3.3.3 CDPD Network Application Services

Network application services are services that add value or content to a user's activities above and beyond basic data carriage. The end-user is typically quite aware of these value-added services and often must explicitly subscribe to them. These services in CDPD could leverage off of

---

10. Mobility management and radio resource management provide functions of both network services and network support services.

the mobility of the user, such as subscriber location services or limited size messaging services. It is also possible that these services could be independent of mobility, such as advanced messaging capabilities.

The CDPD specification includes technical descriptions of mobility-enhanced value-added services. Other CDPD network application services could be based on the intrinsic broadcast and multicast capability defined in the CDPD System Specification.

Some of these network application services are described in Chapter 8 (limited size messaging, subscriber location service).

3.4 CDPD Design Goals and Considerations

A number of design goals and considerations influenced the architecture of CDPD. These are technical objectives only and are not necessarily indicative of the business objectives of CDPD service providers or other industry participants.

Many of these technical objectives reflect the lessons learned by cellular service providers over their first decade. Since the CDPD initiative originated in the cellular community, these objectives largely reflect the interests of the cellular service providers in developing an open and interoperable standard for mobile data services.

As always, full enjoyment of these applications depends on proper implementation by vendors and intelligent operation by service providers.

3.4.1 Location Independence

The operation and appearance of basic CDPD services to an end-user (called a *subscriber*) or application is intended to be independent of the service provider and location at which those services are made available. If a user is receiving service while located in a different CDPD service provider's coverage area, there should be little, if any, impact on the user or application. This seamless "visiting" should not be confused with "roaming" in the cellular world, which as we have seen has had many bad connotations.

However, CDPD also allows service providers to differentiate their respective service offerings by offering services that add value above and beyond the baseline CDPD services. By defining as little as possible, the CDPD System Specification leaves plenty of invention up to the service providers. Over time, service providers will likely differentiate their CDPD service offerings with these additional capabilities, as well as by the level of service they provide.

3.4.2 Application Transparency

Applications do not have to be modified in order to use CDPD; an explicit goal of CDPD is to have minimal impact on end-devices and applications. CDPD services should be accessed via industry-standard application program interfaces (APIs), which are identical to those employed in conventional networks. According to the CDPD System Specification, "the CDPD Network design shall ensure that no impact is exerted on transport and higher protocols."

However, it is possible that timers (such as TCP restart timeouts, etc.) might have to be altered somewhat for optimal CDPD (or other wireless services) usage. Otherwise, CDPD is intended to be fully compatible with existing data networking applications. Time and again, this objective has been demonstrated with new applications running immediately on CDPD with no more effort required than on a conventional LAN. We do this constantly.

However, this application transparency does not prevent additional services and applications, which could not be provided by conventional data networks (such as remote telemetry or location services), from being supported by CDPD. Many of these services, which are exclusive to mobile solutions, are the economic *raison d'etre* for CDPD and end-users (and thus also for service providers). An example is the limited size messaging capability introduced in the CDPD Forum in mid-1995.

3.4.3 Multiprotocol Support

CDPD was intended from the outset to support more than a single connectionless Layer 3 protocol. This was an important consideration because there were concerns during the early 1990s that IP Class B address blocks would be fully assigned in the near future. The impending shortage of address space (among other reasons) motivated the creation of the IPng committee by the IETF [BRAD96]. The resulting IPv6 protocol standard was drafted in 1994. This protocol will likely also be supported by CDPD as its implementation and usage become widespread.

CLNP was also supported from the beginning of the "CDPD Lite" architecture. Support for CLNP is necessary to support several of the OSI applications, such as X.700 (CMIP) for network management and X.400 (message transport) for accounting information exchange between service providers. CLNP is also key to the intersystem NPDU redirection that lies at the heart of CDPD mobility.

3.4.4 Interoperability

The CDPD System Specification and Implementor Guidelines provide the information necessary to ensure interoperability between the equipment and software provided by multiple vendors.

This in turn minimizes the infrastructure and device costs in a competitive environment. Interoperability between service providers is also supported by one of the three well-defined interfaces in the CDPD specification. Abstract test suite definitions further support interoperability between equipment and software providers and CDPD service providers.

3.4.5 Minimal Invention

One of the goals of the CDPD specification effort was to minimize the overall risk to the fledgling industry by minimizing the invention in CDPD. The fast schedule required that off-the-shelf technology be utilized wherever possible. The bulk of the "invention" in CDPD consists of combining existing technology in a new way, mostly over the RF airlink. CDPD service providers have the ability to reuse existing cellular facilities to support data as well as voice services.

3.4.6 Optimal Usage of RF

Although CDPD architecture is holistic in nature, a key design goal was to make efficient use of the radio channel. Since this airlink is the most precious resource in the system, CDPD design trade-offs consistently favored airlink efficiency at the potential expense of other resources of the system. An example of this is the extensive application of standard data compression (V.42*bis*) technologies to conserve over-the-air transmission at the expense of greater computational loads at either side of the airlink. In Moore's Law we trust.

The raw signalling rate of the airlink is 19.2 Kbps; with Reed-Solomon (63,47) FEC, this amounts to a maximum effective bandwidth of 14.4 Kbps full-duplex before considering channel control overhead. Since the inbound channel is shared via a contention-based access scheme, which further imposes overhead on both the inbound and outbound channels, it is essential that the airlink be used effectively.

Another concern in CDPD development was not "pushing the envelope" of RF technology too far. One of the obvious ways to get around the constraint of the narrow airlink "pipe" would be to employ more sophisticated RF modulation techniques. However, doing so would have increased the cost for mobile devices beyond what commercial users would bear.[11] GMSK is already used in GSM systems around the world and provides the 19.2 Kbps data transmission rate over the air, which provides the basis for CDPD.

---

11. To a large extent, we have always considered the RF technology employed in CDPD to be a "temporary" solution. Once again protocol layering supports the evolution to more sophisticated RF technologies as the costs of these technologies decrease.

3.4.7 Evolutionary Design

The data networking world is evolutionary and so must be CDPD. The definition of CDPD architecture, strictly in terms of OSI reference model layers, coupled with the limited scope of the system definition (i.e., OSI layer 3 and below), allows for evolution of CDPD as well as network technologies supported by CDPD. New applications and transport protocols are immediately operable on CDPD systems because of its support for native IP.

The recent introduction of a hybrid architecture of cellular circuit-switched airlink in the CDPD Forum exemplifies the evolutionary nature of CDPD architecture. Similarly, anticipated support for IPv6 (as it becomes widely adopted) will also be straightforward. Other areas of anticipated evolution include the airlink link layer protocol (MDLP) and airlink security (encryption and authentication); evolution in these areas is supported with version codes, command types, etc.

3.4.8 Open

CDPD has always been intended to be an open system, free from all proprietary technology. In our opinion, the only known aspect of CDPD architecture involving previous intellectual property rights is the use of public key cryptography techniques that underlie security across the airlink. CDPD is based on open standards and protocols; the limited invention in CDPD is also open and freely available.

An open standard provides the basis for multi-vendor interoperability and the resulting economic benefits of competition. It also encourages multiple vendors to participate and compete in the marketplace, driving down costs. Multiple developers working on a common problem are likely to produce the best solution. These benefits are rarely achieved by proprietary solutions.

3.4.9 Secure

CDPD is intended to provide data networking services that are no less secure than conventional WANs. (Of course, the trade press has popularized the notion of insecurity of the Internet, so maybe this isn't such a great objective!) The security capabilities provided by CDPD are integral to the system, not later add-ons.

These security capabilities include confidentiality for both users and their data (via data encryption and the use of temporary IDs for users), user authentication, and the key management necessary to support these capabilities. The design requirement for CDPD was to prevent casual "eavesdropping" of users across the airlink; thus the users of CDPD are no less secure than users of conventional networks. Of course, as a public shared network, end-to-end encryption by applications is always encouraged.

The security capabilities of CDPD are limited to the airlink interface. The specification team always felt that the other primary interfaces of CDPD would be able to leverage off the work being done by network security experts. Network security is an issue that transcends mobile networks; mobility only exacerbates the challenges of key management, authentication, etc.

3.4.10 Simple

The architecture of CDPD is elegant in its simplicity. In particular, the mobility management aspect of CDPD is quite straightforward, by design. [KRIS95] states that simplicity "is one of the most important attributes for a routing protocol." Simplicity in design allows for more rapid development and more reliable operation. The rapid CDPD specification draft to service deployment timeframe indicates the value of simplicity.

3.4.11 Transparent to the Existing Cellular Voice Network

CDPD has always been intended to be an overlay service on the existing cellular voice infrastructure. Maintenance of a high quality cellular voice service is of paramount importance to the cellular voice service providers who provided the initial funding for CDPD specification development. Therefore, it is essential that the introduction of CDPD service not negatively impact the basic cellular voice service offered by cellular service providers.

There are two general concerns about the CDPD overlay. First is the voice service degradation that could result from RF interference by CDPD RF transmitters. Because CDPD is transparent to the AMPS network (i.e., the AMPS system is unaware of and does not require modifications for CDPD), CDPD must operate in a way that does not interfere with the cellular voice system. This has proven to be a significant constraint on CDPD design, influencing features such as channel hopping.

The second general concern about the CDPD overlay is the removal of cellular voice capacity required to dedicate AMPS channels to CDPD service. This concern is addressed by the channel hopping capability of CDPD in which a CDPD base station utilizes currently-idle AMPS channels to provide CDPD services. An RF "sniffer" is included in the cell site infrastructure to enable the CDPD channel stream to "hop" to a new physical AMPS channel whenever cellular energy is detected on the channel used by CDPD. An anticipatory algorithm could also be used to minimize the frequency of involuntary channel hops.

The channel hopping mode of operation relies on proper cellular engineering practices, in which it is assumed that the busy hour call blocking probability is approximately two percent.[12] Using an Erlang B distribution (a standard engineering practice in telephony), one can see that approximately twenty to thirty percent of all channels must be available at any instant (on average) to provide the two percent blocking service level of quality. It is this set of idle channels that CDPD is intended to operate with in the channel hopping mode.

---

12. With the more than forty percent compound growth rate in the North American cellular subscriber population during the early 1990s, maintaining a busy hour performance level of two percent blocking has proven to be a significant challenge. Most CDPD service providers have resorted to dedicating RF channels for CDPD service. This short-term sacrifice is offset to some degree by the growing capacity gain provided by digital voice services.

3.5 The CDPD Architectural Approach

The approach taken by the CDPD specification team assumed that all objects could be defined by their interfaces and functions. Initially this philosophy was applied to the entire system.

Upon examination of the basic design goals and considerations of the CDPD network, the specification team found that they could be satisfied with a network providing an "over-the-air" interface to the mobile devices, an external interface to land-line hosts, and an inter-service provider interface to link multiple cooperating CDPD service providers.

This philosophy led to the development of the "CDPD cloud,"[13] depicted in Figure 3.3. With this model, it is necessary and sufficient to fully define the CDPD network by specifying the detailed interface to the mobile devices, external networks, and other CDPD networks. Within the CDPD network "cloud," the necessary support functions of mobility management and data delivery can be defined separately.

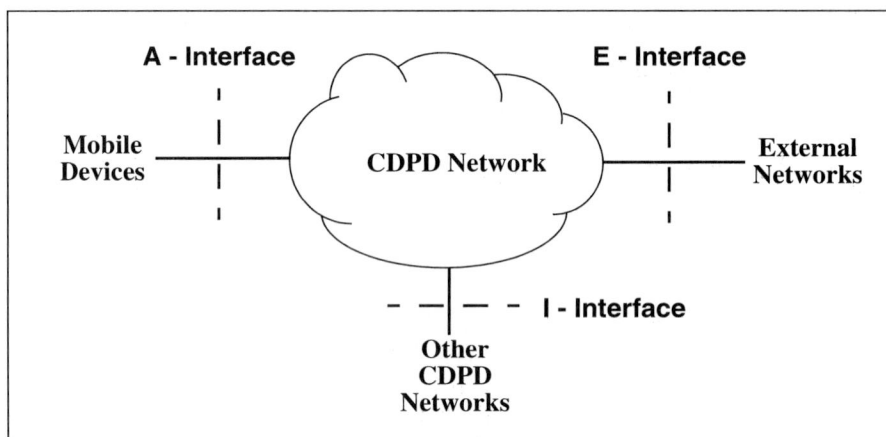

Figure 3.3   CDPD Interface Model

Although this "cloud" approach addresses the stated requirements of the CDPD network, it does not address the practical side of developing a new network service. Any new network service deployment requires the development of new network infrastructure equipment. The technical specification of the new service must also define these components.

While the "cloud" approach to network system specification defines all the necessary information for network equipment development, it may result in vastly different internal network architectures. Different equipment vendors may conceive of different sets of equipment to provide

---

13. No presentation of network technology is complete without at least one "cloud" diagram, so here it is!

the same functionality and interfaces. This is true regardless of the level of detail attained in the system specification, assuming it doesn't go so far as to specify an actual implementation.

Some of the service providers expressed concerns about the "cloud" approach of system specification. They recognized that this approach could result in networks that interoperate (over the I - Interface) but cannot share internal components. They were concerned that the RF equipment of one vendor would only operate with network routing equipment from the same vendor. This type of limitation would severely restrict a service provider's flexibility in equipment vendor selection. Indeed, most of these service providers have already lived under these types of captive marketing approaches in the cellular telephony world. They did not want this vendor-dependence to continue.

It was the service provider's initial discomfort with this aspect of the CDPD "cloud" that drove the specification team to then define individual components within the CDPD network. Some of these components are depicted in Figure 3.4.

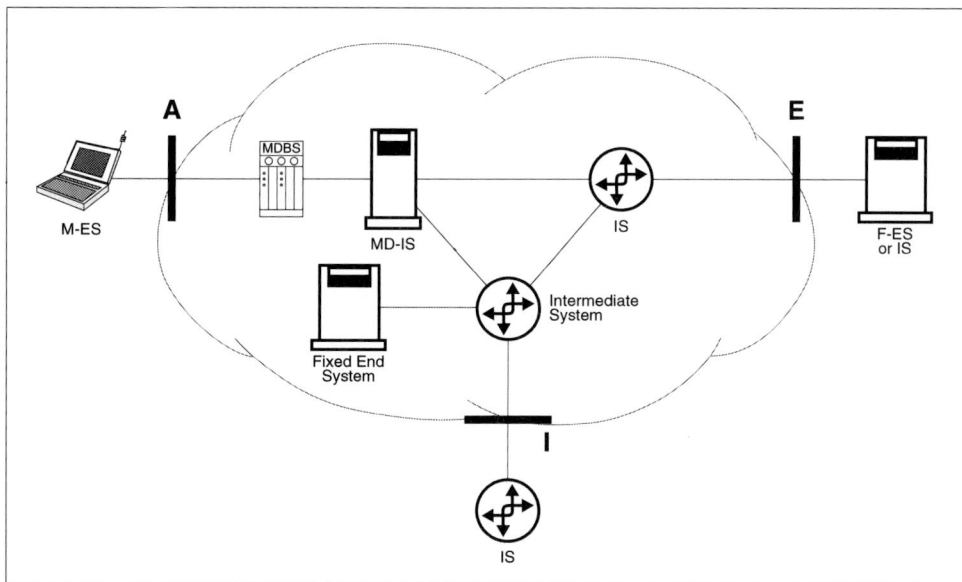

Figure 3.4   CDPD Network Layer Reference Model

3.6 The Three Key CDPD Interfaces

CDPD architecture defines three key external interfaces, as depicted in Figure 3.4. Because these interfaces—"A", "E," and "I"—form the logical boundaries for a CDPD service provider's network, they are essential to the proper operation of CDPD.

Other lesser interfaces are defined within the CDPD service provider "cloud." However, since these internal interfaces are under the control of a single CDPD service provider, their specifications could be considered to be recommendations rather than requirements.

Although this may sound contrary to our previous discussion, flexibility is required in internal interfaces because of the different network implementation approaches favored by the various CDPD service providers. It is important to differentiate between technical specification and implementation requirements.

Each of the interfaces defined in the CDPD specification includes a profile representing the protocols supported or required at each layer in the OSI Reference Model. An example of these profiles is displayed in Figure 3.5. Well-defined primitives at each layer request services of the layer below; the services provided to each layer consists of the collective set of services provided by all of the underlying layers.

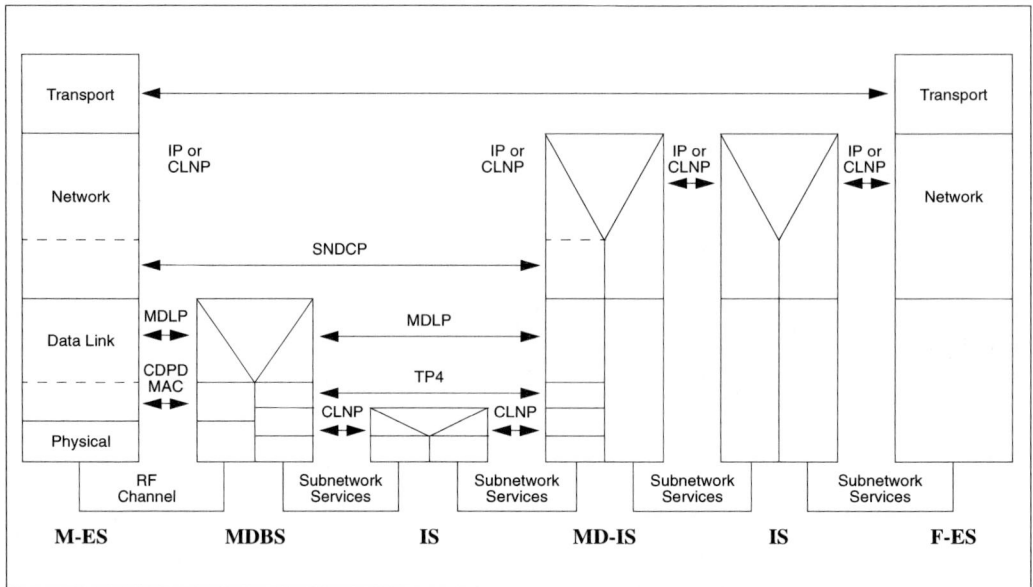

Figure 3.5 CDPD Example Interface Profiles for Network Services

3.6.1 The A-Interface

The *A-Interface* or *airlink* is the interface between the CDPD mobile device and the CDPD network and contains much of the "invention" of CDPD. This is the point at which CDPD network services are accessed by a subscriber and is described in detail in Chapter 5 (network access). This interface is defined by Parts 400 through 409 in the CDPD System Specification. Although the airlink receives much attention, this is only one part of the overall CDPD system architecture.

3.6.2 The E-Interface

The External or E-Interface of CDPD is the means by which CDPD interoperates with the rest of the world and is key to the provision of CDPD network services. Conventional data networking protocols are used for data carriage between CDPD and external data services such as the Internet, VANs, wide area transport providers, or private networks.

The Layer 3 protocols supported at the E-Interface include the same connectionless protocols as within CDPD—IP and CLNP. IPv6 is likely to be supported at a later time as it matures. Other protocols, such as APPN (via MPTN) or IPX, could be supported either via encapsulation (say within IP packets) or via protocol translation gateways. Either of these techniques is outside the scope of the CDPD specifications.

Border gateway protocols such as BGP-4 and IDRP are also recommended at the E-Interface. This is necessary because the E-Interface specifies a boundary between two autonomous systems— that of a CDPD service provider and that of an external party. Initially, static routing is likely to be employed at the E-Interface for CLNP traffic.

The E-Interface is intended to be no different than the interface to any other autonomous system. All of the issues of security, routing, name-to-address translation, etc., apply. The fact that the CDPD service provider supports mobility is transparent to the E-Interface, by design.

3.6.3 The I-Interface

As we discussed in Chapter 2, the North American cellular service environment is partitioned into markets that are served by a multiplicity of service providers. Seamless nationwide coverage (a goal of CDPD) requires these service providers to be capable of supporting each others' customers. Seamless coverage also requires the capability for a transparent and smooth transfer from one system to its neighbors.

The Inter-service provider or I-Interface defines the means by which the CDPD service providers can collectively provide a seamless nationwide service. From a purely technical view-point, there is nothing preventing CDPD service from being offered worldwide.

The I-Interface supports the same protocols as the E-interface plus the *Mobile Network Location Protocol* or *MNLP*. This protocol is the means by which mobile users from one system are supported by another system and is a key piece of the CDPD mobility management scheme. Additional protocols for network management (CMIP) and accounting (X.400-based) are also defined for the I-interface. All of the protocols across the I-interface are based on CLNP.[14]

---

14. Routing of reverse channel IP packets from a visiting mobile back to a host in its home system could be directly routed using standard IP-based protocols, in which case the interface between the two service providers would function as an E-interface. But forward-direction packets would be redirected from the home to the serving via CLNP encapsulation, as discussed later.

3.7 CDPD Network Elements

The successful operation of any communications network requires cooperating system components. These network components or entities perform predefined and a previously agreed upon functions. The components must also communicate with each other in a predefined manner.

The component entities defined by the CDPD architecture (see Figure 3.6) include several that are unique to CDPD and others that are standard "off the shelf" components. Since the CDPD network is an overlay on the existing cellular network, it only made sense to leverage off the existing infrastructure. The CDPD network model defines component elements reflecting the cellular network, and is illustrated in Figure 3.6.

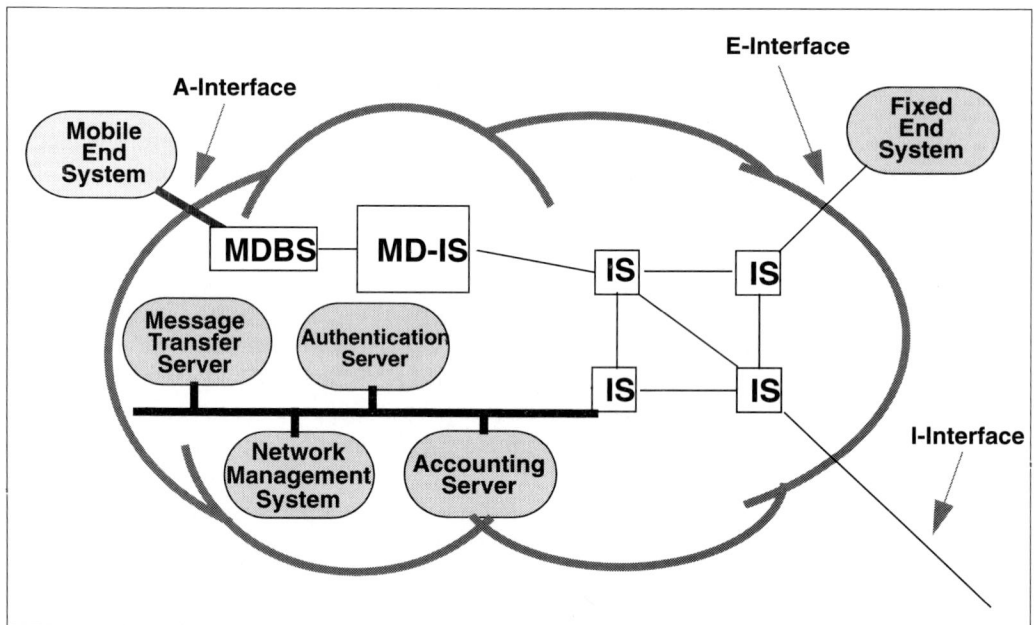

Figure 3.6   CDPD Network Elements

In a typical cellular telephone network, cell sites are deployed throughout the coverage area. At each cell site, a base station transmits and receives RF signals from the cellular telephones through an antenna tower. The demodulated signals are then digitized and placed on voice communications channels of a multiplexing channel. These are typically 1.544 Mbps T1 connections that can carry up to 24 voice calls, each one occupying a 56 kbps digital channel. The voice circuits terminate at a mobile switching center (MSC), which interfaces with the land-line telephone network.

The design of the CDPD system is aimed at minimizing the changes in network operation and maximizing the reuse of the existing cellular network infrastructure. Given this constraint, the next specification team objective was using the system's resources effectively. Without a doubt, the most precious resource is the radio spectrum. Beyond the radio resource, the precious system resources to consider are the physical plant and the communications links.

Many people may not immediately realize that the collection of cell sites constitute a significant investment by cellular service providers.[15] Many cell sites have to be constructed, while others involve ongoing leasehold arrangements. In addition, the antenna tower space is also tied with space, height, zoning, and licensing issues. Furthermore, each base station typically has a T-1 circuit dedicated to carrying its traffic.

The CDPD system architecture reuses these components by specifying a piece of additional infrastructure equipment at the existing cell sites. This new piece of equipment, named the Mobile Data Base Station (MDBS), can use the existing antenna feeds and towers. Furthermore, the functionality of the box has been limited to allow small compact designs that can fit within most existing cell sites. Recent designs can be deployed in microcell environments.

The MDBSs handle the RF communications to and from the mobile devices and relay the data to and from more centralized CDPD network infrastructure equipment. This communication path can reuse channels on the existing cellular communications links. In most cell sites, there are more than enough channels to justify the deployment of a T1 connection. However, there are typically a few unused channels in these T1 links. The MDBS can use the idle channels for CDPD data. Once all the CDPD data channels are brought back to the MSC site, they can be "groomed" off to the CDPD central infrastructure equipment, the Mobile Data Intermediate System (MD-IS).

With this design approach, the CDPD specification team defined the conceptual reference model depicted in Figure 3.7. In the following sections, each of the identified components are described.

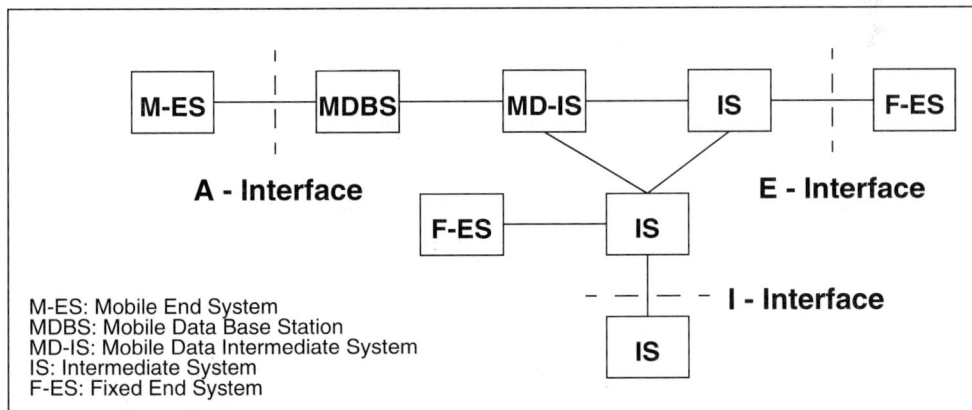

Figure 3.7   CDPD Reference Architecture

---

15. As mentioned in Chapter 2, a typical cell site costs approximately one million dollars or more for initial construction and introduction into service. With an industry total numbering over 18 thousand sites, more than $18 billion have been spent thus far on cellular infrastructure.

3.7.1 The Mobile End System (M-ES)

In OSI terminology, an *End System*, or *ES*, is a network node that is the ultimate source and destination of NPDUs. This is the same as a host in Internet terminology. The *Mobile End System* or *M-ES* is any network host that happens to be mobile (i.e., CDPD radio and software-equipped). Example M-ESs could include telemetry devices, personal communicators, and personal computers. Even communicators in vending machines (which don't actually move) could be considered to be M-ESs.

The M-ES is a network device with protocols specified up to, and including, Layer 3. The M-ES has a Layer 3 address that is globally unique in both the CDPD and conventional networking environments. M-ESs are true mobile hosts and CDPD networks are extensions of IP-based (and CLNP-based) networks, such as the Internet. There is no need for gateways as in other wireless packet data services.

Applications on the M-ES access the network via conventional means—sockets, TLI, NDIS, and ODI are a few example APIs. Standard APIs and protocols are emphasized, especially at the M-ES; this allows immediate portation of applications from existing PCs to CDPD.

Both full and half duplex M-ESs are supported by CDPD. This allows low-cost devices with only a single radio to provide mobile data services to low traffic-generating applications, such as the previously-mentioned vending machines.

The M-ES architecture consists of three distinct functional blocks, as illustrated in Figure 3.8: the subscriber unit, the subscriber identity module, and the mobile application subsystem.

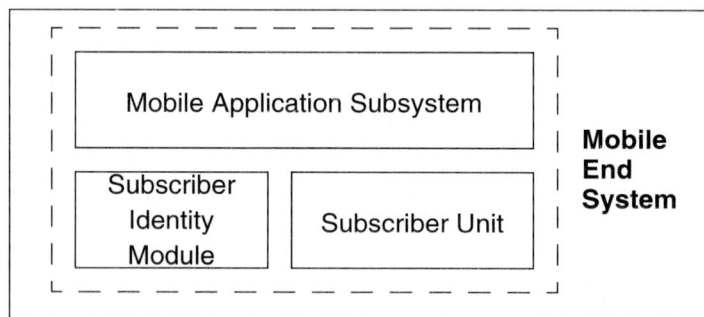

Figure 3.8   Mobile End System Architecture

The *Subscriber Unit* (*SU*) constitutes the portion of the device that establishes and maintains data communications with the CDPD network infrastructure. It achieves this through proper execution of the CDPD airlink protocols, which extend from the physical layer to the network layer. Also included are administrative layers above the network layer and the layer management entities necessary to ensure proper cooperation between the M-ES and the network.

The *Subscriber Identity Module* (*SIM*) is the repository of identity and authentication credentials for the network address in use at the M-ES. Every subscriber device must have the proper authentication credentials and identity. This function was separated from the rest of the M-ES functions to enable implementation of removable SIM cards as in GSM. This is in consideration for users that may find it easier to carry a small smart card with all the necessary identity information than to carry a complete Mobile End System.[16] The specification used to define the SIM is based on the appropriate GSM standards.

The *Mobile Application Subsystem* (*MAS*) is the portion of the M-ES that contain all protocols at the network layer and above. This is what gives the M-ES something interesting to communicate with. The application is whatever needs mobile network connectivity—email, remote database access, vending machines, etc.

M-ESs span a wide range of feature sets and form factors. Some of the units currently available support the CDPD protocols only, while others also provide AMPS cellular modem capability. Still others support voice communications with the addition of a handset.

Along with varying form factors, M-ESs also come with different power source options. Some require large external power sources such as what would be available in a vehicle. Others supply their own power through internal batteries. Still others draw on the power source of a laptop or notebook computer.

3.7.2 The Mobile Data Base Station (MDBS)

The *Mobile Data Base Station* or *MDBS* is the system end of the MAC sublayer over the airlink. The MDBS arbitrates activities on the channels it hosts at the MAC sublayer much like an Ethernet hub. It relays frames at the LLC sublayer. This device is physically located at cell sites.

The MDBS is the network infrastructure device that bridges the different media between the Mobile End System and the CDPD network. The MDBS communicates with the M-ESs through the airlink physical interface. It performs all the necessary modulation of the data bits onto the RF channel. It also demodulates the RF signal into digital bits of data. These operations are carried out within the specifications and rules required to operate on the cellular frequency bands.

In a CDPD system, multiple mobile devices share the use of a single radio channel. To ensure proper sharing of the RF channel, a medium access control mechanism is used to arbitrate access to that channel. An MDBS is an active participant in the CDPD medium access control scheme,

---

16. With the increasing miniaturization of the CDPD modems, it is unclear if removable SIM cards will ever be produced. Indeed, for the removable SIM concept to gain acceptance, manufacturers need to produce CDPD devices with the proper interfaces to accept SIM cards. One possible use for SIM card devices is in fleet operations. In this case, it may be beneficial to deploy mobile units with SIM slots into each fleet vehicle, while the drivers are assigned individual SIM cards. This way, each driver is uniquely identified by his or her network address.

Digital Sense Multiple Access (*DSMA*). Once the data stream is successfully received and decoded by the MDBS, it relays the Link Layer frames between the M-ES and the MD-IS.

The MDBS is Layer 3-addressable for network management and radio resource management purposes. In terms of user data, the MDBS is little more than a Layer 2 relay between the RF and the conventional networking worlds. For user traffic at Layer 3, the MDBS is a "phantom" element.[17]

3.7.3 The Mobile Data Intermediate System (MD-IS)

The *Mobile Data Intermediate System* or *MD-IS* is the focal point of CDPD mobility management. It has two functions in its role as a mobility-enabling router—the mobile serving function and the mobile home function.

The *mobile serving function* or *MSF* of the MD-IS provides the system end-point of the LLC sublayer MDLP link, opposite the mobile. This connection-oriented link serves as the foundation for the registration of mobiles to the system. When a mobile announces itself to the system, it is the mobile serving function that receives this registration request.

The *mobile home function* or *MHF* provides the anchor for the mobility of the M-ES. Whenever some network entity sends packets destined to the M-ES, the packets are routed in the conventional manner to the mobile home function, which then forwards them to the mobile serving function (which could be located in another MD-IS), based on previously exchanged messages between the mobile serving and mobile home functions.

The MD-IS is the most important data networking entity in the CDPD system. These devices are responsible for most of the mobility management functions of the network. The MD-ISs perform the functions necessary to track the local access point of the mobile devices. In other words, the MD-IS deals with the determination of and tracking of the exact radio coverage cell each M-ES is operating from.

The MD-IS is responsible for presenting an interface to the external networks on behalf of all the M-ESs in the CDPD network. This interface is necessary to ensure that hosts wishing to communicate to any M-ES can traverse the external networks and enter the CDPD network at the proper point of presence.

The MD-IS is also responsible for routing all network traffic to the appropriate M-ES destination. The MD-ISs within a CDPD network must cooperate to ensure this task is achieved irrespective of whether the M-ES is in a local area, or if it is at the far end of the continent.

Finally, since the CDPD network is a commercial public data network, the routing nodes—the MD-ISs—must also perform the necessary administrative functions such as usage accounting.

---

17. Strictly speaking, in terms of user data transmission, the MDBS is a link layer relay and is not part of the network layer architecture. However, it serves an important role in this wireless mobile data network and deserves attention here and in the CDPD System Specification.

3.7.3.1 The MDBS-to-MD-IS Interface

The MDBS/MD-IS Interface is an internal interface between the MDBS and the MD-IS. Since this interface is internal to the CDPD "cloud," it is recommended rather than specified. Proprietary solutions have no need to adhere to this interface definition. However (CDPD service providers beware!), allowing a proprietary solution here is tantamount to losing control of one's system architecture.

This interface is specified for the sole purpose of an open system definition. This allows a multiplicity of vendors for each side of the interface in a more or less plug and play manner. There was much discussion amongst members of the CDPD specification team regarding the need for any specification of this interface. In the end, this interface definition met the needs of the CDPD service providers wishing to order equipment from their vendors.

3.7.4 The Intermediate System (IS)

The *Intermediate System* or *IS* is a fancy name for a network router.[18] It is standard OSI terminology and function. In CDPD, ISs handle packet forwarding for both IP and CLNP connectionless Layer 3 protocols, just as in conventional data networks. Typically, a packet traversing between networks will be handled by several ISs on its journey. MD-ISs must also support IS functionality.

In addition to the packet forwarding protocols—IP and CLNP—supported by the ISs, they must also support routing information exchange protocols (in order to function as routers, unless static routing alone is used—a bad choice for dynamically changing networks!). The internal routing information exchange protocols defined by the CDPD specification include OSPF for IP and IS-IS for CLNP. External gateway routing information exchange protocols include BGP-4[19] for IP and IDRP for CLNP. It is wise, whenever possible, to have ISs supporting integrated IS-IS to prevent the "ships in the night" phenomenon, as described in [PERL92].

The CDPD network is a multi-protocol network. This means that the CDPD network is intended to support routing of multiple network layer protocols, including IP and CLNP. The archi-

---

18. When we began work on the CDPD system specifications, it was clear that we needed to use concise terminology. We were not interested in unnecessarily inventing new terms, so we used existing terminology as much as possible. We chose the ISO terminology as a base, not because we were "ISO-bigots" but because we were not as familiar with them, and thus less likely to be burdened with unspoken and differing interpretations that could cause confusion. Besides, OSI terminology sounds much more sophisticated.

19. BGP-4 (Border Gateway Protocol, version 4), in support of classless interdomain routing (CIDR), is essential for efficient allocation of the somewhat limited IP address space to M-ESs, due to the "permanence" of these address assignments. In the future, one could expect CDPD support for the IPv6 (formerly IPng) protocol.

tecture of CDPD allows future extensions for additional connectionless network protocols, such as IPv6. All ISs used in the CDPD network must also support multiple network layer protocols.

For the purpose of providing interconnection between a CDPD network and external networks, and between two CDPD networks, some level of security protection is valuable. For this requirement, the ISs at the borders of the CDPD network are further required to provide security filtering and access control functions, whose definition is beyond the scope of the CDPD System Specification.

3.7.5 The Fixed End System (F-ES)

The *Fixed End System,*[20] or *F-ES,* is a conventional network node, which could be either external to the CDPD service provider network, such as a transport layer peer of an M-ES, or internal, such as the servers that provide network support or application services. The only purpose in explicitly defining an F-ES is to distinguish between a conventional network host and a mobile host.

External F-ESs are the hosts that most CDPD subscribers should be familiar with. They are typically the systems hosting the applications the mobile user wishes to access. Some examples of these F-ESs might include: an inventory system at a home office, an electronic mail server for a road warrior, and a user's favorite World Wide Web site. The most significant thread through these F-ES descriptions is that they are simply common hosts that support standard network layer protocols.

Internal F-ESs are hosts much like external F-ESs. The primary difference is that internal F-ESs operate within the boundaries of the CDPD network. As such, they conceivably are under the control of the service provider and can thus be presented with additional internal network data. Such data may include usage accounting information, mobile location information, subscriber authentication information, etc.

Internal F-ESs allow CDPD service providers to operate administrative servers and value added servers without the need for nonstandard communications protocols. This capability is representative of the CDPD network architecture's flexibility. This flexibility results from the use of standard network protocols and adherence to the ISO Open System Interconnect reference model.

3.7.5.1 The Accounting Server (AS)

The *Accounting Server,* or *AS,* is an internal F-ES that serves two basic functions—collection and distribution of usage accounting data. Subscriber activity is recorded at the serving MD-IS over

---

20. In the spirit of political correctness, some of us wanted to call the F-ES a "Mobility-Challenged End System." Fortunately better judgement prevailed on the CDPD specification team and "F-ES" was established.

a configurable time period, then flushed to the AS. The AS then collates the detailed accounting records and distributes them to the appropriate peer accounting servers.

The distribution of detailed accounting records to home accounting servers is called the *serving accounting distributor,* or *SAD,* function. The reception and redistribution of these records at the home accounting server is called the *home accounting distributor*, or *HAD,* function. Other AS functions are defined in CDPD to enable near real-time accounting, separate accounting for large customers, and separation of accounting (business) from network (operation) customer relationships.

The usage accounting capability is described in Chapter 7 and defined in Part 630 of the CDPD System Specification and Part 1023 of the CDPD Implementor Guidelines.

3.7.5.2 The Authentication Server

The *authentication server* is an internal F-ES that is intended to support the authentication function in CDPD. Since this function can be implemented in many different ways, it is not required to be a separately addressable entity; it could in fact be contained within the MD-IS. Authentication is discussed in Chapter 6 and defined in Parts 406 and 640 of the CDPD System Specification.

3.7.5.3 The Directory Server

The *directory server* is an internal F-ES that provides support for directory services within the CDPD network. Directory services are used primarily for network management and other support services. Like the authentication server, this can be implemented in many different ways. Depending on the needs of a CDPD service provider and its customers, the directory server could support either DNS or X.500 capabilities, or both. Directory services are described in Chapter 7 and defined in Part 610 of the CDPD System Specification.

3.7.5.4 The Network Management System

The *network management system* is the means by which a CDPD service provider operates the CDPD network. Network management includes configuration management, fault management, performance management, and other functions. Like other servers, it can be implemented in many different ways. Typically, network managers run in stand-alone processors because of the resource-intensive nature of their activities. Network management is discussed in Chapter 7 and defined in Parts 700 through 750 of the CDPD System Specification.

3.7.5.5 The Message Transfer System

The *message transfer system* is the means by which CDPD accounting and other messaging functions are supported. CDPD accounting is supported by an X.400 messaging model, which is embodied in the message transfer system entity. It can be implemented in many ways and is discussed in Chapter 7.

3.8 CDPD Mobility Management

The central capability of CDPD is its ability to get data to a mobile device or application regardless of its location. This capability is called *mobility management*. CDPD mobility management is provided by two protocols: the *Mobile Network Registration Protocol,* or *MNRP,* and the *Mobile Network Location Protocol,* or *MNLP* .

MNRP is the means by which a mobile announces its presence (including authenticating itself) to the serving system (via the *End System Hello,* or *ESH*, message). MNLP is the means by which the serving system notifies the home system for the mobile that it is providing service to the mobile.

The CDPD mobility management scheme is based on triangular routing of NPDUs via encapsulation from a home MD-IS (the mobile home function) to the current serving MD-IS (the mobile serving function). This packet redirection is displayed in Figure 3.9.

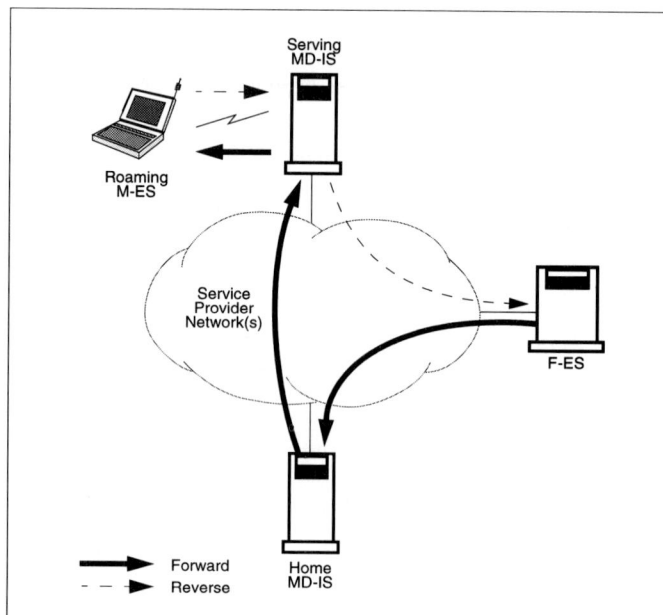

Figure 3.9 CDPD Traffic Flows

By using the home system as the network anchor for the M-ES, the outside world of networked applications can always access the mobile the same way they access any host—conventional routing technology is sufficient to get data packets to the home system. The CDPD mobility management scheme takes over from there, forwarding the data packets via encapsulation to the current system serving the M-ES. This solution is identical to an early Mobile IP Task Force solution, which is elegant in its simplicity.

Although there are pathological cases in which this redirection of packet traffic is highly inefficient, the CDPD specification team elected this solution because the speed of WAN networks is ever-increasing and their costs decreasing. A solution that might be more efficient in the pathological cases would be generally less efficient in accommodating moving users in the cellular environment.[21]

The CDPD mobility management scheme is defined by Parts 500 through 507 of the CDPD System Specification and is described in Chapter 4.

3.9 CDPD Radio Resource Management

Closely associated with mobility management is *radio resource management* or *RRM,* the process that ensures that the optimum radio channel is used by an M-ES. Optimum means that the channel provides the most reliable performance while not interfering with either other CDPD or cellular users. Non-interference with cellular voice customers is of paramount importance, since CDPD is a service overlaid on the existing cellular voice network.

Contrary to cellular voice systems, in which cell handoff is controlled by the system,[22] the CDPD system requires that the mobile device manage its own use of radio resources. This is necessary because of the bursty nature of the packet-switched access to CDPD services; the mobile generally does not transmit long enough for the system to accurately measure its RF reception from multiple MDBSs.

---

21. The particular example of concern to the Mobile IP task force was the scenario in which two travelers from the US were in Amsterdam and wanted to share data. The round-trip path for the data packets would go from Amsterdam to the US and back to Amsterdam. Since CDPD was developed under the auspices of North American cellular carriers, this was considered to be an extreme case and not representative of the mobility CDPD was originally intended to address. Quite frankly, we look forward with great anticipation to the day that this becomes a significant issue.

22. In TDMA the mobile assists the system by evaluating RF channel quality and sharing this information with the system. This seems to be the best way to handle RRM, since it is the mobile which is best situated to determine the best channel to use.

The CDPD system periodically broadcasts information to assist the mobile in evaluating its current channel against alternative channels provided in adjacent cells. Prior to transmitting, the M-ES evaluates alternative channels to ensure that it uses the best channel. In a properly tuned system, the best channel will be in the same cell as the channel assigned to a similarly located cellular voice handset.

The radio resource management scheme in CDPD also controls the power level used by the mobiles by broadcasting a so-called power product. The theory is that RF signals are reciprocal between two points; if one transceiver informs the other transceiver of the power level it is transmitting, the second transceiver can calculate the power level it must use, based on the received signal strength.

CDPD radio resource management is defined by Part 405 of the CDPD System Specification [CDPD95] and is described in Chapter 5.

3.10 CDPD Security

CDPD provides security across the airlink sufficient to prevent casual eavesdropping and fraud. Up to 128 encryption techniques can be supported by the system; currently, only the RSA RC4 stream cipher is specified [RSA-92]. A variation of the Diffie-Hellman electronic key exchange is used to dynamically create the encryption keys to be used by the system and the mobile across the airlink.

Once in encrypted mode, the mobile must *register* its network address along with authentication credentials before it can receive services from the system. The credentials are compared by the M-ES's home system with its record for that M-ES network address. This procedure establishes the authenticity of the M-ES network address to the system. The CDPD security scheme could be enhanced in the future to provide capabilities such as authentication of the system by the M-ES.

CDPD security management is defined by Part 406 of the CDPD System Specification and is described in Chapter 6.

3.11 CDPD Accounting

As mentioned earlier, CDPD defines an accounting scheme that is very general and capable of supporting many kinds of service provider and customer relationships. The basic idea is to functionally separate accounting (business) relationships from networking relationships—i.e., the accounting home for a CDPD subscriber need not be the same as the networking home for that subscriber.

The flow of accounting information is capable of supporting mobile users, while minimizing the coordination between service providers. Usage information such as packets and bytes transferred at Layer 3 is captured by the serving MD-IS. Each CDPD service provider only needs to know the presentation title of the HAD associated with each block of Layer 3 addresses that are in use by M-ESs. X.400 provides the basis for ensuring reliable delivery of accounting data from one accounting server (the SAD) to another (the HAD).

CDPD accounting is defined by Parts 630 and 1023 in the CDPD System Specification and Implementor's Guidelines, respectively, and is also described in Chapter 7.

3.12 Summary

This chapter has presented an overview of CDPD technology, a major milestone in internetwork mobile data communications. The mobility management and network access of CDPD will be discussed in more detail in the following two chapters. Later chapters will discuss CDPD security, network management, and accounting.

4 *Mobility Management in Wide-Area Networks*

One set of messages of the society we live in is: Consume. Grow. Do what you want. Amuse yourselves. The very working of this economic system, which has bestowed these unprecedented liberties, most cherished in the form of physical mobility and material prosperity, depends on encouraging people to defy limits.
                    —Susan Sontag (b. 1933), U.S. Essayist, (1989).

The American Heritage Dictionary of the English Language[1] gives the following two definitions for "Mobility."

1. The quality or state of being mobile.
2. The movement of people, as from one social group, class, or level to another.

However, this entry does not identify the relationship between the two definitions. In today's world, upward mobility is often closely tied with physical mobility. Moreover, high productivity often associated with upward mobility means that there is a demand for continuous contact and communications while mobile.

The best example of this is evidenced in the incredible adoption of cellular telephones by the business community. Nowadays, a successful business person without a cellular telephone or a pager is indeed an endangered animal! With increased dependence on data access, the need for mobile communications has now entered the data arena.

In this chapter we discuss the first of the aspects of mobility—mobility management—in CDPD systems. Chapter 5 will cover CDPD network access, the second aspect of mobility.

---

1. *The American Heritage® Dictionary of the English Language, Third Edition* copyright © 1992 by Houghton Mifflin Company.

4.1 The CDPD Mobility Vision

When someone talks about mobility, what they have in mind can range from being able to move between desktop computers and still access their own account, to the wondrous vision of being continuously connected while anywhere on this globe. Both views are based on the ability to relocate. However, anyone will immediately recognize the great difference in scope: the first situation is not so much a matter of connectivity while in motion as it is account access from multiple locations within a network.

The task and scope of the CDPD specification team can be best understood by first understanding the business interests of the cellular service providers and the common vision of their respective leaders.

Cellular industry leaders wanted to offer a service providing users with continuous connectivity while in motion within the collective nationwide cellular footprint. The vision included movement both within cities and across city coverage boundaries. In the future, this coverage area was expected to become international in scope.

The vision also required that users of the service be able to move from one area to the next without extensive user intervention (and preferably none). The cellular service providers envisioned a ubiquitous cellular data service providing seamless connections even while in motion between cities.

However, the service was not intended to be all things to all people. The goal of CDPD was wide area mobility. CDPD was never intended to be a high capacity (multi-megabit per second throughput) mobile wireless local network. Wide area mobility was considered to be more important than throughput.

In terms of scope of coverage, CDPD was intended to meet terrestrial data communications needs only. This includes stationary use at a desk or in a vehicle. It also includes connectivity and communications while moving at speeds that range between typical pedestrian traffic and vehicular highway traffic (but not necessarily limited to 65 MPH). However, CDPD was never intended for aviation use.

4.2 The CDPD Mobility Approach

Given this vision, how did the CDPD specification team design a service that provides nationwide connectivity with continuous communications within major metropolitan areas? The design approach taken divides the challenge of providing mobile data services into the two aspects of mobility management and network access.

The first aspect is called *mobility management*. This function is responsible for all the activities that allows the network to track the current location of each and every active mobile device.

The issues of mobility management are generic in nature and are the same issues that challenge any mobile data communications network.

Every mobile data communications network requires a method for a mobile device to announce its location. Every mobile data network also requires mechanisms for maintaining a current, up-to-date database of the mobiles' respective locations. Furthermore, every network must incorporate a means of directing traffic to the correct location for the mobile device.

The second aspect of mobility is *network access*. This is the mechanism used to connect a mobile to the network while allowing movement. The CDPD system is wireless and as such must balance the design goals of speed and reliability with the constraints of physics and radio technology.

Network access specifically addresses the limitations set by the design criteria for the system. The CDPD network was intended to use the North American *Advanced Mobile Phone System* (*AMPS*) infrastructure. This requirement imposed certain design constraints, which we discuss in the following chapter.

4.3   CDPD Mobility Management Scope

The ability of a CDPD mobile host to freely roam within a potentially vast coverage area requires continuous tracking of the mobile host's location by the network. Although different tracking techniques may be fashioned, each impacts applications wishing to contact the mobile host in its own way.

As we described in Chapter 1, two dimensions of mobility are defined by frequency of movement and span of movement. From the mobile user's perspective, these are geographic concepts. One user may consider how frequently he or she travels from one business district of a city to another. A different user may view frequency and span in terms of their weekly need to operate from two office locations within a campus. The road warrior may think in terms of daily movement between cities or weekly movement between continents!

On the other hand, the network designer considers frequency and span of mobile movement in network infrastructure terms. Whether the movement is from city to city or from room to room, its system impact depends on how the coverage area is configured; this is a topological consideration.

If the entire city area is effectively covered by a single radio site, then all physical movement of mobile users within the city is invisible from a network perspective. The only noticeable relocation would be movement of mobile users from one city to another. However, if each building in a city commands its own radio coverage sector, then any movement into and out of a building would constitute a relocation event that must be tracked by the network.

Given that each mobile relocation that is visible to the network introduces management overhead, why would the network designer not construct a single all encompassing radio coverage area? Well, unfortunately, we live in a physical world where physical laws apply. Current technology does not allow effective radio coverage of a large area while providing low error, high speed, high capacity data communications with low power/low cost devices. So to satisfy a target of system capacity and performance, geographic areas of typical modern cities must be divided and served by distinct radio coverage zones.

In the cellular telephone system, these zones were originally designed to approximate the honeycomb structure of hexagonal cells. This layout permitted non-interfering reuse of a small set of radio frequencies. The standard configuration relied on a reuse pattern of 7 or 12 frequencies as described in Chapter 2. This approach allowed each frequency to be re-deployed at a radio site that is close by but far enough away that the two transmitters would not cause insurmountable interference.

This approach served the cellular carriers well—at least in the early years. As time went by and users began to appreciate the value of being constantly in contact, more users signed on to the cellular network. To handle the increasing traffic, cellular carriers subdivided cells into smaller units. These smaller coverage areas are typically one third or one sixth of the original cell and are called sectors.

The CDPD system was designed as a data network transparently overlaid on the cellular system, as depicted in Figure 4.1. As such, it adheres to the radio constraints of the cellular telephone network. The CDPD network infrastructure uses radio coverage areas that are equivalent to the cellular sectors. Therefore, in CDPD, the mobility of importance is the relocation of users from one radio coverage sector to another.

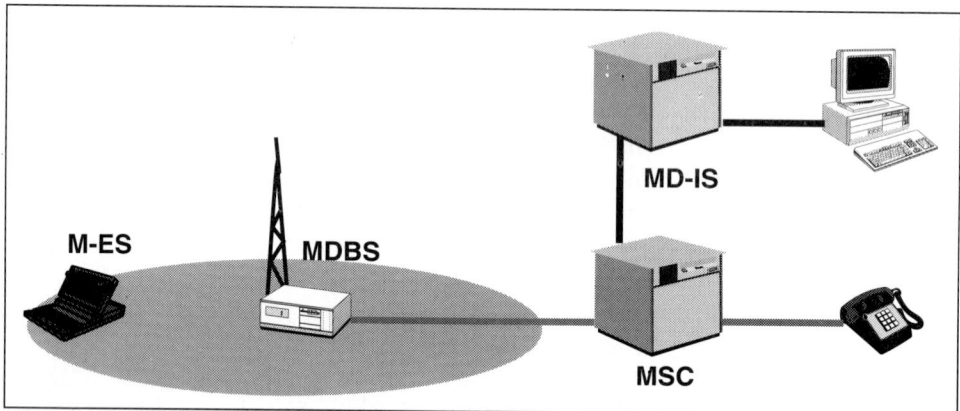

Figure 4.1   CDPD Cellular Network Overlay

Beyond cellular sectors, the CDPD system also approximates the cellular telephone system in aggregating the radio coverage sectors into regions that are served by a single *Mobile Switching Center* (*MSC*). In CDPD parlance, this is equivalent to a single routing area.

At a higher level, various cellular service providers offer service to each city. Movement of a cellular telephone user between cities is handled through "hand-off" of the user from one carrier in one city to the carrier in the next city. An analogous situation exists within CDPD. The CDPD network routing domain approximates the city to city hand-off.

4.4 CDPD Mobility Management Functions

Within the CDPD network, mobility management is separable into three functions. These are:

- •Mobile Identification

  For the network to properly locate a mobile end system, the mobile device must first announce its current location to the network.

- •Mobile Validation and Access Control

  Prior to providing service to a mobile end system, the network must verify that the mobile end system is declaring its true identity. This validation avoids misrouting data packets to the incorrect mobile end system. The home system for the mobile must also verify that the mobile is authorized to receive service while in its current location.

- •Traffic Redirection

  Once a valid mobile end system has been identified and tracked, the network must perform the routing services to direct traffic to the correct mobile end system.

These functions are very similar to the road warrior scenarios described in chapter 1. For example, in these scenarios, the administrative assistant performs the following functions:

- • Keeping track of the whereabouts of the road warrior; and
- • Forwarding messages to the road warrior.

On the other hand, the road warrior has the following responsibilities:

- • Recognizing the need for a change of location;
- • Changing location; and
- • Informing the administrative assistant of the new location.

For efficient operation, the road warrior and the administrative assistant would probably establish a shorthand method of communicating all the pertinent information. For example, the traveller would ensure that the local phone number, fax number, and postal address were communicated back quickly and accurately. The administrative assistant would verify that the caller is as identified and update the location information for redirecting any future messages.

This simple analogy demonstrates the basic responsibilities or functions within each entity of the communications network. The means of transferring information between network entities are the communications protocols defined within the system.

The following sections will examine the functions of each of the CDPD network entities, and describes the protocols used between the entities to provide mobile data communications services.

4.5 CDPD Routing Architecture

Let us begin by discussing the conceptual entities that define the routing hierarchy and architecture used in the CDPD network. These elements are illustrated in Figure 4.2.

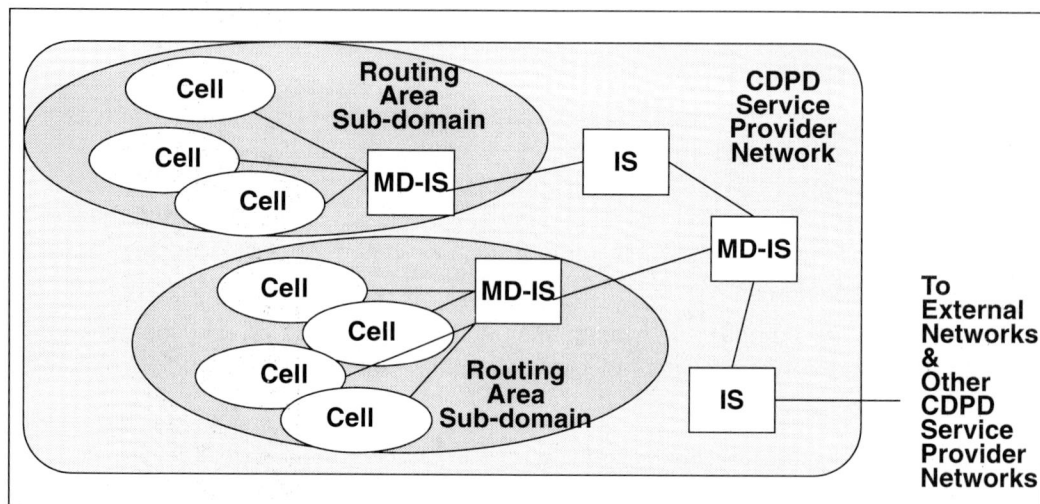

Figure 4.2   CDPD Network Routing Architecture

In order to provide a viable structure to the routing problem, it is necessary to partition the network into manageable sections. On the physical level, we rely on radio coverage limitations to define the smallest unit of control. Each radio channel in a cell coverage area is a single distinct entity, much as an Ethernet LAN is a distinct subnet.

Multiple M-ESs may be sharing such a *channel stream*. A channel stream represents a single *subnetwork point of attachment (SNPA)* to the CDPD network. The M-ESs sharing it are much the same as hosts on an Ethernet LAN, from both an operational and a networking perspective.

Multiple channel streams may operate over a single radio coverage area called a *cell*. In the cellular telephony world, a CDPD cell may be equivalent to a sector.[2] Each CDPD cell is controlled by a *Mobile Data Base Station* or *MDBS*.[3]

---

2. A CDPD cell might or might not share boundaries with an AMPS cell or sector. Depending on the frequency plan in use, a CDPD service provider might instead elect to utilize a "booming" CDPD frequency plan, in which a CDPD cell covers multiple AMPS cells or sectors. This has been done by many CDPD service providers to reduce deployment costs.

Typically, multiple MDBSs are controlled by a single *Mobile Data Intermediate System* or *MD-IS*. An MD-IS managing the data links over the radio channel to M-ESs is a *serving MD-IS*. All cell coverage areas under the control of a single serving MD-IS is called a *routing area sub-domain*.

The collection of routing area sub-domains under the management of a single operating authority is a *CDPD service provider network*. CDPD service provider networks may be interconnected through the specified I-Interface. The collection of all interconnected CDPD service provider networks is referred to as the *CDPD network*.

4.6 CDPD Protocol Architecture

Now that we have outlined the network components and the conceptual routing architecture, let us examine the protocol architecture. In Figure 4.3, a diagram of the protocol stacks used in CDPD communications is presented.

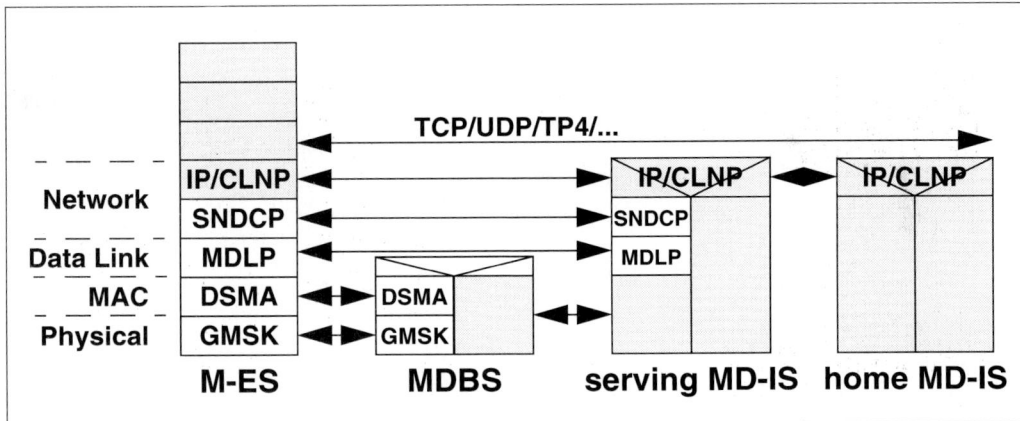

Figure 4.3   CDPD Protocol Architecture

The M-ES is an end system or host, and therefore must contain the complete 7 layer protocol stack. At the physical layer, the M-ES uses a digital radio modulation scheme called *Gaussian*

---

3. To be precise, in a sectored cell, a single common MDBS might control the activities in each of the sectors, which are treated as independent CDPD cells. This is how vendors of MDBS equipment have implemented their solutions, in order to reduce the costs per cell site for a CDPD service provider.

Minimum Shift Keying (GMSK),[4] which is a filtered variant of Frequency Shift Keying (FSK) modulation. The next sublayer is the medium access control mechanism, which provides support for channel sharing by multiple M-ESs. CDPD uses *Digital Sense Multiple Access (DSMA)* for this purpose; DSMA is related to and resembles the *collision sense multiple access* (*CSMA*) scheme of Ethernet.

The data link is managed by a link access protocol named *Mobile Data Link Protocol (MDLP)*. This protocol is derived from the standard *Link Access Protocol* on the *D* channel (LAPD) from ISDN. Above the data link, the *Subnetwork Dependent Convergence Protocol (SNDCP)* provides the functionality necessary to interwork with the supported network protocols. Above this, the standard *Internet protocol* (*IP*) and *Connectionless Network Protocol* (*CLNP*) suites operate at Layer 3.

The MDBS in the CDPD network functions as a data link relay. As such, it cooperates with the M-ES over the airlink by performing the GMSK modulation function and by managing the DSMA medium access control mechanism. The MDBS retrieves MDLP data link frames and relays them between the serving MD-IS and the M-ES.

The serving MD-IS interoperates with the MDBS via conventional data networking infrastructure for carriage of the MDLP frames. The serving MD-IS is the peer entity to the M-ES data link; the M-ES and the serving MD-IS operate the end-points of the MDLP data link connection. Above the data link, the serving MD-IS performs the peer SNDCP function. The network packets are then passed up to the network layer routing function. At Layer 3, the home and serving MD-ISs function much the same as special mobility-aware routers.

From this discussion and from Figure 4.3, it should be clear that the CDPD network provides a network layer routing service. All protocol data units at the network layer and above are carried and delivered without alteration. CDPD provides a special media—radio—but does not define a gateway architecture.

4.7 CDPD Support Protocol Architecture

While the CDPD network provides an NPDU routing service, support protocols are used and routed in parallel to enable mobility. This set of support protocols is illustrated in Figure 4.4.

---

4. Both GMSK and DSMA are defined for AMPS-channel implementations of CDPD. Alternative airlinks are under development in the TDMA Forum and the CDMA Forum, but as of our publication deadline have not been formally released. These alternative airlinks are likely to utilize other physical and MAC layers than GMSK and DSMA.

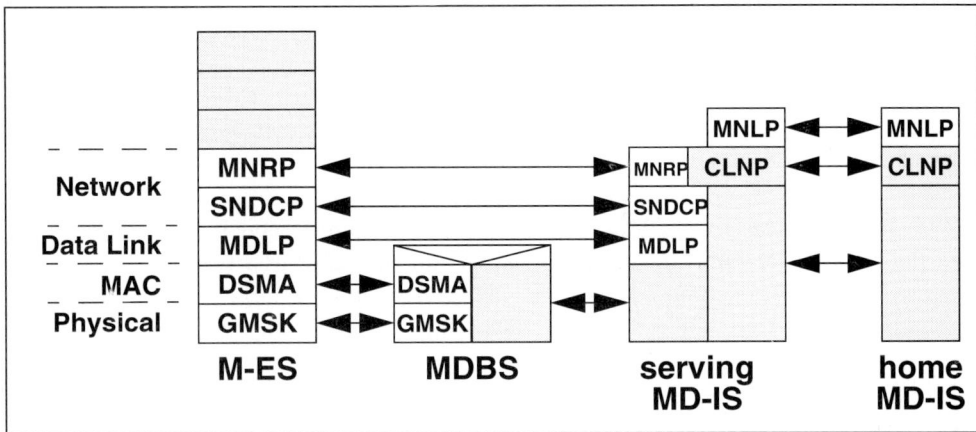

Figure 4.4   CDPD Support Protocol Architecture

The *Mobile Network Registration Protocol (MNRP)* operates over the airlink and is used by the M-ES to identify itself to the network. It is also used by the serving MD-IS to inform the M-ES of its intent to provide service. MNRP also allows the serving MD-IS to query the mobile device and the device to perform a clean deregistration (disconnection) from the network. MNRP is defined by Part 507 of the CDPD System Specifications.

Within the infrastructure, the *home MD-IS* (which functions as the M-ESs routing anchor) and the serving MD-IS communicate through the *Mobile Network Location Protocol (MNLP)*. The serving MD-IS and the home MD-IS must cooperate to provide mobile network routing. This is achieved through location information and authentication information sharing using the MNLP. MNLP PDUs are transported via CLNP PDUs. MNLP is defined by Part 501 of the CDPD System Specifications.

4.8 CDPD Mobility Management Operation

The CDPD system was created with seamless mobile communications in mind. To this end, a method of efficient and effective data relay to the mobile unit is required. This mobility management mechanism must also allow transparent communications to the user. In other words, the user should not be inconvenienced just because he or she is in an area not operated by their home service provider. Given this requirement, the user's location should always be accessible from the home relay service.

If we revisit our Chapter 1 road warrior, Gary, who is attending a conference in a distant city, most of his time will be spent in the hotel housing the conference. He could phone his administrative assistant each and every time he changes conference rooms. That way the administrative assistant could always redirect his calls to that particular conference room. However, this involves a lot of long distance calls and is quite inefficient!

In another mode of operation, Gary could simply inform the hotel concierge of every room change. Now, when there is a message for Gary, the administrative assistant simply relays the message to the hotel concierge, who then relays it to the appropriate conference meeting room. This more localized form of tracking Gary's whereabouts is clearly more efficient than the previous mechanism.

With this administrative redirection arrangement, the hotel concierge is responsible for tracking the local whereabouts of Gary. The home administrative assistant only needs to know that Gary is still in the same hotel. Within the CDPD Network, the serving area entity is equivalent to the hotel concierge, while the home area administration entity performs the role of the administrative assistant. The serving area entity is the serving MD-IS.[5] The home entity is the home MD-IS.

The following sub-sections present the operation of CDPD mobility management. Through this discussion, we will clarify how the mobile units announce their presence to the network and how the infrastructure components cooperate to route data to the mobile units. In addition, we shall define the home MD-IS and the serving MD-IS.

4.8.1 Mobile Identification to Network-End System Hello (ESH)

The first event necessary for a successful mobile data connection is for the mobile unit to announce its current location to the network. This is achieved through several message transactions between CDPD network components, as depicted in Figure 4.5.

The M-ES initiates the process by transmitting a simple registration message to the CDPD network. The network uses this transmission to update the data base it uses to track the mobile's location. The CDPD network must ensure that it is tracking the genuine mobile. This requires that the M-ES send both its identification and its associated authentication credentials.

---

5. Early versions of the CDPD System Specification defined a network entity called the "Mobile Data Intermediate System." With CDPD System Specifications preliminary release 0.8, we introduced the concept of a serving area entity and a home area entity. Unfortunately, there was concern that confusion may result from the appearance of a "new" network component. Therefore, instead of creating yet another acronym, we opted for the notion of a "serving MD-IS" and a "home MD-IS." To our dismay, this has also caused some confusion. Some readers misinterpreted the names to mean that if a M-ES is in its "home" area, it would only interact with the "home MD-IS." This is not so. A perhaps better definition of function involves the mobile home function or MHF and mobile serving function or MSF; these definitions provide clarity in the case of a single MD-IS supporting both at home and visiting mobiles.

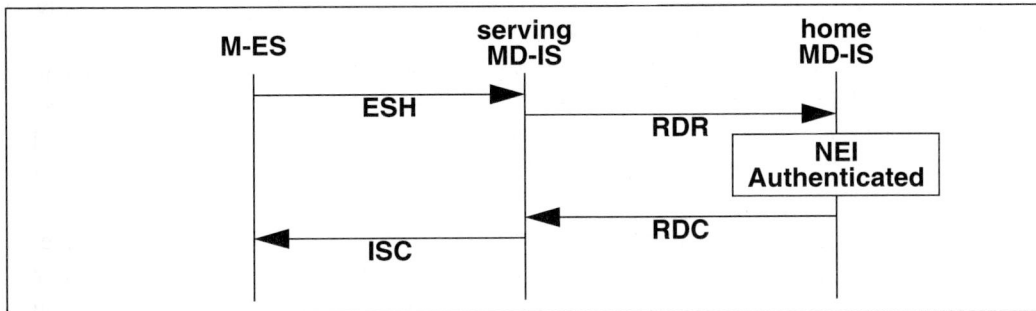

Figure 4.5   M-ES Registration

This exchange of information is accomplished through the transmission of an *End System Hello (ESH)* message (see Figure 4.6), which is part of MNRP. This message contains the mobile's "permanent" network address, called the *Network Entity Identifier (NEI)*, and the associated authentication credentials. In most cases, the NEI is simply an IP address assigned to the mobile.

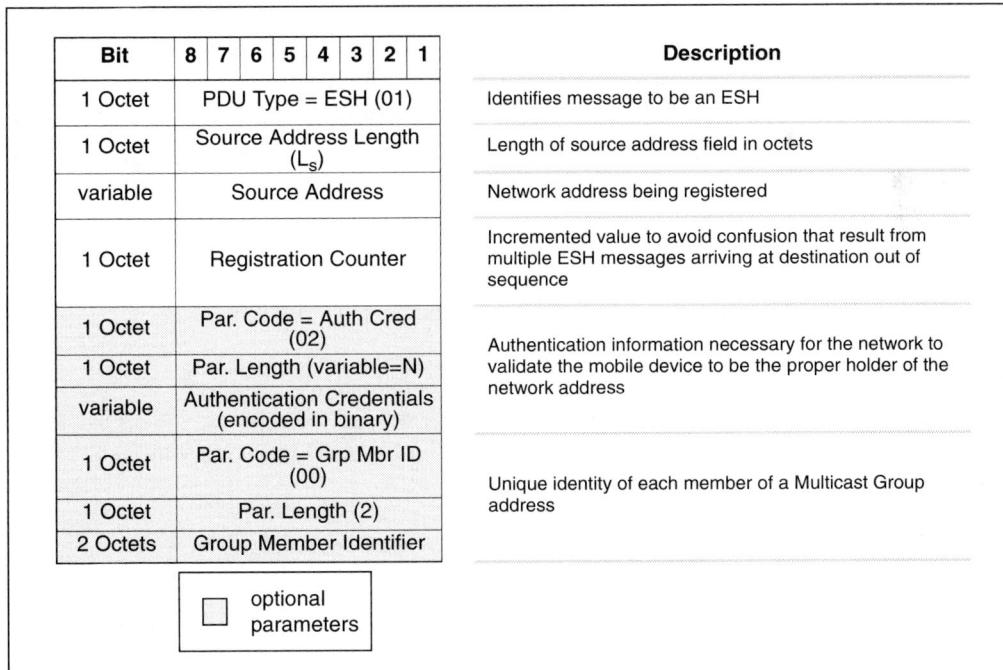

Bit	8	7	6	5	4	3	2	1	Description
1 Octet	PDU Type = ESH (01)								Identifies message to be an ESH
1 Octet	Source Address Length (L$_s$)								Length of source address field in octets
variable	Source Address								Network address being registered
1 Octet	Registration Counter								Incremented value to avoid confusion that result from multiple ESH messages arriving at destination out of sequence
1 Octet	Par. Code = Auth Cred (02)								Authentication information necessary for the network to validate the mobile device to be the proper holder of the network address
1 Octet	Par. Length (variable=N)								
variable	Authentication Credentials (encoded in binary)								
1 Octet	Par. Code = Grp Mbr ID (00)								Unique identity of each member of a Multicast Group address
1 Octet	Par. Length (2)								
2 Octets	Group Member Identifier								

□ optional parameters

Figure 4.6   End System Hello (ESH) Message Format

The *authentication credentials* consist or a randomly generated number, called the *Authentication Random Number (ARN)*, and a sequence number, called the *Authentication Sequence Number (ASN)*. The ARN is generated by the CDPD network and is assigned to the NEI associated with the M-ES. The ARN must be supplied by the M-ES on succeeding registration attempts of that NEI.[6] The authentication process is generally under the control of the home MD-IS, and is described in Chapter 6.

Both the mobile unit and the network maintain two sets of ARN/ASN tuples for each NEI. The purpose of a second set of authentication credentials is to handle the rare situations when the network and the mobile fall out of synchronization with respect to authentication data.

This can happen if, for example, at the moment the network issues a new ARN to an M-ES, it becomes unreachable due to poor radio coverage. Shortly afterwards, the mobile unit may enter a good coverage area in another routing domain which causes it to send in a new registration attempt. In this instance, the ESH sent by the mobile will contain authentication credentials that are older than those expected by the network. By ensuring that the network maintains the two most recent sets of authentication credentials, the network can always recognize the older credentials, validate them, and resynchronize with the mobile.

4.8.2 Mobile Redirection Request (RDR)

The MD-IS that is operating in the mobile serving area receives the ESH from the M-ES. On receipt of the ESH message, this serving MD-IS records the radio coverage location of the M-ES and provides the M-ES identification information to the appropriate home network's MD-IS. The primary purpose of this data transfer is to instruct the home MD-IS to redirect data destined for the M-ES through this serving area. Thus, this serving MD-IS to home MD-IS notification is called the *Redirect Request (RDR)* message.

The data carried in the RDR message (see Figure 4.7)includes all registration information provided by the M-ES. This data allows the home MD-IS to confirm that the M-ES is a valid device. Other information, such as the serving area location is also sent in the RDR message to the home MD-IS.

Since CDPD is a public data network, other considerations may determine whether a unit is to be authorized to use the network. Things such as the subscriber's account status, the usage limits defined by the user at subscription time, etc., provide the basis for the home MD-IS decision to permit access. Rejection of the M-ES may also be based on geographic parameters, such as an M-ES which should not receive service outside of its home city, or a serving area that is also covered by a more preferred service provider. This control by the home MD-IS of access to the CDPD network is called *access control*.[7]

---

6. An M-ES might have more than one NEI assigned to it, especially if it belongs to one or more multicast groups. Each NEI must be separately registered, authenticated, and tracked by the system.

Bit	8	7	6	5	4	3	2	1	Description
1 octet	PDU Type = RDR (01)								Identifies message as RDR
1 octet	Registration Sequence Count								Incremented value to avoid confusion that result from multiple ESH messages arriving at destination out of sequence
1 octet	Source Address Length (L_s)								Length of network address field in octets
variable	Source Address								Network address being registered
1 octet	Forwarding Address Length								Length of Forwarding Service address in octets
variable	Forwarding Network Address								Address of Forwarding Service for this mobile NEI
1 octet	Par. Code = Auth Cred(02)								Authentication information necessary for the network to validate the mobile device to be the proper holder of the network address
1 octet	Par. Length (variable)								
variable	Authentication Credentials								(Encoded in binary)
1 octet	Par. Code = Grp Mbr ID(00)								Unique identity of each member of a Multicast Group address
1 octet	Par. Length (2)								
2 octets	Group Member Identifier								
1 octet	Par. Code = Loc'n Info (09)								
1 octet	Par. Length (6)								
2 octets	Wide Area Service Identifier (WASI)								Identifier for serving network "brand name" and service provider identity. Allows home network to assess whether this is the best network to serve the mobile
2 octets	Service provider Identifier (SPI)								
2 octets	Service Provider Network Identifier (SPNI)								

☐ optional parameters

Figure 4.7   Redirect Request (RDR) Message Format

7. If the serving MD-IS and the home MD-IS belong to service providers who have no business arrangement, the serving MD-IS may not bother sending the RDR message. In this case, the serving MD-IS could possibly return a negative result code to the M-ES in the ISC message. Usually, however, the serving MD-IS would be expected to try to provide service and the home MD-IS would make the go/no-go decision.

Once the M-ES authentication and access control decisions have been made, the home MD-IS must indicate this status to the serving MD-IS. Again, we emphasize, the registration, authentication and access control mechanisms operate on a per-NEI basis. If the M-ES uses more than one NEI, each must be separately registered and authenticated.

4.8.3 Confirmation of Service-Redirect Confirm (RDC)

The home MD-IS uses the *Redirect Confirm (RDC)* message to relay the decision on whether it is willing to redirect data traffic for the indicated M-ES. The home MD-IS sends the RDC message to the serving MD-IS that requested data redirection on behalf of the indicated M-ES.

The RDC message (see Figure 4.8) contains the information that identifies the M-ES being tracked by the network, the decision of the network to grant or deny support for that M-ES, and updated authentication credentials, if appropriate. The updated authentication credentials are not mandatory and depend on the security policies of the home service provider.

If the CDPD network has agreed to service the M-ES, then the home MD-IS updates its location data base entry for that mobile. The data maintained for each mobile NEI include the following:

- Mobile Network Entity Identifier
- Mobile Serving Function address (serving MD-IS address)
- Registration counter

The purpose of the first two entries are obvious. The *registration counter* is a monotonically incrementing value[8] used to detect duplicate or delayed RDR messages. The table of such tuples for all M-ESs managed by a single home MD-IS is the *Location Directory*.

On receipt of the RDC message from the home MD-IS, the serving MD-IS examines the result indication. If the home MD-IS grants support for the M-ES, the serving MD-IS updates its local data base and allocates resources to service the M-ES. If the home MD-IS denies support for the M-ES, the serving MD-IS discards information about the M-ES and frees resources reserved for that device.

---

8. Given the fixed size of the data field, it "wraps around" to zero after reaching the maximum value.

Bit	8	7	6	5	4	3	2	1	Description
1 octet	PDU Type = RDC (02)								Identifies message as RDC
1 octet	Registration Sequence Count								Incremented value to avoid confusion that result from multiple ESH messages arriving at destination out of sequence
2 octets	Des'n Address Length (L$_s$)								Length of network address that requested registration
variable	Destination Address								Network address of mobile unit that requested registration
1 octet	Par. Code = Auth Update (03)								Optional parameter to update the authentication credentials to be used by the M-ES on future registration attempts
1 octet	Par. Length (variable)								
variable	Authentication Credentials								
1 octet	Par. Code = Grp Mbr ID(00)								Unique identifier for each Multicast group member
1 octet	Par. Length (2)								
2 octets	Group Member Identifier								
1 octet	Par. Code = Result Code (04)								Result indicator from registration attempt
1 octet	Par. Length (1)								
1 octet	Result Code								
1 octet	Par. Code = Config Tmr (05)								Timer value of maximum time M-ES may operate without re-registration
2 octets	Par. Length (2)								
2 octet	M-ES Config Tmr (secs)								
1 octet	Par. Code = Addr. Mask (06)								Optional parameter to update serving MD-IS to use new redirect service address for the specified address range (Mask is encoded in binary)
1 octet	Par. Length (variable)								
variable	Address Mask								
1 octet	Par. Code = Home Info (08)								Information about the home network for accounting system purposes
1 octet	Par. Length (variable)								
variable	Home Info Code								

☐ optional parameters

Figure 4.8   Redirect Confirm (RDC) Message Format

4.8.4 Confirmation to M-ES - Intermediate System Confirm (ISC)

Once the serving MD-IS receives the RDC message from the home MD-IS, indicating whether or not to provide service to the mobile user, it must relay that decision to the M-ES. The serving MD-IS achieves this through the transmission of the *MD-IS Confirm (ISC)* message.

The ISC message (see Figure 4.9) contains the mobile address (NEI) that is being acknowledged, the results indication, and optionally, updated authentication credentials.

Bit	8 7 6 5 4 3 2 1	Description
1 octet	PDU Type = ISC (03)	Identifies message to be ISC
1 octet	Dest'n Address Length (L$_s$)	Length of network address field
variable	Destination Address	Network address of mobile that requested registration
1 octet	Registration Counter	Incremented value to avoid confusion that result from multiple ISC messages arriving at destination out of sequence
1 octet	Par. Code = Auth Update(03)	Optional parameter for the network to update the authentication credentials to be used by the M-ES on future registration attempts
1 octet	Par. Length (variable)	
variable	Authentication Credentials (encoded in binary)	
1 octet	Par. Code = Result Code (04)	Result indicator from registration attempt
1 octet	Par. Length (1)	
1 octet	Result Code	
1 octet	Par. Code = Config Tmr (05)	Timer value of maximum time M-ES can operate without re-registration
1 octet	Par Length (2)	
2 octets	M-ES Configuration Timer (in seconds)	

☐ optional parameters

Figure 4.9   MD-IS Hello Confirm (ISC) Message Format

If the received RDC indicates an agreement by the home MD-IS to provide service to the mobile unit, the serving MD-IS must update its local data base regarding the mobile. The data maintained for each mobile within the serving MD-IS's area include the following:

- Mobile Network Entity Identifier
- Subnetwork Point of Attachment (the identifier for the radio channel the mobile is currently using)
- Registration counter

The purpose of the first two entries is obvious. The registration counter is a monotonically incrementing value used to detect duplicate or delayed RDC messages. The table of such tuples for all M-ESs currently hosted by a single serving MD-IS is called the *Registration Directory*.

On receipt of a successful ISC, the M-ES is aware that the CDPD network recognizes its identity and location. The M-ES is also assured that data packets addressed to it will be delivered through the CDPD network. This constitutes a successful mobile registration.

On the other hand, the M-ES may receive an ISC indicating an unwillingness or inability by the CDPD network to serve its data routing needs. This would typically require the mobile user to intervene in resolving any outstanding network or subscription issues. Some of the reasons for refusal to service a registration request are associated with authentication failure or lack of a business agreements between the two CDPD service providers.

4.9 CDPD Mobile Data Routing

Once the M-ES has announced its location and the CDPD network has validated it, the network can forward data packets to the M-ES. In the following pages, we shall describe the process by following the activities necessary to route a network packet from an external host to the mobile device.[9]

4.9.1 Home MD-IS

Prior to the providing its *packet forwarding* function, the home MD-IS for the mobile unit must announce its function to external networks. The intent is to ensure that all reachable hosts direct data traffic for the mobile unit towards the home MD-IS. To achieve this, the home MD-IS advertises itself as the shortest path to the mobile's network layer address. This is typically accomplished by the home MD-IS participating in conventional routing information exchanges with its nearest neighboring routers.

Once this has been accomplished and this routing information has been propagated to the external networks, the external host can successfully send data to the mobile unit. The external host proceeds according to standard networking operation. It sends a network packet with the mobile unit's address as the destination and its own address as the source.

This data packet is directed through the intervening networks to reach the home MD-IS in the conventional manner. Once received by the home MD-IS, it must be *redirected* to the correct serving MD-IS. Unfortunately, the home MD-IS cannot act as a simple router and transmit the

9. Mobile to mobile communications is also possible and is supported in the same manner as from an external host. In other words, network data packets from mobile hosts do not receive special routing support. All network data packets destined for a mobile device must first be redirected through the designated home MD-IS for that M-ES.

original data packet. If the data packet were to be transmitted without modification, it would be looped back towards the home MD-IS since all other routers have been informed that the home MD-IS is the best next node for the message.

To circumvent this loop, the home MD-IS alters the data packet by *encapsulating* the original data packet within a new data packet. The new data packet is addressed to the mobile serving function at the appropriate serving MD-IS. The address of the mobile serving function associated with this particular mobile NEI is retrieved from the *Location Directory*, which is maintained through the mobile registration process described in Section 4.8.1. This encapsulation process is sometimes referred to as *tunneling*,[10] and is depicted in Figure 4.10.

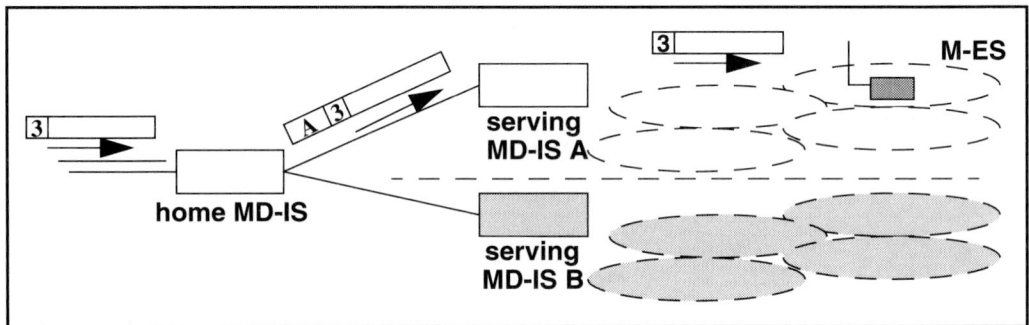

Figure 4.10   Home MD-IS and serving MD-IS

Before closing our discussion of the home MD-IS, we should note that this functionality is further abstracted in the CDPD specification. To avoid too much association between functionality and implementation, the CDPD specification define the mobility management operation at the home MD-IS as the *Mobile Home Function* or *MHF*. Although we use home MD-IS and MHF almost interchangeably in our discussion, it should be noted that there are nuances to each of these terms.

4.9.2 Serving MD-IS

Once the data packet arrives at the serving MD-IS, it must be transmitted over the radio network to the M-ES. However, the M-ES will not respond to the address of the encapsulation

---

10. As we discussed in Chapter 1, there are basically two methods to accomplish the packet redirection needed to support mobility: encapsulation and simply changing the packet's destination address. The CDPD specification team elected to go with encapsulation because we felt that it was a "cleaner" design. Changing the packet destination address would require insertion of the M-ES's NEI somewhere in the packet to enable the serving MD-IS to correctly handle the packet.

packet. The serving MD-IS must de-encapsulate the data packet from the home MD-IS prior to relaying it over the radio network. This is accomplished through the *packet redirection* function within the serving MD-IS.

The serving MD-IS reconstructs the original data packet through de-encapsulation and examines the ultimate destination address. This address is matched against the entries in its Registration Directory and the appropriated subnetwork point of attachment is determined. The original data packet is then transmitted to the radio coverage cell area identified via one or more data link frames.

The mobile unit receives the data packet over the radio connection. The data packet it receives is the unaltered original network packet sent by its peer host. Figure 4.11 illustrates the protocol events over time.

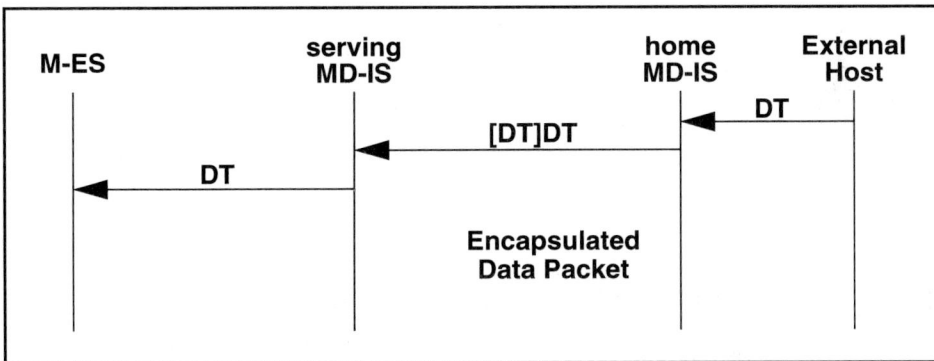

Figure 4.11   CDPD Data Routing

We have just presented an overview of the fundamentals of the data redirection and forwarding operation used to support data mobility. However, the CDPD network must also be able to handle seamless dynamic relocation of the mobile device to a new subnetwork point of attachment.

As in the case of the home MD-IS, so goes the serving MD-IS. In the serving MD-IS, the mobility management function is referred to as the *Mobile Serving Function* or *MSF*.

4.10 Intra-Area Mobility

Within the CDPD network, there is a distinction between two slightly different levels of mobility. *Inter-area cell transfer* refers to movement of the mobile unit from a cell in one routing area to a different cell in a different routing area. *Intra-area cell transfer* refers to the movement of a mobile from one cell to another cell, both of which are in the same routing area.

Why is this distinction useful? It has to do with ensuring that the network is optimized for effective use of the most precious resource, airlink bandwidth. Because movement is most often between cells in a local geographic area, it makes sense to optimize this case.

In the CDPD routing architecture described in Section 4.5, we have defined the structure of cells and routing area subdomains. The cells are radio coverage areas that can be small. In fact, within a downtown core region, a mobile user can traverse several cells during a few minutes. This type of movement across cells will likely be occurring often and the system must handle them efficiently.

On the other hand, a routing area subdomain typically spans tens or even hundreds of cells. Mobile unit movement between routing area subdomains should be relatively infrequent. This is especially true with proper network design that encompasses each major traffic corridor within a single routing area subdomain, etc.

Given these concerns about moving M-ESs, the CDPD system has been designed to accommodate fast relocation between cells. Relocation between routing area subdomains requires more administrative interaction, as described in the following section.

In the CDPD network architecture, each routing area subdomain is controlled by a single serving MD-IS, as illustrated in Figure 4.2. In addition, the network protocol architecture, depicted in Figure 4.3, illustrates that the mobile data link is established between the M-ES and the MD-IS. In other words, the MDBS does not participate in the data link connection other than as a relay function.

This means that even as the mobile unit relocates from one cell to another cell controlled by the same MD-IS (illustrated in Figure 4.12), the end-points of the data link connection are not disturbed. Since the data link end-points have not changed even though the cell location has been altered, it is not necessary to disconnect the data link. Therefore, in the CDPD network, this type of mobile relocation can be handled simply with a recognition of a change in the subnetwork point of attachment.

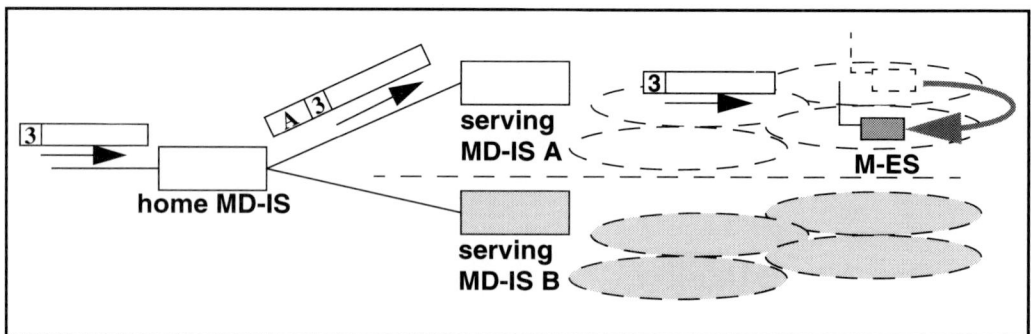

Figure 4.12 Intra-area Mobility

The CDPD system establishes this new subnetwork point of attachment by the detection of traffic for an existing data link connection on a new subnetwork point of attachment. That is, the

M-ES announces its movement to a new cell by ensuring that some data link frame is sent in to the network via a channel in the new cell.

If the M-ES relocates to a new cell and immediately has data traffic to transmit, it simply sends the data. The MD-IS, on receipt of data traffic for a data link connection from a new cell, recognizes that the M-ES has relocated and updates its registration directory to record the move. If the M-ES relocates to a new cell but has no data traffic to transmit, it transmits a *Receiver Ready (RR)* MDLP frame. This RR frame triggers the MD-IS to recognize the movement.

This mechanism provides a very efficient method of apprising the network of the mobile's movement. When the mobile unit has data traffic to send, this method does not incur any over-head.[11] If the mobile unit does not have data traffic to send at the time of the relocation, a very small data frame is transmitted.

Once the serving MD-IS updates its Registration Directory, the process is complete. Since the movement is fully within the scope of control of the serving MD-IS, there is no requirement to inform the home MD-IS of this movement. From this point onward, the serving MD-IS will redi-rect the data packets destined for that M-ES through the new cell. The protocol events are illustrated in Figure 4.13.

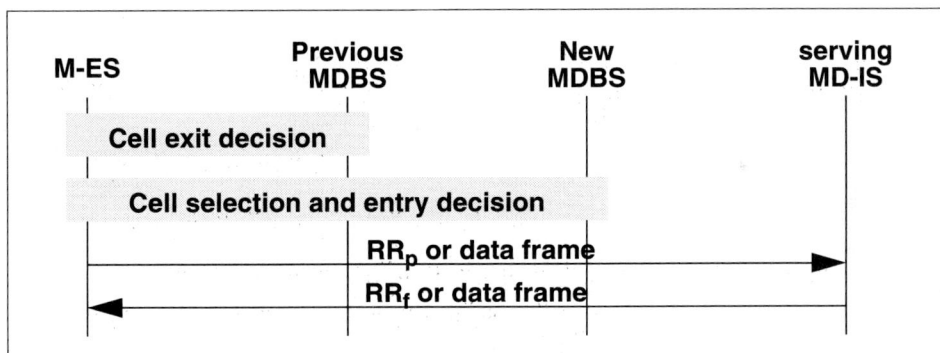

Figure 4.13   Intra-area Cell Transfer Protocol Events

4.11 Inter-area Mobility

When the M-ES moves from a cell within one routing area subdomain to a cell in a different routing area subdomain (illustrated in Figure 4.14), the above intra-area cell transfer mechanism is

---

11. Except for retransmissions of data traffic lost due to the movement between cells.

insufficient. In this instance, the data link end-points are no longer valid. On the movement from one routing area subdomain to another, the serving MD-IS has changed. This means that a new data link must be established between the M-ES and the new serving MD-IS. The re-establishment of the data link and the associated administrative authentication functions must be performed for this type of movement.

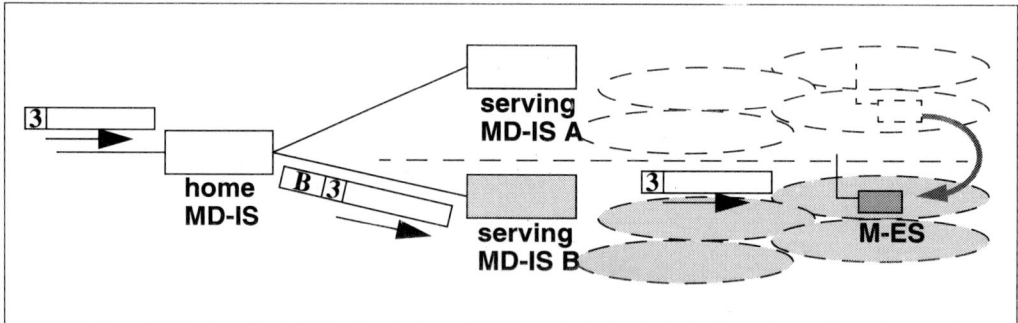

Figure 4.14   Inter-area Mobility

On sensing that relocation has occurred from one routing area subdomain to another routing area subdomain, [12] the M-ES initiates establishment of a data link. [13] Once the data link is established, the M-ES must register its address (or addresses). [14] This is necessary since the new serving MD-IS is unaware of the active network addresses at the M-ES. The M-ES must execute the normal registration process involving ESH, RDR, RDC, and ISC messages as outlined in Section 4.8.

On successful re-registration of the M-ES at the new serving MD-IS, the Location Directory at the home MD-IS is updated. The update reflects the fact that any future network data packets received, destined for the mobile unit's NEI, are now redirected toward the new serving MD-IS. The protocol events are illustrated in Figure 4.15.

---

12. The M-ES recognizes movement across cell boundaries and routing area subdomain boundaries through interpretation of Radio Resource Management broadcast data and messages. Radio Resource Management is discussed in the next chapter.
13. Data link establishment also involves exchange of encryption keys and initiation of data encryption. These are described in the chapter 6.
14. There is no theoretical limit on the number of NEIs used by an M-ES. But practical limitations do apply, usually as a result of the IP protocol stack implementations that have been ported to M-ESs.

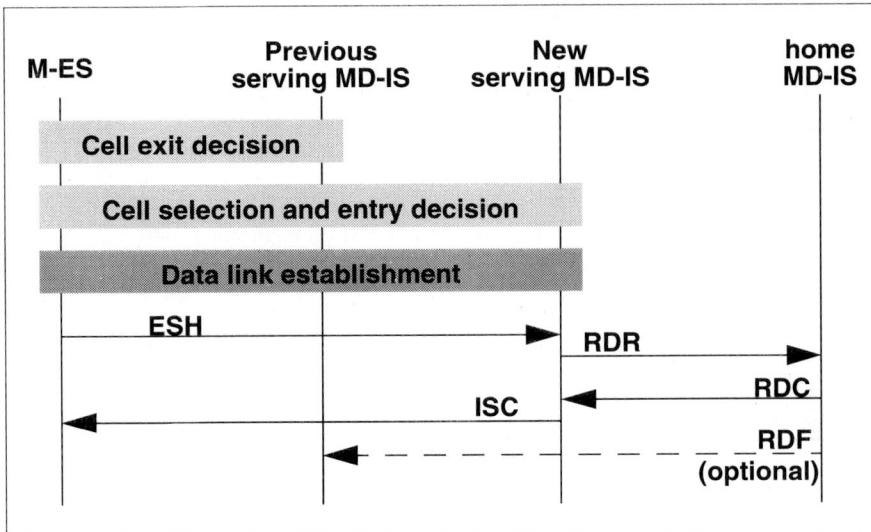

Figure 4.15   Inter-area Cell Transfer Protocol Events

4.12 Other Administrative Operations

The operation of a network such as the CDPD network requires cooperation of multiple network components. This cooperation is achieved through exchanges of administration information and routing update information. Most of the protocol exchanges were described in Section 4.8, however, other exchanges are necessary for complete management of the routing data. These protocol exchanges and procedures are described here, while other exchanges relating to lower layer functionality are detailed in the Chapter 5.

4.12.1 Redirect Flush

When a mobile device relocates from one CDPD serving area to another serving area, the network infrastructure is made aware of the movement through the re-registration of the mobile unit in the new serving area. In this instance, the serving MD-IS in the new routing domain is informed of the entry of the mobile device. However, the serving MD-IS in the previous routing domain is not informed by the mobile unit of its departure.

In this instance, it is possible that the previous serving MD-IS is unnecessarily holding network resources for the departed M-ES. These resources may include the Temporary Equipment Identifier (TEI), [15] data buffer allocation, timer resources, etc. While these resources are usually not excessively taxing on the network, it is preferable to ensure that the most efficient use of the infrastructure is maintained.

To support resource efficiency, the home MD-IS, on receipt of a successful registration attempt from the serving MD-IS in the new routing domain, may notify the serving MD-IS in the previous routing domain of this event. This is achieved via a *Redirect Flush (RDF)* message (see Figure 4.16), which informs the previous serving MD-IS that the home MD-IS will no longer route data packets, destined to the identified NEI, towards it. Since there is no longer any requirement to reserve resources for that NEI, the previous serving MD-IS may then release all resources held for it. This was illustrated in Figure 4.15 as an optional transmission.

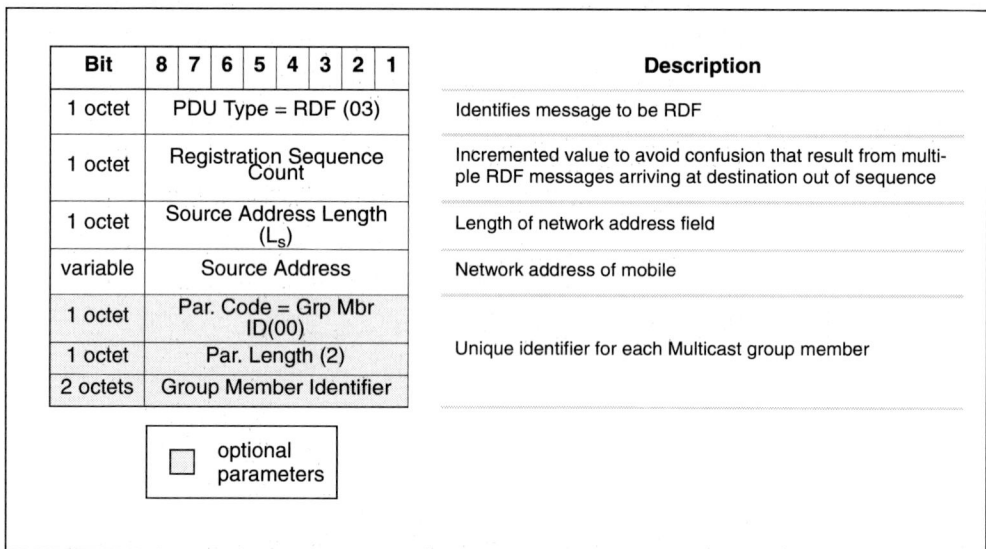

Bit	8	7	6	5	4	3	2	1	Description
1 octet	PDU Type = RDF (03)								Identifies message to be RDF
1 octet	Registration Sequence Count								Incremented value to avoid confusion that result from multiple RDF messages arriving at destination out of sequence
1 octet	Source Address Length (L_s)								Length of network address field
variable	Source Address								Network address of mobile
1 octet	Par. Code = Grp Mbr ID(00)								
1 octet	Par. Length (2)								Unique identifier for each Multicast group member
2 octets	Group Member Identifier								

☐ optional parameters

Figure 4.16   Redirect Flush (RDF) Message Format

4.12.2 Redirect Query and End System Query

When a mobile device registers its NEI, it must provide the associated authentication credentials. These credentials are verified against the NEI to credentials association maintained by the

---

15. The TEI is described in Chapter 5.

network. If the network maintained credentials agree with those provided by the M-ES, the network will authorize access by the mobile device.

This mechanism works well in most instances. Since the mobile device and the network must share a common understanding of the credentials, the network is protected from use by fraudulent devices. However, even with the mandatory data encryption[16] over the airlink, the RF nature of the CDPD system means that the authentication credentials can be intercepted by other devices within the RF coverage area.

To address this concern, the CDPD system additionally allows the network operator, concerned with security attacks by fraudulent devices, to periodically update the authentication credentials. The network may issue new authentication credentials in the response to any registration attempt. Once issued, the mobile device is required to provide the new credentials on subsequent registration attempts. By instituting this type of authentication credentials updates, the probability of fraudulent unit discovery is increased.

In addition, the CDPD system specifications defines that any mobile device must periodically provide its authentication credentials to the network. The maximum amount of time a mobile is allowed to operate without execution of the registration process is defined as the *Configuration Timer*. This value is conveyed from the network to the mobile device by an optional field in the ISC message (see Figure 4.9). If a mobile fails to issue an ESH message prior to expiry of its Configuration Timer, the serving MD-IS may consider the M-ES as unreachable and sends a *Redirect Expiry (RDE)* message (see Figure 4.17) to the home MD-IS.

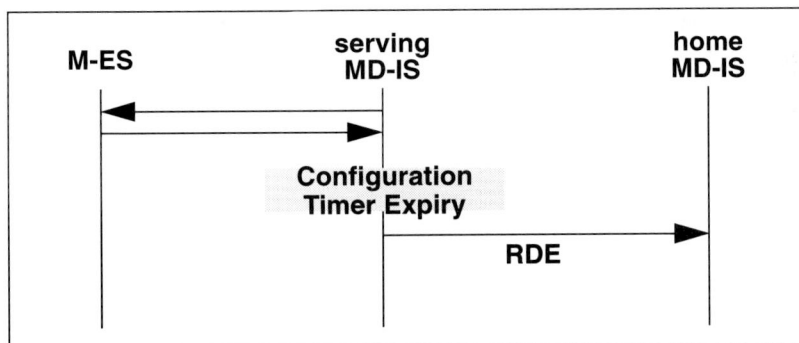

Figure 4.17   Configuration Timer Expiry Protocol Events

If the home MD-IS wishes to confirm that a particular M-ES[17] is still reachable, it may send a *Redirect Query (RDQ)* (Figure 4.18) to the serving MD-IS identified in its Location Directory.

---

16. The security goals and mechanisms within the CDPD system are detailed in chapter 6.
17. To be exact, the home MD-IS and the serving MD-IS are verifying their ability to reach the NEI on the M-ES.

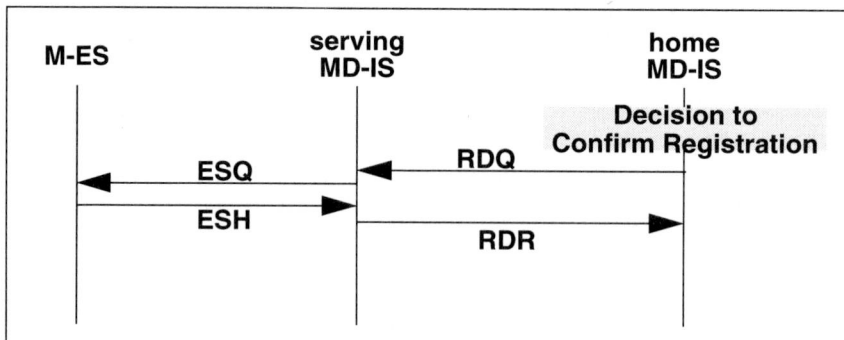

Figure 4.18   Redirect Query Protocol Events

If the serving MD-IS determines from its Registration Directory that the NEI is no longer active, it returns an RDE message to the home MD-IS. If the Registration Directory indicates that the NEI specified is registered, the serving MD-IS in turn, sends an *End System Query (ESQ)* to the M-ES.

When the M-ES receives an ESQ message for an active NEI,[18] it must respond with an ESH message. The serving MD-IS processes the ESH message using the normal mechanism by issuing the corresponding RDR message to the home MD-IS. If the home MD-IS does not receive any response to the RDQ message, it may assess the NEI as unreachable and remove its entry from the Location Directory. It optionally may send a RDF message to the serving MD-IS to release unneeded resources.

4.13 Support Data Structures

So far in this chapter, we have discussed the various mechanisms and procedures that effect the routing of data packets to a mobile device. We have concentrated on the message types and the message exchanges. We have not discussed the data structures necessary to support these functions. In many ways, the CDPD system operates a distributed data base to manage the location information of all the mobile users, which is analogous to conventional router networks.

In this section, we will discuss three of the databases that are concerned with mobility management within the CDPD network. Although there are other equally important data structures, such as subscriber profile information within the network, we shall not discuss them.

---

18. An active NEI is an address that is currently registered on the network.

4.13.1 Home Domain Directory

The first data structure we discuss is the *Home Domain Directory*. Even though it is an essential part of the network, casual observers of the network may not be aware of its importance, or at least be unfamiliar with how this data base is initiated and maintained.

When a mobile device initiates a registration request with the CDPD network, it provides its NEI to the serving MD-IS. Given this NEI, the serving MD-IS must pass the supplied associated authentication credentials to the appropriate home MD-IS for validation. The question is then, how does a serving MD-IS determine the proper home MD-IS for this particular NEI? The Home Domain Directory maintained at each serving MD-IS provides this information.

To support the large and increasing number of mobile NEIs within the CDPD network, it is not sensible to provide a one-to-one lookup table for each and every possible NEI. Instead, the Home Domain Directory is maintained as address ranges. Each Home Domain Directory entry consists of a tuple of three values. The first two values are NEI address and an associated address mask. The combination of the two values allows the system to establish a NEI address range. The third value in the tuple is the address of the associated Mobile Home Function. This is the address of the function within the home MD-IS responsible for any NEI that falls within the NEI address range.

In normal operation, the mobile unit starts by initiating the registration of a specific NEI. The M-ES sends an ESH message to the serving MD-IS containing the NEI and its associated authentication credentials. The serving MD-IS, on receipt of the ESH message, examines its Home Domain Directory for a match between the address range and the supplied NEI. Once the correct tuple is located, the associated Mobile Home Function address is used as the destination address of the constructed RDR message.

This mechanism requires that the Home Domain Directory be complete. If the Home Domain Directory is incomplete, registration attempts with unrecognized NEIs cannot be serviced. However, with the large number of NEIs anticipated and the expected growth of the CDPD infrastructure, it is unreasonable to expect all serving MD-ISs to be manually updated with the most up-to-date home domain information. There must be support for dynamically updating Home Domain Directory information.

In the CDPD system, the concept of dynamic updates to the Home Domain Directory is supported through an optional data field in the *Redirect Confirm* (*RDC*) message. This is best illustrated through an example scenario.

In the following example (see Figure 4.19), all NEIs within the address range of 198.76.0.0 to 198.76.255.255 (hexadecimal $C6.4C.00.00_x$ to $C6.4C.FF.FF_x$) were originally homed at a Mobile Home Function with address 198.12.34.56 (hexadecimal $C6.0C.22.38_x$). As the network grew, the home domain was partitioned into separate devices such that a new MHF was added. This new MHF acts as the home for NEI address range 198.76.80.0 to 198.76.95.255 (hexadecimal $C6.4C.50.00_x$ to $C6.4C.5F.FF_x$) and has an address of 198.12.34.58 (hexadecimal $C6.0C.22.3A_x$).

Tuple #	Area Address	Address Mask	Location Update Service Address
34	...	...	...
35	198.76.0.0 (C6.4C.00.00x)	255.255.0.0 (FF.FF.00.00$_x$)	198.12.34.56 (C6.0C.22.38$_x$)
36	...	...	...

Figure 4.19   Example Home Domain Directory—Initial State

Now when a mobile unit with address 198.76.84.32 (C6.4C.54.20$_x$) registers with the serving MD-IS, the *Home Domain Directory* (*HDD*) at the *Mobile Serving Function* (*MSF*) has not yet been updated with the new MHF information. The MSF thus examines its Home Domain Directory entry and finds a match in the original entry. The Mobile Serving Function sends an RDR message to the original MHF of 198.12.34.56 (C6.0C.22.38$_x$). The original MHF now forwards the RDR to the new MHF. The new MHF has the option of responding with an optional field in the RDR message. This optional field contains the new HDD tuple for future use. This would contain an NEI address of 198.76.54.32 (C6.4C.50.00$_x$), an address mask of 255.255.240.0 (FF.FF.F0.00$_x$).

On receipt of the RDC from the new MHF, the MSF updates the Home Domain Directory to reflect the updated home domain information. This is illustrated in Figure 4.20. It is imperative that the search order through the HDD is managed correctly. The MSF must search through the HDD in ascending order of generality. In other words, it must check for address matches that are more specific in nature prior to matches of wider scope. This is analogous to conventional routing tables

In the example (illustrated in Figure 4.20), a mobile registering the address 198.76.84.32 (C6.4C.54.20$_x$) must be matched with the HDD tuple 35. If the MSF manages the search order such that it attempts to match the NEI with tuple 35 prior to tuple 36, the correct match would be detected. If the MSF attempts the match with tuple 36 prior to tuple 35, then the resultant RDR would be sent to the original, and incorrect MHF.

Tuple #	Area Address	Address Mask	Location Update Service Address
34	...	...	...
35	198.76.80.0 (C6.4C.50.00$_x$)	255.255.240.0 (FF.FF.F0.00$_x$)	198.12.34.58 (C6.0C.22.38$_x$)
36	198.76.0.0 (C6.4C.00.00$_x$)	255.255.0.0 (FF.FF.00.00$_x$)	198.12.34.56 (C6.0C.22.38$_x$)
37	...	...	...

Figure 4.20   Example Home Domain Directory—Updated State

Now the question begs, how does the HDD get established initially? The intent in the CDPD Network is to establish a central addressing authority, the *CDPD Network Information Center (CDPD NIC)*. This authority is responsible for the assignment and allocation of network addresses for all CDPD network service providers.

As each CDPD network service provider initiates its service offering, it registers its address allocation with the CDPD NIC. At the same time, the service provider registers an initial default MHF address. The service provider may also attain the current initial HDD containing all the default HDD tuples of the existing registered CDPD service providers. At this time, this process is still in development. The final operating procedure may deviate from this initial concept.

4.13.2   Registration Directory

The next data structure to be considered is the Registration Directory. This is the data base maintained by the Mobile Serving Function to track the location of each mobile network address within its routing domain.

The Registration Directory (Figure 4.21) is the repository of information that associates each registered NEI with the channel stream it is operating on. The Registration Directory tuples consist of the mobile unit's NEI, the mobile unit's subnetwork address, and a registration sequence counter value.

Tuple #	Network Equipment Identifier	Subnetwork Address	Registration Sequence Count
23	...	...	...
24	198.76.84.32	3	14
25	198.76.76.23	25	46
26	...	...	...

Figure 4.21   Registration Directory

The Mobile Serving Function uses the Registration Directory for two main purposes. The first use is as a routing table for data packets routing towards the M-ES. When the MSF receives a data packet destined for a mobile unit, it first decapsulates the forwarded packet from the Mobile Home Function. The MSF then examines the NEI of the decapsulated packet and searches its Registration Directory to determine the proper subnetwork address for packet redirection.

For data packets in the reverse direction, the Mobile Serving Function uses the Registration Directory to verify that the NEI is a valid registered address. On receipt of a data packet from the M-ES, the MSF compares the source address in the data packet and the subnetwork address against the entries in the Registration Directory. There must be a match in the Registration Directory.

If there is a match with an entry in the Registration Directory, the received data packet is submitted to the data network for eventual routing to its destination. If no match is found in the Registration Directory, the data packet is discarded and will not be routed. This procedure is to ensure that mobile devices cannot inject data traffic into the network with fraudulent addresses.

The registration counter value is used to reduce the possibility of varying network delays resulting in a registration error. This may be the result of a mobile unit relocating from one routing area to another while in the midst of a registration attempt. An example is a mobile initiating a registration attempt in routing area A, then due to movement, relocates immediately to routing area B. The mobile may have sent an ESH message in routing area A and immediately initiated another ESH message in routing area B.

In this instance, if the home MD-IS receives the serving MD-IS generated RDR messages in the same order, that is the RDR from routing area A arrives prior to the RDR message from routing area B, no confusion results. However, if the RDR message from routing area A suffers a longer transit delay and arrives after the RDR message from routing area B arrives, then the Mobile Home Function may be led to believe that the mobile unit has exited routing area B and re-entered routing area A!

To reduce this type of error, the mobile unit increments a registration counter value on each successive registration attempt. The registration counter value is included in the ESH message. The serving MD-IS, on receipt of the ESH message, records the registration counter value, and includes it in the generated RDR message to the Mobile Home Function. This allows the MHF to ignore RDRs that have been delayed and arrive out of sequence.

This shows why it is necessary for the MHF to maintain the registration sequence counter value; it does not immediately explain why the MSF must also maintain a record of the registration sequence counter value. There are really two reasons. The first purpose of the MSF maintained registration sequence counter value allows a Mobile Home Function to issue a *Redirect Expiry* (*RDE*) message to specifically release an out of date Registration Directory entry without fear of inadvertently deleting a new registration attempt by the same mobile NEI.

The second use of the registration sequence counter value in the Registration Directory is related to the possible networking connection between the RF cells and the serving MD-IS. While the original intent was for the serving MD-IS to be geographically close to the base sites, the specifications allow these to be separated by large distances and interconnected through an extensive routing network. In such configurations, it is necessary to protect the Mobile Serving Function from being misled by ESH messages that arrive out of sequence from different cells.

4.13.3 Location Directory

The Location Directory is the data base that is maintained by the Mobile Home Function. It's main purpose is to act as the routing information table for the MHF to determine the address of the re-address server for each mobile NEI.

The Location Directory (Figure 4.22) associates each M-ES NEI with the *readdress server* forwarding address. This is the address to forward the encapsulated data packets for the identified

NEI. On receipt of a data packet destined for a mobile NEI, the Mobile Home Function consults its Location Directory. If an entry with the requested NEI is found, the MHF encapsulates the data packet and redirects the packet towards the readdress server forwarding address indicated in the Location Directory. If there is no entry found in the Location Directory matching the destination address of the data packet, the requested mobile NEI is not registered and the data packet is discarded. The Mobile Home Function may return an ICMP packet to indicate the inability to deliver the packet.

Tuple #	Network Equipment Identifier	Readdress Server Forwarding Address	Registration Sequence Count
23	...	...	...
24	198.76.84.32	198.73.80.13	14
25	198.76.76.23	198.73.80.13	46
26	...	...	...

Figure 4.22   Location Directory

The registration counter value is maintained in the Location Directory to reduce the possible incorrect routing of packets due to varying delays encountered by RDR messages from different Mobile Serving Functions. This mechanism is described in the preceding section.

Unlike the Registration Directory, the Location Directory information is not involved in the relay of traffic initiated from the mobile unit. This is because the data packets sent from the M-ES need not traverse the Mobile Home Function prior to delivery to their destination.

Figure 4.22 illustrates two separate NEIs being associated with a single readdress server forwarding address. In practice, there are likely to be a large number of NEIs associated with each readdress server.

4.14 Multicast Group Management

While defining the CDPD System Specification, it became apparent that an early adopter of this mobile data communications technology would be the fleet manager. Public safety organizations have been using private mobile wireless data communications systems for over a decade. Other fleet services, such as package courier services, have benefitted from the competitive advantage a mobile data system provides. These mobile data users would greatly benefit from a "multicast" service.

Before we proceed, we should clarify that CDPD multicast services is not the same as IP multicast. The services are different, although both are forms of multicast communications.

4.14.1 CDPD Multicast Service Definition

The purpose of the CDPD multicast service is to support organizations and applications that have a need to send the same data to a group of subscribers. This group of subscribers may be dispersed across the network at separate geographic locations. The message will be of lower priority. It is not deemed necessary to guarantee delivery of the message to all members of the group.

Multicast is typically used for some informational bulletin of minimal significance, similar to paging information services. In other words, the service is geared towards inexpensive but possibly unreliable delivery. For those applications requiring reliable group delivery, higher protocol layer distribution list functionality should be utilized.

4.14.2 Multicast Registration

Before providing service to any multicast group, there must be a mechanism for the mobile devices that belong to that multicast group to announce their presence and service requirements to the network. In CDPD, a single network address (*Network Entity Identifier* or *NEI*) is used for all members of each multicast group. This common NEI is known to the CDPD network as a multicast NEI. Any network packet that contains the multicast NEI as the destination address is automatically routed to all members of the group. The CDPD network handles all replication of the packet as necessary to distribute to all group members.

The extensions necessary for this registration mechanism is the use of an additional parameter named the *Group Member Identifier (GMID)*. The GMID is assigned to each device in a way that assures uniqueness among members of the same group.

When a mobile device registers a multicast NEI, it must submit an ESH message with the optional GMID parameter along with the associated authentication credentials.[19] When the serving MD-IS receives the ESH with the GMID parameter, it builds the associated RDR and forwards the authentication information to the home MD-IS.

The main difference at this point involves the treatment of the Registration Directory. In the multicast case, the serving MD-IS allows for the possibility of multiple entries to reference a single NEI value. Under the reference of the single multicast NEI, there will be multiple subnetwork addresses, each associated with one or more unique GMID values.

---

19. Release 1.0 of the CDPD System Specification failed to include the ability to validate individual multicast group members. We initially felt that since multicast address are not allowed to initiate data packets, there is really no security risk. However, a mobile could demand and cause the transmission of forward channel multicast frames. If the mobile device is not authenticated, it is possible to cause unnecessary forward channel traffic. Moreover, without group member authentication, it is not possible for the service provider to repudiate claims that the forward traffic is invalid. Now, if the service provider cannot accurately account for the traffic and accurately control the channel usage, they can't run the network. Thus, the need for individual group member authentication.

4.14.3 Multicast Authentication

On receipt of the multicast RDR from the serving MD-IS, the home MD-IS validates the registration attempt based on the NEI, GMID, and authentication credentials. Each unique GMID within a single multicast NEI has its own stream of authentication credentials.Once validated, the home MD-IS responds with a RDC message containing the proper multicast NEI and GMID data.

Once again, the home MD-IS extends the Location Directory structure to allow multiple entries under the same NEI value. Each entry within the multicast NEI value is a unique GMID and associated data forwarding service address.

4.14.4 Multicast Data Redirection

When the home MD-IS receives a data packet destined for the multicast NEI, it must redirect as many copies of the data as is necessary to reach all members of the multicast group.

The home MD-IS references the Location Directory. It examines the entries associated with the multicast NEI and sends one copy of the data packet to every data forwarding service reported to have group members of the multicast NEI. Each copy of the data packet is encapsulated as per normal point-to-point data traffic.

4.14.5 Multicast Data Forwarding

On receipt of an encapsulated data packet for a multicast NEI, the serving MD-IS examines its Registration Directory to determine the location of the group members. The data forwarding service then sends a copy of the decapsulated packet on each subnetwork point of attachment that has a group member of the multicast network address.

The data packets are transmitted on the appropriate cells on a broadcast channel. This ensures that all mobiles belonging to the multicast group can have access to the data packet.

The actions of multicast redirection and forwarding are illustrated in Figure 4.23. In this example, MDBS 11 and 12 are within the routing domain of serving MD-IS 1. Similarly, MDBS 21 and 22 are within the routing domain of serving MD-IS 2. A multicast NEI has been assigned and some of the group members have registered from cells in MDBS 11, MDBS 12, and MDBS 22. No group member of that multicast NEI have registered from MDBS 21. When the external host sends a data packet to the multicast NEI, the home MD-IS replicates that NPDU and sends one copy to each of MD-IS 1 and MD-IS 2. MD-IS 1 decapsulates the data and sends one copy of the original NPDU to each of MDBS 11 and MDBS 12. MD-IS 2 decapsulates the data and sends a copy of the original NPDU to MDBS 22 but does not send any copy to MDBS 21. This shows how the network infrastructure has distributed the multicast NPDU through the most efficient distribution method. Furthermore, it shows how the external host can send identical copies of an NPDU to multiple recipients with a single transmission.

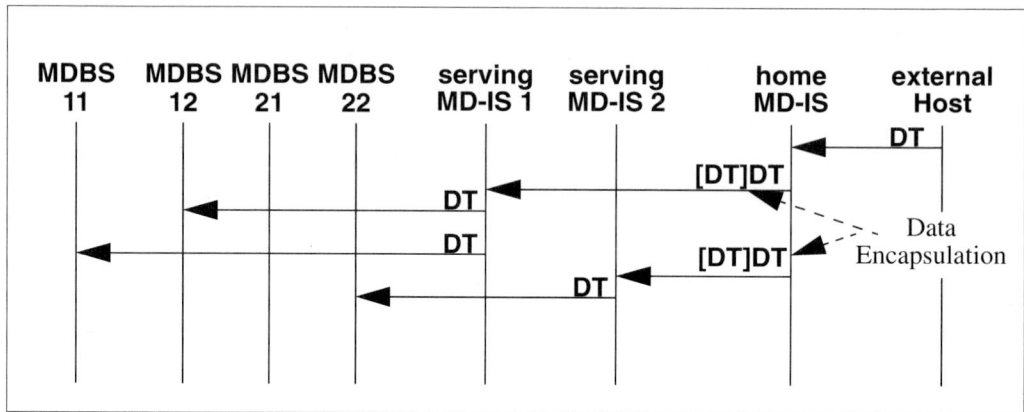

Figure 4.23   Multicast Data Redirection and Forwarding

4.14.6 Multicast Service Characteristics

The use of broadcast services with the two tier distribution process ensures that the most efficient mechanism is used to reach all group members. Only one copy of the data packet is sent between each pair of MD-ISs. Only the serving MD-ISs that are hosting group members receive the distribution. Only one copy of the data packet is broadcast on every channel that contains one or more group members. Only the cells that have reported registered group members receive the broadcast.

The use of broadcast channels for distribution of multicast data packets disallows the return of receipt acknowledgments. There is no receipt confirmation returned to the sender. If acknowledgment of receipt is necessary from all members of the group, the application will need to institute its own application layer mechanism. If guaranteed delivery is necessary for a collection of mobile users, then message handling system distribution list mechanisms should be used instead.

The broadcast nature of the multicast data distribution also disallows data link layer encryption. The possibility of unrecoverable loss of data frames disallows useful operation of services that demand data stream synchronization such as encryption. If secure data is necessary in a multicast situation, application layer encryption may be used. The CDPD network will not interfere with such schemes.

4.15 Broadcast Addresses

During our discussions of multicast service, we defined a separate service capability. This service is similar to multicast in that the same data is transmitted in one or more radio coverage areas. However, unlike the multicast service, the radio coverage areas are selected and defined based on geographic coverage rather than mobile membership. In other words, the CDPD broadcast service provides the ability for a single message to be sent in a specific part of the city regardless of which mobiles are within the coverage area. This allows services, such as the broadcast of road conditions on cells that cover a stretch of highway. It would also allow advertisements to be broadcast to specific geographic areas with target demographics.

This geographic based broadcast service does not rely on tracking of membership within the cell. There is no registration and authentication requirements. The technical considerations to provide this service then becomes a degenerate case of the CDPD multicast service. The same mechanisms used in CDPD multicast to provide data redirection and data forwarding can be used. The problem then becomes one of network provisioning. Since there is no mobile registration, there is no easy mechanism to establish the correct entries within the Location Directories or the Registration Directories. The appropriate values to affect the correct data routing must be established through network provisioning procedures. Unfortunately, the CDPD specifications process does not address these issues. To date, we are not aware of any CDPD broadcast service being established.

4.16 Selection Rationale

The preceding sections have provided much detail into the operation of the CDPD network. We have discussed the mobility management mechanism and the associated protocols. However, the CDPD network design, like all network designs, involved engineering decisions. Two of these decisions have at times come under scrutiny. These involve the use of CLNP as the network backbone protocol and the implementation of three-legged routing for mobility management. The following two subsections discusses these choices.

4.16.1 CLNP

The CDPD infrastructure uses CLNP to carry the MNLP protocol data units and to tunnel the data packets from the home MD-IS to the serving MD-IS. With the wide adoption of IP and the slow uptake of the CLNP based networks, why did the specification team select this ISO based protocol?

Prior to a discussion on the rationale for this choice, it should be stated that it does not impact any user traffic. In particular, since the CDPD network is a multi-protocol network that only uses the tunnel between infrastructure components, this selection does not affect the mobile devices. This decision only impacts the CDPD service providers.

There were two main reasons for the selection of CLNP. The first influence is from the concern over exhaustion of the address space. The second concern was over the need for secure and comprehensive network support services.

When the specifications were being formulated in late 1992 and early 1993, there were wide-spread concerns with the eventual exhaustion of IP address space. There were predictions that address space would be consumed within two or three years. Efforts were under way to define an evolution of the Internet protocol, fondly dubbed IPng or Internet Protocol next generation. This effort was intended to solve a number of ills but one of the major drives was the extension of the address space. There were three major approaches being proposed and convergence was not in sight.[20] In 1993, there was a vision that CLNP would be able to solve the address space problem. Indeed, there were strong proponents for the adoption of CLNP as the replacement for IP. The CDPD specification team could not afford to wait for the resolution of the IPng debate and decided to adopt CLNP as the network infrastructure protocol. This allowed immediate relief from address space issues.

The second concern was with the need for secure and comprehensive network support services. CDPD networks are commercial public data networks and must be well supported in terms of network management, accounting and directory services. These services often require transfer of sensitive data between the infrastructure nodes and thus need secure and consistent facilities to allow distinct CDPD service providers to interconnect and share information. The service providers indicated a preference for using the ISO/OSI protocols for these services. CLNP is the natural lower layer protocol.

From the security perspective, CLNP was also perceived as a more secure alternative. Provision of data confidentiality for the tunnel and authentication of the two ends of the tunnel could be accomplished by referring to Network Layer Security Protocol. The equivalent was not possible in the IP universe.

4.16.2 Triangle Routing

As we have learned through our years, everything has a cost. So what is the cost of the method of mobility management selected for CDPD? Well, the most discussed topic in this mobility management scheme is the criticism of what is called "triangle redirection" or "dog-leg routing." The criticism centers around a perceived inefficiency in the necessity of data always traversing the "home" location prior to reaching the mobile unit.

Consider again our road warrior Gary, who has a "home" in, say, California. While Gary is visiting Miami, he needs to get some data from the branch office in New York. Given the mobility management method of CDPD, data packets from the New York computing facility must first be sent to the California "home" before it is redirected to Gary's location in Miami. This is obviously less efficient than if the New York computing center communicated with Gary through a direct link from New York to Miami.

---

20. In the end, IPv6 was established in July of 1994.

However, this inefficiency eliminates the need for the New York computing facility, or any other computing facility for that matter, from having to deal with the establishment and maintenance of a link to the mobile unit. This transparency of mobility to end-user applications (and the rest of the world) is one of the chief design goals of CDPD.

Furthermore, the perceived inefficiency of the triangular redirection has much less impact on actual performance than is perceived. Typical routing patterns of applications across the Internet involved many—on the order of ten to twenty—router hops.[21] A few more hops for the triangular redirection are not perceivable to the user of an application, which is typically not that delay sensitive. Only in the most pathological cases is this likely to have an impact.

Using a more direct path between the mobile and its corresponding host, while appearing more efficient, would greatly complicate mobility management. Multiple mobility-aware routers would have to participate, caching redirected packets, etc., to support in-motion mobiles in a connectionless world.

In conclusion, the goal of a transparent interface to the existing connectionless networking world dictated the redirection scheme of triangular routing. This is a minimal overhead for most data applications that have lower data rates and will be burst in nature. The circuit resources are shared by many users and thus relatively inexpensive. This scheme provides a simple way to communicate with in-motion mobiles using conventional connectionless data protocols, such as IP.

4.17 Summary

In this chapter we have presented the mobility management scheme of CDPD, including the high level objectives and design criteria, the architecture and protocols, the sequence of events and data structures necessary to support a mobile host, and, finally, the multicast service of CDPD. In the next chapter, we shall discuss the second aspect of mobility—mobile network access.

---

21. If you don't know what we mean, try using the traceroute utility!

5 *Accessing the Mobile Network*

All animals are equal but some animals are more equal than others.
—George Orwell, *Animal Farm*, 1945.

In Chapter 4 we discussed how network packets are routed from a host application to a Mobile End System attached to a CDPD network. However, we did not cover any details about how the mobile device attaches itself to the network, and in doing so, how it shares the precious airlink resources with other mobile devices on the channel.

In CDPD, mobile devices attach to the network infrastructure via radio frequency channels. However, this requires many steps, from the creation of an analog waveform on a transmitter to transporting data packets. To perform these operations, the CDPD system relies on a collection of layered protocols. This collection of protocol layers that span the physical channel to the network layer is called the *A-Interface*.

In this chapter, we shall delve into some of the logistics, protocols, and procedures associated with getting a Mobile End System onto the network via the A-Interface.

5.1 The A-Interface

The A-Interface, or *airlink,* is the most visible of the required CDPD interfaces and is key to the provision of CDPD network services to mobile hosts. This is the interface between the mobile end-user and the CDPD system. Because of the numbers of mobile units (projected to be in the millions before the end of the decade) and the fact that they are owned and configured by end-users, getting the A-interface correct is essential to the success of the CDPD technology. This is where the bulk of the "invention" in CDPD is located.

The A-interface is the profile of protocols between the M-ES and MDBS stacks in Figure 5.1. One of the more interesting aspects of this interface is the separation of network-side endpoints for the MAC and LLC sublayers. The shaded area in the figure highlights the protocols and services described in this chapter and defined in the 400s series of Parts[1] of the CDPD System Specification.

---

1. Parts 400, 401, 402, 403, 404, 405, 406, 408, and 409 define the airlink interface.

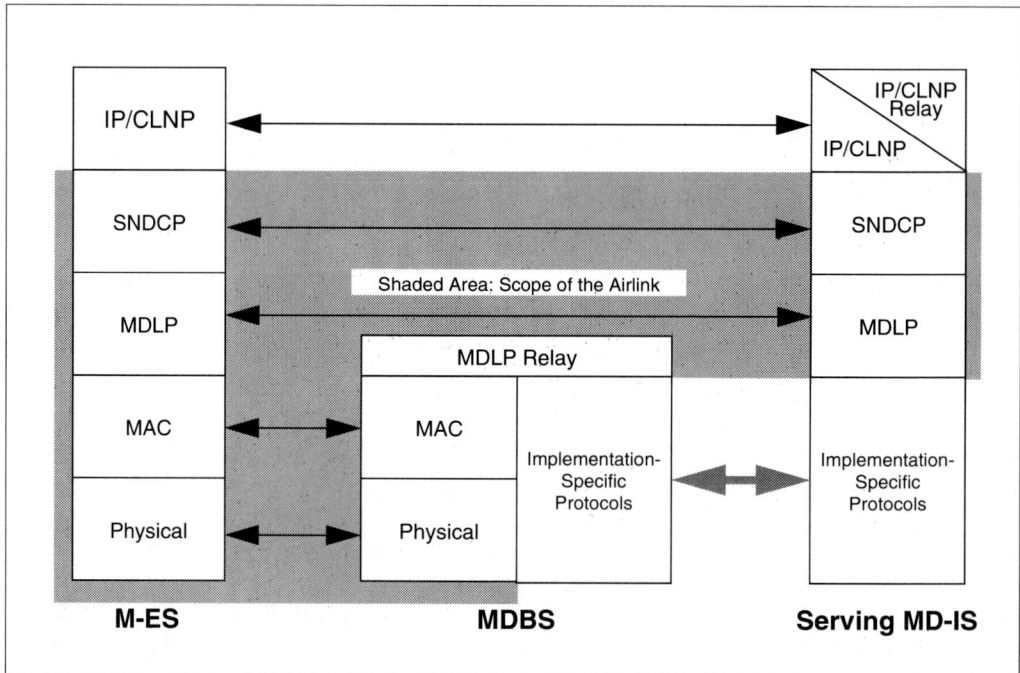

Figure 5.1   Airlink Protocol Profile

In the following sections, we examine each layer of the A-Interface protocol stack. In our discussion, we will build up from the physical layer and progress towards the network layer.

5.2 The Airlink Physical Layer

The Airlink physical layer consists of two distinct one-way RF channels, as depicted in Figure 5.2. The *forward channel* is directed from the network to the mobile hosts. The *reverse channel* is directed from the mobiles to the network. These 30 KHz channels are the same as those used for analog cellular voice (AMPS) systems, as specified in EIA/TIA-553, located in the 800 MHz region of RF spectrum.

Digital transmission is used; the CDPD channels use Gaussian filtered Minimum Shift Keying (GMSK) modulation at a 19.2 Kbps transmission rate. This GMSK modulation uses a $B_bT=.5$ with a modulation index of 0.5. The power levels used are consistent with EIA/TIA-54 and 55. GMSK is a form of frequency-shift keying (FSK) modulation.

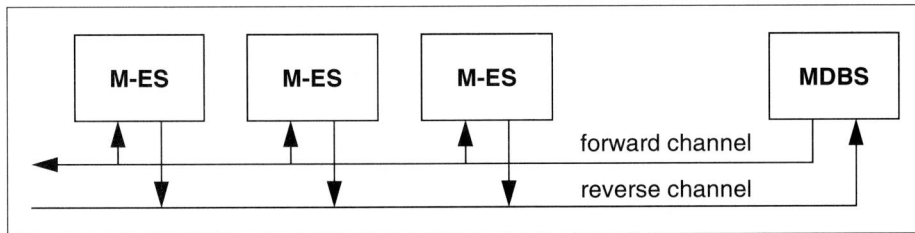

Figure 5.2   Physical RF channels

For most of us, these names and numbers are not meaningful. They aren't even information that we can easily work into a cocktail party conversation![2] Suffice it to say, the modulation scheme is different from typical cellular data modems. The selection of modulation scheme was based on the need to provide high data rate over the air while fitting the RF emission spectrum into the standard 30 kHz channel.

Furthermore, the RF modulation scheme must be robust enough to operate in metropolitan environments under typical cellular RF engineering constraints. Finally, the modulation method had to be easy to implement in terms of available hardware technology. This final limitation restricts the modulation scheme from being the "megabit per second" killer that requires multiple DSP chips and a 12 volt automotive battery.

The CDPD airlink physical layer is defined in Parts 400, 401, 408, and 409 of the CDPD System Specification [CDPD95] and remained largely unchanged between Release 1.0 and Release 1.1 of the specification. The reader interested in greater detail on the physical layer design should refer to [WONG95] and [PAHL95].

5.3 Shared Channel Environment

With the physical modulation scheme defined, the next layer is responsible for managing individual mobile unit use and access of the available radio spectrum. This is called *Medium Access Control* or *MAC*.

On the cellular network, each cellular call is assigned a pair of frequencies, typically called the RF channel, for the duration of the call. The RF channel remains dedicated for the user's conversation even if both parties are experiencing a long and awkward moment of silence. This is reasonable for voice communications systems. Human conversations suffer greatly if each party's

---

2. Unless, of course, it is a gathering at the CDPD Forum membership meeting!

voice is delayed in transit.[3] If the cellular system released and reacquired the channel through the duration of the call, the inconsistent delays would be unacceptable to the subscribers. The cellular telephone system therefore dedicates an RF channel to each call. This is extremely expensive use of the precious RF channel resource.

In contrast, CDPD is a data communications system, and variable delays of individual data packets is quite acceptable. With this in mind, the CDPD system was designed with the *Local Area Network* (*LAN*) shared channel model of operation. The CDPD mobile unit only transmits on the RF channel when it has data packets to deliver.

During periods when the mobile unit does not have any data packets to send, it turns off its transmitter and allows other mobile units to access the RF channel resource. In this manner, the precious RF resource can be shared by many devices. More efficient use of the RF channel can be accomplished.

There are many different ways to share a channel, RF or otherwise. Many of these methods have been used in the Local Area Network environment. In the following, a few of the common channel sharing methodologies are discussed briefly.

5.3.1 Approach 1: Token Passing

In a *token passing* system, a data packet of transmission authorization, the *token*, is transmitted from one unit to another. Only the device that possesses the token is allowed to transmit on the channel. Once the unit is finished with its transmissions, or if it has reached a predetermined maximum transmission time limit, it relinquishes the token and passes it to its "downstream" neighbor.

This mechanism provides a very orderly sharing of the channel resource. It relies on the ability of each device to unambiguously pass the token to the next appropriate unit. It works well within a network where the collection of units are well organized and the next token holder is correctly identifiable. Figure 5.3 illustrates two types of token passing networks.

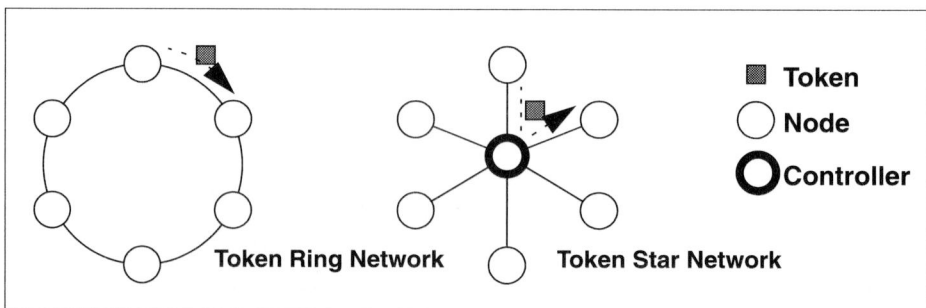

Figure 5.3   Token Passing Networks

---

3. You can experience this on overseas long distance calls that are routed through communications satellites. The quarter second round trip delay to the satellite can make conversations quite awkward.

The CDPD network architecture does not support this type of orderly passing of a token. The membership of the RF cell is not static. Mobile units enter and depart from the cell at will. This means that mechanisms must be added to allow new entrants into a cell to announce their presence. There must also be mechanisms for the controller of the token to recover from a mobile that departs with the token.

For these reasons, CDPD does not use token passing mechanisms to manage sharing of the RF resource.

5.3.2 Approach 2: Demand Assigned with Reservation

Another approach to resource sharing is termed *demand assigned with reservation* scheme. Essentially, the channel is allocated on demand. When a mobile unit identifies itself to the network controller as requiring channel resources, the controller allocates a portion of the resource to that user. Typically, this is done on a time allotment basis, but it is also possible to assign the channel on a frequency assignment basis. Indeed, the cellular telephone system works on this scheme in terms of its assignment of channel pairs (frequencies) per call. Figure 5.4 and Figure 5.5 illustrate these two medium access control methods.

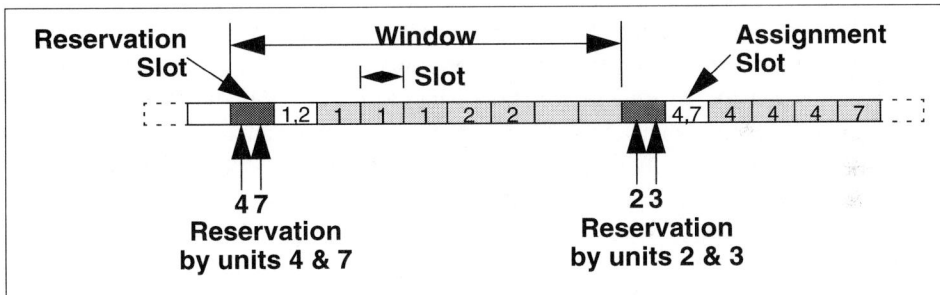

Figure 5.4   Time Based Demand Assigned with Reservation Example

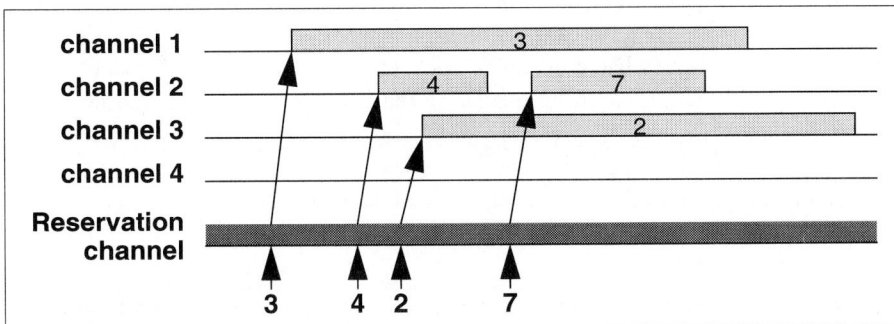

Figure 5.5   Frequency Based Demand Assigned with Reservation Example

A common method of time slot based Demand Assigned Multiple Access scheme involves the partitioning of a channel resource into multiple time slots. Users that have data to transmit are allocated individual time slots within a larger time window. A unit that has been allocated a particular slot within the window will transmit its data during the set time slot and not any other time. This method allows the central controller to manage the transmissions from multiple units without fear of collisions.

To determine how to allocate the time slots, there must be a mechanism for the mobile units to indicate their need to access the channel. With a potentially large population of mobiles in a single RF coverage area, a polling mechanism would be too slow and inefficient. Typically, a contention based mechanism is used by the mobile units to indicate a need for a time slot. Even if polling were feasible, mobiles would have to use some contention mechanism to announce their presence in order to have time slots assigned.

A Demand Assigned with Reservation approach requires the mobile units to contend for a "reservation" channel. It further requires the central controller to sort through the reservation traffic and formulate an assignment of slots for the next available transmission window. This process introduces a slot assignment delay. This delay is significant. If all the mobiles engage in only short transmissions, the delay may be several times the actual transmission period of the data. If all the mobiles have long transmissions, then the ability to demand continual use of a slot will reduce the effect of the reservation delay.

The CDPD system does not use the demand assigned with reservation scheme. The CDPD system is expected to support a traffic profile that contains a significant amount of short bursty transmissions from the mobiles. In addition, the movement of the mobile units may result in unusable statically assigned slots when a unit moves out of the coverage area.

5.3.3 Approach 3: Slotted Aloha [4]

The preceding two approaches were based in controlled access authorization mechanisms. Lest the reader think that all channel access mechanisms rely on orderly exchange of access privileges, there are alternate approaches. One of such founding methods was developed at the University of Hawaii and is fondly called the Aloha scheme.

In the *Aloha* network, all devices transmit on a single uplink frequency to a communications satellite. The satellite relays what it receives back towards the ground devices on a downlink frequency. However, instead of carefully managing the channel resource so that no device's transmission collides with another, the devices are allowed to access the channel on a free for all basis. Whenever a device has data to transmit, it does so without regard for condition of the channel. If a transmission collision occurs, the transmitting device learns of it through lack of acknowledgement

---

4. An excellent presentation of Aloha and slotted Aloha may be found in [KLEI76].

from the peer entity. When such transmission loss is noticed, the transmitting device repeats the data transmission at a later time.

As the reader may postulate, the effectiveness of such a system is limited at best. If there are few devices, each with little data to transmit, then the probability of collisions is minimal. In this case, the low overhead approach to channel sharing is indeed very reasonable. However, if there was a large device population, or if the devices all have a large amount of data to transmit, then collisions could become problematic. Indeed, collisions result in retransmissions, which increases traffic load and result in greater probability of collisions. This snowballing effect can cause the eventual collapse of the channel. Theoretically, using Poisson[5] arrival rates for the data and infinite retransmissions[6] by devices, such a channel may only reach 18 percent of channel capacity before collapse occurs.

To address this low maximum throughput, the Aloha scheme was altered by forcing synchronized access. This means that all devices are still allowed to transmit whenever they have data, however, every device must start their transmissions at predefined times. This effectively reduces the probability of collision by half, which doubles the maximum effective channel capacity to 36 percent.

This type of medium access mechanism, though enjoying low protocol overhead, is unacceptably inefficient for a public data network. Much of the problem lies in the devices' lack of knowledge of the channel status prior to initiating data transmission.[7] The approach discussed in the next subsection incorporates such assessment of channel status. CDPD uses neither Aloha nor slotted Aloha mechanisms.

5.3.4 Approach 4: Carrier Sense Multiple Access with Collision Detection (CSMA/CD)

The CDPD approach to media access control closely follows that of the more familiar *Carrier Sense Multiple Access with Collision Detection (CSMA/CD)* scheme. The CSMA/CD scheme is typified by the implementation in the ubiquitous Ethernet systems. In this scheme, a unit on the network may transmit on the channel whenever it has data to send *and* the channel is not already occupied by another unit.

---

5. The Poisson distribution is commonly used to model event arrivals in queuing analysis. [KLEI75]
6. Real networks typically will not allow infinite retransmissions. Finite retransmissions along with disconnection of the link will result in performance different from the theory.
7. This ignorance of channel status results in an enlarged collision window, which in turn decreases the probability of successful transmission, causing the eventual breakdown of the shared channel.

In CSMA/CD, a unit on the channel wishing to transmit a block of data must first assess the state of the channel. If the channel is found to be unoccupied and available, the unit may start its transmission. If the channel is occupied, the device must wait a certain amount of time before attempting to access the channel again. This is the *carrier sense* portion of the methodology.

If two units find the channel unoccupied at the same time, they may both transmit, in which case, there would be a *collision* of their transmissions and the likelihood is that neither transmission would be successfully decoded by its intended recipient. In this case, a collision detection mechanism triggers both units to stop their current transmissions. Both units must then wait a random amount of time before attempting to reaccess the channel. This is the *collision detection* portion of the scheme.

The amount of random time a unit must wait before reaccessing the channel is the *back-off* time. This random value is chosen from an exponentially growing maximum value with each successive retry of the same transmission.

The CSMA/CD mechanism bases its performance on the ability of each unit to sense the transmission of another unit sharing the channel. While this is easy to achieve on a baseband transmission medium such as on a LAN, it is much more difficult and unreliable on the CDPD radio channel. The CDPD network uses two distinct frequencies for the forward and reverse channels. For a mobile unit to directly detect another mobile unit's transmission, it must configure its receiver to capture the signal. This adds complexity, cost, size, and power consumption to the mobile device.

Furthermore, even if every mobile unit was designed to receive transmissions by other mobile units, the performance would be unreliable. This is because most mobiles are low power units that operate at ground level. The transmissions from these units, while adequately received by base stations with high antennae and high gain circuitry, may not be detectable by other mobile units. These effects make CSMA/CD an inappropriate mechanism to deploy directly in the CDPD network.

However, it is recognized that the basic concept of CSMA/CD has much merit in an RF based multiple access network. Another media access mechanism based closely on CSMA/CD is indeed used in the CDPD network.

5.4 The Airlink MAC Sublayer

The CDPD network uses the concepts of CSMA/CD with a modification to address the dual split frequency nature of the channel. In the CDPD system, forward channel transmission (from the MDBS to the M-ES) is on a different frequency than reverse channel transmission (from the M-ESs to the MDBS). Within each cell, there is a single forward channel transmitter (the MDBS) and multiple reverse channel transmitters (M-ESs). Channel access contention only occurs among the M-ESs.

With the two frequency duplex channel, an M-ES is only receiving radio transmissions from the MDBS and is not receiving radio transmissions from other M-ESs. In other words, a reverse channel carrier sense mechanism is not possible or reliable. To address this aspect of the CDPD system, a digital indicator is provided on the forward channel in order to indicate reverse channel traffic status. This indicator, the *BUSY/IDLE* indicator, is set whenever the MDBS senses reverse channel transmissions. This indicator is interspersed into the continuously transmitting forward channel and provides functionality similar to the carrier sense mechanism in CSMA/CD.

Another flag on the forward channel, the *Decode Status*, provides an indication as to whether the most recently transmitted reverse channel block has been successfully decoded by the MDBS. This provides a functionality similar to the collision detection mechanism within CSMA/CD.[8] The use of these digitally encoded flags gives the mechanism the name *Digital Sense Multiple Access (DSMA)*,[9] sometimes irreverently referred to as "dismay."

For the DSMA mechanism to operate efficiently, the MAC layer must exhibit the following characteristics:

- The transmissions must be segmented into blocks of fixed length.
- The transmitted blocks must include a mechanism for detection of reception errors.
- The mobile units must be able to quickly and reliably determine the Busy/Idle status of the channel.
- The start of transmissions for mobiles must be synchronized to reduce the collision window.
- The mobile units must be able to quickly determine the success of the most recent transmission.

To address these requirements, the CDPD MDBS continuously transmits on the forward channel. The transmission is block oriented with interspersed Busy/Idle flags and Decode Status flags. These flags are further encoded with the synchronization word. This is illustrated in Figure 5.6.

5.4.1 Reed-Solomon Blocks

In the DSMA access scheme, data transmissions are grouped into fixed length blocks. In CDPD, this blocking requirement has been tied with the need for reliable transmissions. A forward error correcting Reed-Solomon (63,47) code block is used to provide for both needs.

---

8. The Decode Status flag actually provides a bit more data since any error that results in decode failure by the MDBS is fed back to the mobile units via this flag.
9. Actually, the full description of the airlink MAC protocol in CDPD is "slotted non-persistent DSMA with collision detect." Yikes!

A Reed-Solomon (63,47) code block consists of 63 symbols, each 6 bits in length. Of these 63 symbols, 47 symbols are data, the remaining 16 symbols form the forward error correcting code. This means that each Reed-Solomon encoded data block can carry 282 = 47 * 6 bits of data link layer data. Detailed explanation of the performance of Reed-Solomon codes is beyond the scope of this book. Interested readers should examine the excellent discussion in [LIN-83].

Without delving into exact performance computations and proofs, we can state that the Reed-Solomon codes provide both error detection as well as error correction. However, there is a trade-off between error correction capability and error detection effectiveness. The selected Reed-Solomon (63,47) code allows development of algorithms that correct up to 8 symbol errors per block. However, in the interest of better undetected symbol error performance, the CDPD specifications suggest use of algorithms that correct only up to 7 symbol errors.[10] This brings the undetected symbol error rate to a vanishingly small 2.75×10^{-8}.

5.4.2 Busy/Idle Indicator

The next requirement for DSMA is the ability for the mobile device to quickly and accurately determine the status of the reverse channel. The ineffectiveness of each M-ES to directly detect the transmission of other M-ESs has already been raised. The DSMA solution is for the reverse channel status to be indicated as a digital flag on the forward channel.

In CDPD, this Busy/Idle flag is transmitted once every 10 symbols of the forward channel transmission. The purpose of this frequency of transmission is to ensure that mobile devices have up-to-date information on the reverse channel status. This mechanism provides the reverse channel status every 3.125 milliseconds and is the basis for collision avoidance in CDPD channels.

The careful reader may have noticed that the Busy/Idle flag is a binary flag (either "busy" or "idle"), yet the indicator itself is 5 bits in length! This may at first seem at odds with the much repeated concern about the conservation of radio channel bandwidth. Surely, the designers could have used a single bit flag! Well, it is not an oversight. To ensure that mobile devices can make fast and accurate channel access decisions, the flags must be robust in the noisy RF environment. However, this robustness must not come at the expense of processing latency. This eliminated the protection of the Busy/Idle flag within the Reed-Solomon block.[11]

---

10. Although the Reed-Solomon (63,47) encoding could be used to correct up to 8 symbol errors, doing so would raise the probability of undetected symbol error to approximately 1.2×10^{-5}. It was the desire to avoid undetected symbol errors that drove our adoption of Reed-Solomon coding rather than convolutional coding in CDPD.

11. Rapid collision detection reduces the size of the collision window of DSMA (in CDPD) to 2 microslots (the parts of the block that lie between control flags). Students of contention protocols will recognize that it is the minimization of the collision window that is most responsible for increasing the efficiency of a contention protocol.

Instead, the control flags are repeated and must be interpreted by the mobiles via a majority voting (or better) algorithm—three out of five bits in each flag for the reverse channel busy/idle determination. Analysis showed that under the expected channel characteristics a 5 bit encoding is adequate.

5.4.3 Decode Status Flag

The Busy/Idle flag helps keep a mobile from transmitting while another unit is already operating on the channel. However, it does not prevent two or more units from starting their transmissions at the same moment. In such an instance, two or more units may have sensed the channel status as idle, and simultaneously decided that the channel was ready to accept its transmission. Another indicator must be used to efficiently recover from this collision condition.

The Decode Status flag is used for this purpose. On reception of a Reed-Solomon block, the MDBS executes the decoding algorithm. Typically during normal channel activity, the received block suffers less than 7 symbol errors and is successfully decoded. However, if a collision has occurred, there will be more than 8 symbol errors and the decoding process will fail. In CDPD, the MDBS transmits an indicator on the forward channel to announce the success or failure of decoding the most recently received block.

After transmitting a Reed-Solomon block, the mobile unit monitors the forward channel in search of the Decode Status flag even as it continues to transmit the next block. If the flag indicates successful reception of the transmitted block, the mobile is assured that it can continue to transmit. On the other hand, if the flag indicates a failure to decode the previous block, the mobile must assume that channel conditions were not favorable, perhaps due to a collision, and immediately cease transmission. The immediate cessation of transmission on decode failure is to ensure that a collision condition isn't allowed to persist.

Once again, while the Decode Status is a binary indicator, repetition encoding is used to increase the robustness of the indicator. The Decode Status flag is a five bit value that transmitted as five single bits, each separated by 59 bits. The Decode Status indicator is not contained within the forward channel Reed-Solomon blocks themselves in order to hasten the collision detection process of a transmitting mobile.

Figure 5.6 illustrates how the Busy/Idle flag and the Decode Status flags are bitwise exclusive-ORed with a forward channel *synchronization word*. The purpose of the synchronization word is to allow the mobiles to correctly determine where in the forward frame they are as they receive symbols from the system. Thus, the forward channel synchronization word is evenly interspersed amongst forward channel Reed-Solomon blocks; this can be done because the forward channel is continuously transmitted. The reverse channel also needs a synchronization word, which occurs at the beginning of any (burst) transmission by a mobile.

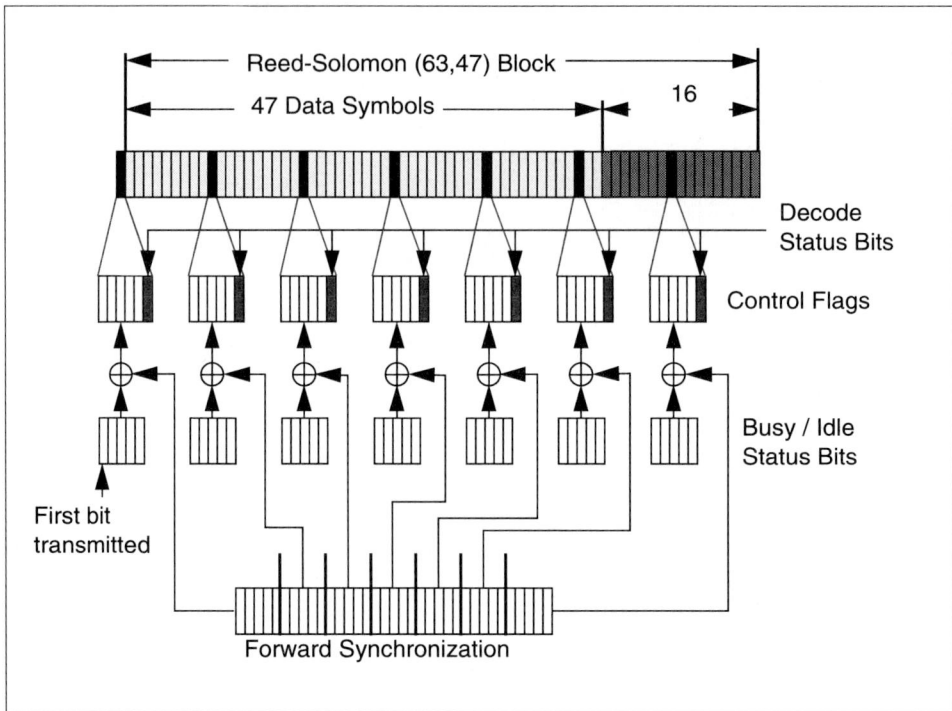

Figure 5.6   Forward Channel Transmission Structure

5.5 M-ES State Machine

The previous section described the various flags that are combined with the forward channel data. These flags, or indicators, are used by the mobile devices to manage their medium access. This and the following sections detail the procedure followed by the mobile device when it has data to transmit. The state machine for the M-ES is shown in Figure 5.7. Initially, the M-ES is in the Idle state.

When a mobile device has data to deliver, it must transmit Reed-Solomon encoded blocks on the reverse channel. Before the mobile attempts transmission, it must first "listen" to the control flag transmitted by the system on the forward channel. If the reverse channel is busy, the mobile enters the Defer state, "backs off" for a random time interval, and then tries again (i.e., "listens" to the reverse channel status again). The random backoff action is the "non-persistent" part of the MAC protocol; the entire listen-before-transmission procedure comprises the "collision-avoidance" aspect of the protocol.

If the reverse channel is idle, the mobile enters the Transmit Blocks state and transmits on a block by block basis. A continuation field is used by the mobile to inform the network that it intends to continue transmission (see Figure 5.8); this allows greater synchrony between the state of the

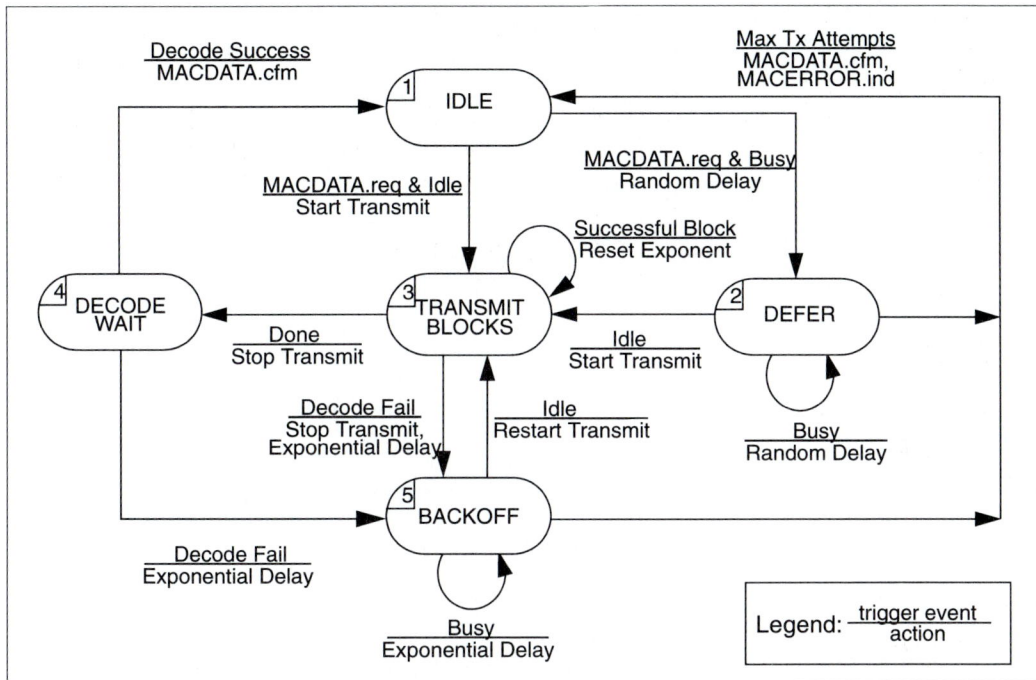

Figure 5.7   M-ES Procedure for Reverse Channel Access

reverse channel and the broadcast reverse channel control flag.[12] As each block is received by the system, it is decoded and the results of the decode activity are transmitted on the forward channel in the Decode Status portion of the control flag.

While the M-ES is transmitting, it examines the Decode Status flag associated with each block transmitted. If a decode failure is encountered, the mobile stops its transmission and enters the Backoff state. While in the Backoff state, the M-ES waits a random amount of time and then assesses the channel in an attempt to restart its transmission. If the channel is found to be idle, it re-enters the Transmit Blocks state and restarts transmission. If the channel is found to be busy, the mobile remains in the Backoff state and waits another random period before assessing the channel status again.

Once the last block has been transmitted, the mobile cannot return to the Idle state immediately. It must enter the Decode Wait state and wait for the Decode Status flag associated with the final block. If the flag indicates a success, the mobile can then return to the Idle state. If the final

---

12. It is this synchrony between the state of the reverse channel and the broadcast control flag that reduces the amount of "busy hang" time. *Busy hang* is the state that exists when the reverse channel is actually idle but a mobile awaiting transmission believes it to be busy because the flags indicate it to be busy. The size of the busy hang interval limits the efficiency of the shared medium of the reverse channel.

block was not received successfully, the mobile proceeds to the Backoff state and waits a random delay period before again assessing the channel status.

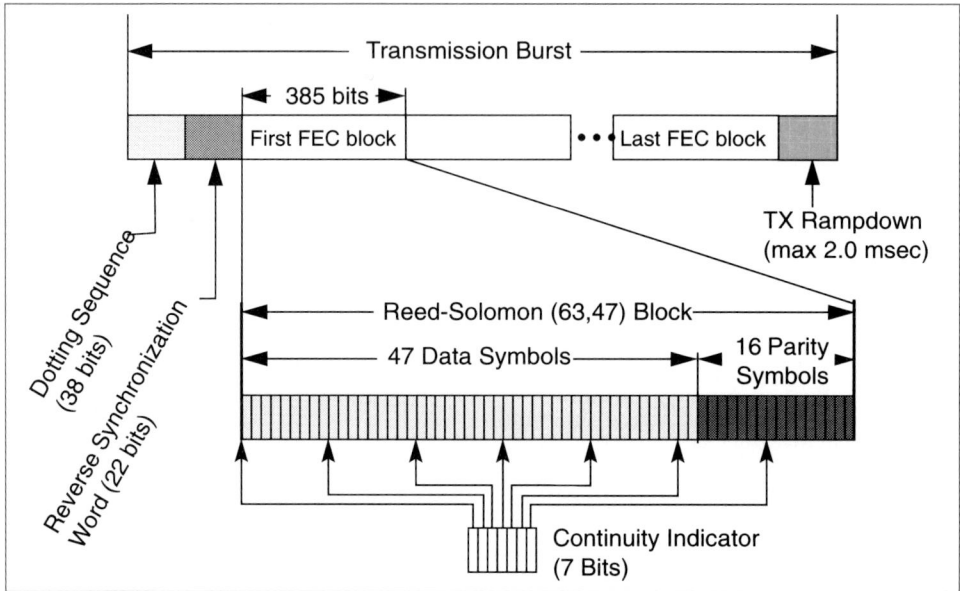

Figure 5.8 Reverse Channel Transmission Structure

The forward and reverse channel relationship is displayed in Figure 5.9. The airlink MAC sublayer is defined in Parts 400 and 402 of the CDPD System Specification [CDPD95] and remained essentially unchanged in CDPD Release 1.1.

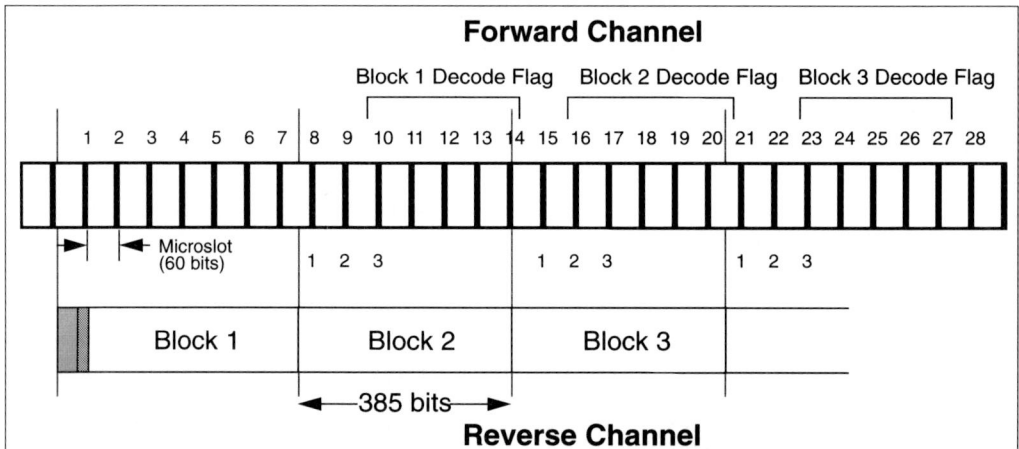

Figure 5.9 Decode Status Flag Timing Relationship

5.6 Airlink MAC Parameters

The above description of the M-ES state machine identified several wait times and retransmission events. To allow tuning of the mechanism, several parameters are defined. These include the following:

- Min_Idle_Time
- Min_Count
- Max_Count
- Max Blocks

Each one of these parameters is described in the following sections.

5.6.1 Min_Idle_Time

The Min_Idle_Time parameter specifies the minimum amount of time a mobile must wait after it has finished one transmission burst before it is allowed to start transmission of a succeeding burst. This time is included in the system to ensure that all mobiles sharing a channel have an opportunity to access the channel. If a mobile was allowed to continuously transmit without pause, no other units would be able to access the channel.

One common misperception about the Min_Idle_Time parameter is that it must be non-zero. This understanding fails to take into account the need for a mobile to await the complete reception of the Decode Status indicator for the final block. The requirement that a mobile must receive this final Decode Status indicator forces the mobile to stop transmission for a period of at least 7 microslots. The Min_Idle_Time parameter thus indicates an additional period of quiescence for the mobiles.

The service provider can adjust this parameter to accommodate the traffic profile on the channel. If there are a large number of long transmitting mobiles on the channel, then a larger Min_Idle_Time period may help spread the channel usage among them. This has to be adjusted with care because lengthening the Min_Idle_Time period reduces individual throughput.

5.6.2 Min_count and Max_count

The Min_count and Max_count parameters define the limits of back-off delay periods. To understand the use of these parameters, the reader must first be familiar with the exponential back-off delay mechanism.

On the first instance of a decode failure, the mobile must stop transmission and wait a random period before attempting to restart the transmission. The delay period is chosen as a value evenly distributed between 0 and the current maximum delay value. If on expiry of the delay period chosen, the channel is found to be in use, the mobile must repeat the back-off. However, the delay period must now be chosen from a value evenly distributed between 0 and twice the previous maximum delay value. For example, if the first decode failure resulted in a delay period being chosen as a number evenly distributed between 0 and 16 microslots, [13] then the next back-off delay period would be chosen as a number evenly distributed between 0 and 32 microslots.

The Min_count specifies the exponent (of two) of the shortest delay period distribution (*i.e.*, the first backoff interval). That is, if the Min_count is 4, on the first decode failure the mobile must select a back-off delay period as a value evenly distributed between 0 and 16.

The Max_count specifies the exponent of the largest delay period distribution (*i.e.*, the last backoff interval). This maximum value limits the mobiles from extending the back-off delay to unreasonable amounts of time. This means that even if the channel is so busy that a mobile has to "back-off" repeatedly, it will not result in excessive delay. If the Max_count is set at 8, then the mobile will, at most, select a delay value from a number evenly distributed between 0 and 256 microslots.

5.6.3 Max_blocks Parameter

The Max_blocks parameter specifies the maximum number of Reed-Solomon blocks that a mobile may transmit in a single burst. This system parameter allows the system operator to ensure that no single mobile can continuously transmit and prevents other mobiles from accessing the channel.

The default setting for the Max_blocks parameter is 64. This allows a mobile with approximately 2 kilobytes of network packet to be able to transmit it in a single burst. Of course, mobiles with shorter data can cease transmissions as soon as their data has been transmitted. If this parameter is reduced, each mobile will occupy the channel for a shorter burst and more quickly relinquish the channel for use by other mobiles. However, this comes at a cost of throughput efficiency to the mobile with long data packets to transfer. Increasing this parameter provides better support for the long data user but may introduce excessive channel access delays to other mobiles on the channel.

5.7 Half Duplex Mobiles

In the discussion of the MAC layer functionality thus far, there has always been an assumption that the mobile is a full duplex device. By this we mean that the mobile is expected to be able to receive and interpret the forward channel status flag while it is in the process of transmitting reverse channel blocks. This is not always a valid assumption.

---

13. A microslot in CDPD is equal to the transmission time of 60 bits at the 19,200 bps.

Full duplex devices require two radio sections. One section of the mobile device RF circuitry is used to receive forward channel transmissions, while a separate section of the circuitry simultaneously transmits on the reverse channel. The duplication of some RF circuitry adds cost, size, and power demands on the device.

However, one of the requirements of the CDPD specification was the accommodation of lower cost devices that only use a single RF section. This single RF section can be used either for transmission or reception, but not simultaneously. The delay of the decode status flag from the reverse channel block transmission allows this type of RF circuitry switching quite effectively. After the transmission of a single Reed-Solomon block, the half duplex mobile immediately switches the RF circuitry to receive the associated decode status flag. This restricts the mobile to transmit a maximum of a single block in a burst.

Some enterprising reader may postulate that it is really not necessary to always receive the decode status flag. The reasoning may be that even if the decode status flag indicates failure, the worst that can result is a greater inefficiency due to the need to push the error recovery to the higher protocol layer. In other words, one may gain MAC layer efficiency under most conditions while intermittently suffering more expensive recovery at the data link layer. The trade-off may seem reasonable.

Unfortunately, this introduces two different problems. The first is related to MAC layer operation efficiency, the second is related to radio channel regulatory issues.

The DSMA scheme gathers much of its channel efficiency gain over Aloha type schemes through greater shared knowledge of the channel condition. A critical part of the operation is the quick detection of channel collisions. The maximum channel capacity is directly related to the size of the collision window. If a half duplex device transmits a long burst without regard for the decode status flag, it would significantly increase the collision window of the entire system. So, from a channel efficiency point of view, it is unacceptable to allow the half duplex device to transmit more than a single block at a time.

The RF spectrum used by the CDPD system was originally assigned for use by cellular operators for voice communications. These RF channels are thus allocated with voice traffic receiving top priority. As such, all data mobiles must relinquish the channel to voice users. In fact, the regulations require that all data transmission on these RF channels be terminated within 40 milliseconds of the initiation of voice transmissions.

In CDPD, each Reed-Solomon block on the reverse channel is 385 bits long. This translates into 20.5 milliseconds at 19,200 bps. Accounting for the initial preamble and synchronization bits, the transmission of two blocks would exceed the 40 milliseconds limit. For a half duplex device, it is not possible to sense the initiation of voice transmissions during data block transmissions. Therefore the half duplex mobile must stop data transmissions after every single block to allow sensing of the RF channel state.

This restriction of a single Reed-Solomon block, maximum transmission by half duplex devices, severely limits the service the MAC layer may provide to upper layers. Some of these limitations will be discussed in the following section on the data link protocol.

5.8 The Airlink Data Link Protocol

The data link protocol is the peer-to-peer communications layer that provides data transfer between nodes directly linked by the physical channel. In the CDPD system, the data link layer entities across the airlink are the *Mobile Data Intermediate System (MD-IS)* and the *Mobile End System (M-ES)*. Although some people believe that the end points of the data link layer are the M-ES and the *Mobile Data Base Station (MDBS)*, the MDBS functions strictly as a link layer relay and does not participate in any data link layer activities.

The CDPD system airlink is asymmetric. By that we mean that a single MD-IS operates by transmitting on the forward channel while the reverse channel is shared by multiple M-ES units. The forward channel does not require access control and coordination since there is only one MD-IS per cell, while the reverse channel supports multiple mobile units. This is called a multi-drop link.

When the data link for CDPD was designed, a robust mechanism was desired. Towards this end, existing protocols were drawn upon as a base. *The Link Access Procedure - D (LAPD)*[14] was selected for this purpose. This is a multidrop protocol with effective, and more importantly, well implemented procedures.

The *Mobile Data Link Protocol,* or *MDLP,* is the protocol used at the *Logical Link Control (LLC)* sublayer on the Airlink. In this protocol a separate logical link is maintained between each mobile and the MD-IS. It is based on LAPD

The network-side endpoint for the LLC sublayer is the MD-IS; the user-side endpoint is the M-ES. Each end of the link (i.e., the mobile and the system) maintains state information for that link. The link—which maps one-to-one to a single mobile—is identified by a variable-length *temporary equipment identifier* or *TEI*. The TEI is between one and four bytes in length, which allows for both reduced airlink resource consumption and enhanced user privacy. The MDLP frame format is displayed in Figure 5.10 and is delimited by the standard HDLC[15] frame flags.

A sliding window protocol is used to detect missing frames at each end of the link. Each frame header contains the transmit number for that frame and the number of the next frame expected to be received by the transmitter. Up to the maximum window size (128) number of frames may be outstanding (i.e., unacknowledged) in either direction at any point in time. Procedures for establishing and recovering the MDLP multiple frame mode of operation are displayed in Figure 5.11.

---

14. *Link Access Protocol on the D-channel (LAPD)* is an ISDN-standard protocol, which defines the link operation for multiple "dumb" terminals sharing a common physical link to a "master" ISDN device. This standard was deemed ideal for the purposes of the CDPD channels with the following extensions: longer and variable-length IDs for the mobiles, Selective REJect capability for more efficient use of the airlink, no parity word because of the strong Reed-Solomon encoding, sleep mode for mobile's battery life conservation, and multicast capability for groups of mobiles.

15. High Level Data Link Control.

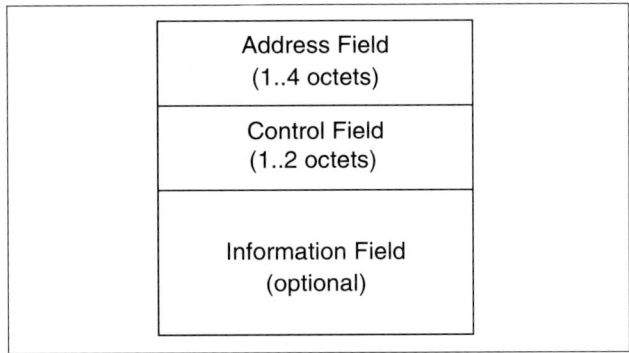

Figure 5.10　MDLP Frame Format

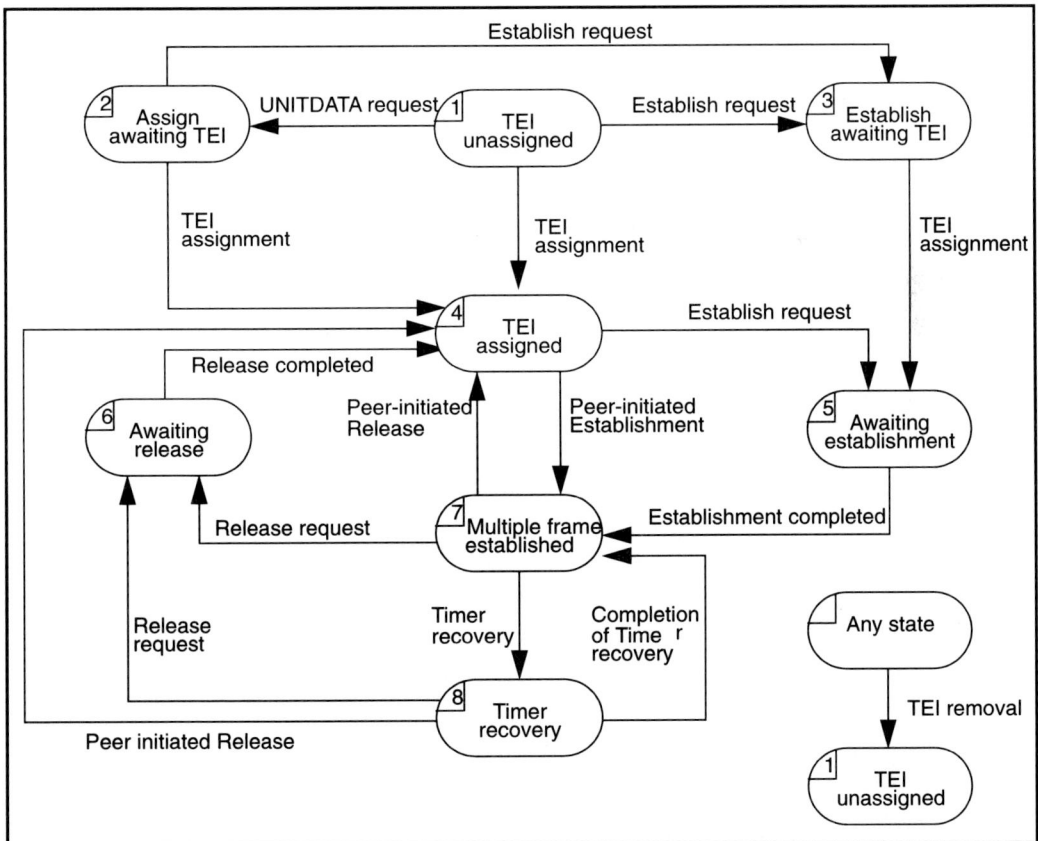

Figure 5.11　Overview of States of the Point-to-Point Procedures

Reception of frames is indicated either implicitly via the next expected frame number in a frame header or more explicitly via a Receive Ready frame. Implicit acknowledgement is more efficient for the precious airlink resource and is preferred in the protocol specification. Frames that are detected as missing are individually re-requested via Selective REJect (SREJ) messages.

The MDLP protocol provides Layer 2 support for mobility. As long as the mobile remains active on a single CDPD system (mobility area), the MDLP link is maintained even as the mobile unit moves about from cell to cell.[16] This is part of the provision for Type 3 Mobility in CDPD.

The airlink LLC sublayer is described in Parts 400 and 403 of the CDPD System Specification [CDPD95], and was extensively enhanced in Release 1.1.[17]

MDLP procedures are not discussed in detail in this book. The interested reader should refer to the CDPD System Specifications Release 1.1 for proper reference. Much of the procedure is similar to the Link Access Procedure family of protocols. Readers familiar with LAPD should find MDLP easy to grasp. The following sections cover the more significant deviations from LAPD found in MDLP.

5.8.1 Selective Reject

When LAPD was adopted as the basis for development of the link layer protocol appropriate for CDPD, some unique characteristics of the RF channel were recognized. The first and foremost concern is the scarcity of bandwidth and the noisiness of the channel. The question for any RF channel is not so much whether data will suffer from errors, but rather, how often it will suffer from errors. In the CDPD system, the MAC layer uses Reed-Solomon forward error correction coding to minimize retransmissions. However, channel conditions may still cause some blocks to be undecodable and thus require the retransmission of one or more link layer frames.

The LAPD protocol institutes a windowing mechanism with retransmission request to address frame errors. The mechanism requires that a sender repeat all frames from the errored frame onward. This method of error recovery was deemed too costly on the precious airlink. Since the RF channel may suffer bursty errors, it is quite likely that only a small number of frames of the current transmission window will be in error. In this case, retransmission of frames subsequent to the errored frame may be unnecessary and wasteful.

MDLP departs from the retransmission of all subsequent frames mechanism of LAPD and introduces a selective reject mechanism.[18] With this mechanism, the receiver transmits an SREJ frame for

---

16. The "system" referred to is the MD-IS, or more precisely, the *Mobile Serving Function* of the MD-IS. The range of control for an MD-IS is a mobility area.

17. Enhancements to MDLP included the replacement of the XID parameter negotiation process with the negotiation taking place during the TEI request/assignment process, additional timers to enhance performance, and clarifications of procedures for handling various error recovery situations.

each missing frame. The sender then only retransmits the frame identified by the SREJ frame. Subsequent frames are not retransmitted unless individually requested by another SREJ frame.

5.8.2 Removal of CRC

Once again, in the interest of preserving precious radio channel resource, the CDPD specification team examined the utility of every field in the link layer protocol. In the LAPD protocol, as in most link access procedures, a cyclic redundancy code is used to detect errors in the link layer frames. It is the detection of errors within a frame that triggers the reject/repeat mechanism. However, link access procedures are generally performed over simple physical links where errors may be introduced.

In CDPD, the radio channel is recognized as unreliable and prone to errors. To address this, the MAC layer protocol uses the Reed Solomon forward error correcting code to minimize need for retransmission.

The MAC layer is also able to detect errors upon receipt of Reed-Solomon blocks. Furthermore, the MAC layer is defined so as to not forward a received data frame to the logical link control layer if that frame has been corrupted by an undecodable block. In other words, the LLC layer will not receive an incorrect link layer frame.[19] Instead, incorrect link layer frames are discarded by the MAC layer.

Given this error control performance of the MAC sublayer, it was felt that the 2 octets of CRC at the LLC sublayer could be eliminated. The LLC sublayer recognizes the need for retransmission when it senses lost frames through sequence number gaps.

5.8.3 Addition of ZAP

The shared nature of the CDPD radio channel raises another concern. If a single mobile operates improperly and continually transmits, ignoring the maximum block size transmission burst

---

18. We not only introduced the selective reject mechanism, we removed the normal reject mechanism. We had long and difficult discussions about whether we should retain the normal reject mechanism to reduce the chance of destabilizing existing protocol software base (we anticipated most developers would start from a LAPD implementation). In the end, we felt that if the normal reject mechanism was retained, there may be little incentive for the developers to use the selective reject mechanism, then our intent of a more efficient error recovery mechanism would be foiled.

19. To be precise, the probability of a block being decoded with an undetected error and passed to the LLC layer is 1.2×10^{-5} (assuming 8 symbol correction at cell edge of 17 dB C/I) and 2.75×10^{-8} (assuming 7 symbol correction at cell edge of 17 dB C/I). The CDPD specification recommends 7 symbol correction.

restriction, it would block all other mobiles on that channel from accessing the channel. This is understandably of grave concern. To address this concern, the CDPD specification team added a new frame type into MDLP.

The Zap frame is defined to cause the mobile recipient to disable all transmissions for the period of time indicated by the message. The concept is to allow the network operator to send the errant mobile unit a "zap" command to remove it from the radio channel.

Of course we all realize the flaw in this approach. If a mobile unit is malfunctioning to the point that it is continually transmitting, what is the likelihood that it will observe the zap frame? The CDPD specification team discussed it for a period of time, then decided that it at least gives the network operator one last chance to correct the problem. It remained in the specification.

5.8.4 Sleep Mode

The most complex addition to the link layer protocol is the addition of *Sleep Mode* operation. This mode of operation is to enable the mobile units to periodically power down its components to conserve power. These periods of inactivity or sleep can help mobile devices extend their battery life significantly.

So why does the link layer protocol need to get involved in the power conservation of the mobile unit? It turns out that with current technology, one of the more power hungry components in a wireless modem is the radio. The radio can draw a significant amount of current even when it is only receiving. So, to minimize battery drain, the mobile unit must periodically turn off its receiver circuitry. This means that during periods of sleep, the mobile cannot be contacted. If the network infrastructure did not participate in support of the mobiles' sleep periods, transmission timers could expire, retransmission counters could be exceeded, and the link could be disconnected. These are clearly undesirable.

To support the mobile's sleep periods, the link layer is allowed to be placed into a suspended state. During this state, all timers associated with a data link are suspended. Timers are restarted on resumption of the mobile's active operation.

The above concept is simple enough. However, for such a link state suspension mechanism to operate, there must be synchronized mutual understanding of the start and end of the mobile's sleep periods. Furthermore, there must be mechanisms to "wake" the mobile when there is outbound data for the device.

5.8.4.1 When Is the Mobile Asleep?

The first question is how does the network determine that the mobile is "sleeping"? The CDPD specification reverses this question by asking how could the network infrastructure know that a mobile is not in sleep mode? This turned out to be very simple and is illustrated in Figure 5.12.

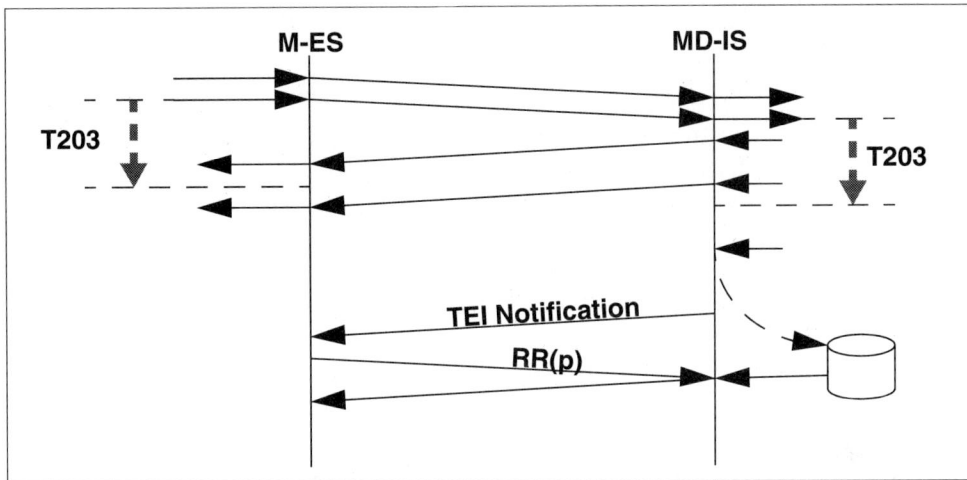

Figure 5.12   Sleep Mode Operation

If we just received a transmission from the mobile device, we can be quite sure that it is not sleeping. This simple (negative) indicator is embodied in the timer value called the *Inactivity Timer T203*. If the mobile hasn't transmitted any data for an amount of time equal to T203, it will go to sleep. This implies that if the network has not received any transmissions from the mobile unit for a period of time equal to T203, it also assumes that the mobile has entered sleep state. Now, both the mobile and the network can use T203 to determine the start of the mobile's sleep state.

This means that if the network has data to send to the mobile within T203 seconds since receipt of data from the mobile, then it can send the data with good expectation that the mobile will be listening. If, however, the network has data to send to the mobile after T203 seconds since the last receipt of data from the mobile, then it must suspend the data link, put the data in temporary storage, and send it to the mobile after the receipt of a transmission from the mobile.

5.8.4.2 How is the Mobile Awakened?

Now, what if the mobile does not have any data to send? How does the network "wake" the mobile? The CDPD system uses the simple mechanism of requiring the sleeping mobile to periodically wake up to check for outbound data destined for it. This is accomplished through the periodic broadcast of a *TEI Notification* message.

The network periodically, at every *T204* seconds, broadcasts a list of TEIs that have outbound data frames pending. The mobile, prior to entering sleep mode, listens for at least one TEI Notification message. Within the message, the T204 value is announced. The mobile keeps track of this value and manages the timer to be in synchronization with the network. After it has entered sleep mode, the mobile must turn on its receiver in time to capture and process the next TEI Notification message.

If the mobile's TEI is not within the list of the TEI Notification message, it returns to sleep mode and leaves the link state suspended. If it finds its TEI value within the list of the message, it resumes the data link and transmits a data frame inbound to announce its active state. When the MD-IS receives the inbound data frame from the now active mobile unit, it resumes the appropriate data link, retrieves the data frames from temporary storage, and delivers them to the mobile.

This simple mechanism has several failsafe mechanisms. The MD-IS will only issue a TEI within the TEI Notification message a maximum of N203 times. If the mobile does not respond after its TEI has appeared in N203 + 1 consecutive TEI Notification messages, the data frame is discarded. This protects the MD-IS from maintaining data for mobiles that have powered down. This is not intended to be a store-and-forward mechanism.

Further, if a mobile has relocated from one cell to another cell within the same routing area, it is required by radio resource management function to indicate its new location through the transmission of a Receiver Ready frame with poll bit set (RR(p)). The receipt of this frame triggers the MD-IS to recognize the new location of the mobile, as well as the fact that it is no longer in sleep mode. This allows the network to deliver data frames to mobiles that have relocated during their sleep period.

5.9 SNDCF: Protocol Convergence

Above the Mobile Data Link Protocol is the Subnetwork Dependent Convergence Function (SNDCF). This sublayer performs the function of mapping the services provided by MDLP to those expected by the network layer protocols. Since these are operations applied to the network layer packets rather than a protocol in the purest sense, this sublayer is more properly referred to as a function rather than a protocol.[20]

The two types of services performed by the SNDCF allows for the data link characteristics. The first type of service bridges the gap between the requirements of the network layer and the service characteristics of the data link layer. These bridging functions include:

- managing the difference between the maximum data link frame size of 130 octets and the maximum network data packet of 2048 octets; and

- managing the use of a single data link connection by multiple network layer connections.

---

20. Unfortunately, in [CDPD93] and [CDPD95], SNDCF is called a "protocol" with the obvious acronym "SNDCP." We're splitting hairs here... 'nuf said!

The second type of service performed by SNDCF focuses on providing more efficient and appropriate utilization of the data link. The specific service characteristics of concern are:

- high value of data link resources; and

- shared physical medium.

The next two subsections discuss the SNDCF bridging functions of segmentation and reassembly, and multiplexing.

5.9.1 Segmentation and Reassembly

To address the difference between the maximum protocol data unit sizes, the SNDCF provides a segmentation and reassembly service. Each network layer data packet is examined prior to its submission to the data link layer unit for delivery. Any network data packet that is larger than 128 octets in length is split into multiple units or segments. A SNDCP header is prepended to each segment. The header provides information to allow reassembly of the data segments by the receiver.

There are two types of data link services that may be used by the SNDCF. The SN-Data PDUs (Figure 5.13) are conveyed over the acknowledged data link service. The SN-Unitdata PDUs (Figure 5.14) are conveyed over the unacknowledged data link service. Since the acknowledged data link service provides reliable sequenced data frame delivery, the SNDCF header only needs an indicator to signal the last segment of a network layer packet. On the other hand, SN-Unitdata headers must provide both a sequence number and a segment number. This allows the receiver to reliably reassemble the complete network data packet, or recognize the loss of segments.

Bit	8	7	6	5	4	3	2	1
Octet 1	M[a]	K[b]	Compression Type		Network Layer Protocol Identifier			
Octet 2	Data Segment							
Octet N								

a. M=0 -> last data unit in a complete SN-Data PDU sequence.

b. Parity of encryption/decryption key.

Figure 5.13   Encoding of SN-Data PDU

Bit	8	7	6	5	4	3	2	1
Octet 1	M[a]	Reserved			Network Layer Protocol Identifier			
Octet 2	Sequence Identifier				Segment Number			
Octet 3	Data Segment							
Octet N								

a. M=0 -> last data unit in a complete SN-Unitdata PDU sequence.

Figure 5.14 Encoding of SN-Unitdata PDU

5.9.2 Multiplexing

To manage the sharing of a data link connection by multiple network layer protocols, the SNDCF prepends the data segments with a Network Layer Protocol Identifier (NLPI). Currently, the defined NLPI values are presented in Table 5.1.

Table 5.1 Network Layer Protocol Identification

NLPI	Network Layer Protocol Entity
0	Mobile Network Registration Protocol
1	Security Management Entity
2	Connectionless Network Protocol (CLNP) [ISO-8473]
3	Internet Protocol (IP) [RFC-791]
4...15	Reserved for future use

The following subsections describe the SNDCF services that handle the unique data link characteristics, including header compression, data compression, and encryption.

5.9.3 Header Compression

We can never say it enough: the radio link is a precious resource. Network layer protocols are typically not aware of this concern and as such, can be inefficient users of the link layer resources. The subnetwork *dependent* sublayer is the intended service to address these issues.

5.9.3.1 TCP/IP Header Compression

The first approach to providing more efficient network layer protocol data unit transfer comes from a tried and tested method. This is the packet header compression technique made popular by Van Jacobson [VANJ90]. This mechanism comes from the examination of the combined TCP/IP headers of a connection. It was found that much of the data within the TCP/IP header were either static (*e.g.* source and destination addresses), or changed in a highly predictable manner (*e.g.* sequence number). Using this knowledge, a header compression technique was developed.

This method is illustrated in Figure 5.15. Basically, the header of sequential protocol data units of a TCP/IP connection are expected to proceed in the normal predictable manner. Therefore, instead of transmitting the expected information in all TCP/IP PDUs, the header field is replaced with a single octet that identifies any header information that has changed unpredictably. If no header data has changed unpredictably, only that single octet is sent. If one or more header information fields have changed in an unexpected manner, the bits of the first octet identifies the changed header field. The new header field values are then provided, in order, in the octets immediately following the TCP checksum. The complete specification of the procedures and header encoding can be found in [RFC-1144]. This mechanism can reduce the TCP/IP header to 3 octets from up to 40 octets uncompressed.

Bit	8	7	6	5	4	3	2	1
Octet 1	0	C	I	P	S	A	W	U
Octet 2	Connection Number (C)							
Octet 3	TCP Checksum							
Octet 4								
•••	Urgent Pointer (U)							
	delta (Window) (W)							
	delta (Ack) (A)							
	delta (Sequence) (S)							
Octet N	delta (IP ID) (I)							

Figure 5.15   Encoding of a Compressed TCP/IP Protocol Header

5.9.3.2 CLNP Header Compression

A similar header compression technique has been applied to the other network layer protocol supported by the CDPD network, the *Connectionless Network Protocol (CLNP)*. In fact the potential savings are even higher given that CLNP network addresses can be 20 octets in length.

Figure 5.16 shows a typical CLNP header for a data PDU.[21] The header size, using an ISO Data Country Code NSAP-Address format is a minimum of 57 octets! However, during the

---

21. This assumes the subsets, mandatory functions, and optional functions specified by [IGOSS-1] and [NIST-500-206] are in effect. (i.e. inactive subset is not used, non-segmenting subset is not used, use/non-use of checksum is configurable, and option fields are permitted)

exchange of PDUs between two endpoints, many of these fields will remain constant or change by small amounts.

Octet	Field
1	Network Layer Protocol Identifier
2	Header Length Indicator
3	Version
4	Lifetime
5	SP | MS | ER | Type
6	Segment Length
7	
8	Header Checksum
9	
10	Destination Address Length
11	Destination Address
•••	
m-1	
m	Source Address Length
m+1	Source Address
•••	
n-1	
n	Data Unit Identifier
n+1	
n+2	Segment Offset
n+3	
n+4	Total Length
n+5	
n+6	Options
•••	
p	

Figure 5.16   Typical Uncompressed CLNP PDU Header

For the lifetime of an association between two NSAP pairs, the following fields remain constant:

- Network Layer Protocol Identifier
- Version

- Destination Address Length Indicator
- Destination Address
- Source Address Length Indicator
- Source Address

These fields never need to be transmitted in a compressed header.

As for the remaining fields, knowledge about the specific underlying data link and network topology is used. For example, since the CDPD data link layer entity provides an indication of the length of a received frame, the segment length field need not be sent.

Furthermore, the connection between the serving MD-IS and the M-ES is unique. For network layer PDUs destined for a mobile device, this link is the final hop. For network layer PDUs originated at the mobile device, this is the first hop and thus the serving MD-IS is aware that it should be the initial first hop value. This implies that the Lifetime field is redundant and does not need to be transmitted over this link.

The Header Checksum, which protects individual hops from a corrupted header, is redundant because MDLP provides its own error detection. However, the receiver at the serving MD-IS must track whether use or non-use of the Header Checksum is employed and must be able to regenerate the proper checksum value as appropriate.

The above considerations allow the elimination of 49 octets of the header. While the remaining 8 octets are likely to change, they either do not change all the time or they only change by small amounts. Given these characteristics, the CDPD SNDCF uses a change mask mechanism to identify the fields that have changed. The sender of a compressed header will send a change mask indicating what fields changed from the previous PDU. This is followed by an update of the field value, relative to the previous PDU.

The format of the compressed CLNP header is illustrated in Figure 5.17. The first octet of the compressed CLNP protocol header is the change mask. Each of bits 1 to 7 of the mask identify one of the parameter fields that exhibit extraordinary behavior. The definition of the change mask bits are shown in Table 5.2. Most of these bits are self explanatory. There are two bits that merit further expansion. These are the *Address-Pair Index changed* bit and the *Data Unit Identifier change other than +1* bit.

The *Address-Pair Index* parameter identifies a particular association of source address and destination address. The sender of the CLNP PDU assigns a unique *Address-Pair Index* value to each source-destination address pair. The assignment of a specific Address-Pair Index value is conveyed to the receiver in the first octet of a *UNCOMPRESSED CLNP* message.[22] Once the *Address-Pair Index* has been established, subsequent *COMPRESSED_CLNP* messages are expected to be for the same source-destination address pair. This is indicated by the *Address-Pair Index changed* bit of 0. On the other hand, if the *Address-Pair Index changed* indicator bit is set to 1, then the *Address-Pair Index* for the current CLNP NPDU is found in the first octet of the compressed header. If a CLNP NPDU with a new source-destination address pair needs to be sent, an *UNCOMPRESSED CLNP* message is transmitted. This message carries the new *Address-Pair*

---

22. A *UNCOMPRESSED CLNP* message is different from an unaltered *CLNP* message.

Index value for the specific source-destination address pair. Even though the Address-Pair Index parameter field has been defined to be 8 bits, the CDPD system specification limits its use to 4 bits. This is to reduce the memory requirements on the implementations.

Bit	8	7	6	5	4	3	2	1
Octet 1	0	C	I	E	M	S	L	H
	Address-Pair Index (C)							
	delta (Data Unit Identifier) (I)							
	Segment Offset (S)							
	Total Length (L)							
Octet n	Header Length (H)							
Octet n+1	Options							
•••								
Octet p								

Figure 5.17   Encoding of Compressed CLNP Header

Table 5.2   Change Mask Bit Definitions

Bit	Meaning if Set to 1
C	Address-Pair Index changed
I	Data Unit Identifier change other than +1
E, M	Copies of CLNP ER, MS flags
S	Segment Offset field present
L	Total Length field present
H	Header Length field present

The next parameter to discuss is the *Data Unit Identifier Delta.* This parameter in a NPDU identifies an Initial PDU and its Derived PDUs for segmentation/reassembly by CLNP. The value sent in the compressed header field is the difference between the current and previous NPDUs. Since the normal operation results in an increment of the *Data Unit Identifier,* absence of the *Data Unit Identifier Delta* value implies an increment of 1 (not unchanged). If the *Data Unit Identifier* is unchanged or has increased by more than one, or has decreased by one or more, then the *Data Unit Identifier change other than +1* mask bit is set to 1, and a signed 8 bit integer is provided in the *Data Unit Identifier Delta* field. If the delta is beyond the range of -128 to +127, then an uncompressed packet is sent.

5.9.4 V.42*bis* Data Compression

Beyond the NPDU header savings, Release 1.1 introduced compression of the data content. In the spirit of not inventing new technology when existing methods will suffice, the V.42*bis* data compression technique was adopted. The compression algorithm relies on efficiently encoding data prior to transmission such that strings of user data octets are represented by a sequence of code-words in fewer bits. The reader with greater interest in V.42bis data compression technique should refer to [CCITT-V.42*bis*].

To establish data compression between the two endpoints, the control parameters must be negotiated. In the CDPD system, these parameters are negotiated by the Layer Management Entity at initial data link connection creation. Once the link is established with these parameters, they remain unchanged for the duration of the data link connection.

5.9.5 Data Encryption

The foregoing sections have described the mechanisms used to ensure the efficient use of the RF resource. The other link characteristic to address stems from the broadcast nature of radio transmissions.

When the MDBS or the M-ES transmits its data, devices other than the intended recipient can intercept the information. It is therefore important to protect that data so that only the intended recipient may correctly interpret the message. The CDPD system relies on data encryption for this protection.

On the establishment of a data link, the mobile device and the CDPD network infrastructure transfer information to create a shared secret. The shared secret is then used to generate a cypher stream to encode the transmission. Since other parties on the RF channel do not possess the shared secret, they cannot decypher the information. The mechanisms used to establish the shared secret are described in Chapter 6.

The CDPD System Specification Release 1.1 allows up to 127 encryption algorithms to be assigned. Currently, there is only one defined, the RC4 algorithm [RSA-92].

5.10 How Data Moves Through Layers

The preceding sections detailed the various functions that the SNDCF performs. However, the order of operation is important and to ensure maximum efficiency, and compatibility, data must be operated on in the prescribed order. Within the SNDCF sublayer, the data transformation operations are depicted in Figure 5.18.

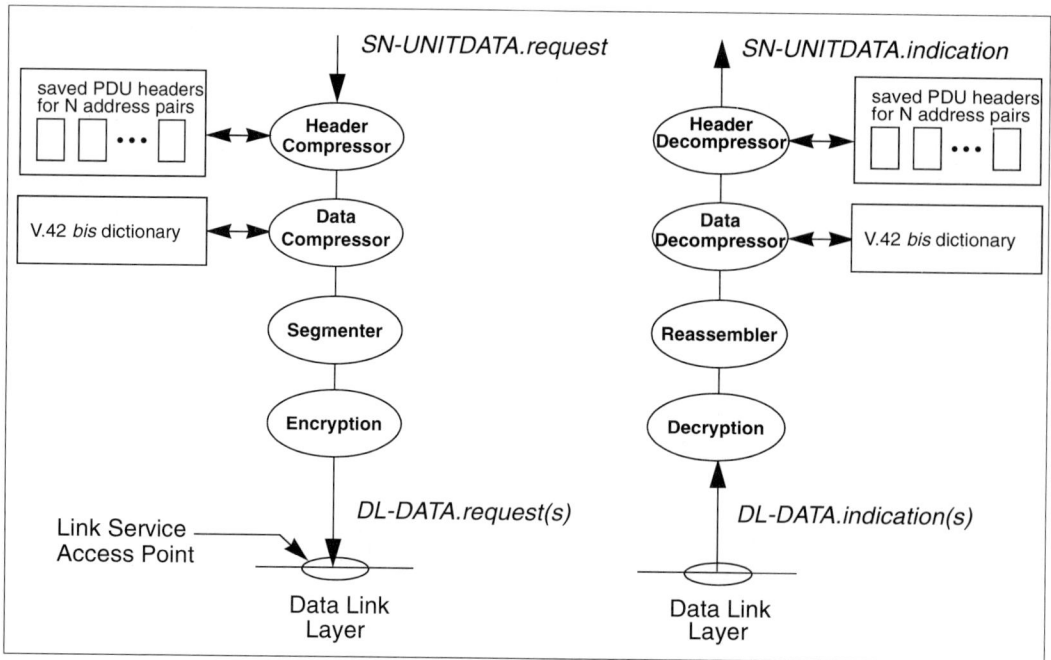

Figure 5.18   SNDCP Model for use of Acknowledged Data Link Services

When data packets are passed to the SNDCF, the compression algorithms are applied. Following that, the data is segmented. This order of operation avoids segments that are then altered in size due to compression. Next, the segments are encrypted.

The encryption must be performed after data compression. In a way, data compression and encryption operate at odds to each other. Data compression looks for and takes advantage of patterns in the data stream. Encryption on the other hand, attempts to "randomize" the data. Therefore, encrypted data do not gain much from data compression techniques. In the CDPD system, data must be compressed prior to encryption, to allow achievement of the greatest efficiency.

Figure 5.19 further shows how all the data transformations are linked together within the CDPD system. The Network layer data packet is passed to the SNDCF. After compression, segmentation and encryption, the encrypted segments are passed to the data link layer. The Data Link Layer adds the proper framing headers and passes the sequence of frames to the MAC layer. The MAC layer concatenates the frames into a bit stream with frame flags between the data frames. Bit stuffing is performed to guarantee data transparency. This data bit stream is then broken into data blocks of 282 bits. The Reed-Solomon Forward Error Correction Code is appended to the 282 bit data block to form Reed Solomon (63,47) blocks of 378 bits. These Reed-Solomon blocks are then transmitted over the radio channel in accordance with the MAC protocol engine, taking into account the contention resolution and error recovery mechanisms.

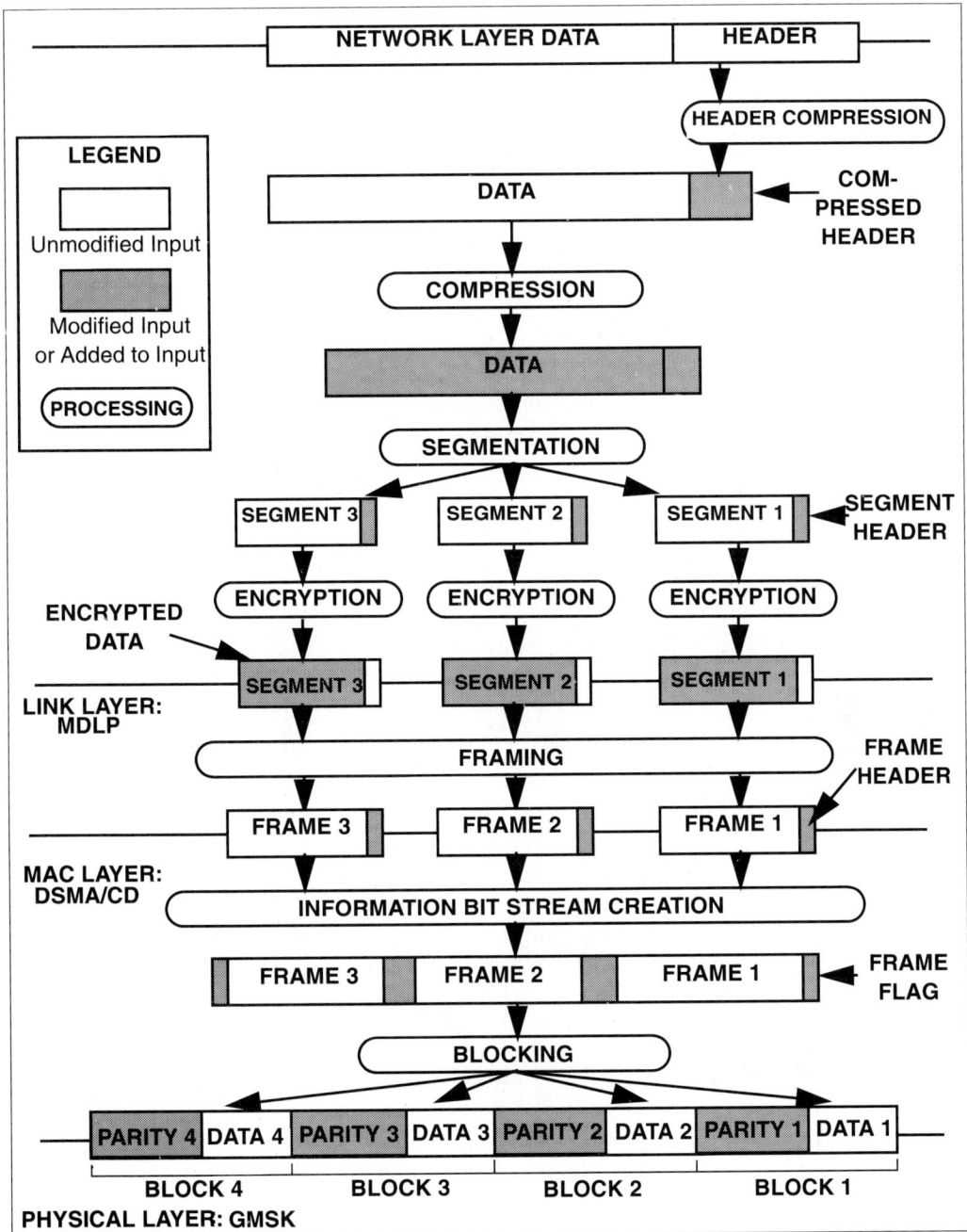

Figure 5.19　Packet Transformation Data Flow

It looks like a lot of processing and manipulation. However, each operation is necessary and addresses a specific characteristic of the radio data link.

5.11 Radio Resource Management

The preceding sections have dealt with how the mobile device accesses the CDPD network. The emphasis has been on establishment and operation of a data link through a shared RF channel. However, the topic of how the mobile locates the "proper" RF channel to use has not been addressed.

To handle this topic, we must first define what is meant by "proper." In principle, a CDPD coverage area boundary is identical to the cell boundary perceived by cellular telephone users, in both physical space and frequency space. This is depicted in Figure 5.20. In addition, cellular telephone users should not have to be aware of the presence of CDPD. The most important result of these two requirements is that CDPD transmissions must not interfere with cellular telephone service.

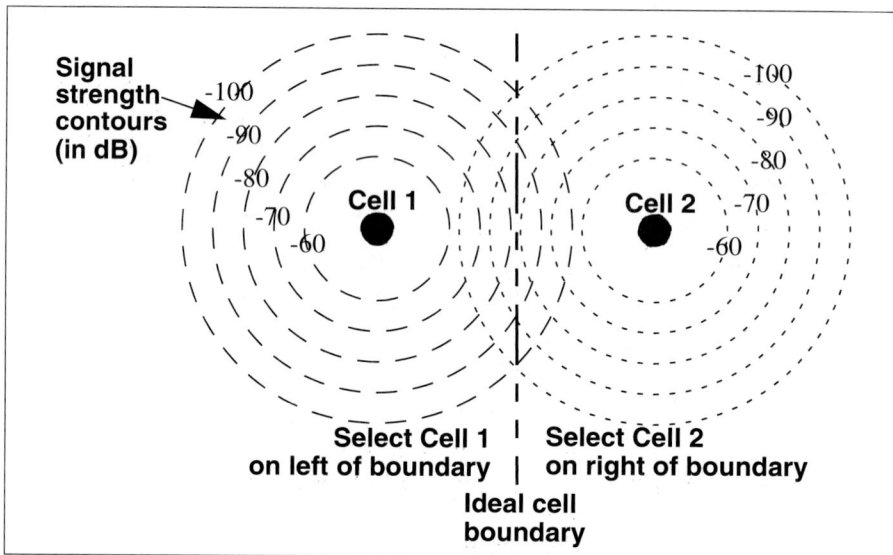

Figure 5.20   Theoretical Cell Selection

In the development of the CDPD System Specification Release 1.1, the specification team examined a collection of cell coverage scenarios. These included differing terrain, vegetation, and population density. From the diverse set of data collected, it became obvious that the theoretical view of cell boundary definition is unrealistic. An example of a real world cell is illustrated in

Figure 5.21. From the illustration, one can see that if the mobile operates with a selection threshold of -90 dB, it may transmit on the Cell 2 channel while well into the center of Cell 1. On the other hand, if the threshold is set at -80 dB, then the mobile may enter areas where both Cell 1 and Cell 2 are considered unacceptable. This thus creates a coverage hole.

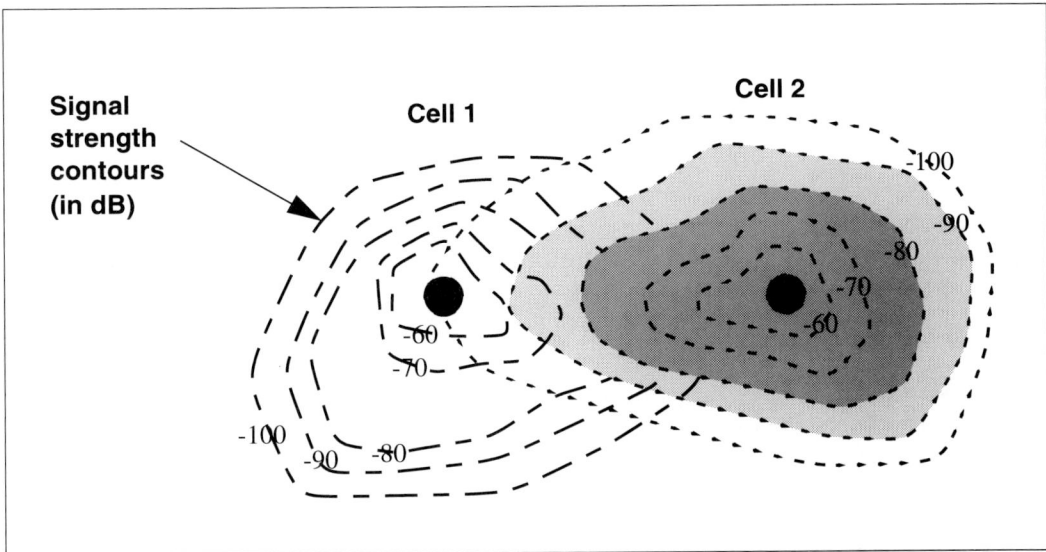

Figure 5.21   Example of Absolute Received Signal Strength Based Selection

From the various measurements, it became obvious that a single variable algorithm, such as received signal strength, would not satisfy all variations. So instead of using an algorithm that relied on a single parameter, the specification adopts an approach that provides the M-ES with a large collection of parameters. These parameters help direct the M-ES to make the decision most appropriate for the coverage area characteristics.

The basis for the CDPD Radio Resource Management mechanism is that the M-ES selects the best channel. By this we mean that the M-ES must locate the strongest CDPD RF channel instead of settling on any channel with sufficient signal strength. Specific terrain effects may result in the M-ES successfully receiving the forward channel from an adjacent cell with good performance. This condition may confuse the M-ES into acquiring and operating on the channel from the distant cell. However, this condition results in the M-ES causing unacceptable interference with other CDPD mobiles and cellular telephones operating on the same RF channel frequency. By requiring the M-ES to select the best or strongest channel, the device will locate the stronger local cell's channel even though the distant channel provides an adequate signal level. This is illustrated in Figure 5.22.

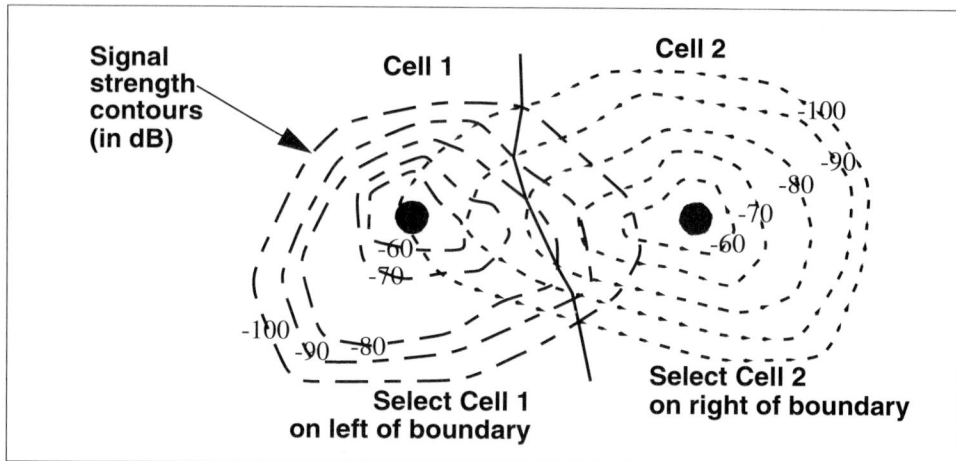

Figure 5.22   Example of Comparative Received Signal Strength Selection

In addition to selecting the best channel, the CDPD specification allows for some decision modifying parameters. For example, the "select the best channel" algorithm would ideally create a boundary between two cells at the locus of points where the signal strength from both cells are equal. As the mobile device crosses this imaginary equi-power line,[23] it would switch to operate on the channel from the adjacent cell. However, this may not be desirable behavior for the specific terrain. For example, if this imaginary line falls on a major thoroughfare, then mobile units travelling on this road will be continually moving from one cell to another. This generates undesirable traffic overhead. To address this condition, a hysteresis value is broadcast to the M-ESs. This RSSI Hysteresis value instructs the mobile devices to stay on its current channel until the difference between the current channel and the adjacent channel exceeds this broadcast value. An example of the "sticky" region using a 10 dB is illustrated in Figure 5.23.

Another way to address the above scenario is to relocate the boundary such that it does not fall on the roadway. This is accomplished in the CDPD specification by the use of a RSSI[24] Bias value. This bias value is used by the M-ES when it compares the signal strength of the current cell and the adjacent cell. A negative RSSI Bias value instructs the M-ES to apply greater preference to the current cell's signal strength, thus effectively increasing the current cell's size.[25] This also

---

23. In the real world of RF shadow effects and varying reflectors around the mobile device, measurements will fluctuate between 5 dB to 8 dB. So the line of equal power between the two cells "jumps" around a long term average.
24. Recieved Signal Strength Indication.
25. It seems counter intuitive that a negative value favors the current cell. Unfortunately, that is how the equation for the algorithm was documented.

means that the current cell's coverage size can be reduced by a positive RSSI Bias value. An example of the use of the RSSI Bias value is shown in Figure 5.24.

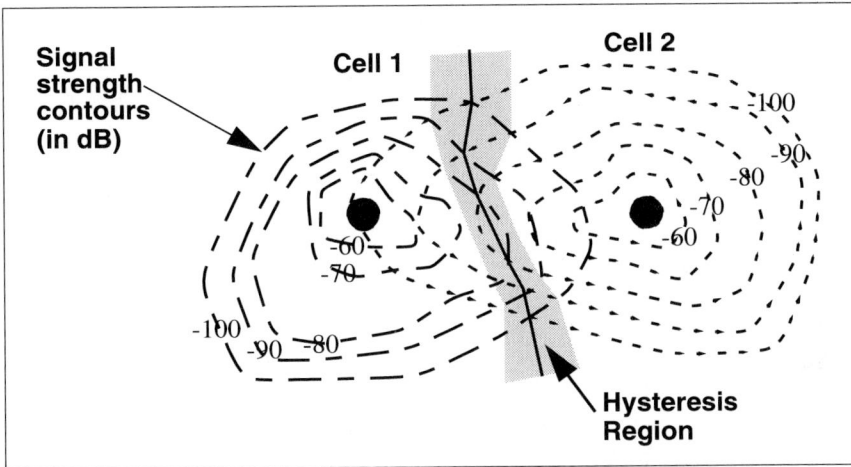

Figure 5.23   Example of Hysteresis Region of 10 dB

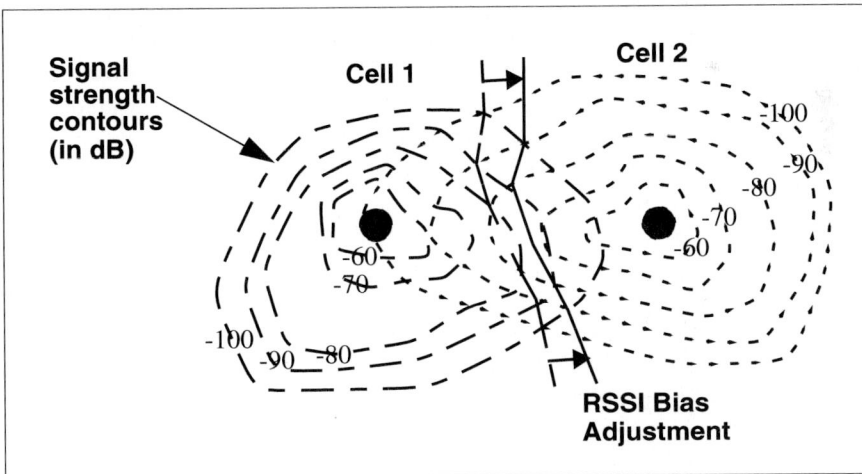

Figure 5.24   Example of Received Signal Strength Parameter of -10 dB

The last parameter for radio resource management is concerned with interference management and not with cell selection. This is the *Maximum Power Level* parameter. This parameter is used by the network to ensure that any mobile operating within a particular cell must not exceed the broadcast Maximum Power Level. In CDPD, the mobiles dynamically adjust their transmission power level based on the signal strength it measures from the forward channel. The concept is that as the mobile moves away from the cell site antenna, the signal it receives weakens. This also means that for the base site to receive the mobile adequately, the mobile must increase its transmission power. The reverse is true also. As the mobile moves closer to the base site, it reduces its transmission power.

So why do we need a maximum power level limit? Once again, terrain effects come into play. In various parts of the country, there are cells situated in valleys between plateaus or mesas. The cell site may be situated at or near the bottom of the valley. As the mobile moves away from the base site and towards the crest of the mesa, it must increase its transmission power. However, if it is operating at peak power as it moves over onto the mesa, the flat terrain will allow the mobile's transmission to irradiate far and wide. This could result in unacceptable interference in distant cells using the same RF channel. Under these circumstances, the mobiles operating in the valley cell must be governed with a maximum power level chosen to minimize the unwanted interference effects on the mesa.

5.11.1 Model of Operation

In the CDPD system, the mobile device has the responsibility of selecting the "best" RF channel to use. However, there are two issues to address. First, the mobile device must possess the necessary data to make a valid decision. Unfortunately, much of this data is not directly accessible by the mobile device. The network infrastructure must pass the pertinent data to the mobiles.

The second issue is one of efficiency. Since the mobile is required to always operate on the "best" channel, it must frequently compare the current channel with possible alternate candidates. Unfortunately, most, if not all, mobile devices will only have a single receiver, which means that when a mobile is assessing an alternate channel, it is unable to receive data broadcast on its normal data channel. Therefore, the algorithm must contain mechanisms to improve the efficiency of alternate channel scanning.

The CDPD system address these two concerns with a series of broadcast messages. The messages are transmitted periodically and consists of the following:

- Channel Stream Identification message
- Cell Configuration message
- Channel Quality Parameters message
- Channel Access Parameters message

The Channel Stream Identification message is illustrated in Figure 5.25. Its purpose is to identify the channel stream to all M-ESs able to receive its signal. The content of the message uniquely identifies the channel stream by the Cell Identifier and channel stream identifier tuple. The remainder of the PDU specifies the business relationship identifiers. Multiple CDPD service providers may select to operate under a single brand identity. The *Wide Area Service Identifier (WASI)* indicates this "branding" of the service. The *Service Provider Identifier (SPI)* specifies the business entity that is operating this network. These parameters have more to do with access control than with cell selection during movement of the mobile. The business relationship identifiers may be used by the mobile to determine if the current network is an appropriate one to access. The remaining fields contain the Power Product and Max Power Level parameters. These are used to direct the proper setting of dynamic power control mechanisms within the mobile devices.

Bit	8	7	6	5	4	3	2	1
Octet 1	Link Management Entity Identifier = 42							
Octet 2	Type = Channel Stream Identification (0)							
Octet 3	Protocol Version							
Octet 4	Dedicated	Capacity	Channel Stream Identifier					
Octet 5	Cell Identifier (= Service Provider Network Identifier + Cell Number)							
Octet 6								
Octet 7								
Octet 8								
Octet 9	Service Provider Identifier							
Octet 10								
Octet 11	Wide Area Service Identifier							
Octet 12								
Octet 13	Power Product							
Octet 14	Max Power Level							

Figure 5.25　Channel Stream Identification Message

The Cell Configuration message is illustrated in Figure 5.26. The MDBS of a cell transmits multiple cell configuration messages. It sends one Cell Configuration message containing data for itself and one Cell Configuration message for each and every one of its neighbor cells. Each Cell Configuration message contains a cell identifier. For the cell identified in the message, the following are indicated:

- The reference channel to be used for received signal strength comparisons. The need for a reference channel is discussed in greater detail in the following sections.
- The Effective Radiated Power Delta (ERP Delta). This is used to adjust for the difference between the power level of the reference channel and the actual

power level of the CDPD data channel. The need for this parameter and its use is discussed in greater detail in the following sections.

- The Received Signal Strength Bias (RSSI Bias). This value is used to weigh the signal strength comparison between the CDPD channel in the current cell versus that of the indicated adjacent cell.

- The Power Product is the mobile dynamic power control parameter to be used in the cell identified in the message.

- The Maximum Power Level is the mobile dynamic power control parameter to be used in the cell identified in the message.

- The CDPD Channel List is a list of all RF channel numbers allocated for CDPD use in the cell identified.

- Other miscellaneous indicators to allow mobile optimization of the scanning function.

Bit	8	7	6	5	4	3	2	1
Octet 1	Link Management Entity Identifier = 42							
Octet 2	Type = Cell Configuration (1)							
Octet 3	Cell ID (= Service Provider Network Identifier + Cell Number)							
Octet 4								
Octet 5								
Octet 6								
Octet 7	Face	0	Active Channel Streams		Area Color Code			
Octet 8	Reference Channel							
Octet 9	ERP Delta							
Octet 10	RSSI Bias							
Octet 11	Power Product							
Octet 12	Max Power Level							
Octet 13	Dedi-cated	Reserved						
Octet 14	RF Channel Number 1							
.....	(RF Channel Numbers 2 to N-1)							
Octet 2N+12	Dedi-cated	Reserved						
Octet 2N+13	RF Channel Number N							

Figure 5.26   Cell Configuration Message

With the information from a full set of this data for all adjacent cells, a mobile device can quickly and effectively determine if the current channel is the most appropriate one. The basic scan algorithm involves a measurement of the signal strength of the reference channel of the adjacent cell. The received signal strength of the adjacent cell reference channel is then adjusted by the *Effective Radiated Power* (*ERP*) Bias value associated with that cell.[26] The resulting adjusted RSSI is compared against the received signal strength of the current cell. If the comparison indicates the adjacent cell is preferred, the mobile will need to perform a cell transfer procedure to move to that adjacent cell.

So, what is a "reference channel" and why is it necessary? In the CDPD system, each adjacent cell may use any one of approximately 300 RF channels. To scan all of them would be very time consuming. Given the Cell Configuration message about the adjacent cells, a mobile will need to scan the RF channels allocated for CDPD use. However, since the CDPD channel may change RF channels to avoid voice communications traffic, a scan action may miss the channel being used for CDPD data. The radio resource management mechanism identifies a continuously transmitting RF channel located at the same CDPD base site. This reliable RF signal allows the mobiles to quickly measure the signal strength from the specified adjacent cell. Unfortunately, these continuously transmitting RF channels may be operating at a different power level than the CDPD data channel it is used to represent. To allow the M-ES to account for this difference, an adjustment value called the *Effective Radiated Power Delta* (*ERP Delta*) is associated with the reference channel. After the mobile measures the signal strength of the reference channel, it subtracts the ERP Delta value. The result is a good approximation of the signal strength of the actual CDPD data channel from that base site.

The above description answers the question as to why there is a reference channel. It doesn't explain what a reference channel may be. The two characteristics a reference channel must have are that it must be a continuously transmitting signal and that it must be co-located at the CDPD base site. Both of these requirements may be met by either a dedicated CDPD data channel or a cellular telephone control channel.

Once the pertinent RF channel information is known about the possible adjacent channels, it is important to ensure that the mobile devices perform the scans at a rate appropriate for the current cell. The Channel Quality Parameters message (Figure 5.27) provides the necessary guidance to the mobile devices. The data broadcast includes the following:

- RSSI Scan Time
- RSSI Scan Delta
- RSSI Hysteresis

---

26. The comparison is carried out according to the following formula:
    If $RSSI_{curr}$ + RSSI Hysteresis > $RSSI_{RefCh}$ - ERP $Delta_{R-C}$ + $Bias_{Adj-Curr}$
    then stay in current cell, otherwise the current cell is not the "best".
    The use of the RSSI Hysteresis value is discussed in a later section.

- RSSI Average Time
- BLER[27] Threshold
- BLER Average Time

Bit	8	7	6	5	4	3	2	1
Octet 1	Link Management Entity Identifier = 42							
Octet 2	Type = Channel Quality Parameters (2)							
Octet 3	RSSI Hysteresis							
Octet 4	RSSI Scan Time							
Octet 5	RSSI Scan Delta							
Octet 6	RSSI Average Time							
Octet 7	BLER Threshold							
Octet 8	BLER Average Time							

Figure 5.27   Channel Quality Parameters Message

First and foremost, the mobile must decide on a delicate balance between frequent channel assessment and low overhead. However, without general knowledge about the cell topography and size, it is difficult for an M-ES to define effective scan triggers. Typically an M-ES would scan for alternate channels if the current channel's signal deteriorates significantly. However, it was found that there are many cell layouts where the channel's signal does not drop significantly even when a mobile has moved well into the coverage area of an adjacent cell. To handle this situation, a mobile must assess the adjacent channels periodically regardless of the current channel's signal history. The network operator can use the RSSI Scan Time and RSSI Scan Delta to direct the mobiles to use values appropriate for each cell. For example, a cell that is small, relative to the normal movement speed, could scan more frequently—a smaller RSSI Scan Time. A cell that suffers from excessive RF shadowing effects should ignore sudden fluctuations in signal strength—a larger RSSI Scan Delta.

The RSSI Hysteresis value is the amount of signal improvement that an M-ES must experience before it moves to the alternate channel. This parameter is useful for network operators to alleviate excessive cell transfers at some cell boundaries due to topography.

The RSSI Average Time parameter inform the mobiles on what length of time to average the signal strength readings to achieve reliable measurements.

The remaining parameters direct the mobiles to search for an alternate RF channel when the current signal, though strong, suffers from other channel degradation effects, such as interference. These effects appear as channel impairments that increase the block error rates. The BLER Threshold sets the percentage block error rate that should be considered appropriate for operation

27. Block Error Rate

within the current cell. The BLER Average Time instruct the mobile device to take the average of block error performance over the specified period of time.

The last message broadcast by the MDBS is the Channel Access Parameters message shown in Figure 5.28. This message contains the important parameters associated with the Medium Access Control function. Adjustment of these parameters for each cell may be necessary to account for cell size and traffic profile and loading.

Bit	8	7	6	5	4	3	2	1
Octet 1	Link Management Entity Identifier = 42							
Octet 2	Type = Channel Access Parameters (5)							
Octet 3	Max Tx Attempts							
Octet 4	Min Idle Time							
Octet 5	Max Blocks							
Octet 6	Max Entrance Delay							
Octet 7	Min Count							
Octet 8	Max Count							

Figure 5.28   Channel Access Parameters Message

Once the mobile device has accumulated all this data, it observes the received signal strength of the current signal. If the received signal strength changes by more than the RSSI Scan Delta value, it initiates scanning of all the neighbor cells. If the received signal strength has not changed by more than the RSSI Scan Delta for a period of time equal to RSSI Scan Time, it also initiates scanning of all the neighbor cells.

For each adjacent cell identified by the Cell Configuration messages received, the mobile assesses the signal strength of the reference channel. The comparison between current cell signal strength and adjacent cell signal strength is made. If the adjacent cell is considered to be a better cell, the mobile must initiate cell transfer procedures. If the current cell is considered to be better than all neighbor cells, the mobile must stay within the current cell.

This is a simple and logical algorithm to provide local mobility management.

5.12 Channel Hopping

In Section 5.3, we discussed the sharing of the precious radio channel resource among CDPD mobile devices. In this section, we discuss the sharing of the radio resources by the CDPD network and the cellular telephone network.

The CDPD network is designed to operate as an overlay on the existing cellular voice system. Figure 5.29 illustrates the AMPS cellular system as using a frequency based demand assignment reservation scheme. As a call request is made, it is assigned to an available channel. The channel is freed on completion of the call.

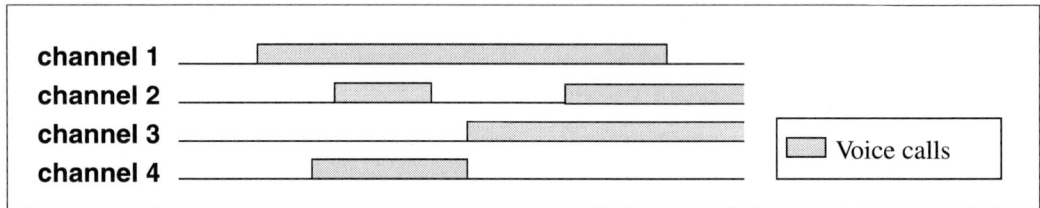

Figure 5.29   Cellular Channel Assignment

In order to ensure that a cellular call request can be serviced, cellular service providers deploy a large number of radio channels at each cell site. Using queueing analysis and typical telephony traffic models, cellular carriers attempt to engineer the radio channel layout to achieve a low *blocking factor*. The blocking factor is the probability that no channels are available to service a new call request. Using the typical target value of 2 percent blocking,[28] theory shows that there would be significant excess channel capacity even during the typical busy hour.

The CDPD system design exploits this characteristic and attempts to make use of this excess capacity. *Channel Hopping* is the concept of using the unused radio resource between voice calls. In order to eliminate the need to alter the voice system's operation, the data channel is managed by moving or hopping among the unused cellular channels. Figure 5.30 illustrates this operation. In effect, this is an attempt to "create" an RF data channel out of otherwise unused and unusable radio resource.

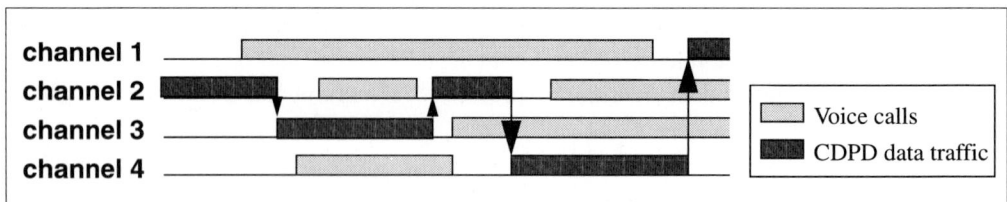

Figure 5.30   Channel Hopping example

---

28. Given the explosive growth of cellular subscribership, it is not always possible to maintain such a low blocking factor. Cellular carriers are continually adding infrastructure, dividing cells, and other technologies to keep up with the demand.

The CDPD system was designed as a transparent overlay on the cellular telephone network. As such, the CDPD system must not rely on the cooperative programming of the voice equipment. In other words, it must not require interaction with the cellular telephone infrastructure equipment to determine which radio channels are appropriate for use. The CDPD infrastructure equipment must devise methods to create the data channel.

The basic approach involves the MDBS to move the data traffic to different channels over time in order to avoid impacting voice traffic. This could be achieved through the MDBS "learning" the channel assignment algorithm of the cellular system and continually moving to the channel least likely to be assigned next. This is known as a *planned channel hop*. Unfortunately, this involves much intelligence, since different cellular manufacturers use vastly different algorithms for selecting the next (voice) channel assignment. Futhermore, manufacturers may evolve their channel assignment algorithms and thus require even more intelligent[29] MDBSs to evolve along with them.

The unlikelihood of creating the perfect planned hop algorithm means there will be instances where a voice call is assigned to a channel already occupied by CDPD data traffic. The CDPD specification addressed this problem by requiring that MDBSs use a device to sense the initiation of a voice call. This device, called the *Sniffer,*[30] continually monitors the RF channel for non-CDPD transmissions. When it detects a non-CDPD transmission, it immediately[31] terminates the CDPD transmission and moves the CDPD traffic onto a different unoccupied channel. This is an *unplanned hop*.

The two channel hopping mechanisms are not without problems. The inefficiencies introduced by a need to change frequencies and cause all the mobile devices to reacquire the new channel is obvious. Unfortunately, there are other effects.

First, the CDPD forward channel is a continuously transmitting channel. As such, it adds energy to the RF environment. Some of the cellular telephone infrastructure equipment continually monitors the RF energy of the available channels. If it senses significant energy on any of its allocated channels for a set minimum period of time, it declares that channel as noisy and prevents if from being used for voice calls.[32] To ensure that the CDPD traffic channel doesn't cause this type of "channel sealing," the CDPD channel must hop very frequently, sometimes often enough to seriously impact the efficiency of the channel.

Second, the channel hopping concept was created with the promise of creating RF spectrum. However, some researchers are skeptical about this claim. They have argued that in many cellular systems today, the limiting factor is interference. In their claims, the cellular system's capacity will be reduced by the addition of RF energy into the system, regardless of whether it is stealing time

---

29. AI experts within the cellular community started salivating.
30. What a name!
31. Within 40 milliseconds.
32. Instead of a sniffer, the MDBS is also a stinker.

between calls or not. In their presentations, they claim that a hopping channel will cause the same capacity reduction impact as dedicating a single channel for use by CDPD.

Finally, it should be noted that the ability to operate in a "hopping mode" relies on the assumption of low voice channel blocking rates. With the rapid growth of cellular adoption in the early 1990s, this assumed condition is often not met, especially in environments that are attractive to cellular voice usage, such as busy highways and airports. When the voice channel blocking rates rise significantly above about 5 percent or so, the hopping algorithms are unable to find a vacant channel to run on and the CDPD channel goes into a temporarily quiescent state. When this occurs, mobiles are forced to either find another channel or drop their virtual connection (and any running applications).

The specification team felt that these considerations placed important questions on the validity of the channel hopping approach. However, the field trial did provide some level of proof that the concept is usable. Furthermore, it was an important mechanism that was conceptually well accepted by the cellular carriers in terms of limiting the impact on their voice operations.

As of this writing, some CDPD service providers have trial channel hopping sites. These have operated well in periods of light voice traffic. However, current usage has been low and the true effectiveness of channel hopping will not be tested until CDPD traffic increases. It is worthwhile to note that many of the CDPD service providers have decided to operate with dedicated CDPD channels.

5.13 Circuit-Switched Cellular Digital Packet Data

The astute reader may object to the title of this section. It seems inappropriate to fashion a title that contains circuit switch concepts with a packet data network! Furthermore, what is this topic doing in a section of network access? This strange marriage of the two technologies is discussed in this section.

In 1995, a few members of the CDPD Forum saw an opportunity to add to the CDPD System Specification through the definition of a new complementary service. The thought was that if CDPD services could be available through the existing cellular voice telephone connections, the requirement for nationwide coverage would be instantly realized.

With the goal of developing a complementary standard to allow mobile devices to access the CDPD network through cellular voice telephone circuit switched connections, the group examined the CDPD system architecture. It became quickly obvious that the layered communications architecture has provided a great flexibility to accomplish this.[33]

---

33. We have often heard that a layered communications architecture design is important. However, the development of CS CDPD is concrete proof that such design techniques are valid and useful.

The development team examined the CDPD system architecture on a layer by layer basis. The resultant architecture, shown in Figure 5.31, is based on the following considerations.

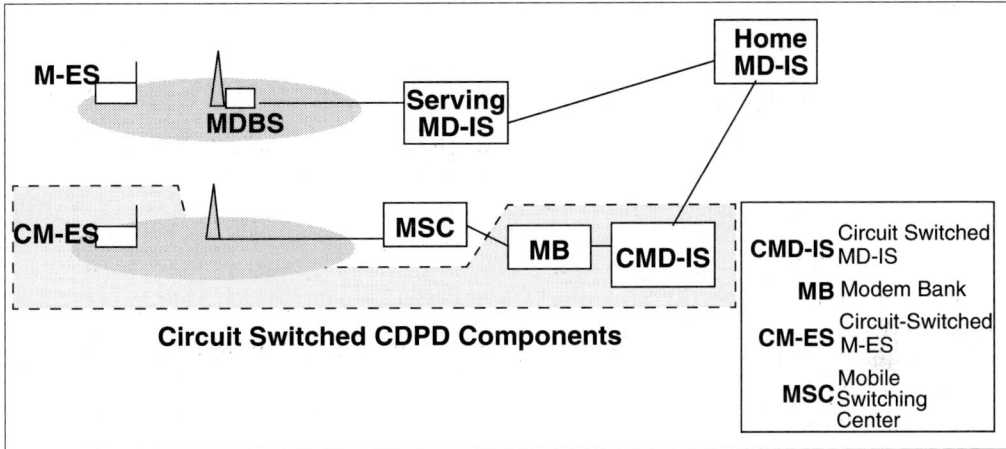

Figure 5.31   Circuit Switched CDPD Components

The physical layer was first examined. There really wasn't much to decide here. Since the intent is to make use of the cellular telephone voice channel, the GMSK modulation scheme cannot be used without changes. Furthermore, since there are already cellular modem devices available, with mass manufactured chip sets, it makes much more sense to rely on that technology. All through the design of CDPD, the philosophy has been to define new technology only when necessary. The development team wisely chose to use the developments of the cellular telephone modem industry.

The data link layer in CDPD is divided into two sub-layers, the Medium Access Control sub-layer and the Logical Link Control sub-layer. In the Circuit Switch CDPD system, the use of individual circuits for each mobile means that there is no sharing of the RF channel in use. As such, there is no need for a Medium Access Control function.[34]

The Logical Link Control function is responsible for establishment and management of a point-to-point connection between the CS CDPD mobile device and the CS CDPD network. The basic requirements of this layer include:

- Reliable delivery of data frames
- Sequenced delivery of data frames
- Link establishment and disconnection

---

34. To be exact, the system makes use of the cellular telephone system's frequency-based demand assigned multiple access scheme.

Much of these requirements are already satisfied by the typical modern day modem equipment. Current modem technologies typically include end-to-end protocols and procedures to provide error detection and correction, call establishment, and disconnection. However, the development team identified additional control parameters that are necessary for efficient operation within the CDPD network. These additional functions are used to ensure transparent operation to the mobile user and efficient use of the RF channel. The requirements were extensive enough to require the establishment of the *Circuit Switch CDPD Control Protocol* (*CSCCP*[35]) to be used on top of widely available reliable modem protocols. The CSCCP is discussed in greater detail in the next section.

Above the data link layer, there is the Network Layer. The lower sub-layer of the Network Layer is the *Subnetwork Dependent Convergence Function* (*SNDCF*). The SNDCF is specifically defined to address mismatch in service requirements of the Network Layer and service characteristics of the Data Link Layer. In the early stages of CS CDPD system design, there were considerations to alter the CDPD SNDCP. However, as the system design progressed, it became obvious that the SNDCP need not be modified. Some minor adjustments in terms of maximum frame size may have provided some efficiency gains, but general consensus was reached that such gains were small and may make implementation of dual mode devices more complex. SNDCP is not changed.

Since the SNDCP is not changed, protocols at the Network Layer and above are also unchanged. This ensures transparency of application operation between CDPD and CS CDPD.[36]

5.13.1 Circuit Switch CDPD Control Protocol

The purpose of the Circuit Switch CDPD Control Protocol is to provide the services necessary to maintain efficient CDPD mobility management function on circuit switched data modem technology. The goals for this protocol are:

- Use of circuit switched connection
- Efficient use of circuit switched technology
- Continual connection to network
- Efficient circuit switched backbone connections
- Robust connection

To address these design goals, the specification team developed the following CS CDPD messages:

- Connection Request
- Connection Response

---

35. It is usually of concern when we have to resort to acronyms of acronyms!
36. Isn't layering wonderful!

- Reconnection Request
- Reconnection Response
- SNDCP Data Packet
- SNDCP Unitdata Packet
- Link Reset
- Link Reset Acknowledge

The use of these message to achieve the design goals may best be illustrated through examples of connection events. The events presented include the following:

- Initial connection (by the mobile)
- CS CDPD M-ES initiated reconnection
- CS CDPD MD-IS initiated reconnection
- Redirection
- Redirection with override
- Link Reset

5.13.1.1 Initial Connection

The CS CDPD connection begins with the connection request by the mobile device. Within the CS CDPD specifications, the mobile device is called the CS CDPD Mobile End System or CM-ES. Just as in CDPD, the CM-ES must initiate the connection.

The CM-ES starts by selecting a dial code from the list programmed into the device by the service provider. Using an appropriate dial code, the CM-ES establishes a circuit switched data connection. The peer end point of this circuit is the CS CDPD MD-IS or CMD-IS. The CM-ES then sends a Connection Request message carrying the following parameters:

- CM-ES Equipment Identifier
- V.42*bis* data compression parameters
- Duration time
- Cellular System Identifier (AMPS System ID)
- Dial code

The CMD-IS responds with a Connection Response message containing the following parameters:

- CMD-IS Identifier
- Service Provider Network Identifier (SPNI)

• Wide Area Service Identifier (WASI)

• V.42bis compression parameter response

• Result code

This exchange of messages (see Figure 5.32) allows the CM-ES and the CMD-IS to identify themselves to each other and establish compression negotiation parameters. In addition, the CM-ES informs the CMD-IS of the dial code to use in order to contact the CM-ES.

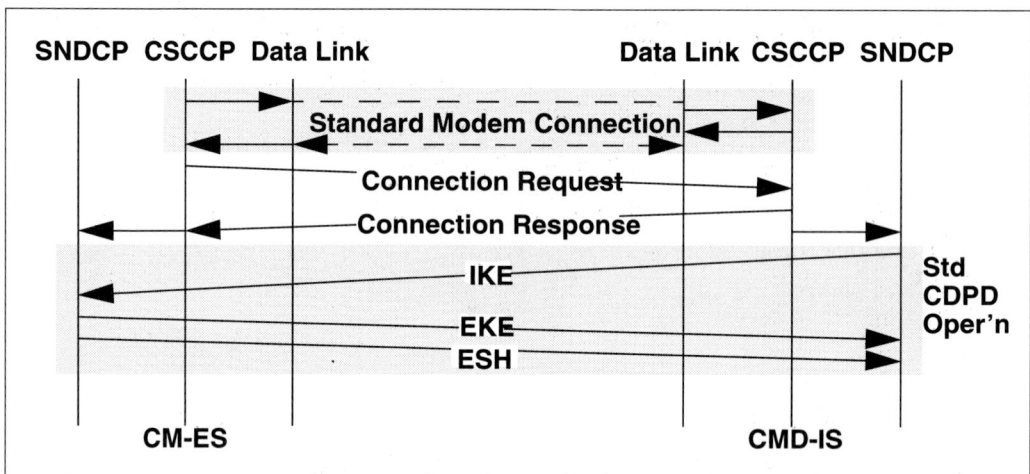

Figure 5.32   CM-ES Initial Connection

Once a successful connection has been established, the CMD-IS initiates the exchange of encryption keys. From this point forward the communications process proceeds as in standard CDPD.

This interchange of messages achieves the first goal of establishing a circuit switched connection.

5.13.1.2 CM-ES Initiated Reconnection

After the connection has been established, data transfer between the CM-ES and the network proceeds. For most connections, there are periods of inactivity. On a circuit switched connection, these periods are wasteful, since the link cannot be shared by other devices. To account for this data traffic characteristic, the CM-ES disconnects after a predetermined idle period and suspends the data link connection.

When the CM-ES has data to send after having disconnected, it must initiate reconnection procedures. This is accomplished by the CM-ES selecting an appropriate dial conde and establishing a circuit connection. However, unlike the initial connection, the CM-ES sends a Reconnection

Request message (see Figure 5.33) which contains only the CM-ES Equipment Identifier (EID). This EID allows the CMD-IS to quickly ascertain this to be a reconnection by a previously connected device. Therefore, there is no need to repeat the exchange of data compression parameters and AMPS system ID. The CMD-IS responds with a Reconnection Response carrying the CMD-IS ID. This allows the CM-ES to quickly confirm that it has reconnected to the same CMD-IS.

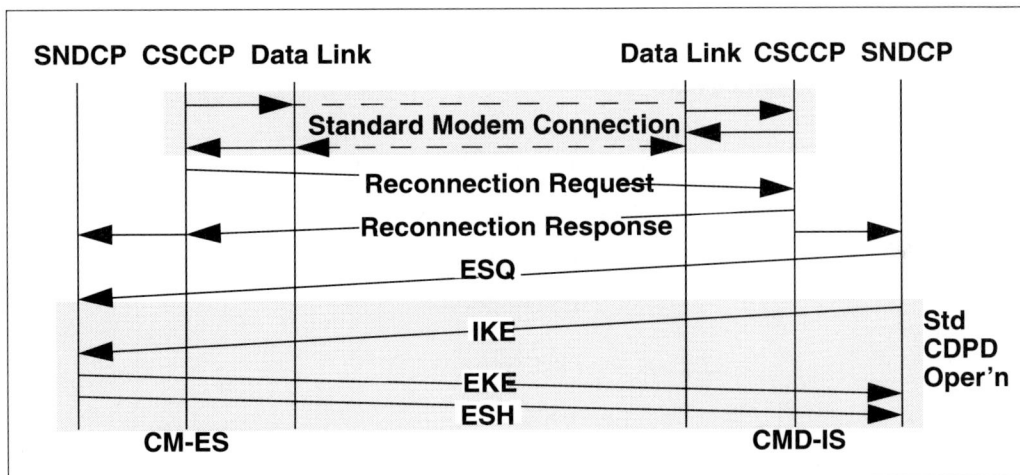

Figure 5.33   CM-ES Initiated Reconnection

Once the reconnection message exchange has been successful, the two peer entities resume the suspended data link connection.

The only other deviation from the CDPD system is the use of an End System Query message to force the exchange of registration data and authentication credentials. This is an added precaution to avoid fraudulent access.

This procedure achieves the second goal of efficient use of the circuit switch technology. There is no need to keep the circuit switched connection active when there is no data to transfer.

5.13.1.3 CMD-IS Initiated Reconnection

After the data link is disconnected due to an extended idle period, it is possible that the network needs to deliver data to the CM-ES. In the usual circuit switch connection scenario, this is not possible. The mobile user must periodically "check-in" for data. However, the CS CDPD designers wanted to offer connection service similar to CDPD. In which case, the network must be able to initiate reconnection to the CM-ES.

One of the optional parameters provided by the CM-ES during initial connection is a dial code. This dial code is to be used when the network wishes to initiate reconnection. Therefore, when the CMD-IS has data to send to the CM-ES, it establishes a circuit switch connection using the earlier supplied dial code. Once connected, the CMD-IS sends a Reconnection Request message (see Figure 5.34) containing the CMD-IS ID. If the CM-ES finds the CMD-IS ID acceptable, it responds with a Reconnection Response containing the CM-ES ID. Once again, the two peer entities resume the suspended data link connection. The End System Query is sent by the CMD-IS to cause registration and authentication.

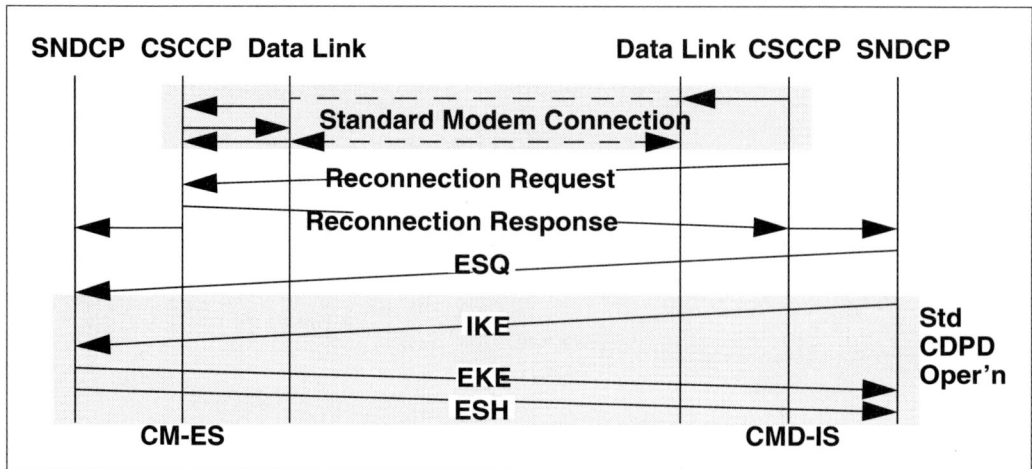

Figure 5.34   CMD-IS Initiated Reconnection

The procedure achieves the third goal of allowing the CM-ES to be logically continually connected to the network without the need to maintain the circuit switch link.

5.13.1.4 Redirection

Due to the mobile nature inherent in CDPD devices, it is possible that a CM-ES relocates to an area where the dial code normally used is not the optimal path through the infrastructure. This can result if the service provider has a local point of presence through a local modem bank (see Figure 5.35), or that the service provider has an alternate CMD-IS at the local system (see Figure 5.36).

In these cases, it may be more efficient for the mobile to use the different set of dial codes to access the network. This is provided for in the CSCCP through the Redirect result code.

The procedure occurs on the initial connection request. The CM-ES proceeds with an initial connection request but the CMD-IS responds with a Connection Response message containing the optional parameter to indicate a Redirect directive. Along with that directive, a list of alternate dial codes is provided.

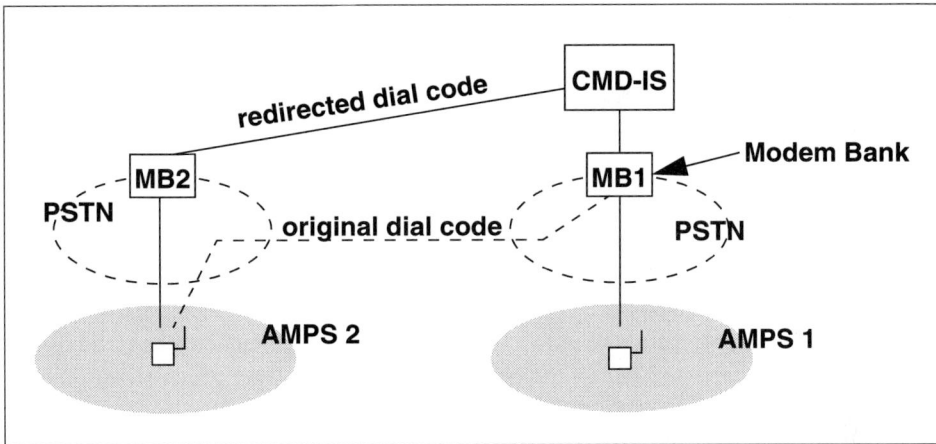

Figure 5.35   Redirect to Local Modem Bank

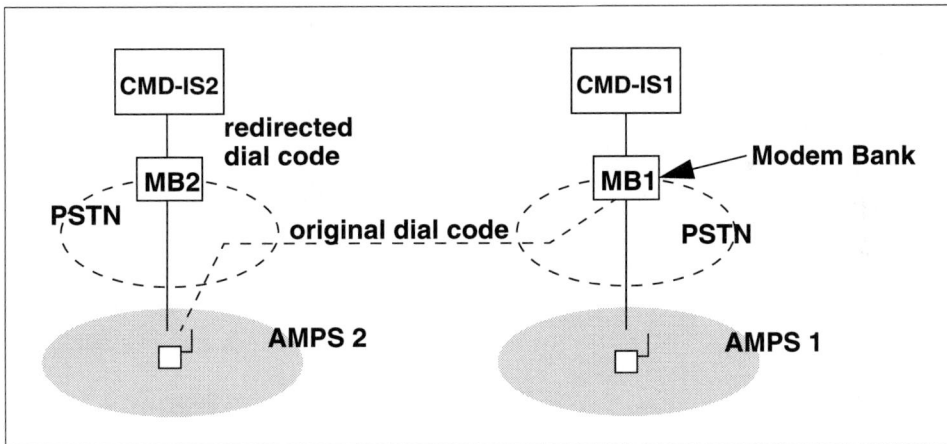

Figure 5.36   Redirect to Local CMD-IS

The CM-ES, barring other problems, disconnects from the CMD-IS and attempts to re-initiate connection requests with one of the new dial codes. If, for some reason, the new dial codes are not operational, the CM-ES may retry the connection with the original dial code and issue a Redirect Override indicator. If the CMD-IS cannot accept any connection requests, it may issue a Forced Redirection command.

This procedure allows the service provider to instruct the mobile device to access the network at the most efficient point of presence.

5.13.1.5 Robust Connections

Even though the CS CDPD system has been built on using reliable data transfer mechanisms available from current modem technologies, errors may rise from various internal connection points. To address these errors, the CS CDPD specification included an error recovery mechanism.

The mechanism is achieved in two steps. First, the data transferred is contained in the CSCCP SNDCP Data Packets. These messages contain both a simple checksum and a sequence number. The receiver of each message verifies the checksum. If a checksum failure is detected, the link is reset by the receiver issuing a Link Reset message (see Figure 5.37). This Link Reset message contains the sequence number of the failed packet. The peer entity then responds with a Link Reset Acknowledge packet containing its next expected sequence number. Once the Link Reset message and the Link Reset Acknowledge messages are exchanged, the two entities reset their sequence numbers to 0 and restart the exchange of SNDCP Data packets from the point of the failure.

This procedure corrects the small residual error probability of the link.

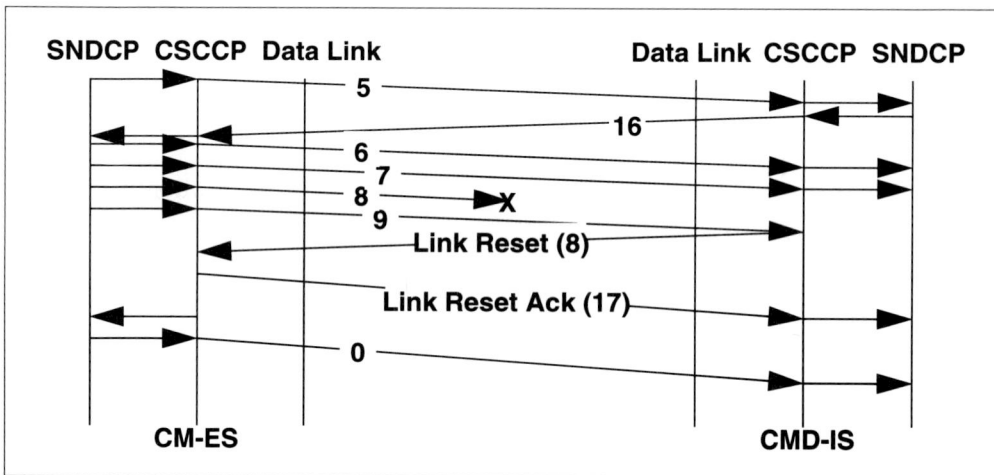

Figure 5.37   CSCCP Link Reset Procedure

5.14 Summary

This chapter has presented the CDPD network access mechanism. The Medium Access Control and Logical Link Control protocols and procedures were described, as was the Subnetwork Dependent Convergence function and Radio Resource Management in CDPD systems. A brief discussion of the Circuit Switched CDPD system concept and protocols was also presented as an important extension to the packet-switched native mode of operation.

Our goal in this discussion was to provide the reader with some insight into how the CDPD devices (M-ES and CM-ES) access the network and maintain a connection. Now that we have presented the basic data carriage capabilities of CDPD, we shall move on to CDPD support services, beginning with security features.

6 *Mobile Data Network Security*

Even a paranoid can have enemies.
—Henry Kissinger, *Time*, January 24, 1977

In this chapter we first provide the necessary background on security, oriented towards internetwork mobility. The security services provided by CDPD are discussed next. Although we begin our discussion with a general description of security concepts and issues, it is not our intention to provide a complete description of security technology. Rather, our objective in this chapter is to provide background information about security issues in the mobile WAN in general and CDPD in particular.

Security is a highly specialized field with its own well defined terminology, structure, and discipline. Much of the background information presented in this section is based on Security Architecture of OSI Reference Model and Authentication Framework of X.509. For readers interested in more formal and detailed discussions of security technology, excellent presentations can be found in works such as [KAUF95].

We close this chapter with a discussion of CDPD's security considerations.

6.1 Introduction

No discussion of wide area networks would be complete without including security issues. It seems as if every publication of industry trade magazine contains one or more articles on recent security breaks. As long as bad guys want to break into systems for fun and profit, security is likely to remain an important system architectural consideration.

What is security? [ISO7498-2] defines *security* to be *the minimization of vulnerabilities of assets and resources*, such as information data software. Information, in this definition, includes data supporting the security measures themselves, such as passwords and encryption keys. A security vulnerability is any weakness that could be exploited to violate a system or the information it contains.

The possibility of such an exploitation is called a *threat*. This potential violation of security—resulting in destruction, theft or loss, disclosure of information, or interruption of services—can be either intentional or accidental. Accidental threats can be caused by things like software bugs or system malfunctions.

Threats can be further categorized as being either passive or active. A *passive* threat would be something like wiretapping, in which the system operations and services provided to users remain unaffected. However, there are usually ramifications to this activity that are experienced at a later time, usually away from the threatened system.

Active threats are things like malicious changes to a system's routing tables or user data. Typically, the consequences of an active threat are more directly associated with the threatened system.

An intentional threat—either active or passive—which is realized is referred to as an *attack*. An attack may result in service disruption, modification of messages or data, or unauthorized access and masquerade.

Wide area networks are subject to more security threats because of their exposure relative to more contained systems. If these WANs are public networks, available to a wide unrestricted user base, their exposure is increased due to key management and authentication issues. Mobility adds a further dimension of security risks because of the lack of physical security inherent to these systems.

6.2 Security Policy

Attentive readers will note that the definition of security calls for minimization rather than elimination of system vulnerabilities. This is because perfect technical security, like perfect physical security, is simply not possible.

Every system has security vulnerabilities—ways in which system security can be compromised. Eliminating all such security risks is generally quite difficult and expensive. Trying to do so is tantamount to overkill—the expense of protecting a system exceeds the value of what is being protected.

A far more reasonable security objective is to *make the cost of an attack high enough to discourage such an attack*. Raise the bar high enough that making an attack is not worth the price. In this sense, the decision to secure (attack) or not secure (attack) a system is reduced to a cost-benefit analysis by (both) the system owner (and the cracker).[1]

From a cracker's perspective, the cost-benefit analysis is essentially the inverse of that for the system owner/operator. We prefer to adopt the analysis of the system operator:

1. Identify the vulnerabilities of the system.
2. Analyze the likelihood of threats carried out exploiting these vulnerabilities.

---

1. We share the sentiment expressed in [KAUF95] that "hacker" should be reserved for master programmers who are honest. "Cracker" is a derivative from "safe cracking," romanticized in print and reel, which is unfortunate.

3. Assess the consequences of the realization of each potential threat.
4. Estimate the cost of each such attack.
5. Estimate the cost of potential countermeasures designed to thwart each such attack.
6. Select those countermeasures that can be justified by a cost-benefit analysis. The collection of such countermeasures collectively constitutes the security system.

Thus, determining a *security policy* for a system consists of identifying the types of potential threats, the mechanisms for confronting these threats, and the costs associated with such mechanisms. A security policy defines those mechanisms whose implementation singly, or in combination, provides adequate security at a reasonable cost. Absolute security is not the goal—the cost of securing a system is as important as the risk of not securing it in a security policy.

A security policy is not static. Technology advances, and with it, so do the bad guys. What was once secure will not be secure tomorrow—increases in computing speed and cryptanalysis algorithms allow crackers to steadily advance their ability to break into systems. Security mechanisms must similarly advance to stay at least one step ahead. System security is a moving target.

6.3 Security Threats

In any computing or communication system, there are entities—people, applications, programs, etc.—which are *authorized* to use the system. Authorization is specific to both the entity and the actions of that entity such as accessing data. I can withdraw money from my bank account at an ATM,[2] but I am not authorized to withdraw from someone else's account.

Attacks on a system can be categorized as insider or outsider attacks. *Insider attacks* involve legitimate users of the system behaving in an unintended or unauthorized manner. When I attempt to withdraw funds from someone else's account at the ATM, I am conducting an insider attack on the system. Most serious security threats seem to be from insiders, which is reminiscent of the old Pogo comic strip conclusion "We have met the enemy and it is us!"

Outsider attacks are conducted by non-legitimate users of the system. If I try to access funds at another bank (at which I have no account) at the ATM, I am likely conducting an outsider attack.

---

2. Automated teller machine, not a much-hyped link layer protocol.

The most common types of attacks are summarized as follows:

1. *Masquerade:* This is when an entity pretends to be a different entity. For instance, authentication sequences can be captured and replayed after a valid authentication sequence has taken place. In this way, the capturing entity assumes the identity of the entity whose authentication was compromised. A masquerade is thus usually used with some other form of active attack.

2. *Replay:* This occurs when a message, or part of a message, is repeated to produce an unauthorized effect. For example, a valid message containing authentication sequences can be replayed by another entity in order to authenticate itself (as something that it is not).

3. *Modification of Messages:* This occurs when the content of a data transmission is altered without detection and results in an unauthorized effect, as when, for example, a message "Allow Karen Jones to read confidential file 'accounts' "is changed to "Allow Tim Smith to read confidential file 'accounts'."

4. *Denial of Service:* This occurs when an entity fails to perform its proper function or acts in a way that prevents other entities from performing their proper functions. Examples are general, targeted suppression of messages and/or traffic, or generation of extra traffic or messages intended to disrupt the operation of the network.

5. *Trapdoor:* When an entity of a system is altered to allow an attacker to produce an unauthorized effect on command or at a predetermined event or sequence of events, the result is called a trapdoor. An example is modification of the password validation process so that, in addition to its normal effect, it also validates an attacker's password.

6. *Trojan Horse:* When introduced to a system, a Trojan Horse has an unauthorized function in addition to its authorized function. A relay that also copies messages to an unauthorized channel is a Trojan Horse.

6.4 Security Services and Mechanisms

Having identified the relevant security threats to a system, the system operator can apply various security services and mechanisms to confront these threats and implement a desired security policy. In this section we provide a general description of such services and techniques. The science behind these methods is researched and developed as part of the broad discipline of *Cryptography.* Cryptography embodies the mathematical principles, means, and methods for the transformation of data in order to hide its information content, prevent its undetected modification, and/or prevent its unauthorized use. Cryptographic functions may be used as part of encipherment, decipherment, data integrity, authentication exchanges, password storage and checking, etc. to help achieve confidentiality, integrity, and/or authentication.

The following subsections summarize some key security services and mechanisms.

6.4.1 Encipherment and Data Confidentiality

Encipherment is a security mechanism that involves the transformation of data into some unreadable form. Its purpose is to ensure privacy by keeping the information hidden from anyone for whom it is not intended, even those who can see enciphered data. Decipherment is the reverse of encipherment. That is, it is the transformation of encrypted data back into some intelligible form. Encipherment is performed on *cleartext* (intelligible data) to produce *ciphertext* (encrypted data whose semantic content is not available). The result of decipherment is either cleartext, or ciphertext under some cover.

Encipherment can provide confidentiality of either data or traffic flow information and can play a part in, or complement, other security mechanisms.

Encipherment and Decipherment require the use of some secret information, usually referred to as a *key*, which directs specific transformations. This is one of two cryptovariables used: The other is the *initialization variable*, which is sometimes required to preserve the apparent randomness of ciphertext.

Encipherment techniques can be *symmetric* or secret key, where knowledge of the encipherment key implies knowledge of the private decipherment key and vice versa, or *asymmetric*. In asymmetric algorithms, generally one key is called *public* (because it is publicly available), while the other is called *private* (because it is kept secret). Once a private key has been compromised, the system (or at least the use of that private key) is no longer secure. Both encipherment techniques are used to provide the data confidentiality service.

Modern cryptographic systems also provides mechanisms for authentication, for instance, through digital signatures that bind a document to the possessor of a specific key or digital timestamps that bind a document to its creation at a given time. In general the existence of an encipherment mechanism implies the use of a key management mechanism.

6.4.1.1 Public Key Cryptography

Figure 6.1 illustrates a simple public key cryptographic system that provides data confidentiality. When Alice wishes to send a secret message to Bob, she looks up Bob's public key in a directory, uses it to encrypt the message, and sends it off. Bob then uses his private key to decrypt the message and read it. No one listening in can decrypt the message. Anyone can send Bob an encrypted message but only Bob can read it. Clearly, one requirement is that no one can figure out the private key from the corresponding public key.

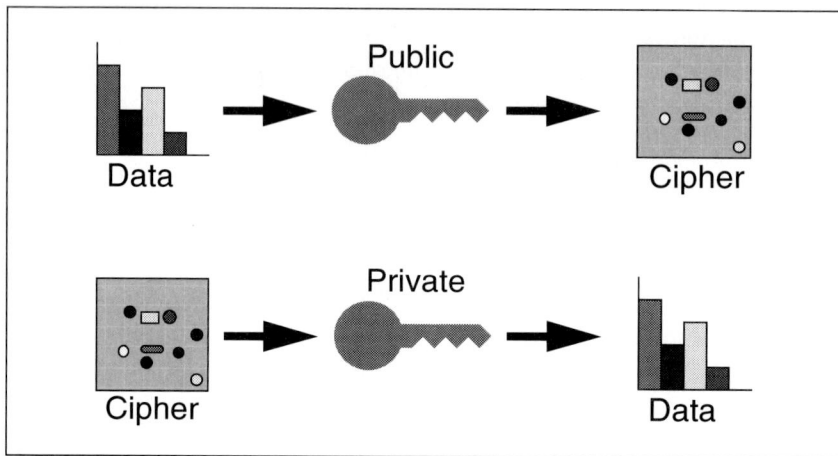

Figure 6.1   A Public Key Cryptographic System (PKCS)

6.4.2 Digital Signatures

Digital signature is the process of binding some information (e.g., a document) to its originator (e.g., the signer).

The essential characteristic of a digital signature is that the signed data unit cannot be created without using the private key. This means that:

1. The signed data unit cannot be created by any individual except the holder of the private key.
2. The recipient cannot create the signed data unit.
3. The sender cannot deny sending the signed data unit.

Therefore, using only publicly available information—the public key—it is possible to identify the signer of a data unit as the possessor of the private key. It is also possible to prove the identity of the signer of the data unit to a reliable third party in case of later conflict.

Thus, a digital signature attests to the contents of a message, as well as to the identity of the signer. As long as a secure hash function (a function that is easier to compute in one direction than the opposite direction) is used, one cannot take away a person's signature from one document and transpose it on another one, or alter a signed message in any way. The slightest change in a digitally signed document will cause the digital signature verification process to fail. However, if a signature verification fails, it is, in general, difficult to determine whether there was an attempted forgery or simply a transmission error.

In short, a digital signature mechanism involves the two procedures of signing a data unit and verifying the signed data unit. The former process uses information that is private (i.e. unique and confidential) to the signer. The second process uses procedures and information that are publicly available but from which the signer's private information cannot be deduced.

Figure 6.2 illustrates a digital signature mechanism. To sign a message, Alice appends the information she wishes to send to an enciphered summary of the information. The summary is produced by means of a one-way hash function (h), while the enciphering is carried out using Alice's secret key (E). Thus the message sent to Bob is of the form:

$$X\{info\} = info + Xs[h(info)]$$

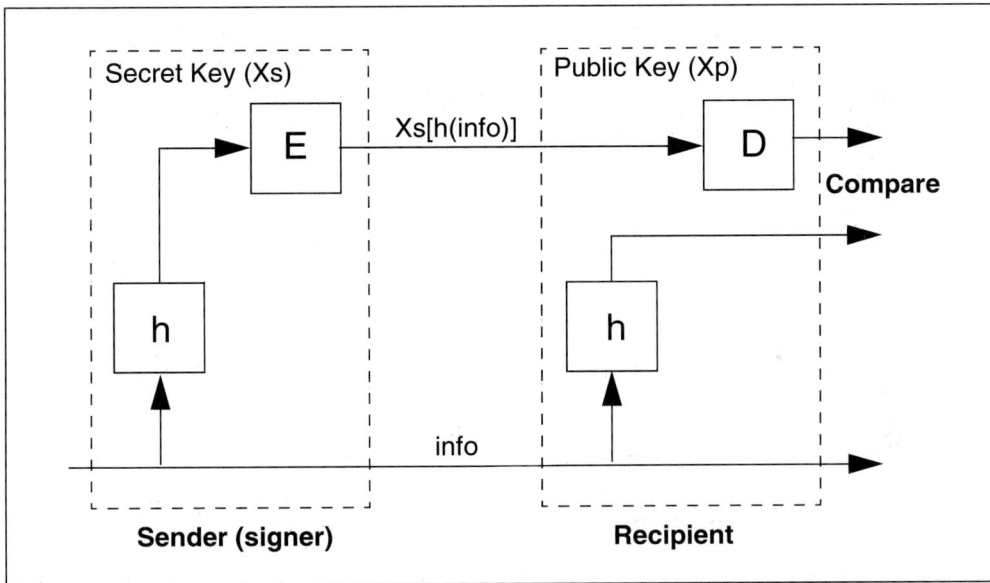

Figure 6.2   A Digital Signature Mechanism

The encipherment, using the secret key, ensures that the signature cannot be forged. The one-way nature of the hash function ensures that false information, generated so as to have the same hash result (and thus signature), cannot be substituted.

In his turn, upon receipt of Alice's message, Bob verifies the signature by applying the one-way hash function to the information and comparing the result with that obtained by deciphering the signature, using the public key of Alice. If these two are the same, it is verified that Alice is the "true" sender of the message. It should be clear and imperative that for the authentication to be performed correctly, both Alice and Bob must be using the same hash function.

6.4.3 Authentication

Authentication is defined by [KAUF95] as "the process of reliably verifying the identity of someone (or something)."

Authentication can be "One-Way" or "Two-Way."[3] Each of these is described below.

- *One-Way Authentication:* Involves a single transfer of information from one user (A) intended for another (B) and establishes the following:
  - the identity of A and that the authentication token was generated by A;
  - the identity of B and that the authentication token was intended to be sent to B; and
  - the integrity and originality (the property of not having been sent two or three times) of the authentication token being transferred.

- *Two-Way Authentication:* Involves, in addition, a reply from B to A and establishes, in addition, the following:
  - that the authentication token generated in the reply was actually generated by B and was intended to be sent to A;
  - the integrity and originality of the authentication token sent in the reply; and
  - (optionally) the mutual secrecy of part of the tokens.

Corroboration of identity is often established by demonstrating the possession of a secret key. Authentication may be accomplished by applying symmetric or asymmetric cryptographic techniques.

When using private keys (symmetric) corroboration of identity is often based on a "shared secret."

When using public keys (asymmetric), authentication is accomplished based on digital signatures and digital timestamps. Since the digital signature binds the possessor of the private key with a document, and the timestamp can be verified to protect against replays, corroboration of identity can be established by combining digital signature and a timestamp.

6.4.4 Traffic Flow Confidentiality

Cryptographic protocols are designed to resist attacks and also, sometimes, traffic analysis. A specific traffic analysis countermeasure, *traffic flow confidentiality*, aims to conceal the presence or absence of data and its characteristics. This is important because knowledge of the activity can be as useful to the bad guys as the content of the activity itself.

---

3. Also called bilateral authentication.

If cyphertext is relayed, the address must be in the clear at the relays and gateways. If the data are enciphered only on each link, and are deciphered (and are thus made vulnerable) in the relay or gateway, the architecture is said to use *link-by-link confidentiality* (or encipherment). If only the address (and similar control data) are in the clear in the relay or gateway, the architecture is said to use *end-to-end data confidentiality* (or encipherment). End-to-end encryption is more desirable from a security point of view, but considerably more complex architecturally.

Furthermore, traffic padding can be used to provide various levels of protection against traffic analysis. This mechanism can be effective only if the traffic is protected by a confidentiality service.

6.4.5 Data Integrity

Data integrity is the property of data that has not been altered or destroyed in an unauthorized manner. It is achieved via a calculated cryptographic *checkvalue*. The checkvalue may be derived in one or more steps and is a mathematical function of the cryptovariables and the data. These checkvalues are associated with the data to be guarded. If the checkvalue is matched by the value calculated by the data recipient, data integrity is assumed.

Two aspects of data integrity are: the integrity of a single data unit or field, and the integrity of a stream of data units or fields. Determining the integrity of a single data unit involves two processes, one at the sender and the other at the receiver. The sender appends to the data unit a quantity that is a function of the data itself. This quantity may be supplementary information such as a block code or a cryptographic check value and may itself be enciphered. The receiver generates a corresponding quantity and compares it with the received quantity to determine whether the data has been modified in transit.

Protecting the integrity of a sequence of data units (against misordering, losing, replaying, and inserting or modifying the data) requires, additionally, some form of explicit ordering such as sequence numbering, time stamping, or cryptographic chaining.

6.4.6 Key Management

Key management encompasses the generation, distribution, and control of cryptographic keys. It is implied by the use of cryptographic algorithms. Important points to be considered are:

1. The use of a lifetime based on time, use, or other criteria, for each key defined, implicitly, or explicitly. The longer a key's lifetime, the greater the probability that the key will be compromised by the bad guys.

2. The proper identification of keys according to their functions so that they are used only for their intended function. The greater the key's exposure (to multiple applications) the greater the probability that the key will be compromised.

3. Physical distribution and archiving of keys. This is both a logistics and security issue, especially in distributed systems such as WANs.

Points to be considered concerning key management for symmetric key algorithms include:

1. The use of a confidentiality service in the key management protocol.
2. The use of a key hierarchy ("flat" hierarchies using only data-enciphering keys, multilayer key hierarchies, etc.)
3. The division of responsibilities so that no one person has a complete copy of an important key.

For asymmetric key management, confidentiality services are used to convey the secret keys. Additionally, an integrity service (or a service with proof of origin) is needed to convey the public keys.

6.4.7 Access Control

Access control mechanisms are used to enforce a policy of limiting access to a resource to only those users who are authorized. These techniques include the use of access control lists or matrices, passwords, capabilities, and labels, the possession of which may be used to indicate access rights.

6.4.8 Network Layer Security Considerations

6.4.8.1 Network Layer Security Protocol (NLSP)

NLSP is an international standard that specifies a protocol to be used by end systems and intermediate systems in order to provide security services in the network layer. It is defined by ISO 11577. Much of the material appearing here is from the American National Standards Institute (ANSI), which is the official U.S. representative to ISO.

NLSP specifies a series of services and functional requirements for implementation. The services, as defined in ISO 7498-2, are:

• peer entity authentication
• data origin authentication
• access control
• connection confidentiality

- connectionless confidentiality
- traffic flow confidentiality
- connection integrity without recovery (including data unit integrity, in which individual SDUs on a connection are integrity protected)
- connectionless integrity

The Procedures of this protocol are defined in terms of:

- requirements on the cryptographic techniques that can be used in an instance on this protocol; and
- requirements on the information carried in the security association used in an instance of communication.

Although the degree of protection afforded by some security mechanisms depends on the use of some specific cryptographic techniques, correct operation of this protocol is not dependent on the choice of any particular encipherment of decipherment algorithm that is left as a local matter for the communicating systems.

Furthermore, neither the choice nor the implementation of a specific security policy are within the scope of this international standard. The choice of a specific security policy, and hence the degree of protection that will be achieved, is left as a local matter among the systems that are using a single instance of secure communications. NLSP does not require that multiple instances of secure communications involving a single open system use the same security protocol.

NLSP supports cryptographic protection either between End Systems (and in this case resembles the *Transport Layer Security Protocol - TLSP*) or between Intermediate Systems that are located at the borders of security domains. This latter aspect makes NLSP quite appealing to those who would like to provide security services; not by securing each and every system in a domain, but by forcing all external communications to transit through a small set of secure systems (assuming that communications within the domain need no security services). In this sense, one can see NLSP as supporting (at the domain level) administrative policies (mandatory security), while TLSP is more tuned towards discretionary communication policies.

6.5 CDPD Security

The CDPD network is a public commercial wide area mobile data communications network. As such, services must be available, which provide security for both the subscriber and the network service provider. In many respects, CDPD represents a worst case scenario of security challenges, which must be met for commercial viability.

6.5.1 CDPD Security Design Goals and Tradeoffs

Both the CDPD service provider and the subscriber have a stake in the security of the system. For the CDPD service provider, it is imperative that fraudulent use of the network be minimized. This is addressed through *Mobile End System (M-ES)* authentication services.

For the CDPD subscriber, it is important that communications be protected from casual eavesdropping. This threat is particularly bothersome on the airlink because of lack of physical security. In the CDPD network, data link confidentiality is provided through encryption of subscriber data over the airlink.

6.5.1.1 Security Functions Supported

The security services provided across the CDPD airlink support the following security functions for all subscribers:

- Data Link Confidentiality

  All information contained in the information fields of SN-DATA PDUs,[4] including the network entity identifiers[5] or NEIs of M-ESs, is transmitted across the airlink in an encrypted form, once secret keys have been determined.

- M-ES Authentication

  Each NEI used by the M-ES is separately authenticated by the CDPD network to ensure that only the authorized possessor of the NEI is using the NEI.

- Key Management

  All secret keys required to operate the encryption algorithms supporting the first two functions are managed by the CDPD network.

- Upgradeability

  The CDPD network can support upgrade or replacement of the algorithms used to support the first three functions.

- Access Control

  The CDPD network can support restrictions on access by or to different NEIs, such as restrictions by location, screening lists, and so on. Access control is not specifically an airlink function and is under control of the home MD-IS for an NEI.

---

4. Subnetwork data protocol data units
5. NEIs are most commonly IP addresses.

6.5.1.2 Security Functions Not Supported

The security services across the CDPD airlink do not support any other security functions, including the following:

- Bilateral Authentication

  The security services do not validate the CDPD network to the M-ES across the airlink. The security services do not support bilateral authentication of the NEIs of the source and destination network entities.

- End-to-End Data Confidentiality

  The security services do not provide end-to-end data confidentiality. They only provide data confidentiality over the airlink.

- Data Integrity

  The security services do not provide protection against modification of encrypted data transmitted across the airlink.

- Non-repudiation

  The security services do not provide protection against repudiation of commitments entered into by a user of the security services.

- Traffic Flow Confidentiality

  The security services do not provide protection against monitoring of the volume of data exchanged by users of the security services.

Users of the airlink security services who require any of these other security services must provide them by other means.

6.5.2 CDPD Authentication

Since the CDPD system is public data network, there is always concern regarding network security. The greatest concern is in the area of network integrity from fraudulent users. The NEI authentication mechanism provides a method of conducting a validity check during the registration process.

In CDPD, authentication procedures are defined to validate the NEI claimed by each M-ES at registration time. These procedures are modelled as being performed by a *Mobile Network Registration Protocol* (*MNRP*) *Management Entity* (*MME*). An MME is resident in each M-ES and also in the MD-IS.

In the event that an M-ES is implemented with separable *Subscriber Identity Modules* (*SIMs*), the authentication functionality in the M-ES is supported in the SIM. We stress that it is the network layer entity (NEI) which is authenticated, not the physical device (EID)!

6.5.2.1 Authentication Process

The authentication procedure is an integral part of the NEI registration process. The process is started immediately after link encryption is established but prior to transfer of user data. This ensures that the authentication parameters are protected from casual eavesdropping and that user data is exchanged with the bona fide user.

In the authentication process, each M–ES maintains two variables for each NEI that may be authenticated. These are the *Authentication Sequence Number (ASN)* and the *Authentication Random Number (ARN)*. The triplet formed by the NEI, the ASN, and the ARN forms the *authentication credentials* for the NEI.

Whenever an M-ES registers an NEI on the CDPD network, it transmits the NEI's current credentials over the encrypted link. On receipt of the M-ES's credentials, the serving MD-IS forwards them to the home MD-IS using the Mobile Network Location Protocol. The home MD-IS compares these credentials with the expected values for this NEI.

If the credentials are verified, the home MD-IS informs the serving MD-IS of the authentication success. In addition, the home MD-IS may optionally generate a new ARN, increment the ASN, and return the new credentials to the M-ES via the serving MD-IS.

If the credentials received from the M-ES are found to be invalid, the home MD-IS informs the serving MD-IS of the authentication failure. In this instance, the serving MD-IS refuses the registration attempt by the M-ES, denying service to the M-ES.

This may be the result of a mobile device malfunction, network infrastructure malfunction, or a fraudulent unit attempting to access the network. The network service provider must then deal with the discrepancy. If the network service provider is aware of a system failure that may have caused the mismatch of credentials, it may decide to allow the service to the mobile despite the lack of ARN validation. This would be a choice to ensure that a valid customer does not perceive a disruption in the service.

Aside from the authentication exchanges that result from M-ES registration attempts, authentication exchanges may be initiated by the serving MD-IS at any time. This mechanism allows the network to periodically verify the credentials of any M-ES, through a challenge-response process.

In the event that the authentication exchange is not completed, the M-ES can use the immediately preceding credentials to register an NEI. This fallback capability is important in a mobile environment.

6.5.2.2 Authentication Philosophy

The basic concept of CDPD's authentication mechanism relies on the network verifying the mobile unit's knowledge of a shared "truth." This truth, or authentication credentials, is generated by the network and is assigned to a mobile network address. At any time, if the network wants to validate the mobile unit, it challenges the mobile device to divulge its assigned authentication credentials. Only mobile devices that respond with the correct authentication credentials are considered valid.

M-ES authentication is also based on the notion of establishing a shared historical record of all interactions between the M-ES and the network. This use of a historical concordance protects against theft of permanent authentication parameters, which would be more difficult to detect. It also provides a fallback capability whenever the authentication process is interrupted, resulting in an inconsistency in authentication parameters.

The specification team recognized that such authentication credentials have a finite lifetime. If a mobile unit's authentication credentials were static over time, the secret could be copied and used to mimic the valid unit. To prevent this, the CDPD specification team defined the ability for the CDPD network to, either periodically or at the service provider's discretion, update a mobile unit's authentication credentials. In this way, any particular authentication credential only has value during the period of time deemed useful by the network operator.

However, the CDPD specification team recognized the possibility of legitimate instances causing the authentication data to be out of synchronization. For example, if the network sent an ARN update to the mobile device just as the subscriber turned off the power to the unit, there is a possibility that the network believes the new ARN is in effect, while the mobile unit is still operating on an older one. When the user turns on the mobile unit at a later time, the M-ES will supply an out-of-date ARN.

To handle such circumstances, CDPD specifies that both the mobile unit and the network maintain the two most recent values for the ARN. In addition, a binary indicator (the ASN) is used to identify whether the "odd" or the "even" ARN is being supplied. The addition of this short history allows the system to survive situations such as this.

6.5.2.3 Authentication Opportunities

There are several instances where normal network activity can generate opportunities for updating of the authentication credentials. First and most common, every time a mobile device initiates a new registration attempt, the home MD-IS may optionally include new authentication credentials in the *Redirect Confirm* (*RDC*) message returned to the serving MD-IS. In turn, the serving MD-IS relays the new authentication credentials to the M-ES through the *MD-IS Confirm* (*ISC*) message. This is depicted in Figure 6.3.

If the mobile device has not relocated to a new routing area for an extended period of time, the configuration timer will trigger a forced re-registration to allow the M-ES to inform the network of its continuing connected status. During these forced re-registration exchanges, the home MD-IS has yet another opportunity to update the M-ES with new authentication credentials.

If the home MD-IS wishes to update the M-ES with new authentication credentials prior to expiration of the configuration timer and the M-ES has not relocated to a new routing domain, the home MD-IS needs a mechanism to command the M-ES to activate the re-registration procedure. This is accomplished with the *Redirect Query* (*RDQ*) and the *End System Query* (*ESQ*) messages.

The RDQ message is sent by the home MD-IS to the appropriate serving MD-IS, which in turn sends a ESQ message to the specific M-ES.[6] The receipt of this message instructs the M-ES to initiate a registration procedure for the NEI identified. During this registration procedure, the home MD-IS has the opportunity to assign and convey new authentication credentials for the NEI.

---

6. To be correct, the ESQ message is directed to an active NEI within the M-ES. Authentication credentials are associated with the NEI and not with the M-ES device.

Given the above discussion, it appears that the best approach is to update the authentication credentials as often as possible. This can certainly be achieved by setting a short configuration timer value and, on every forced re-registration exchange, assign new authentication credentials. There are two problems with this approach. The first and obvious difficulty is the increased network overhead of the high level of registration traffic. The second less obvious, but much more devastating problem, involves the current technology for updateable permanent storage.

Since the authentication credentials for each NEI must be maintained in synchronization with the network, the M-ES must be able to maintain the current authentication credentials even during periods when the device is powered off. The most common current technology to achieve this is the use of "flash ROM."[7] Unfortunately, these devices have a limited write cycle lifetime. Typical devices are specified to provide approximately 30,000 write cycles before write failures causing bit errors will occur. This means that if new authentication credentials are assigned every 6 minutes, the device may fail to operate within 3 to 4 months.[8] This is unacceptable.

The CDPD System Specifications Release 1.1 provides guidance that the authentication credentials update frequency be set at once every 24 hours.

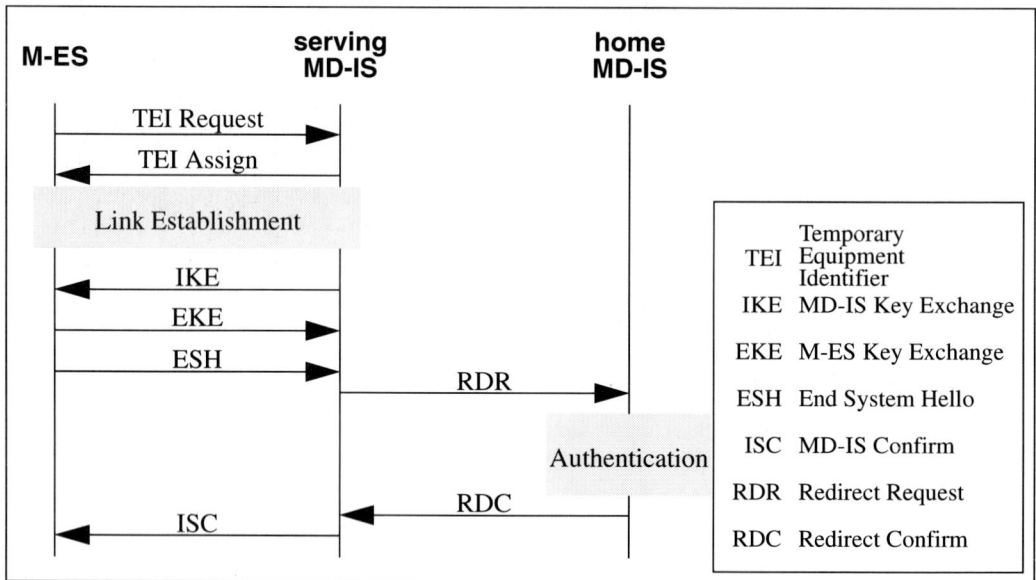

Figure 6.3   CDPD Security Protocol Events

---

7. Read Only Memory.
8. Some of the early networks were configured with this high authentication credentials update rate. Better understanding of the issues through this experience has corrected the problematic network configurations.

6.5.3 CDPD Confidentiality

To provide data link confidentiality, all information contained in the information fields of SN-Data PDUs, including NEIs of the M–ESs is transmitted across the airlink in an encrypted form.

The procedures necessary for SN-PDU confidentiality include:

- exchange of secret keys to be used for encryption and decryption; and
- encryption and decryption of the data.

Key exchange procedures are required for management of the encryption function. These procedures are performed by a *Security Management Entity* (*SME*) in the M-ES and the MD-IS. The key management function is based on the Electronic Key Exchange procedure of Diffie and Hellman, described in [DIFF76].

On assignment of a *Temporary Equipment Identifier* (*TEI*), but prior to the establishment of a LLC link,[9] the M-ES generates a secret random quantity $\mathbf{x}$, while the MD-IS generates a secret random quantity $\mathbf{y}$. The MD-IS also generates two public quantities, a base $\mathbf{a}$, and a modulus $\mathbf{p}$. The modulus $\mathbf{p}$ must be a prime number larger than the base $\mathbf{a}$. For CDPD, both $\mathbf{a}$ and $\mathbf{p}$ are 256 bits long.

With these values, the serving MD-IS initiates and controls the key exchange procedure. It transmits the triplet consisting of ($\mathbf{a}$, $\mathbf{p}$, and $\mathbf{a^y}$ mod $\mathbf{p}$) to the M-ES. The M-ES in turn replies with the value ($\mathbf{a^x}$ mod $\mathbf{p}$) to the MD-IS. Through this interchange, both the MD-IS and the M-ES generate a *shared secret* value ($\mathbf{a^{xy}}$ mod $\mathbf{p}$). This is depicted in Figure 6.4.

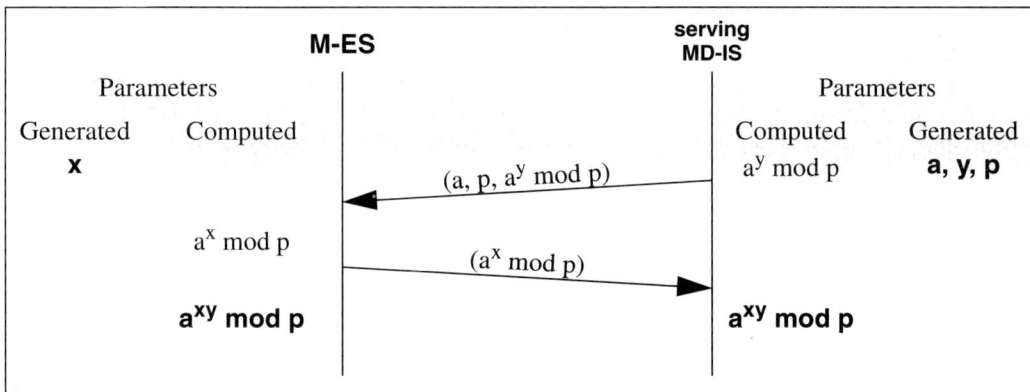

Figure 6.4   CDPD Key Exchange

Using the shared secret, the M-ES and the MD-IS each generate two encryption keys. The first key is used by the MD-IS to encrypt data transmitted in the forward channel and used by the

---

9. More precisely, key exchange is done prior to establishing the multi-frame mode in MDLP.

M-ES to decrypt the data received. The second key is used by the M-ES to encrypt the data transmitted in the reverse channel and used by the MD-IS to decrypt the data received.

The CDPD System Specifications releases 1.0 and 1.1 dictate the use of the RC4 encryption algorithm, described in [RSA-92]. It is a stream cipher that generates a stream of pseudo-random data from the *key* called the *keystream*. Each consecutive bit of keystream is exclusive-OR'd with a bit of data to be encrypted. Data is decrypted by applying the same process to the received data.

Future releases of the CDPD System Specification may incorporate additional encryption algorithms. The definition of CDPD key exchange mechanisms allow the specification of up to 127 (plus cleartext) such encryption algorithms.

6.5.4 CDPD Privacy

Privacy is provided in CDPD networks by the use of temporary identifiers, local dynamic key management, and encryption and access control.

A TEI is used to identify an active M-ES across the airlink. The TEI is a layer 2 identifier included in the header of every MDLP frame exchanged between the M-ES and the MD-IS. Aside from the one-time exchange of physical equipment identifiers (EIDs), to unambiguously assign the TEI, the TEI is the only identifier of the M-ES that is transmitted in the clear.

Since the registration (including authentication credentials) is conducted via MDLP frames, whose data fields are encrypted, use of a dynamically assigned TEI is necessary to uniquely identify the mobile to the network and yet maintain privacy.

Key management is another process that supports privacy in CDPD networks. By dynamically computing local keys based on random information exchanged between the M-ES and the MD-IS, the problem of distributed key management across a large internetwork is avoided. The key exchange, based on the Diffie-Hellman EKE algorithm, is difficult to meaningfully intercept. Since the keys are used locally and associated with TEIs, there is no chance of a key being compromised.

Access control prevents unauthorized use of resources, including use of resources in unauthorized manners. By preventing unauthorized resource usage, CDPD provides better privacy to users and their data.

6.6 CDPD Security Design Rationale

Security is one of those areas of the CDPD specification that has received the most comments and criticisms. Does CDPD have security vulnerabilities? Of course—see Section 6.2, Security Policy.

We[10] have never postured CDPD as a high-security system.[11] However, we believe that the CDPD security objectives, summarized in subsection 6.5.1, CDPD Security Design Goals and Tradeoffs, and described in Part 405 of the CDPD specification, have in fact been met. One can perhaps quibble over whether or not the security objectives we outlined are sufficient.

In this section we discuss various considerations that shaped the design of CDPD security.

6.6.1 CDPD Security Objectives

The CDPD specification team spent a significant amount of time identifying requirements and clearly defining the goals and objectives for CDPD security. The specification team drafted several revisions of documents enumerating explicit goals and objectives as well as a list of security services that were explicitly being excluded. The service providers that were funding the CDPD development effort reviewed and approved the set of goals and objectives that are enumerated in Part 405 of CDPD specifications and summarized in subsection 6.5.1.

The basic principal driving the formation of these goals is expressed below:

"What happens inside of the CDPD network can be trusted. What happens outside of the CDPD network cannot be trusted."

Furthermore, CDPD security was designed to protect against passive attacks. Active attacks that involve masquerading the CDPD network and are likely to disrupt service are detectable and require significant effort on the part of the "Bad Guys." For these reasons, protecting against active attacks is not one of the CDPD security objectives.

6.6.2 One-Way vs. Two-Way Authentication

The objective for authentication in the CDPD specification is limited to M-ES authentication. This is defined as each NEI being used by the M-ES to be separately authenticated by the CDPD network. This is to ensure that only the authorized possessor of the NEI is using the NEI.

Bilateral Authentication was explicitly excluded as an objective. In other words, CDPD security services do not include authentication of the CDPD network to the M-ES across the airlink.

Lack of bilateral authentication makes CDPD vulnerable to the so-called man-in-the-middle attack (because the system is never authenticated by the mobile). The specification team was well aware of this vulnerability.[12]

---

10. "We," in this context, refers to the entire CDPD specification team, not just us!
11. A "High" level of security is in the eye of the beholder. What qualifies as a high-security system to a security expert is generally prohibitively expensive to anyone else.
12. One of the purposes of enumerating the non-goals for CDPD security was to acknowledge potential vulnerabilities.

This vulnerability was pointed out in [FRAN95], based on a technical analysis. The design of CDPD security meets its objectives; it is just that bilateral authentication was deliberately excluded. The man-in-the-middle attack involves an active attack. Masquerading the CDPD network on a large scale is likely to be difficult and easily detectable.

We believe that this vulnerability does not impose a significant security threat. We agree that over time the bad guys are likely to exploit this weakness, which will necessitate evolution of the airlink security mechanisms.

Our main concern, in 1993, was the possibility of fraud, based on passive eavesdropping as had occurred in the AMPS cellular systems. Our primary objective was to protect the end-users' identity as well as their data. We designed the system with end-user confidentiality in mind. Since the system provides for many encryption and authentication types, we now believe these concerns will prove to be largely unfounded.

6.6.3 The Tunnel's Data Confidentiality and Authentication

Because the mobility tunnel falls within the CDPD network to some extent, it is already protected and does not require the level of security that is necessary between the home agent and the foreign agent in Mobile IP.

Even though securing the network layer of the CDPD network infrastructure is not explicitly specified in the CDPD specifications, the designers of CDPD specifications recognized that providing data confidentiality and authentication for the mobility tunnel was important. *Network Layer Security Protocol (NLSP)*, which can be considered an adjunct to CLNP provides comprehensive security services.

[FRAN95] observes that the I-interface between CDPD service providers is also in the clear, enabling essentially the same type of man-in-the-middle attack as over the airlink. This attack also results in capture of the M-ES's security credentials and subsequent cloning.[13]

Our assumption has always been that the CDPD service providers will have to work together to secure the I-interface. Some people believe that a technical specification should answer all implementation questions. We respectfully disagree.

6.6.4 Considerations for Use of PKCS

Use of *public key cryptography (PKCS)* was considered for authentication in CDPD. The specification team chose not to use PKCS for a number of reasons. Incorporation of private keys in devices would have complicated provisioning[14] of mobile devices. Furthermore, the requirement

---

13. Although doing this would require decoding of CLNP datagrams—a relatively minor security mechanism!
14. Provisioning refers to the process of activating a new user on the network.

for private keys also presents difficulties and would have increased the cost of producing generic ready to use consumer electronic devices.

M-ES authentication is based on a historic shared secret between the device and the network that requires no pre-assignment of secret keys in M-ESs, which simplifies mass production of devices and activation of users.

6.6.5 Consideration of Other Approaches

[FRAN95] has suggested challenge-response schemes for bilateral authentication, authenticated key exchange, and authenticated MSF/MHF interaction (the MNLP protocol). There is no doubt these ideas have merit. However, some global system perspectives temper our enthusiasm for these mechanisms; at some point the cure becomes worse than the disease.

CDPD has always been intended to be a dynamic, mobility-supporting data internetwork. Speed of system access is important to end-users. Limited complexity is important for rapid cost-effective implementation and deployment. Overhead must be limited because of both airlink bandwidth limitations and the degree of interactions necessary between serving and home mobility functions.

Perhaps, one could criticize the design point of in-motion access to CDPD services. After all, just how many database accesses will a person do while driving on the freeway? However, it is this goal-in-motion access that implies the need for rapid connection to and transfer between potentially independent CDPD systems. One only need think of New York City to fully appreciate the possibility of rapid intersystem cell transfers.

6.6.6 End-to-End Security Services

As far as E-interface security goes, we have always been of the impression that this is essentially identical to conventional internetwork security concerns. There are many technically-savvy people working on this issue, so why should we tackle it? Since this is a strictly conventional internetworking interface, the general solution—combination of routing filters, firewalls, etc.—applies.

As far as end-to-end application security goes, well, that is a Layer 7 issue. CDPD is a Layer 3 system.

7 Mobile Network Support Services

I get by with a little help from my friends
—John Lennon & Paul McCartney, 1967

Support services are necessary for the operation of any shared system or WAN, especially in a commercial offering. These services are not always visible to users of the network—in fact, they probably shouldn't be—but they are essential to the operation of such a network. The need for support services is amplified in a large public mobile data network, such as CDPD, because the opportunities for failure, fraud, and unaccounted resource usage are much greater from an operational perspective than in non-mobile networks.

Our goal in this chapter is to present both an overview of the support services necessary for any mobile WAN and a description of how these services are provided in CDPD. Security services are considered to be support services and are separately described in Chapter 6. We shall continue the discussion with network management, usage accounting, message handling, directory services, and subscriber profile maintenance services. The inclusion of these support services in the basic system definition of CDPD is a distinguishing feature of this system.

7.1 Support Services Overview

In addition to the security services discussed in Chapter 6, many other support functions are required, which are themselves supplementary to basic data carriage in a mobile data network. A network operator has to be able to run and manage the network; this becomes ever more important as the size of the network grows. A network operator also must be able to account for network resource consumption for cost allocation and capacity planning purposes. Feedback on network performance is always better received from monitors rather than potentially disgruntled users. Finally, functions such as message handling and directory services are essential to supporting other network services.

7.2 CDPD Support Services

In addition to the security services described in Chapter 6, CDPD support services include network management, usage accounting, message handling, directory services, and subscriber profile maintenance services. These support services can generally be assigned to one of two categories:

- support services for CDPD Network Services; or
- support services for CDPD Network Application Services.

Support services for CDPD Network Services (introduced in Chapter 3) may themselves be located in the application layer, but are intended to support the Layer 3 operations of the network. These services include:

- Services that support M-ES authentication (described in Chapter 6)
- Services to maintain subscriber profiles (used to provide customized services and access control for subscribers)
- Network management
- Usage accounting

Support services for CDPD Network Application Services (introduced in Chapter 3) are generally provided at the application layer and include the following:[1]

- Directory services (application entity title to presentation address translation)
- Services to maintain subscriber profiles (used to provide customized services and access control for subscribers)
- Network management
- Usage accounting
- Message handling services (MHS)

The following sections will describe these support services and how they are provided in CDPD. In some cases, most notably network management, these services could themselves be the subject of an entire book. Thus, we shall not aim at a complete description but only present an overview that highlights the aspects of support services most impacted by mobility.

---

1. There is some overlap between these two lists. This is because support functions tend to be general purpose in nature and address multiple support needs.

7.3 Network Management

Building a large data network is difficult. Operating it reliably on an ongoing basis is even more difficult. As a network grows in size, scaling issues and their associated complexities eventually predominate all other operational considerations. It is essential to have the right tools available to be able to efficiently operate such a large network.

The issues of scale are not the only challenge of operating large networks. Most existing large networks have evolved over time and support a variety of old and new equipment. They must also support a large number of protocols. This makes centralized management and administration of such networks nearly impossible.

Faced with these challenges, the data networking industry and various standards bodies have published specifications of how to operate large networks; this is called *network management*. Among the published standards for network management are *SNMP* (*Simple network management Protocol*), *DCE* (*Distributed Computing Environment*) and *CMIP* (*Common Management Interface Protocol*). There is a reason for the use of adjectives such as simple, distributed, and common— making a very difficult activity easy is a seductive vision indeed.

The OSI vision of network management—CMIP—is very elegant and sophisticated. Unfortunately, it is a challenge in and of itself to figure out how this vision is supposed to be implemented. However, the OSI model is a useful tool, which may be used to describe any management system, and so we will begin with an overview of the OSI systems management framework.

7.3.1 Overview of System Management Framework

The OSI systems management[2] architecture describes the relationships of management functions, managed objects, and communication protocols to functional areas. These relationships are defined in *OSI Reference Model - Management Framework* [ISO-7498-4], *OSI System Management Overview* [ISO-10040] and *Telecommunications Managed Networks (TMN)* [CCITT M.30].

The three major types of systems management specifications are:

- systems management functions specifications,
- managed objects specifications, and
- communication protocol specifications.

---

2. Network management is called "systems" management in OSI terminology, which does not distinguish between computers and networks. Throughout this chapter (and quite possibly the entire book as well), when we refer to "management" we mean management of networks, not people.

These specifications define abstract entities and operations, which are capable of meeting the requirements in each of the systems management functional areas. We will now review these specification types in order.

7.3.1.1 Systems Management Functions

A *systems management function* is defined as a set of related services that collectively provides for the manipulation of managed objects to accomplish a specific purpose of systems management. Informally, a managed object is a representation of something that needs to be managed. Management is accomplished by manipulating the managed object in certain specific ways.

One example is the *object management function*, which provides the ability to create, delete, examine, and modify managed objects. Another example is the *state management function*, which provides the ability to examine changes in state and the ability to monitor the overall operability of managed objects.

A given systems management function may satisfy more than one requirement. Some requirements might involve more than one systems management function to satisfy them. Therefore, a many-to-many relationship between systems management functions and requirements is typical.

7.3.1.2 Managed Objects

A *managed object* is the systems management view of a resource that is subject to management, such as a layer entity, a connection, or an item of physical communication equipment. Thus, a managed object is the abstraction of such a resource that presents its properties as seen by (and for the purpose of) management. These properties are referred to as *attributes*. The resource that is represented by the managed object might be physical (e.g., a processor) or logical (e.g., a state table in memory).

An essential part of the definition of a managed object is the relationship between these properties and the operational behavior of the resource itself. Another part of the definition of a managed object is the specification of the set of management operations that can be performed upon it and the effect that these management operations have upon the managed object and its attributes.

Managed objects can also emit notifications, which contain information concerning the occurrence of an event associated with the managed object. This is how alarms are activated in an operational system.

7.3.1.3 Management Communication Protocols

The interactions between the management system[3] and the managed system are realized through the exchange of management information and control. The rules governing these interactions

---

3. The "management system" is the application running on one or more computers, which controls the systems management activities. Of course, the management system must itself be managed.

are the *management communication protocols*. Management functions and managed objects are components of the communication protocol.

Management communication protocols can be either connection-oriented or connectionless, depending on the services provided by the underlying communication protocols. SNMP operates via UDP/IP in a connectionless mode of operation. CMIP operates via TP4/CLNP in a connection-oriented mode. All of the issues of reliability and security associated with connection-oriented and connection-less protocols, which we discussed in earlier chapters, factor into network management operations.

7.3.2 Systems Management Functional Areas

The requirements to be satisfied by systems management activities are generally categorized into five functional areas:

- fault management
- usage accounting management
- configuration management
- performance management
- security management

These are general functions that should be provided to some extent in any system. The rigor of any of these functions depends on the type of system to be managed and the anticipated circumstances under which it will operate. There is a price to be paid for the services provided in these areas, which might or might not be justifiable. We shall now describe these systems management functional areas.

7.3.2.1 Fault Management

Fault management is the ability to detect, recover, and limit the impact of failures in a system, and is the capability most commonly associated with network management. Because no system is infallible, it is essential that the system be able to detect, report, and recover from failures as quickly as possible. Ideally the impact of failures should remain transparent to users of the system.

However, the operators of a network need to know about the failures so they can take the steps necessary to prevent these failures or worse from occurring in the future. Typically, an error detection and reporting mechanism is based on asynchronous notifications, called *alarms* or *traps*. A local agent[4] detects the failure and reports it to a systems manager,[5] which is then responsible for reporting the failure and taking corrective action.

---

4. The agent is the application that monitors and controls the state and operation of a managed object. It facilitates the management functions for that object under the control of the manager.

In a large network, efficient fault management is required to prevent the network operators from needing an army of personnel just to run and administer the network. Efficiency is also required to prevent the fault management communications from overwhelming the network's data carriage capacity. This is especially true in large networks.

However, because fault management is the means of controlling system failures, it must function in a real-time mode. If a problem is potentially catastrophic to the system, efficiency considerations must evaporate in favor of quick restoration of the system's health.

7.3.2.2 Usage Accounting Management

Usage accounting management is the ability to account for the resources consumed in a system. Whether the system is strictly for internal corporate use or a public commercially available service, it is important to know who is consuming what resources. Resources that must be accounted for include bandwidth on communication links or routers, storage space on servers, or computational effort.

Usage accounting is important for capacity management (staying ahead of the demand curve) as well as for cost allocation and billing purposes. Oftentimes, capacity shortfalls precipitate systems failures and service outages. Usage accounting management can also tandem with security management to detect and prevent fraudulent system usage. Usage accounting management is described in Section 7.4.

7.3.2.3 Configuration Management

Configuration management is the ability to configure a system to be able to operate in a desired manner. This could include provisioning of virtual circuits in frame relay switches, manual creation of static routing tables in routers, etc. Typically, configuration management is best performed at a central site rather than always requiring visits to remote locations; this is an important efficiency consideration in any large-scale distributed system.

7.3.2.4 Performance Management

Performance management is the means by which a system's performance may be monitored. Only by monitoring performance can a system operator know that it is meeting the needs of users; it can be highly embarrassing (and potentially career limiting!) for a network operator to hear about performance issues for the first time directly from the users of the network. Although

---

5. The manager is the application running on one or more computers that monitors and controls overall system operation. Its control is usually exercised via agents, which are more closely attuned to individual objects.

performance monitoring might not require the real-time immediacy of fault management, it shouldn't be too delayed. Oftentimes, system failures initially manifest themselves as performance problems.

7.3.2.5 Security Management

Security management is the ability to control access to the system and its services, while protecting the privacy of its legitimate users. This is described in Chapter 6.

7.3.3 Relationship of Management Specifications to Functional Areas

Management functions are usually defined to be general purpose in nature; in performing management activities, sets of management functions may be combined to fulfill a particular management requirement. Similarly, managed objects are general in the sense that they may be used to fulfill requirements in more than one functional area. Managed objects, their associated management operations, and the communication protocols are used in more than one area whenever this is possible.

In general, the managed entity, known as the *agent*, cannot determine the purpose of the management commands it receives or the notifications that it emits. For example, a managed entity cannot, in general, determine whether its responses to *read error counters* requests will be used for the purpose of fault management or performance management. The agent responds individually to each request from a *manager* individually, without needing any wider context within which to carry out the request. This simple perspective is necessary for the unambiguous definition of an agent's activities and its responses to commands from the manager.

7.3.4 CDPD Network Management

The CDPD network provides comprehensive mobile data communication services to subscribers. To ensure a high level of network availability, the CDPD network is designed to incorporate network management services that allow CDPD service providers to operate the network. The network management services provide timely information to the network operator to detect network faults, to exercise controls to correct faults, and to configure the network for optimal operation.

CDPD network management is defined in Parts 700 through 750 of the CDPD System Specification.

7.3.4.1 CMIP and SNMPv2

The CDPD network management architecture and services uses X.700 for the network and, optionally, *Simple Network Management Protocol* (*SNMPv2*) for mobile devices. CDPD Network Management Model is depicted in Figure 7.1. The X.700 management protocols and functions are specified by the network management Forum set of OMNI*point* 1 documents. These include the *Common Management Information Protocol* (*CMIP*), *Common Management Information Services* (*CMIS*), and the technique of modelling management information as managed objects.

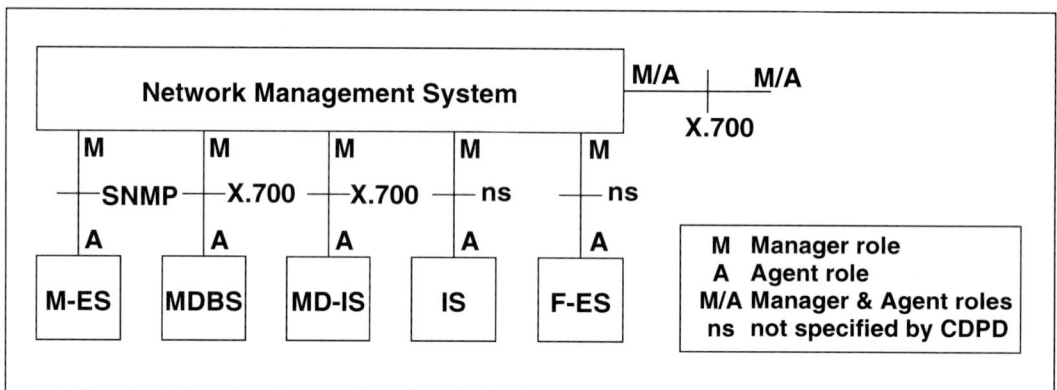

Figure 7.1   CDPD Network Management Model

7.3.4.2 Proprietary vs. Open Standard

Wherever possible, the CDPD System Specification uses existing, standard managed objects defined by the International Organization for Standardization, International Telegraph and Telephone Consultative Committee, and industry groups such as the network management Forum and the Open System Environment Implementors' Workshop. Refinements of standard objects, which are specific to CDPD, are used where appropriate; these objects are defined in the CDPD System Specification as the CDPD Library.

A *Managed Object Ensemble* defines how a collection of managed objects may be used to satisfy management requirements in a particular management context. The following ensembles are defined for managing one of more CDPD systems:

- CDPD MD-IS and MDBS Management Ensemble
- CDPD Inter-Domain Management Ensemble
- CDPD Accounting Management Ensemble
- Generic Equipment Management Ensemble

7.3.4.3 Why CMIP?

One of the more controversial aspects of the CDPD System Specification has been its reliance on X.700 technology to define network management services and functions. Although in some respects this decision could be considered to be arbitrary, several reasons may be offered.

Scalability was the most important factor in the selection of X.700 as the basis for network management. CMIP provides the capability of very powerful and flexible managed object definitions. This, coupled with a rich set of operations, helps to reduce the network traffic necessary to manage large networks, consisting of thousands of MDBSs.

Furthermore, CMIP relies on a connection-oriented transport protocol (TP4/CLNP) to carry commands to agents and responses back to the manager. This helps to reduce overall network traffic because only errored packets require retransmission; with unreliable datagram protocols, critical information must often be transmitted multiple times to assure proper reception.

Another consideration was security. The connection-orientation of TP4/CLNP is inherently more secure than a connectionless paradigm, in which—theoretically, at least—a random or malicious datagram could cause a remote device such as an MDBS to reboot. The TP4/CLNP data carriage, itself, also adds to the security because it is not typically used in the ever-popular Internet.[6] In the future, TP4 could also operate over the network layer secure protocol (NLSP), described in Chapter 6.

The challenge of implementing CMIP-based network management services has prompted some CDPD service providers to provide these services initially via SNMP or other technology. These "shortcut" solutions to management have been implemented in the spirit of rapid CDPD services deployment. After all, network management functionality is more important than the protocol used. Oftentimes, these issues become overshadowed by protocol "religion."

7.4 Usage Accounting

As mentioned previously, usage accounting is the ability to account for the consumption of a system's resources. Usage accounting can be performed in support of internal "customers" in a cost center service or in support of a fully commercial service. In either case, it is important to know which users are consuming which resources for both cost allocation and capacity planning purposes.

Usage accounting functions must be more robust and flexible in a commercial environment, where customers are unlikely to tolerate inaccuracies in billing statements. Usage accounting is even more challenging in the case of large systems because of the larger quantities of usage data that are captured and must be managed.

---

6. An example of the proverbial "security through obscurity."

Usage accounting is not equivalent to billing, but it provides the data necessary for billing. Typically, billing is proprietary and handled by billing services providers. The capability for rendering large numbers of bills is a highly specialized activity that could be distracting to a networking services provider.

7.4.1 CDPD Usage Accounting

The CDPD usage accounting services provide information on how the resources behind CDPD network services are used and by whom. The overall goal of this usage accounting service was to provide automatic, near real-time collection, and dissemination of resource usage data; because CDPD spans service provider domains, a standardized usage accounting information exchange mechanism is essential.

The CDPD system collects network layer airlink usage data for each subscriber to support billing for this resource usage. The accounting service collects this data with supporting information necessary to provide accurate computation of charges. The data collected includes packet count, packet size, source and destination addresses, geographic location of M-ESs, time of transmission, and so forth.

The key resource accounted for in CDPD systems is the utilization of the airlink bandwidth at the network layer. Because the CDPD network provides connectionless, datagram services to M-ESs, the accounting approach is to accumulate statistics about network layer protocol data units (NPDUs) that cross the airlink. Retransmissions at the transport layer and above are not recognized as being redundant and could be double-counted from the perspective of an end-user. It is possible that this retransmission was caused by Layer 4 time-outs resulting from contention or bad RF conditions in CDPD.[7]

Because the accounting mechanisms capture mobile data link utilization, traffic between two M-ESs gets measured twice—once when it traverses the mobile data link from an M-ES to its serving MD-IS and again when it is transmitted from (possibly) another serving MD-IS to the second M-ES. However, the airlink usage for this M-ES to M-ES correspondence is associated with each M-ES' respective airlink (MDLP link).

The CDPD accounting mechanisms do not measure the distance that a particular NPDU travels between its source and destination. They also do not measure traffic that does not cross a mobile data link (e.g., they do not measure traffic between two F-ESs). But then, CDPD is assumed to provide mobile data services, not conventional data services.

---

7. In bad RF conditions, or in a contention situation, multiple attempts may be required to get data packets across the airlink. Even though these multiple attempts are not counted (more than once), they could require enough time that Layer 4 time-outs expire at the mobile or the correspondent host.

CDPD services are offered by a variety of service providers who interact with one another in a variety of relationships. Because no single CDPD service provider covers all of North America, it will often be the case that a CDPD service provider provides service to a visiting M-ES. This is particularly true for nationwide CDPD customers.[8]

To efficiently account for nationwide services spanning multiple CDPD service providers, the CDPD accounting service distinguishes between home CDPD *network* service providers and home *accounting* service providers. A subscriber of CDPD service provider *A* might be served most of the time by service provider *B* (perhaps in a subcontractor arrangement for service provider *A*); CDPD accounting mechanisms support this relationship. There is no need for network service relationships to dictate business (accounting) relationships.

CDPD usage accounting mechanisms, in themselves, do not address pricing, billing, the reconciliation of usage claims among CDPD network service providers, or receivables processing. These functions are accomplished by applications that are outside the scope of the CDPD System Specification. CDPD usage accounting mechanisms exist to capture and distribute CDPD resource usage information in support of the business applications of service providers.

The CDPD accounting service is defined in Part 630 of the CDPD System Specification and Part 1023 of the CDPD Implementor Guidelines.

7.4.2 The CDPD Accounting Model

The CDPD accounting service relies on resource consumption data initially collected in serving MD-ISs. This accounting data is distributed amongst CDPD accounting *correspondents* via a simple one-way peer protocol. This accounting data exchange protocol is layered on top of an X.400-based message transfer system. The accounting protocol has been designed to be relatively independent of the accounting transfer mechanism so that migration to additional transfer mechanisms in the future is possible.

The accounting mechanisms are described by first providing a top-level description of all of the correspondents that participate in the CDPD accounting model, and then establishing the relationships between them. A relationship between two correspondents simply means that the correspondents may send messages to one another. The model is depicted in Figure 7.2.

---

8. The CDPD System Specification distinguishes between a *customer* and a *subscriber* in the same way that the cellular industry does. A *customer* is the entity with which a CDPD service provider has a business relationship. A *subscriber* is the individual actually receiving service. The customer pays the bills on behalf of the subscriber; a typical example would be a large corporation that would be the customer, with many of its employees receiving service as subscribers.

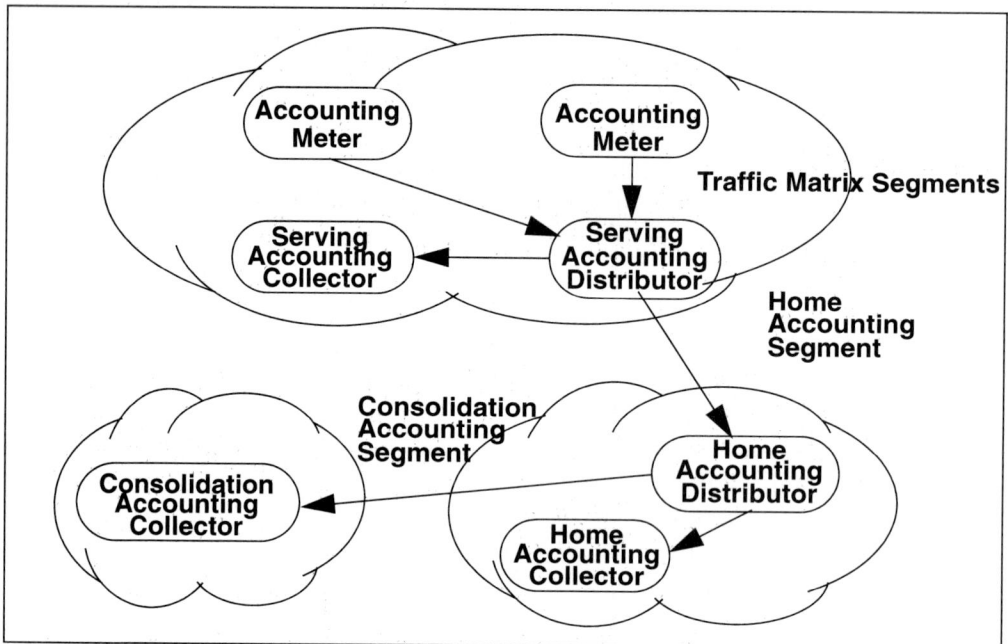

Figure 7.2   CDPD Accounting Model

The entities in the CDPD accounting model include the following components:

•Accounting Meter

An Accounting Meter in a serving MD-IS captures NPDU statistics and delivers these statistics in the format of a traffic matrix to a Serving Accounting Distributor.

•Serving Accounting Distributor

A Serving Accounting Distributor sorts traffic matrix segment rows into home accounting segments, which it then distributes to the appropriate Home Accounting Distributors.

•Serving Accounting Collector

A Serving Accounting Collector stores and processes home accounting segments for the serving CDPD service provider; the data contained in these segments could be used for billing and planning purposes.

•Home Accounting Distributor

A Home Accounting Distributor sorts home accounting segment flows into consolidation accounting segments and distributes them to Consolidation Accounting Collectors, with a copies to a Home Accounting Collector.

- Home Accounting Collector

  A Home Accounting Collector stores and processes home accounting segments.
- Consolidation Accounting Collector

  A Consolidation Accounting Collector stores and processes consolidation accounting segments.

The following subsections will describe these CDPD usage accounting entities.

7.4.3 Accounting Meter

Datagrams (Network PDUs) to and from M-ESs flow through serving MD-ISs and are counted by *Accounting Meters* located in the MD-ISs. Information about each packet is gathered by the Accounting Meter and accumulated in a *traffic matrix*, typically located in a volatile storage location in the serving MD-IS. This information includes the number of NPDUs and NPDU-bytes conveyed successfully across the airlink.

The traffic matrix information also includes the identifier of the cell that served the M-ES and the *Home Tariff Code* provided to the serving MD-IS by the home MD-IS during registration. A new matrix row is created whenever a new M-ES NEI and correspondent NEI pair begin communicating. The traffic matrix is periodically flushed to the Serving Accounting Distributor, a more permanent store for this data.

7.4.4 Serving Accounting Distributor (SAD)

The primary purpose of a *Serving Accounting Distributor* (*SAD*) is to build *home accounting segments* or *HASs*, one for each different home accounting area encountered in the received traffic matrix segments. At some mutually agreed upon interval, the SAD sends these HASs to the appropriate target home accounting areas.[9] The O/R (originator/recipient) address of the HADs are statically preconfigured in the SAD; since there are a limited number of CDPD service providers, each with a single HAD, which has an unvarying address, scaling and flexibility are not concerns.

On receipt of a traffic matrix segment from an Accounting Meter, the Serving Accounting Distributor may choose to add Serving Tariff Code information to the rows of the traffic matrix segments. This information could be used by the Consolidation Accounting Collectors to generate the proper bills to end customers/subscribers. The CDPD specifications define entities and protocols but not implementation nor how this information should be used by service providers.

---

9. Although monthly exchange of HASs between CDPD service providers fits neatly into existing cellular billing mechanisms and practices, the CDPD specifications support much more frequent exchange of this information. Frequent exchange of detailed usage accounting information would assist in preventing fraudulent use of CDPD services by "bad guys."

7.4.5 Home Accounting Distributor (HAD)

A *Home Accounting Distributor* (*HAD*) accepts home accounting segments from potentially multiple Serving Accounting Distributors with the purpose of delivering consolidation accounting segments to the various Consolidation Accounting Collectors and to a Home Accounting Collector in that accounting area.

The Home Accounting Distributor finds the O/R Address of the appropriate Consolidation Accounting Collectors from the subscriber profile maintained by Directory Services. The O/R Address of the Home Accounting Collector is provided to the Home Accounting Distributor by network management.

Having a single HAD (address) defined for each home accounting area means that only one address per service provider needs to be shared with other service providers. Thus, each CDPD service provider has flexibility in their ability to configure and evolve their internal accounting architecture.

There are actually two kinds of HAD—the P-HAD and the R-HAD—defined by CDPD System Specification Release 1.1. These two types of HAD reflect the inter-service provider relationships possible in CDPD. The *P-HAD,* or *primary HAD,* is located in the domain of the CDPD service provider owning the business relationship with the customer receiving service. The *R-HAD,* or *routing HAD,* is located in the domain of the CDPD service provider providing the *mobile home function* (*MHF*), i.e., the mobility support for the subscriber.

This separation of mobility and accounting is necessary to support situations in which one service provider's customer has subscribers that are homed in another service provider's area. For efficiency reasons, there is no requirement that the mobility home be the same as the accounting home. Whenever this situation prevails, the SAD must transmit identical HASs to both HADs for a given subscriber.

7.4.6 Home Accounting Collector (HAC)

The *Home Accounting Collector* (*HAC*) is the final repository of CASs, which have been forwarded by the HAD. The HAC is where CASs are stored and processed by the various applications using accounting data, most notably billing and planning. This is also where the home service provider can verify the activities of its subscribers visiting other service provider domains and audit the corresponding service charges of the serving service providers.

7.4.7 Consolidation Accounting Collector (CAC)

The *Consolidation Accounting Collector* (*CAC*) defines the storage and processing location for large CDPD customers whose subscribers (mobiles) commonly receive service from multiple CDPD service providers. Large nationwide customers would be expected to operate their own CACs to verify the activities of their subscribers and audit the corresponding service charges of the serving service providers.

7.5 Message Handling Service

To support the internal operation of the CDPD network, a reliable store-and-forward messaging service is included in the CDPD System Specification. This messaging service should not be mistaken for other subscriber-visible messaging services that are to be provided through the use of the CDPD network described in Chapter 8. The messaging handling service is intended for internal network operation only.

The primary reason for choosing the message handling service as an element of the infrastructure of CDPD support services was the near-real time requirement for transfer of accounting information between service providers, described in Section 7.4.1.

The CDPD Message Handling System provides a generic message store-and-forward service that is utilized by other CDPD network Services and some CDPD network Application Services. The Message Handling Service is based on the CCITT X.400/ISO-10021 standards published in 1988.

7.5.1 Overview of Message Handling Services

The basic architecture for messaging was originally visualized in the 1984 X.400 Series of Recommendations and is based on the concept of a store-and-forward delivery system. Outside of this delivery system, there are systems used to originate and receive messages, the end-systems in the architecture. The delivery system, called a *Message Transfer Service (MTS)*, consists of systems called *Message Transfer Agents (MTAs)*. The originator/recipient systems are called *User Agents (UAs)*.

7.5.2 Message Structure

A message consists of two basic parts. The first part is referred to as the envelope, the second part is referred to as the content. This structure is depicted in Figure 7.3.

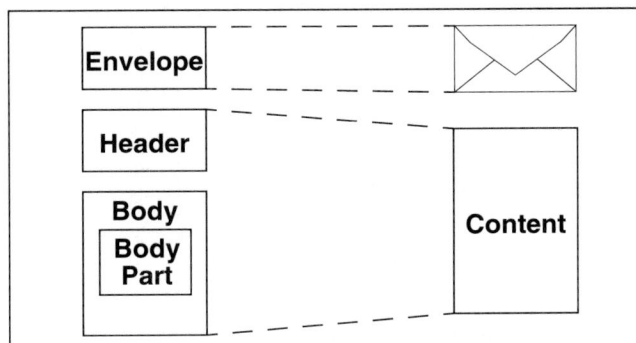

Figure 7.3 Message Structure

The *envelope* contains the addressing information needed to deliver the message. It contains such information as *to: cc:, bcc:, date:*, a list of other nodes the message has "visited" (for loop detection), unique message ID, etc. The envelope is never seen by the recipient application; it is for the use of the Message Transfer Service only.

The *content* is made up of a header and a series of "body parts." The header duplicates much, but not all, of the information on the outside of the envelope. The information in the header is intended for the user application, so it contains items such as *to:, cc:, from:, subject:, date:*, etc.

The vast majority of messages contain a single body part, made up entirely of ASCII text. However, it is often useful to compose a message with text, and then attach a graphics or spreadsheet document. This message would then have two (or more) body parts: one text body part and one (or more) graphics (or spreadsheet) body part.

The separation of the envelope and the content allows for message delivery systems to look at addressing and routing information needed to deliver a message while maintaining the integrity of the contents. It also allows for the contents to be encrypted, if desired, and have no effect on the delivery capability.

7.5.3 Message Transfer Agent (MTA)

The *Message Transfer Service (MTS)* is comprised of the set of nodes that route electronic mail messages, as depicted in Figure 7.4. These transfer nodes are called *Message Transfer Agents or MTAs.*

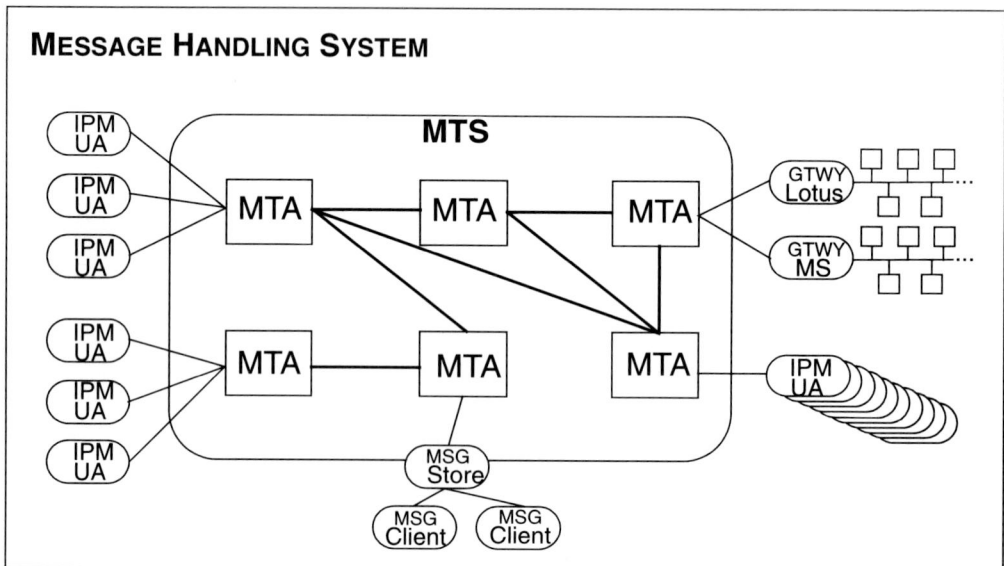

Figure 7.4   MHS Architecture

An MTA has a very limited, but critical, scope of responsibility. Its job is to receive a message, examine the address (routing information) on the envelope, determine whether the message is intended for a UA within its domain, and either deliver it (if the destination is within its domain) or give it to another MTA (if it isn't). One MTA never deletes a message until it receives absolute confirmation that another MTA, a Message Store, or a UA has taken responsibility for the message. This is the fundamental concept of store-and-forward messaging.

MTAs may know of many other MTAs, or they may only know of one other MTA. As long as there exists a path from the originating UA to the recipient UA, the MTS must be able to deliver the message.

An MTA may service UAs in any number of different ways. The MTA could directly deliver mail to UAs within its domain; it could deliver messages to a gateway serving a set of UAs; or it could deliver messages to a Message Store, to be held until a UA requests its messages.

An MTA could serve zero or more UAs. It must deliver the messages regardless of the type of receiving UA. This flexibility of the MTS is what allows new UAs (such as LSM, described in Chapter 8) to be defined without having to build a whole new messaging infrastructure.

7.5.4 User Agent (UA)

User Agents are the end-systems that process messages. There are many different types of User Agents (*UAs*). Originating UAs communicate with recipient UAs of like types. However, gateways do exist that allow unlike UAs to communicate. Protocols, such as *Simple Mail Transfer Protocol* (*SMTP*) provide a common basis for various UAs to exchange commonly formatted (RFC 822) messages.

The most common UA is an *Interpersonal Message* (*IPM*) UA. The IPM-UA is used to process messages intended for humans to view. However, IPM-UAs are not the only User Agents.

7.5.5 Message Store (MS)

A Message Store (MS) spans the boundary between the MTS world and the UA world. MSs don't have any routing or message processing responsibilities. An MS may be thought of as a "holding tank" for messages.

An MS accepts messages from an MTS so that the MTS can get on with its task of moving messages along. However, there are many instances where a UA might not be able to accept a message at a given time. While many UAs are always available (time shared systems, for example), many UAs are systems that are turned off occasionally, or are mobile, such as laptops with a modem connection. Protocols such as POP and IMAP define how these intermittently attached UAs communicate with an MS.

7.6 Directory Services

To support the internal operation of the CDPD network, a directory service was included in the CDPD specifications. This directory service should not be confused with other directory services that are to be provided through the use of the CDPD network to subscribers. It is intended for internal network operation only.

7.6.1 The Directory

The Directory contains a variety of user application-accessible information about the CDPD network and provides for the maintenance, distribution, and security of that information.

The Directory provides the directory capabilities required by applications, management processes, and other entities. Among the capabilities it provides are those of *user-friendly naming*, which allows objects to be referred to by user-friendly names (although not all objects need have user-friendly names),[10] and *name-to-address mapping*, which allows the binding between objects and their locations to be dynamic.

The need for the Directory's capabilities arises from:

- The desire to isolate (as much as possible) users of the CDPD network from its frequent changes. This may be accomplished by placing a level of indirection between users and the objects they access. For example, the Directory allows users to refer to objects by name rather than by address. The Directory provides the necessary mapping service between the object names and addresses.

- The desire to provide a more user-friendly view of the CDPD network. Names are easier for humans to remember and less error-prone than addresses (for most people).

The Directory provides services in the following environment:

- The CDPD network is a large-scale network that is constantly undergoing change:
  - Objects of various kinds enter and leave the CDPD network either singly or in groups.

---

10. Actually, having less user-friendly names adds some measure of security; for this reason it is desirable to not have every network resource name contained in a user application-accessible directory.

- The connectivity of the objects changes, due to the addition or removal of paths between them.
- Various characteristics of the objects, such as their addresses, availability, and physical locations, may change at any time.
- Although the overall rate of change is high, the useful lifetime of any particular object is not short. An object is typically involved in communications much more frequently than it changes its address, availability, physical location, and so forth.
- Objects involved in the CDPD network are typically identified by numbers or other strings of symbols, selected for their ease of allocation or processing, but not for ease of use by human beings.

7.6.2 The Directory Model

The CDPD Directory is a collection of open systems that cooperate to hold a logical database of information about a set of objects in the CDPD network. The users of the CDPD Directory may read or modify the information, or parts of it, subject to having permission to do so. Each user is represented in accessing the Directory by a *Directory User Agent (DUA)*, which is an application process. These concepts are illustrated in Figure 7.5.

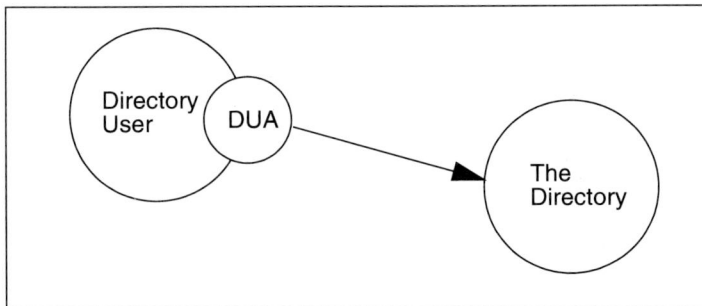

Figure 7.5   Directory and Users

The information held in the CDPD Directory is collectively known as the CDPD *Directory Information Base (DIB)*. The Directory is itself distributed and consists of one or more *Directory System Agents (DSAs)*. Each local database is entirely implementation dependent.

A DSA is an OSI application process that is part of the Directory and provides access to the DIB, to DUAs, and/or other DSAs. A DSA may use information stored in its local database or it may interact with other DSAs to carry out requests. Alternatively, the DSA may direct a requestor (either a DUA or another DSA) to another DSA that may help carry out the request. The interrelationship between DUAs and DSAs is depicted in Figure 7.6.

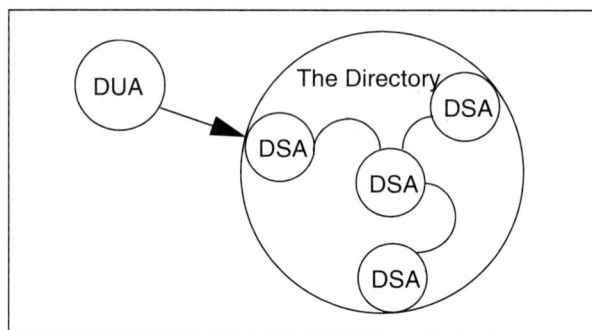

Figure 7.6   Directory Model

The CDPD network views the Directory in the singular and reflects the intention to create, through a single, unified name space, one logical directory composed of many systems and serving many applications. Whether or not these systems actually interwork depends on the needs of the applications they support. Applications dealing with non-intersecting worlds of objects have no such need. The single name space facilitates interworking should interworking needs change later.

The activities of the Directory services requires that the users (actually the DUAs) and the various functional components of the Directory cooperate with one another. In many cases, this requires cooperation between application processes in different open systems. This is accomplished through the use of the standardized X.500 Directory protocols.

The Directory has been designed to support multiple applications, drawn from a wide range of possibilities. The nature of the applications supported governs which objects are listed in the Directory, which users can access the information, and which kinds of access they are allowed.

Applications may be very specific, such as the provision of CDPD subscriber profiles for authorization purposes, or generic, such as the *intersystem communications directory* application in which application names are used to obtain presentation addresses.

The Directory provides the opportunity to exploit commonalities among the applications. For example, a single object may be relevant to more than one application; perhaps even the same piece of information about the same object may be relevant. To support this, a number of object classes and attribute types are defined, which are useful across a range of applications.

7.6.3 The CDPD Directory Service

All services are provided by the Directory in response to requests originating from DUAs. Some requests support interrogation of the Directory; these requests are: Read, Compare, List,

Search, and Abandon. Other requests support modification of the Directory; these requests are: Add Entry, Remove Entry, Modify Entry, and Modify Relative Distinguished Name.

Service requests may be qualified according to service controls, security parameters and filters. Any service may fail, for example, because of problems with the user-supplied parameters, in which case an error is reported. Information is returned with the error, where possible, to assist in correcting the problem.

7.7 Summary

This chapter has described the support services necessary for mobile internetworking and provided in CDPD. These services not only support basic network functionality, they also support applications services, such as those described in the next chapter.

8 *Mobile Applications*

> *Out in the woods,*
> *or in the city;*
> *Its all the same to me—*
> *when I'm drivin' free,*
> *the world's my home;*
> *when I'm mobile!*
>
> —The Who, "Going Mobile, 1971"

The mobile workforce is growing rapidly. As corporations expand, merge, and split, it is often preferable to bring work to workers via telecommuting than vice-versa. This ever-increasing capability for mobile communications has resulted in new job categories, such as *mobile professionals*, who are defined as professionals spending 20 percent or more of their time away from their primary work locations. There are also a very large number of jobs that have always been mobile, such as sales, which are now able to enjoy communications capability essentially everywhere.

The capabilities, size, and cost of mobile computing devices continue to improve, encouraging further growth in the number of mobile workers. These mobile computing devices include modems, notebook computers, personal intelligent communicators, personal digital assistants, palmtop units, organizers, and information managers. However, the inherent limitations of mobile computing devices (e.g., size, computing power, energy usage) have thus far limited the scope of early mobile applications to those that are time sensitive.

It is beneficial for mobile applications to be divisible into a part that travels with the mobile user and a part that remains in place. The part of the application that travels with the user is generally referred to as the *client* and the stationary part is generally referred to as the *server*. The client-server architecture is well-defined and, if followed, allows many applications to work as well for a mobile user as for a LAN user.

In this chapter, we discuss some of the more common mobile applications and the services they require from the network. Several specific value-added services provided in CDPD, such as limited size messaging and the subscriber location service, are also presented.

8.1 Categories of Mobile Applications

There are several ways to look at different types of mobile applications. One perspective might be the means by which applications access information. Another perspective might be more closely associated with the nature of the application itself.

8.1.1 Push or Pull: Mobile Application Information Access

To get information to a mobile device, one of two information access modes must be invoked. Either information is "pushed" onto the mobile device by the server, or the mobile device must "pull" information from the server. The primary difference between these modes of data access is the degree of synchronization required. The "pull" mode of access is synchronous from the perspective of the mobile, while the "push" mode is largely asynchronous. The "pull" is initiated by the mobile client; the "push" is initiated by the server.

An application can be built to access data in either one of these modes. For example, an email application supporting the limited size messaging protocol would have incoming email messages immediately "pushed" onto the client device whenever the device is available to accept the message. However, an email application supporting the *Post Office Protocol* (*POP*) would require the client device to "pull" the message off of the server, usually at the prompting of the user of the client.

Each of these information access modes has its relative advantages and disadvantages. If the information is indeed time critical, then the user would most likely prefer the "push" method because it would be faster than the "pull" mode. However, since we are dealing with small (often hand-held) devices, it might occasionally be preferable to allow the user to decide when and what they would like to download or "pull" onto their device.

8.1.2 Vertical or Horizontal Nature of Mobile Applications

Mobile applications naturally fall into either horizontal or vertical categories. A *horizontal* application is one that is aimed at a broad cross-section of users, without consideration of their job function or how they intend to use the application. email (or messaging) is the quintessential example of a horizontal application, since virtually everyone has a need for it.

A *vertical* application is one that is targeted for a narrow cross-section of users and has little or no applicability to anyone outside of this select group. An application that reports back the inventory of a vending machine to its supplier is an example of a vertical application.

The following sections will discuss some vertical and horizontal applications of mobile data networks.

8.2 Vertical Applications

Vertical applications include those that address functions and business-specific requirements typically associated with a particular industry or a specific company. They are typically categorized into market segments, such as field service, mobile professional, transportation, point-of-sale, telemetry, and government. We will discuss these market segments next.

8.2.1 Field Service

Field service applications have traditionally involved things such as utility services (meter reading, customer service, repair and, maintenance) and high technology manufacturers' representatives. These applications support workers, whose primary work location is "in the field." Thus, data communication capability could be considered mission critical to the performance of these duties.

Some of the earliest wireless data systems were specifically designed and built to support this market segment; *ARDIS* is a prime example of such a system, and is discussed in Chapter 9. The traffic profile for this market segment could be considered light in terms of both frequency and intensity—relatively infrequent transmissions/receptions of relatively modest amounts of data (work orders, schedules, parts' numbers, etc.).

8.2.2 Mobile Professional

Mobile professional applications are horizontal in nature but vertical in terms of sales and support, and the specifics of usage. Although everyone seems to use email in some way, the level of use varies widely and so does the purpose. (Many of us are now so dependent on email that we simply cannot function professionally without it.)

Like the field service market segment, mobile professionals spend a significant amount of their time away from the office. But mobile professionals do typically have an office, and applications must work the same there as on the road. It is not acceptable for a mobile professional to have to do a lot of configuring, to move from the office environment to being "on the road" and vice-versa. Transparent mobility is of paramount importance to this group. This is a relatively new market segment.

8.2.3 Transportation

The transportation market segment is usually focused on fleet management and dispatch functions. "Just where is boxcar number 701149J?" is the type of question that must be answered by this application. Often a wireless medium is coupled with a support technology, such as a *global positioning system* (*GPS*), which may be used to determine the location of a vehicle.

The key consideration of the transportation market segment is coverage—is the mobile communication service available where it is needed? Early systems supporting this market segment include *NexTel* (formerly *Fleetcall*) and other SMR/ESMR systems, which are discussed in Chapter 9.

8.2.4 Point-of-Sale (POS)

Credit card verifications occur now at almost every *point-of-sale* (*POS*) that is established for a non-mobile location. Usually, a phone number is dialed and the credit card number is entered; shortly thereafter, an "accept" or "reject" code is returned and the transaction is completed. This same assurance of payment can now be enjoyed by taxi drivers, package deliverers, espresso-cart vendors, vendors at public markets, and others with mobile wireless communications capability.

The key factors in the POS market segment are reliability, cost, and responsiveness. Financial transactions must be secure and function in an all-or-nothing mode of operation.

8.2.5 Telemetry

Telemetry is another important vertical market segment. Many machines and services operate remotely, where it is often uneconomical to maintain these systems. Being able to have the device "phone home" rather than requiring routine visits by maintenance personnel can greatly extend the scope of such services.

For example, operators of vending machines would benefit from an application that provides remote inventory control. Instead of requiring a worker to personally inspect each machine and perform an itemized inventory, an application could be developed that tracks purchases and sends notifications to the suppliers of the current stock on hand. This would provide much greater efficiencies in stocking remote locations. Although vending machines are generally stationary devices, they are considered a mobile data application because they could be placed anywhere (subject to the availability of power).

Key factors in the telemetry market segment include low cost (both mobile unit and subscription fees) and reliability (of both the mobile unit and the service itself).

8.2.6 Government

A large vertical market segment is that of government agencies. Examples are law enforcement and emergency services. This segment encompasses a wide scope of activities with differing requirements, reflecting the range of missions undertaken by various branches of the government. Thus, key factors could include reliability, ruggedness and fault tolerance (of both the mobile device and the network), and speed. This market is usually geographically bounded and often regional or local in nature. Largely as a result, this has proven to be one of the most prolific early adopters of technology, such as CDPD.

8.3 Horizontal Applications

Horizontal applications are aimed at a broad cross-section of users, irrespective of the particulars of their usage. The solutions deployed to meet these horizontal application needs span both off-the-shelf products and integrated solutions using third-party products as building blocks. We will discuss horizontal applications and protocols in broad terms, focusing on the generic application types rather than on how they are used.

Networks supporting mobility that are compatible with today's Internet can use most of the existing applications that are being used throughout the Internet. However, many of Internet's widely used application layer protocols were not designed with mobility in mind.

8.3.1 Messaging and email

Messaging (sometimes called interpersonal mail, electronic mail, or email) is the generic application name for mechanisms that allow one user to send a "message" to another user or group of users. Marketing surveys continually show that electronic messaging is the dominant application for both local and wide area networks.

There are a number of available electronic messaging options for the mobile user, including the *Post Office Protocol* (*POP*), the I*nteractive Mail Access Protocol* (*IMAP*), the *Simple Mail Transfer Protocol* (*SMTP*), and proprietary client/server protocols. All of the above mentioned protcols are based on open standards. They will be discussed in the following subsections.

8.3.1.1 POP

The intent of the *Post Office Protocol* (*POP*) is to allow a user's client device to access mail from a mailbox server. To receive a message the client "pulls" the message via POP. To send a message the client typically "pushes" the message via SMTP (Section 8.3.1.3), because POP does not specify a mail posting capability.

In this configuration, a subscriber would only be responsible for the POP client. The Post Office Protocol is currently defined by RFC 1460.

8.3.1.2 IMAP

The I*nteractive Mail Access Protocol* (*IMAP*) is the "glue" of a distributed electronic mail system, which consists of a family of client and server implementations. These implementations run on a wide variety of platforms, from small single-tasking personal computing engines to complex multi-user timesharing systems.

Although different in many ways from POP, IMAP may be thought of as a functional superset of POP. Like POP, IMAP specifies a means of accessing stored mail and not of posting mail; this function is handled by a mail transfer protocol such as SMTP.

In this configuration, the user is only responsible for the IMAP client. An example of a IMAP client is *Pine*. The Interactive Mail Access Protocol is currently defined by RFC 1176.

8.3.1.3 SMTP

The *Simple Mail Transfer Protocol* (*SMTP*) provides mechanisms for the transmission of mail. This transmission can be a direct one from the sending host to the receiving host when the two hosts are connected to the same transport service. Alternatively, this transmission can be via one or more relay SMTP servers when the source and destination hosts are not connected to the same transport service.

SMTP comes with all Unix and Unix-like (e.g. Xenix, Linux) operating systems. It is also available as an add-on to almost every other operating system. While, technically-speaking, SMTP can work in mobile scenarios, it will limit the available choices as far as mobile devices are concerned. SMTP is a much "larger" general-purpose solution that requires more resources from a device than other solutions. Implementations of SMTP are often more complicated to configure and maintain than proprietary client/server-based solutions.

The Simple Mail Transfer Protocol is currently defined by RFC 821.

8.3.1.4 Proprietary Client/Server

Proprietary client/server mail systems are usually spawned from a LAN environment. LAN-based messaging systems are not typically client/server-oriented because the client can utilize the server in a much more efficient manner if it knows that it will always have immediate access to that server. Also, the readily available bandwidth encourages more direct interaction without concern for bandwidth. For example, Lotus' *cc:Mail* has been modified to allow users the mobility of a true client/server system by adding a cc:Mail mobile router to the picture. This has allowed users to make remote connections from wherever they can access the server's network.

8.3.2 Limited Size Messaging

The concept of *Limited Size Messaging* (*LSM*) originated in the world of CDPD. While LSM is not limited to a CDPD network (it is designed to work over any IP network), it is the first application that is designed around CDPD's unique network characteristics. The LSM protocol specifications are open specifications, which are reviewed and published by the CDPD Forum.

8.3.2.1 Why LSM?

None of the messaging protcols mentioned above were designed with wirelessness, mobility, and device miniaturization in mind. Design of LSM was highly influenced by these considerations.

There are many electronic messaging solutions on the market today. These solutions often expect a fast connection as well as a large amount of disk space available to store messages of any size. In fact, the direction of email is aimed at being able to exchange larger and more complicated messages with graphic and other (e.g., audio) attachments.

At the other extreme of the messaging spectrum is the paging network. Paging has progressed from purely numeric to very small alpha-numeric messages. The system has historically been one-way, but recently there have been some proprietary two-way paging offerings (as described in Chapter 9).

LSM could be looked upon as an open, standards-based high-end pager, but is really more like a full-service messaging system that is optimized for small messages. LSM is aimed at users who may be using expensive low speed subnetwork and who use energy limited devices (i.e., battery operated), such as a wireless mobile system.

A user may have a permanent computing system where they can review large email documents at their leisure. However, while they are on the move, they need to be kept abreast of any important bulletins that will need their immediate attention. Some messages simply cannot wait for mobile users to find the time to set up a laptop and dial in to check for messages. They must be able to immediately accept messages at anytime on a device that they can carry with them anywhere. This concept is similar to that of cellular phones, except that the device now has the ability to accept electronic messages.

8.3.2.2 What is LSM?

The LSM protocols define a submission and delivery system and a similar set of services as SMTP or X.400. They completely define the rules for *submitting* a message (end-user device to LSM Server) and *delivering* a message (LSM Server to end-user device). LSM improves on these other protocols for this particular environment by highly optimizing the exchanges between the LSM Server and the end-user device, both in terms of the number of bytes and the number of transmissions. Because of the required timeliness of the messages, mailbox access protocols, such as POP and IMAP, are not used.

8.3.2.3 LSM Requirements and Objectives

The requirements that initially drove the LSM protocol suite include:

- LSM extends the existing email-centric messaging world.
- LSM optimizes short messages via efficient encoding techniques.
- LSM respects mobile platform resource limitations, including memory and CPU levels, as well as battery power longevity. This results in a client-light and server-heavy paradigm. Power efficiency is gained by minimizing the number of transmissions by the mobile LSM device.
- LSM is extensible. Different users demand different options, so LSM cannot require every feature to be a part of every message. Likewise, in the future, usage will emerge that is not currently recognized as a requirement. LSM must be extensible enough to handle new, emerging requirements.

8.3.2.4 How LSM Works

A mobile communicator is an LSM device, typically a hand-held device with a CDPD modem. While the device can be turned off, the modem always remains on to accept any incoming messages. Anyone with access to the global messaging world (e.g., the Internet) can send a message to this user, as depicted in Figure 8.1.

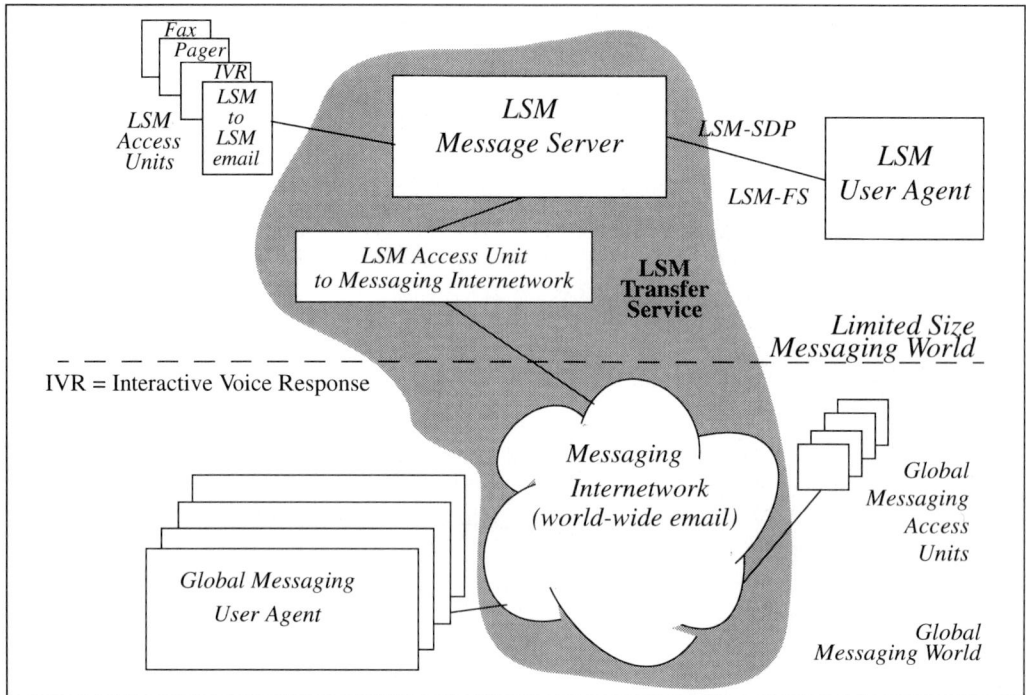

Figure 8.1   LSM World with Global Messaging World

The LSM service provider accepts messages from the global messaging world via standard Internet protocols and delivers them to the user's device via LSM protocols. Since the modem is always powered on and accessible, such messages are accepted at any time and the user notified (possibly in a similar manner as a pager notification) whenever a message arrives.

The user could then activate the LSM device and read the message. The device will most likely have a limited display area and a limited keyboard. This encourages utilization of canned (system or device defined) and embedded (originator defined) responses.

To send a message, the user enters the message, possibly using a canned message, and send it to the LSM service provider via the LSM protocols. The service provider then acts like a standard Internet service provider, forwarding the message via standard Internet protocols.

8.3.2.5 LSM Protocols

The LSM Protocol specifications define the protocols between the LSM client device and the LSM server. LSM requires the *LSROS (Limited Size - Remote Operation Services)* protocol, which was developed in conjunction with LSM. However, LSROS is an independent protocol, as described in Section 8.4.1.

The Limited Size Protocols were designed with three high-level goals:

1. define a new paradigm of limited size messaging;
2. define a remote operations service that could handle messaging and other standard networking applications; and
3. make them an extension of the existing internetworking world.

These goals avoid (whenever possible) the expense and associated problems of "re-inventing the wheel." The LSM Protocols make heavy use of existing technology, including:

- [RFC-822]
- ASN.1
- Basic Encoding Rules
- X.400 and Internet email

The LSM technologies have been thoroughly tested and have proven to be reliable solutions for the problems they address—message format, reliable message delivery, encoding, and compacting. The LSM Specifications support users who enjoy the advantages of this new technology, while remaining connected to the rest of the existing messaging world.

Figure 8.1 depicts the coexistence of the global and limited size messaging worlds. The messaging Internetwork and its estimated 20 million current users are in the lower half of the figure. This world is connected to the LSM messaging world via an *LSM Access Unit*. These access units may be a part of an LSM message server or they may run on a separate processor altogether.

The *LSM Message Server* stores messages and makes decisions (e.g.,formatting, compacting, routing, etc.) based on size and addressing information, on a per message basis.

The LSM Protocols consist of three independent components:

1. *LSM Format Standard (LSM-FS)*

    LSM-FS is responsible for defining the format of a limited size interpersonal message. It defines the "content" encoding (header + body) and the end-to-end envelope. It relies on LSM-SDP (see 2 below) for the transfer of the content to its recipients.

2. *LSM Submission and Delivery Protocol (LSM-SDP)*

    LSM-SDP is responsible for wrapping a limited size interpersonal message in a point-to-point envelope and submitting or delivering it.[1] LSM-SDP performs the envelope encoding and relies on the services of LSROS (see 3 below) for transporting the envelope and its contents. Some of the services of LSM-SDP include: message originator authentication and optional message segmentation and re-assembly.

3. *Limited Size Remote Operation Services* (*LSROS*)
    LSROS is described in Section 8.4.1.

8.3.2.6 Messaging Communication Stacks

LSM is designed to fit within the many protocols already in use for messaging, as well as those already in use for networking. Figure 8.2 illustrates where LSM fits with the other prominent messaging protocols. (Note that the RFCs referenced here are current at the time of this writing, but could be obsoleted or updated at any time.)

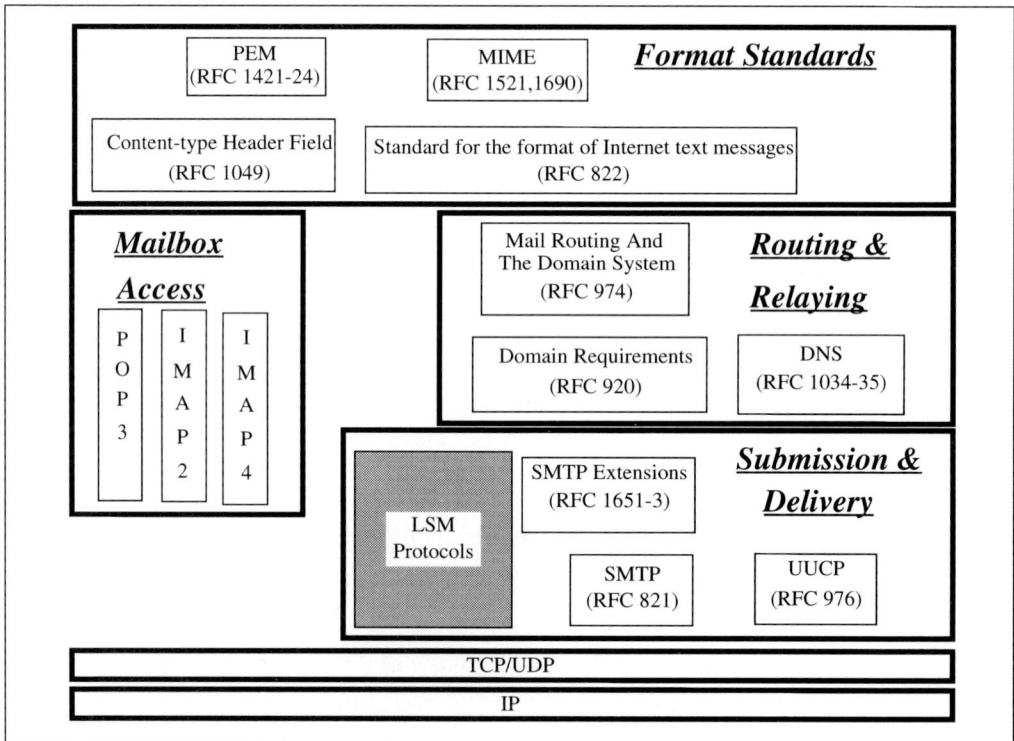

Figure 8.2   Messaging Communication Stack and LSM

1. Remember, *submission* is from client (at the mobile) to the server; *delivery* is from the server to the client.

8.4 Applications-Enabling Protocols

8.4.1 Limited Size Remote Operation Service (LSROS)

Limited Size Remote Operation Services (*LSROS*) defines a notation and the services provided by an application-service element to support interactive applications in a distributed systems environment. The scope of limited size remote operation services is not confined to limited size *messaging*. LSROS is designed to support other applications (i.e., finger/limited directory service) and not just messaging. Transaction-based applications, such as point-of-sale, could also benefit from an LSROS base.

8.4.2 Status Notification Service

In the CDPD Network, most mobile end systems (M-ESs) will only be occasionally connected. There are two main reasons for this:

1. User's choice of not having his/her device connected to the network
2. Unavailability of service (e.g., in an airplane)

The occasionally connected nature of M-ESs introduces the challenge of delivering information to the devices in a timely and efficient manner. Previous solutions to this problem have been generally inefficient. This problem is addressed in an efficient and timely manner by the *Status Notification System* (*SNS*), which provides the current status (active/inactive) of the M-ES to applications wishing to communicate with the M-ES. The occasionally connected nature of M-ESs in the CDPD network is common to other networks that support mobility as well.

8.4.2.1 Why SNS?

In the traditional information exchange model, the originator of information assumes that the recipient is ready and willing to accept the information. The introduction of occasionally connected devices that are often disconnected from the network invalidates this assumption because the occasionally connected devices are often not available for information exchange.

Attempting to communicate with an occasionally connected device suffers from the inherent problems of efficient and timely notification of the availability and desire of the communicating parties. The originator needs to know whether or not the intended (occasionally connected) recipient will be likely to successfully receive the data. Similarly, the recipient needs to know about the originator's intent to transmit data to it. Without this information, network bandwidth and other resources could be wasted in futile attempts to communicate.

Most networks supporting mobility have end systems that are only occasionally connected. The problem of end system status notification is particularly relevant in these networks, which are dominated by occasionally connected mobile end systems.

Both device and network performance is greatly enhanced if the originator knows the current status (e.g., reachable or unreachable) of the occasionally connected recipient and if the occasionally connected recipient knows that the originator desires communication with it. This system provides a mechanism by which each of the communicating parties is efficiently notified about the status of its communications peer.

8.4.2.2 SNS Requirements and Objectives

The requirements driving the SNS protocol include:

- SNS is an optional service that uses home MD-IS knowledge about an M-ES's state of registration.
- SNS allows a corresponding end system (C-ES) to determine the current status of one or more M-ES entities in a quick and efficient manner.
- SNS allows a C-ES to request notification when one or more M-ES entities change status, either becoming active and eligible for communication or inactive and unavailable.
- SNS provides status change notifications to the C-ES entities that have requested notification.
- SNS guarantees timely and reliable delivery of status change notifications, as this directly affects the quality of service when a C-ES is waiting.
- SNS provides notification to an M-ES that a C-ES desires to communicate with it. This is to allow the M-ES to initiate communications at its convenience.

The SNS protocol provides a common mechanism for applications to efficiently communicate with an occasionally connected mobile device. Without SNS, each application would have to separately track the availability of these mobile devices.

8.4.2.3 SNS Model

In the most general case, a *corresponding end system* (*C-ES*) communicates with an *occasionally connected end system* (*OC-ES*) using information provided by the *Status Notification System* (*SNS*). A corresponding end system may be any system other than the *originating end system* (*O-ES*). An example of a corresponding end system would be a mail server that is always available and that can communicate with the OC-ES on behalf of the originating end system (i.e., sender of email). This is depicted in Figure 8.3.

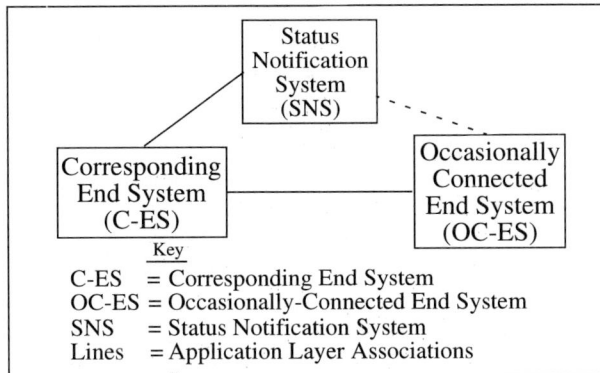

Figure 8.3 Status Notification System Architecture

8.4.2.4 How SNS Works

The first mechanism supporting C-ES communication with the OC-ES can be applied to messaging (e.g., email) applications. The steps involved in sending an email message from an originator to a recipient OC-ES via a message-delivery-system (C-ES), are identified in Figure 8.4.

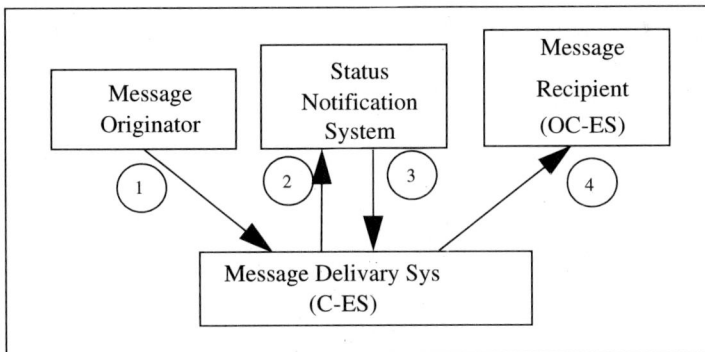

Figure 8.4 Example of messaging to an OC-ES

The following time sequence scenario is depicted in Figure 8.4.

1. The message originator sends a message that arrives at the recipient's message-delivery-system (i.e., mail-box). The message-delivery-system attempts to deliver the message to the recipient but the association between the C-ES (message-delivery-system) and OC-ES (Message Recipient) fails.

2. The message-delivery-system (C-ES) requests from the SNS to be notified of the message recipient's status. Note that this step could either precede or follow Step 1.

3. The OC-ES becomes reachable. The SNS notifies the C-ES of the OC-ES's reachable status.

4. The C-ES uses this information to send the message to its recipient (OC-ES)

8.4.3 Subscriber Area Location Service

This book has dealt with various concepts of routing data packets to mobile subscribers and devices. We have described methods used to track the location of a mobile device. At the same time, these systems and methods have been designed to make this very mobility transparent to the applications on the mobile device and at its peer. In fact, in the interest of greater application attachment ease, knowledge of the mobile device's current location and movements are hidden from systems outside the network infrastructure.

However, in some instances, this very hidden information provides value to applications. For example, if a fleet dispatch operation has current location information about its delivery vehicles, it may be able to construct more efficient dispatch algorithms. In these instances, the vehicle geographically closest to the required pick-up location can be sent.

This type of location information may be provided by use of location tracking equipment on the vehicles that use the mobile data communications system to relay the current position to the dispatch center. External devices such as *Global Positioning System* (*GPS*) receivers or dead reckoning systems can be used for this purpose. These systems require the mobile device to attach to extra equipment, and, in the case of GPS, require the mobile to be able to "see" at least 3 GPS satellites.

An alternative approach available from mobile data systems is to tap the mobility tracking database within the network infrastructure. For example, within the CDPD network, the combination of Location Directory and Registration Directory allow each mobile to be placed at a single RF cell. In fact, this position information is available without the mobile providing any information beyond what is already necessary for maintaining registration with the network. Furthermore, the mobile device need not attach additional location equipment.

The limiting factor in this approach lies in the lack of resolution in the location information. The position can only be determined to the granularity of a coverage cell. In most cases, this coverage area is a 120 degree sector of circle with a radius of approximately 2.5 miles. Some micro-cells within the downtown core may provide greater accuracy, while some rural sites may be much larger.

Even given these considerations, it was felt that the location information maintained by the mobile data network may be of value to some applications. The CDPD specification team defined an approach to provide this data.

8.4.3.1 CDPD Subscriber Area Location Service

The CDPD subscriber Area[2] Location Service uses a messaging mechanism similar to the accounting service. Figure 8.5 illustrates the basic operations.

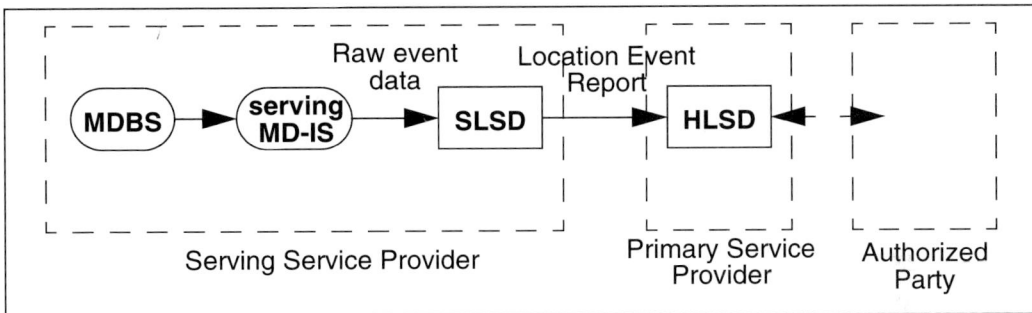

Figure 8.5   CDPD Subscriber Area Location Service

Within the CDPD network, the entity that first notices a mobile device's movement is the serving MD-IS. Whenever the serving MD-IS notices the relocation of a mobile device from one cell to another, it generates an event report.[3] This event report identifies the NEI on the mobile device as appearing in the new cell and is sent to the *Subscriber Location Services Distributor (SLSD)*.

The SLSD reformats this raw location information into geographic information of cell center (latitude and longitude), cell radius, angle of coverage (start degree, end degree),[4] and time of day. The SLSD then sends this event information to the *Home Location Services Distributor (HLSD)*.

The HLSD correlates this information with its local information about a subscriber and its authorized NEIs to determine how to provide the location information to the party authorized to receive this information.

At this point of the system definition, the specification team ran into difficulty. There are several concerns regarding the exchange of information from the CDPD service provider to the authorized party.

From the technology perspective, it was not clear that a single standard for transfer of the location information is possible or appropriate. Indeed, it wasn't clear that consensus could be

---

2. In release 1.1 of the CDPD System Specification, the word "Area" was added to the title of the service. This is in recognition that the accuracy of such an approach is limited to a cell coverage area. The intent was to avoid confusion with systems that provide "pinpoint" accuracy.
3. Event reports are also generated for registration and deregistration events.
4. Remember, these are all approximate since RF is a world of probabilities.

reached on a small number of operational modes. For example, should the authorized party be informed of every movement between cells? Should the authorized party be required to request the latest location information? Should the authorized party be able to request a history of movement? Should the system notify the authorized party only when the movement constitutes a significant event for the application?[5]

Moreover, how should the authorized party be established? Issues of violation of privacy are a strong consideration. Legal opinion was necessary to progress further on this service.

Despite the concerns, the specification team felt it important to capture the direction and the concept. The definition of these messages and procedures is found in Part 1019 of the CDPD Implementor Guidelines.

5. The likely answer is "All of the above." There wasn't enough time to address them all.

9 Non-Cellular Approaches to Mobile Data Networking

Cellular

Doesn't

Pamper

Data

　　　　　　　　—Prominent display in RAM Mobile Data booth at Comdex, 1993.

　　　Increasing demand for mobile data communications has prompted the development of a number of wireless data solutions. Limited primarily by cost of technology and regulatory restrictions, these wireless data solutions include wireless (campus) LANs, ESMRs, private and public wireless packet data services, and satellite-based systems.

　　　This chapter presents a survey of these existing and intended wireless data communications services. But it is only a survey; many fine references—in particular [PAHL94], [PAHL95], [PATE95a], [PATE95b] and [WONG95]—are cited in the bibliography and should be investigated for a deeper understanding of these technologies.

9.1 Background

　　　The demand for wireless data services appears to be inescapable and relentlessly increasing. This demand is driven by both a growing reliance on data communications, especially in the form of email, and an ever-increasing desire for mobility. Recent technical developments are now allowing this demand to be met at a commercially reasonable cost.

In earlier years, wireless data communications were expensive and justifiable only by those willing to pay the price, such as the military, public safety, or other governmental authorities. Other early adopters of wireless data technology had very specific needs, typified by services such as package delivery or taxi dispatch, or applications such as remote telemetry. These early wireless data solutions were typically mission-critical to their customers. They were also typically private, closed systems, which were dedicated to a single purpose rather than serving multiple user constituencies.

Early wireless data communications systems were physical layer-centric by design. Radio-based systems were developed from an RF (radio frequency) technology perspective, with customizations enhancing the efficiency of the scarce resource—the RF channel. These customizations often included shared RF channels, canned messages, and proprietary protocols at all levels. Reminiscent of the early days of computing, applications were developed with full consideration of physical resource limitations; the RF protocols in use were clearly visible to applications, countering today's prevailing design wisdom of layered protocol architectures.

RF bandwidth has always been a key constraint in wireless data systems. Efficient use of limited bandwidth has typically involved the reuse of scarce radio frequencies with geographic separation of simultaneously transmitting-on-the-same-frequency units to prevent interference. This is the architectural basis of current cellular systems, as we discussed in Chapter 2. Increasing system bandwidth is most easily accomplished by subdividing coverage areas, called cells, into smaller cells or microcells, with corresponding decreased transmission power levels.

From the earliest days of commercial wireless data services, expectations have been high for growth of customer bases and revenues. While these high expectations remain largely unsatisfied, there is little doubt as to their eventual fruition: the demand for mobile data communications appears insatiable. As we discussed in Chapter 1, mobility is enhanced by wirelessness. Continuing improvements in technologies as disparate as batteries and digital signal processors are increasing both the effective duty cycle and reliability of wireless data transmission.

The following sections will describe non-cellular approaches to mobile data networking. Non-cellular in this context refers to services and technology provided by organizations other than cellular carriers, which we discussed in Chapter 2.

9.2 Wireless LANs and Metropolitan Networks

Wireless local area networks or LANs have been available since the late 1980s, but the market remains immature due to a dearth of standards and predominance of incompatible proprietary solutions.

By definition, LANs are local in terms of networking technology and thus involve none of the complexities of routing, internetwork address resolution, name-to-address translation, segmentation, and reassembly of data packets, etc. Also, since traditional LANs have been bound by the limitations of physical media, such as the 500 meter maximum coaxial cable length for a traditional 10-BASE5 Ethernet, user mobility has not traditionally been an important consideration.

The traditional motivation for wireless LANs has been the desire for flexibility of user location within a building or campus. With a wireless LAN, a user's workstation is no longer physically constrained to local network taps. This is particularly effective in environments with frequent user moves, additions, and changes (such as point-of-sale terminals in a retail situation), or in situations where installing cabling is either undesirable (such as historic buildings) or unsafe due to construction issues (such as asbestos ceilings). Manufacturing environments, with robot-driven machinery have also found increasing use for wireless communication networks.

Another growing motivation for wireless LANs is the demand for ad hoc user networks, such as sharing of data by attendees at meetings and conferences. Previously, this need was met via the proverbial "Sneakernet," which, despite being a wireless LAN technology, will not be discussed further. One could consider ad hoc networks to be a special case of mobility, but aspects of mobility such as security (authentication) and external accessibility have not been an issue, although they probably should be, considering the rapid deployment of viruses that is possible in these settings.

A third motivation for wireless LANs is the desire to remain "in touch" while moving through a local area such as a building or campus. Roaming software, extending the effective wireless LAN coverage area, has recently become available, allowing mobile users to maintain contact while wandering among overlapping cells. Wireless access points monitor the signal strength of moving hosts and coordinate handoffs from one point to another. However, the rate at which a user is allowed to move is typically limited to pedestrian speed.

Three primary physical technologies have been used in wireless LANs: infrared, narrowband RF, and spread-spectrum RF. Their characteristics are summarized in Table 9.1. [WONG95] provides a fine summary of these physical technologies. Adoption of these solutions has been hampered in the past by a lack of accepted standards and the expense of these solutions relative to their performance.

Table 9.1   Wireless LAN Technology Characteristics

Technology	Infrared	Narrowband RF	Spread Spectrum RF
licensing requirement	No FCC licensing	FCC licensing	No FCC licensing
coverage	No wall penetration—line-of-sight only	Some wall penetration	Better wall penetration
interference risk	No interference	No interference	Interference resistant
standards	IEEE 802.11	No standard	IEEE 802.11

All of these wireless LAN technologies provide "mobility" at OSI Reference Model Layer 2. This allows the benefits of mobility within a highly localized area, defined by the area of coverage for the medium in use. Conventional routing technology could be employed to interconnect these mobile islands. However, as we have seen, the mobility provided by conventional routing technology is limited by static addressing and slow convergence of routing protocols.

9.2.1 Infrared Systems

Infrared systems can be either point-to-point directed infrared solutions or point-to-multi-point diffused infrared solutions. The *directed infrared* solutions tend to be limited by the interconnection complexity of line-of-sight requirements and congestion at key nodes; they are appropriate for token ring LAN architectures, where each host is "directly" attached to both an upstream and a downstream station. *Diffused infrared* solutions tend to be limited by the "interference" of daylight and are appropriate for the shared media nature of Ethernet LANs.

In either case, infrared solutions are physically appropriate only for relatively open areas, such as cubicles; infrared transmission will not penetrate walls. The primary advantages of the infrared systems include freedom from FCC licensing and low cost. Infrared solutions involve interfacing standard computing devices to some form of optical transceiver; as always the API is a key consideration. This technology is likely to continue to be a niche solution strongly supported by its adherents.

9.2.2 Narrowband RF Systems

Narrowband RF systems, such as Motorola's Altair wireless Ethernet system, are able to penetrate some walls but require licensing from the *Federal Communications Commission (FCC)* and tend to be expensive, especially in light of their somewhat limited capacity and coverage. The need for installation of backbone cabling to connect the hubs providing the sometimes limited coverage further reduce the applicability of such solutions.

Altair operates in the 19 GHz RF spectrum and is a closed, proprietary technology providing approximately 3.3 Mbps effective user throughput in a 15 Mbps transmission medium. A derivative product called VistaPoint provides a wireless link for LANs, such as between neighboring buildings at an effective throughput of approximately 6 Mbps. Of course, security becomes a concern whenever the physical barriers of walls are removed as a deterrent to potential network eavesdroppers.

9.2.3 Spread Spectrum Systems

The predominant wireless LAN technology is currently that of *spread spectrum* RF systems, which operate in the Industrial, Scientific, and Medical (ISM) bands at 902-928 MHz, 2.4-2.4835

GHz, and 5.725-5.850 GHz. These frequency ranges are unlicensed by the FCC[1] and so they can be used by many non-LAN applications, such as garage door openers.

There are many vendors of spread spectrum technology. The spread spectrum LAN systems have recently been standardized by the IEEE 802.11 standard.[2] Typically, a low effective user bandwidth solution, this technology provides approximately 1-2 Mbps of usable bandwidth, versus the Ethernet standard supporting transmission rates of 10 Mbps.

There are two forms of spread spectrum technology, both of which spread a baseband signal over a wider range of frequencies in order to achieve resistance to noise and fading and thus gain in performance. It was this resistence to noise (i.e., jamming) that encouraged the development of spread spectrum technology for military applications.

The first spread spectrum technique is called *frequency hopping* spread spectrum, in which the baseband signal is spread by hopping from carrier frequency to carrier frequency within the ISM band in a pseudorandom fashion; both transmitter and receiver must know the hopping sequence and dwell time at each frequency prior to the transmission.

The second form of spread spectrum is called *direct sequence* spread spectrum, in which each transmission is modulated by a pseudorandom binary sequence that serves to spread the waveform spectrum; a correlator at the receiver evaluates the energy at the binary sequence-defined frequencies and despreads the signal prior to decoding it.

9.2.4 Metricom Ricochet

A recent development is the Metricom Ricochet wireless metropolitan network, which is an outgrowth of the ISM band spread spectrum LAN technology. Metricom, founded in 1985, constructs private wireless networks for utilities for wireless data acquisition and monitoring of public utility grid performance. These private networks were collectively called Utilinet, with a protocol that could be licensed from Metricom for other purposes.

Ricochet is a campus or metropolitan network, which is available in a few locations, primarily in Silicon Valley. Rather than pursuing a "Field of Dreams" strategy of universal coverage, Metricom constructs in the locations where specific customers have already been identified.

The high-level architecture of Ricochet consists of metropolitan networks linked together via public switched services. Within a metropolitan area, Ricochet utilizes a mesh of ISM-band frequency hopping spread spectrum RF repeaters, spaced approximately one mile apart.

Ricochet's many RF repeaters are small low cost, low power units, mounted on telephone poles and buildings to reduce deployment costs. The maximum transmit power of the radios is one Watt per ISM band restrictions; this limits reception to the previously mentioned one mile distance and reduces the in-building penetration of the signal.

---

1. These frequencies were originally in Part 18 of the FCC regulations.
2. IEEE 802.11 also has provisions supporting infrared media.

The low-power nature of Ricochet also increases the number of repeaters necessary to cover large metropolitan areas—on the order of 100,000 base stations will be required to cover the top 30 markets. This will also increase the network interconnectivity and scaling complexity; smaller cells means more frequent handoffs. Ricochet is a strictly LAN solution whose capability for wide area network services is limited by lack of definition of an internetworking scheme.

Within a metropolitan area, Ricochet has a flat topology, with distributed intelligence capable of supporting both automatic alternate route selection and peer-to-peer communications between mobiles. Network elements include *Remote Terminal Units* (*RTUs*), *Load Control Transponders* (*LCTs*), and network gateways. Three radio types are used: WAN gates (RS-232-based units at entry-point PCs serving as gateways), network radios (repeaters), and status control radios (which communicate status and control information).

Ricochet frequency hopping is based on a pseudo-random pattern using 240 narrowband channels within the 902-928 MHz band. Radios optimize their frequency hopping by being offset with respect to their neighbors. The same channels are used for both repeater to repeater links and communications between mobile and repeater. Under ideal conditions, the RF technology employed provides a transmission rate of up to 100 Kbps with an effective application rate of up to 38 Kbps.

Ricochet mobility is limited somewhat by the complexities of passing control to the mobile in a distributed system. Mobiles must either be stationary or slow-moving (i.e., less than 10 kph). Small cell sizes limit the speed of communicating mobiles due to handoff failures; the repeaters cannot update their routing tables quickly enough if users move too swiftly. The system design encourages constant connectivity by the mobile device. Direct mobile to mobile communications is supported as long as they are within one mile of one another.

Ricochet repeaters are addressed by latitude and longitude, with color codes used to differentiate between radios; each base station has a *global position system* (*GPS*) receiver. This is a novel way to unite geographic and network locations for routing purposes. Radios build internal node tables, whose entries include coordinate location, ASCII name, signal strength, unique radio address, and frequency hopping algorithm offset.

Packets are routed between radios in the mesh based on latitude and longitude coordinates; this coupled with the dynamics of alternate path decision-making eliminates the need for static routing tables. Each radio also maintains traffic history records, including the number of packets handled and forwarded to each neighbor, the number of retries for each neighbor, the number of hops and time needed for each message, the percentage of successful packet deliveries, etc.

Users can typically expect on the order of 3 or 4 RF hops between meshed base stations before their packets reach a landline access point, as depicted in Figure 9.1. This number of hops could increase to 30 or 40 in large cities, depending on the location of backbone points of presence. The backbone is a frame relay network.

The Metricom protocol is reliable. Data packets are sent with the address of the network radio nearest to the end destination. Packets sent are followed by queries for reception status;

each packet is separately queried. However, this overhead could effectively throttle the total system capacity, especially considering that the same channels are used for both mobiles and repeater links.

Applications access the system in a prioritized manner. Up to 200 packets can be stored by the radios; packets have time-to-live and number-of-routing-hops parameters to help determine which ones to keep. Old messages are discarded by the radios in the mesh, as are those requiring too many RF hops.

The system is self-healing thanks to its distributed intelligence. This helps it recover from outages and control congestion via alternate routing. Alternate paths are selected when the first-choice route is busy or unavailable.

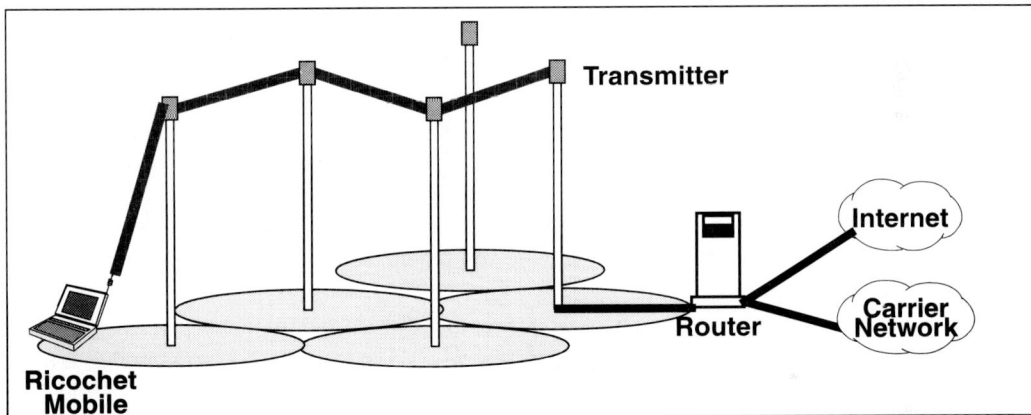

Figure 9.1   Metricom Ricochet

9.3 Paging Systems

Paging systems have traditionally consisted of infrastructure capable of *simulcasting*[3] phone numbers to small portable receivers, notifying subscribers of the need to call whomever initiated the page. Today, these systems are capable of two-way interaction, with subscribers initiating transactions from their portable devices as well as responding to messages by selecting one of a number of canned responses.

_____

3. Simulcast means that the same message is transmitted simultaneously from a number of locations in the network.

9.3.1 One-Way Paging Systems

The traditional paging system provides the capability for a subscriber to receive simulcast messages from the network as long as they are in the coverage area of the paging service provider. Early incarnations of paging services limited the message to a 10-digit phone number and limited the coverage area to a specific market.

Both of these limitations have been extended with text messages (typically limited to about 80 characters in length) and simulcast coverage that is nationwide in scope (typically supported via satellite). With the proper equipment[4] and provisioning, coverage areas can be extended internationally. Partly as a result of these extensions, at year-end 1995 there were some 34 million one-way paging subscribers in the United States.[5]

With increasing simulcast coverage comes increasing contention for a simulcast channel. It is significantly more resource-consumptive to use many transmission channels over a wide area for a single message than just one transmission channel over a single region. Prices for nationwide and international service are commensurately more expensive. This is the price paid for an essentially nonexistent mobility management scheme, in which the mobile is assumed to be everywhere.

A typical one-way paging network consists of a message center that receives messages to be simulcast to one or more mobile receivers. The message center consists of a combination of computers and operators to enter messages into the computers. Messages can originate from people phoning the operators or email.

Messages are formatted per the protocol in use, then forwarded to one or more paging transmitters. The paging transmitters are RF towers, typically located in high places, which transmit messages over a wider area than cellular transmitters. Because one-way paging devices are provided with an excellent "sleep mode" capability by paging protocols, battery life is greatly extended (to approximately one month or more). As a result, these devices are very small and inexpensive. Battery life is further extended by the receive-only mode of operation of pagers, although to a lesser degree.[6]

One-way paging service is much less expensive than two-way service because there is no reverse path (i.e., mobiles never transmit) and they can thus be deployed with fewer larger cells. Fewer cells means lower fixed (infrastructure) costs for service providers. One-way paging systems also benefit from not having to perform mobility management functions—the network doesn't really care where the mobile is or if it is even powered on. The network simply simulcasts the message from all of the paging transmitters included in the service profile for the subscriber.

Each pager receives all messages transmitted on the channel it is tuned to and filters all messages not addressed to it. Pager addresses have traditionally been formatted as 10-digit phone

---

4. For example, Canadian paging systems utilize 1200 baud rates vs. the U.S.'s 2400 baud. For this reason many pager models accommodate both baud rates.
5. Economics and Management Consultants International (EMCI) estimate.
6. Despite its receive-only mode of operation, the perpetual duty cycle of a one-way pager results in a significant power drain over time. Thus, the need for an effective sleep mode.

numbers for user-friendliness reasons; all of these phone numbers would be received by the message center. Now a common number (often an 800 number) is used with the particular pager identified by a *personal identification number* (*PIN*), also often formatted as a 7-digit phone number.

Early one-way paging systems used proprietary protocols to convey the 10-digit phone numbers to pagers. From these proprietary systems evolved the *Telocator Alphanumeric Protocol (TAP)* and associated *Telocator Network Paging Protocol (TNPP)*, with support for 7-bit ASCII text messages.

TAP is used today to access most text paging services, although it is inefficient in its inability to perform multicast transmissions. Instead, it must generate a separate copy for each of the members of a group targeted to receive a common message. TAP also provides no support for binary file exchange (i.e., noncharacter-oriented messages), which limits its ability to support other data applications.

An improved standard called *Telocator Data Protocol (TDP)* has recently been developed by the *Paging Communications Industry Association* (*PCIA*), the primary paging industry trade group. TDP is aimed at addressing the shortcomings of TAP, which it will replace.

TDP supports 8-bit ASCII messages, which are capable of transporting binary files, facsimile, and digitized voice as well as supporting longer messages, error correction, and file compression. TDP provides for packetization of larger messages with reassembly of the messages required at the recipient device. TDP also provides the group multicast capability absent in TAP.

With TDP, subscribers now have the option of either receiving the message directly at the pager or having it forwarded to a mailbox for later retrieval with a spawned short notification message being sent to the pager in near real time. As shown in Figure 9.2, a message originator sends a message from their computer as a binary file to the message processor via the *Telocator Message Entry (TME)* protocol. The message processor packetizes the message and forwards either the message or its notification to the paging transmitter.

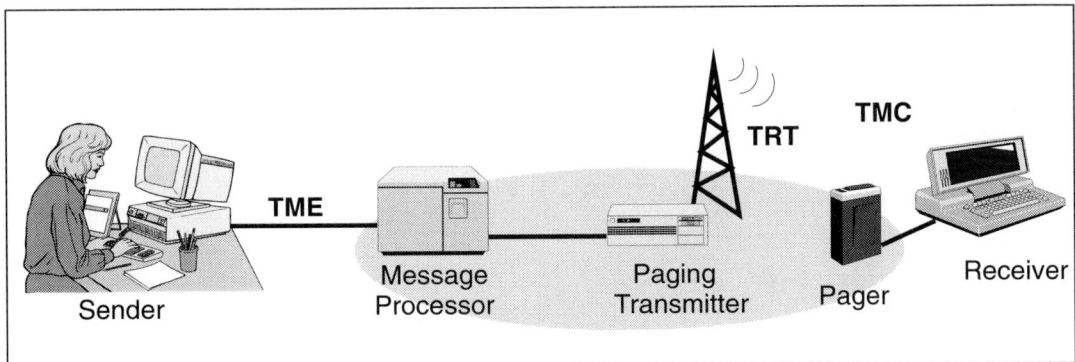

Figure 9.2   Telocator Data Protocol

The paging transmitter broadcasts the packets (or notification) to the recipient pager via the *Telocator Radio Transport (TRT)* protocols. The recipient pager reassembles the packets into the original message (or notification). Finally, the paging receiver uses the *Telocator Mobile Computer (TMC)* protocol to relay the message (or a file) to an application on a computer.

The ability to use TDP is a powerful tool for distribution of messages or data (including software upgrades) to users of mobile computing equipment. It could even be used to update the control software in the pager itself, although complicated by the fact that one-way service—by definition—cannot provide the means for the pager to acknowledge the correct receipt of the message (data) or initiate procedures for error recovery (retransmission, etc.).

Despite these advances in capability and coverage, one-way paging remains a best-effort simulcast service. The embryonic two-way paging services are likely to obsolete one-way paging; in fact the 1994 narrowband PCS spectrum definition includes channels for incumbent one-way paging services to extend their capability to acknowledged paging. After all, who doesn't wonder whether or not their page has actually been received?

9.3.2 Two-Way Paging Systems

In response to the twin demands for two-way messaging capability and a reduced federal budget deficit, the FCC conducted auctions in mid-1994 for *narrowband personal communication services (NPCS)* licenses in the 900 MHz frequency bands.[7] The auctions were a precursor to the subsequent broadband PCS auction (described in Chapter 2) and raised some $613 million for the U.S. Treasury.

The FCC definition of NPCS services is broad, including messaging, two-way paging, voice, and mobile communications. Digitized voice paging services are also expected. Broadcast services are explicitly prohibited under the licensing provisions.

The NPCS licensing involves a complicated channel plan encompassing nationwide, regional, and local coverage areas. Regional license areas are based on the 47 *major trading areas (MTAs)* defined by Rand McNally. Similarly, local license areas are based on Rand McNally's 487 *basic trading areas (BTAs)*.

As displayed in Table 9.2, NPCS licensing includes twelve 50 kHz channels, each paired with a 12.5 kHz channel. These channel pairs are targeted at asymmetric services where messages and data are transmitted outbound to mobiles, which acknowledge receipt of the messages and data. Nine 50 kHz channel pairs are defined for symmetric data and message transmission. Eight

---

7. NPCS frequencies include 900-901, 930-931, and 940-941 MHz bands. Only two of these three frequency bands have been auctioned and assigned. The third is being held in reserve for later assignment.

unpaired 12.5 kHz channels are defined for use by existing paging services for two-way capability. Finally, five unpaired 50 kHz channels are defined. NCS channels may be aggregated up to symmetric 150 kHz channel pairs for services requiring greater bandwidth.

Table 9.2   Narrowband PCS Channels

Licensed service area	Channels available
nationwide	3 (50 kHz + 12.5 kHz) pairs 5 (50 kHz + 50 kHz) pairs 3 unpaired 50 kHz channels
regional (47 MTAs)	7 (50 kHz + 12.5 kHz) pairs 4 (50 kHz + 50 kHz) pairs 2 unpaired 50 kHz channels
local (487 BTAs)	2 (50 kHz + 12.5 kHz) pairs 8 unpaired 12.5 kHz channels for use by existing one-way paging license holders.

Although the media (RF frequencies) have been defined for NPCS, the standards and technology to be used are left to the discretion of license holders. From the NPCS community, two basic standards have emerged—one based on a paging paradigm and the other based on a data networking model. These competing standards offer tradeoffs between system capacity and complexity versus subscriber battery life and simplicity. Other existing and intended paging equipment vendors have proposed alternative standards for use in the NPCS arena, but have since capitulated to the two dominant standards.

9.3.2.1 Motorola ReFLEX

The paging-based standard for NPCS is the extended FLEX™ family of protocols by Motorola. The FLEX messaging protocol has now been augmented by the ReFLEX™ two-way messaging protocol and the InFLEXion voice and data messaging protocol.

As listed in Table 9.3, new FLEX protocols are aimed primarily at asymmetric services, where greater capacity is needed in the forward direction. These protocols support a variety of data types, including binary files, and provide error detection and highly efficient sleep mode for mobiles *a la* one-way paging. These TDP-based protocols provide no security capabilities although they could be added later. As in any proprietary standard, licensing is required for any other manufacturer's products to be able to use these protocols.

Table 9.3   The Motorola FLEX™ Protocol Family

Protocol	Outbound / Inbound Bandwidth	PCS Channel Pair	Purpose
FLEX	2400 / NA bps	NA	One-way text paging
ReFLEX 25	12.8 / 9.6 kbps	50 / 12.5 kHz	Two-way paging / data
ReFLEX 50	25.6 / 9.6 kbps	50 / 50 kHz	Two-way paging / data
InFLEXion	112 / 9.6 kbps	50 / 50 or 50 / 12.5 kHz	High-speed voice and robust data transport

The two-way extensions to FLEX include mobile registration to a particular local area, typically a city. Whenever outbound pages or data are destined for the mobile, all transmission facilities in that local area must participate. In a large city this could require simulcast transmission of the message from dozens or even hundreds of paging transmitters. This makes economic sense only if a few large paging cells can provide the service; otherwise fixed infrastructure costs would be excessive.

Although this simulcast bandwidth requirement is inefficient, it is mitigated somewhat by a much simpler mobility management scheme with support for limited tracking. This allows an efficient sleep mode capability, which in turn extends battery life. Unfortunately, the need for supporting reverse channels for low power mobiles limits the size of cells, increasing the fixed (infrastructure) costs of the network.

Thus, an expensive bi-directional infrastructure is required to support the reverse channels but cannot be efficiently used (in terms of airlink capacity) because of simulcast forward transmission. However, the system retains the benefits of simple mobility management and long battery life, which also result from its paging history.

9.3.2.2 personal Air Communicator Technology (pACT)

The second primary standard for NPCS is the *personal Air Communicator Technology (pACT)*[8] standard developed by AT&T Wireless Services and others. This open CDPD-based messaging standard is oriented toward the data networking paradigm of the IP protocol suite. pACT is a variant of CDPD, with modifications to the airlink and radio resource management definitions.[9]

As in its CDPD heritage, pACT requires no licensing fees and is IP-based. Mobile units are IP-addressable network nodes. pACT preserves the security and mobility management capabilities of CDPD; a mobile device must notify the network whenever it moves to a new channel stream.

---

8. This is pronounced "pact," not "p-act."
9. This extensibility of the CDPD specification is a benefit of an open, layered system definition. Network elements and protocols in the pACT technical specification are the same as in CDPD, but with the leading "Mobility" being replaced by "Personal," e.g., "PD-IS" instead of "MD-IS."

This allows a pACT-based service provider to support much greater collective bandwidth because only a single transmitter is required to transmit to a mobile. The tradeoff is a somewhat reduced battery efficiency at the mobile device, because of the need for more continual reception of the forward channel to support mobility management.

The spectrum efficiency of pACT is offset somewhat by a low speed transmission capability. In support of its symmetric communication architecture, both forward and reverse channels support 8 kbps channel speed on a 50/50 kHz channel pair. This relatively low data rate includes error correction plus the capability for a cellular-type mode of frequency reuse. Each 50 kHz license is implemented as multiple sub-rate transmission channels.

pACT is designed for limited size messages and data. As such, it includes the LSM and SNS protocols standardized in the CDPD Forum. Both symmetric (e.g., peer-to-peer email) and asymmetric (e.g., acknowledged paging) applications are supported by pACT. Message and data store-and-forward capabilities are intrinsic to the system. But pACT is not intended to provide a general purpose mobile data service.

Although pACT mobiles are IP-addressable, the nature of the application—NPCS—suggests that the services are provided via a "closed" system. Therefore, there is no requirement that pACT-based service providers actually use globally-unique IP addresses. However, use of InterNIC-supplied IP address blocks will greatly facilitate the ease with which pACT-based applications can be developed to interact with the rest of the world.

Going forward, it seems likely that applications software developers will increasingly consider NPCS capability essential to the products they create. File compression and, possibly, encryption will likely become increasingly common. Of course, IP-based paging protocols, like pACT, also encourage the trend toward communications and computing commonality.

9.4 Private Wireless Packet Data Systems

Many of us have experienced riding in a taxi. One of the more memorable aspects of a taxi ride—aside from the almost predictable stunt driver nature of the ride itself—is the squawk coming from the taxi's radio. This seemingly crude form of communication is an example of a private land mobile radio system. Other examples of private systems include those used for public safety, utilities, and other applications.

Operating primarily in the 806-824 MHz and 851-869 MHz frequency bands, these private systems are usually conventional non-trunked[10] systems. The channels are 25 KHz in bandwidth.

Specialized mobile radio, or *SMR,*[11] systems are regional trunked radio systems, which means that a number of users (radios) share a common channel, typically provided via a single base

---

10. A trunked system is one with shared RF channels among disparate users.
11. This is pronounced "smur."

station.[12] SMR systems have traditionally been used in small cities for local services such as fleet dispatch and public safety.   Only scratchy-sounding voice has been supported by these analog systems, typically via 12.5 kHz channels, located in the 800 and 900 MHz bands.

Despite limited bandwidth, SMR systems are widely used. According to a 1995 survey of SMR operators and manufacturers, there were more than two million SMR subscribers at year-end 1995, a growth of some thirteen percent over the previous year.[13] This net subscriber growth was actually lower than previous years, largely because of increased congestion of these 800 MHz networks.

This congestion has prompted a recent FCC proposal to auction additional SMR spectrum above 860 MHz in 1997. The proposed auction would allow large SMR service providers, such as Nextel and Pittencrieff Communications, to acquire the contiguous spectrum necessary to compete with other wireless services. A similar auction of SMR frequencies in the 900 MHz bands was held in the winter of 1995-96, largely in support of other SMR participants such as GeoTek.

Contiguousness of frequencies is important for any nationwide wireless service provider. In the late 1980s, Nextel and others began an effort to acquire SMR service providers with the objective of patching together a nationwide coverage. Unfortunately, many of the existing regional SMR services have operated in non-contiguous bands, hampering such a nationwide combination. The spectrum auctions will help this situation.

In the late 1980s, Motorola developed a digital or enhanced SMR (ESMR[14]) system called *Motorola Integrated Radio System (MIRS)*.[15] These systems support two-way data and paging as well as 7200 bps voice. Also available in the ESMR systems, via the PSTN, are 4800 bps circuit-switched data services. New technologies and standards, such as *Enhanced Digital Access Communications Systems (EDACS)*, are encouraging additional vendors to participate in this industry.

So, where are we today? In 1996, Nextel continues its efforts to provide a nationwide ESMR service. With Craig McCaw's 1995 investment in a controlling interest came focus—toward remote and mobile office connectivity rather than the previous horizontal cellular-type services. Today's circuit-switched services are scheduled to be augmented with packet-switched data services in 1997.

Other SMR operators such as GeoTek Communications will also offer integrated voice and data services aimed at dispatch, one-way and two-way messaging, remote point-of-sale, auto vehicle location, and other markets. Until the larger players in ESMR deploy nationwide services, these systems will continue to be regional or even local in nature. Mobility will remain constrained, much as it is with metropolitan networks such as Metricom.

---

12. Like the party lines commonplace in bygone days, the multiple users of the channel determine that the call is their's by the ringing pattern or by the identifier called out. Remember "Car 54, where are you?"
13. American Mobile Telecommunications Association and Economic and Management Consultants International, Inc., estimate.
14. This is pronounced "e-smur."
15. This former proprietary technology was renamed iDEN or integrated Dispatch Enhanced Network in 1995. iDEN may now be licensed from Motorola. MIRS was originally developed for NexTel (then known as FleetCall). Motorola subsequently traded its SMR channels (then amounting to 30% of the channels available in the U.S.) to NexTel in exchange for an equity interest in the company.

9.5 Public Wireless Packet Data Services

The demand for wireless packet data services has spawned the creation of public services, initially dominated by Ardis and RAM Mobile Data. These services are largely based on proprietary technology that can be licensed by other manufacturers. Nonstandard *application program interfaces (APIs)* lessen the attractiveness of porting applications to these services.

Public wireless packet data systems rely on third-party vendors, such as RadioMail, to provide gateways to the rest of the data networking world and perform store-and-forward functions. As a result, customer acceptance of these services has been somewhat slow, with approximately 30K and 40K subscribers on RAM and Ardis, respectively, at mid-1995.[16] These are considered to be public services because they are available on a subscription basis to whomever desires wireless capability.

9.5.1 Advanced Radio Data Integrated System (Ardis)

Ardis was created as a joint venture of Motorola and IBM. This 1990 partnership was intended to leverage the system Motorola had previously created for IBM field service technicians, who still comprise almost one-half of the Ardis subscriber base. Now owned solely by Motorola, Ardis retains its vertical market orientation with an emphasis on host connectivity; applications supported by Ardis include dispatch and field service.

Ardis is an 800-MHz band RF system built with a cellular-type architecture. Cellular architectures are used for one reason—the ability to reuse scarce channels for increased capacity—and Ardis exemplifies this goal. This single-frequency reuse system has up to 6 25-kHz RF channel pairs available in large North American cities (12.5 KHz channels in Europe), but only one so-called Nationwide Channel pair is available for accessing the system.

This limited channel set dictates a mode of operation that limits forward channel capacity. In areas where only a single channel is available, nearby base stations coordinate their transmissions to avoid interfering with one another; in a small cluster of cells only one base station can transmit at a time. This base station coordination is handled by *area communications controllers (ACCs)* upstream in the network.

However, a nice characteristic of the single-frequency reuse scheme is that overlapping cell coverages results in enhanced in-building reception of the reverse channel. Multiple base stations typically receive each mobile-originated packet; an ACC selects the best copy of the packet from these multiple receptions. The ACC then uses an intelligent "path sensing" algorithm to select the best route outbound to the mobile to minimize congestion. This routing algorithm also allows multiple simultaneous transmissions from non-interfering base stations by an Ardis system, gaining capacity of 1.5 to 3 times over a simulcast system.

---

16. The slow acceptance of these services has spurred RAM and Ardis to interconnect their services with those of cellular and CDPD service providers.

A 19.2 Kbps radio link protocol known as RD-LAP is replacing the original 4800 bps MDC4800 protocol (which is still used for Nationwide Channel access). Both protocols are Motorola proprietary although RD-LAP can be licensed by other manufacturers. Four-level FSK modulation with a Gaussian filter is used on the RD-LAP-based system. A three-quarters rate Trellis-coded modulation with interleaving and CRC-32 supports an undetected block error probability of approximately 2^{-32}.

RD-LAP provides a slotted *digital sense multiple access* (*DSMA*) MAC protocol without collision detection by the half-duplex mobiles; higher layers are assumed to recover from errors. The maximum transmission burst is 2048 bytes. A *stop-and-wait* (*SAW*) link protocol is used by the half-duplex mobiles, which limits the throughput enjoyed by an application running over Ardis.

Taking all of this into consideration, the effective data rate for a 512-byte transmission is approximately 6.33 Kbps [WONG95]. The protocol efficiency is 57 percent and 61 percent for 125 and 250 octet messages, respectively.

Ardis is best suited for low bandwidth non-interactive applications; response times generally exceed 5 seconds. Ardis enjoys widespread deployment, providing coverage to some 80 percent of the population of the U.S. and 90 percent of U.S. business areas via more than 1400 base station sites, 35 area communications controllers (ACCs) and 3 message switches, as depicted in Figure 9.3.

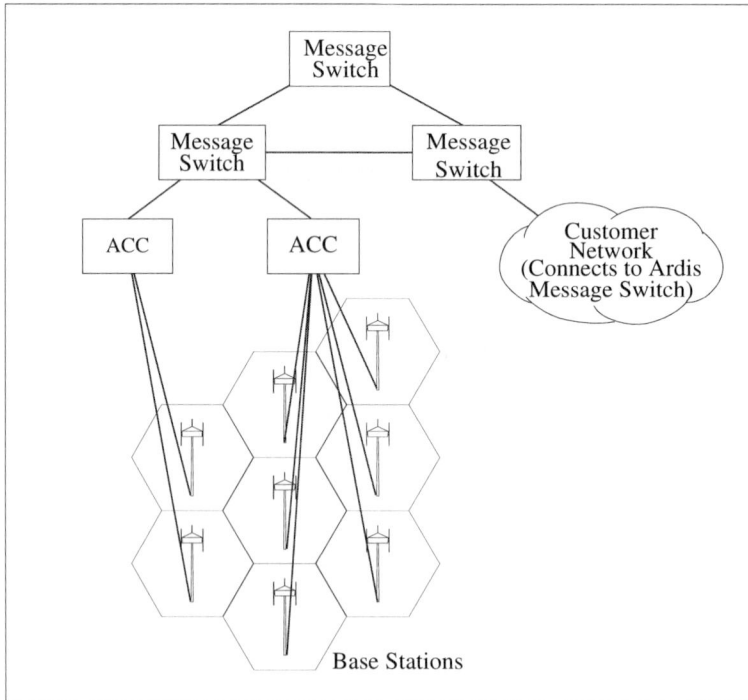

Figure 9.3   ARDIS Architecture

The Ardis architecture defines protocols up to and including Layer 4 in the mobile. A so-called *Native Command Language (NCL)* in the bottom two layers provides a command/response type of transaction protocol between the *Radio Packet Modem (RPM)* and the subscriber's computer. The RPM uses RD-LAP in Layers 2 and 3 to access the network, which is X.25-based. The Ardis communications architecture is depicted in Figure 9.4.

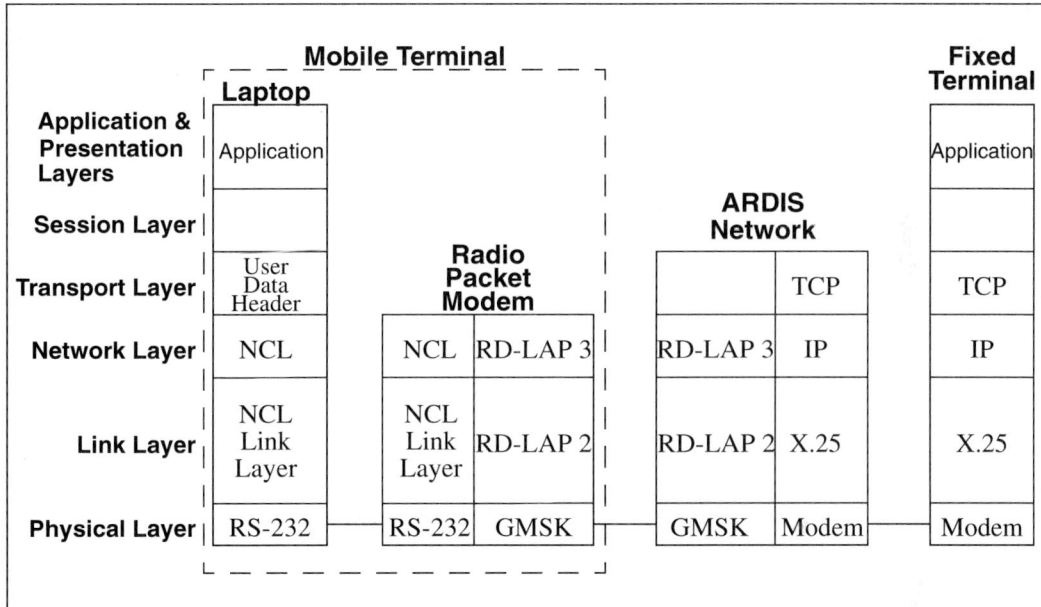

Figure 9.4   ARDIS Communications Architecture

Mobility management in Ardis resembles CDPD. A H*ome Location Register (HLR)* and *Visitor Location Register (VLR)* located in ACCs track the position of each RPM registered with the network. Whenever an RPM recognizes that it is in a new cell (by base station-transmitted information), it sends a registration packet to update the network location database. The serving ACC and VLR coordinate this with the home ACC and HLR, getting authorization prior to granting service.

Ardis provides a Motorola-proprietary security capability, involving authentication and symmetric key exchange. It defines communication protocols up to the Transport Layer of the OSI reference model. No access priorities are defined. Gateways are necessary to interface to the rest of the data networking world because of the nonstandard protocols and APIs in use.

Because the network consists of a single administrative domain, service and performance are consistent everywhere; there are essentially no interoperability or incompatibility problems. Ardis connects with the outside world via dedicated links or VANs (e.g., Advantis). As mentioned previously, the RadioMail service is typically used by subscribers for both store-and-forward and network gateway services.

Ardis features are compared with those of CDPD and RAM in Table 9.4.

9.5.2 RAM Mobile Data (Mobitex)

RAM Mobile Communications is a joint venture of Ericsson and Bell South in the U.S. This public wireless packet data network is based on the Mobitex network, the name by which it is known outside of North America. Mobitex was first deployed in Sweden in 1986 as a joint venture of Ericsson and the Swedish post office for voice and dispatch data services. RAM continues to have a horizontal market orientation with an emphasis on peer-to-peer messaging.

Typical applications of RAM include host access and dispatch. RAM has been widely deployed with over 1000 base stations in operation. RAM has worked with customers to co-finance base stations in remote areas where RAM might otherwise not build-out. RAM now provides nationwide coverage via cellular, paging, satellite, dial-up, and private networks.

Architecturally, Mobitex has always been considered to be a wireless extension of X.25 packet switching networks, consistent with its European telephony roots. Mobitex is a cellular-based system with between 10 and 30 12.5 kHz channels available in markets in the 896-901 MHz band.[17] As a result, airlink capacity has never been a concern. Access to the system is provided by National System Channels, which control access to the particular channel set in operation in any given area; this provides the necessary support for mobility between markets.

Intercommunication is done at the lowest possible level of the tiered hierarchy of base stations, local switches called MOXs and regional/national switches called MHXs, as displayed in Figure 9.5. The MHXs are identical physically to the MOXs but differ in their software soul. A *network control center* or *NCC* handles billing and management functions, but no user traffic. The modular nature of Mobitex architecture supports both small systems and extremely large systems with multiple levels of MHXs and redundant NCCs.

Sufficient intelligence is built into each node allowing intercommunication to be done at the lowest possible level: mobiles can interact directly via the base station (if they are registered to the same base). If a base station doesn't recognize the destination mobile, it will pass the message to the MOX. If the MOX knows the mobile, it will pass the necessary information on the destination mobile to the base station; if the MOX doesn't know of the mobile, it passes the message on to the MHX. Most fixed-location hosts are interconnected physically via land-lines at the local exchanges (MOXs), although the connection is also possible at the base station level. Occasionally the fixed host might also be connected to a main exchange (MHX).

---

17. RAM assembled its nationwide spectrum by purchasing and consolidating SMRs.

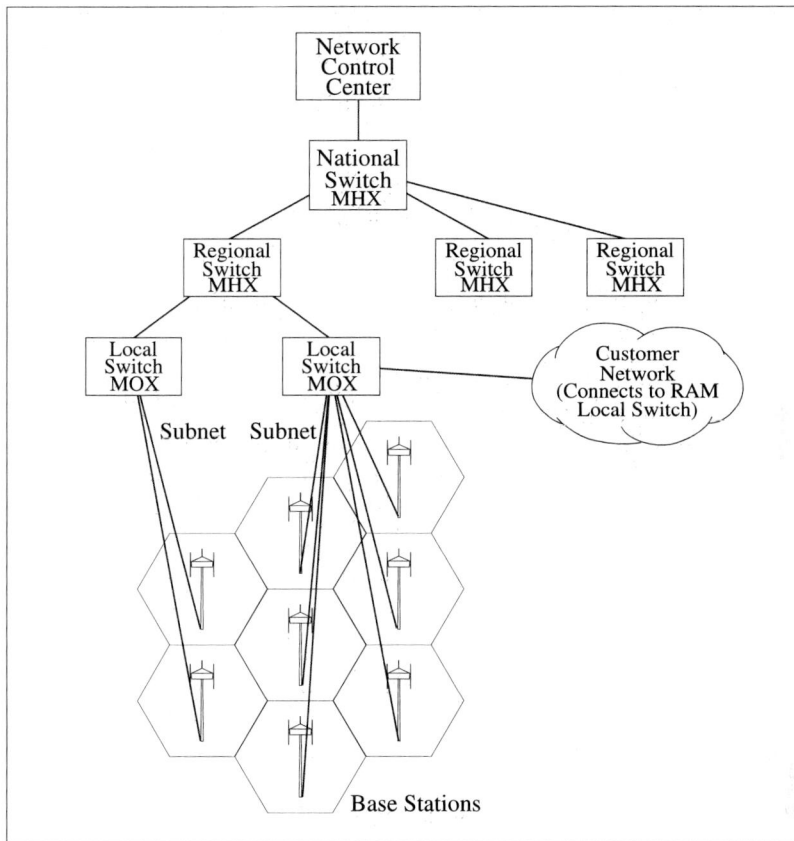

Figure 9.5   RAM Architecture

External hosts can either connect directly to the MOXs or via public X.25 packet data networks. Other fixed host connection alternatives include dial-up gateways (preassigned to minimize PSTN charges), IP gateways (over either X.25 or PPP), and specialized gateways (including 3270 and 5250 emulation).

The 8 Kbps Mobitex MAC layer protocol is open but not a standard. It has two modes of operation—slotted Aloha for short messages and a modified CSMA for longer transmissions. The maximum transmission burst is 512 octets. A combination of a shortened (12,8) Hamming forward error correction with interleaving to a depth of 20 and CRC-16 parity provides an undetected block error rate of approximately 2^{-16}. A selective *ARQ* (*automatic repeat request*) mechanism enables the retransmission of specific blocks.

Like Ardis, the half-duplex Mobitex mobiles have no capability for collision detection and so error recovery must be done at a higher layer. A go-back-N protocol is employed at the *logical link control* (*LLC*) sublayer by the half-duplex mobiles for error recovery.

The effective data rate for a 512-octet transmission is 4.6 Kbps [WONG95]. The protocol efficiency is 51 percent and 55 percent for 125 and 250-octet messages, respectively. Response times are typically over 4 seconds and highly variable. Channel access algorithm parameters such as maximum message length and priority levels can be dynamically adjusted by the network operator to optimize system performance in the face of changing traffic loads.

Protocols at the mobile are defined up through Layer 4, as displayed in Figure 9.6. *MASC* is the *Mobitex Asynchronous Communications* Protocol and *MPAK* is the *Mobitex Packet* assembly/ disassembly protocol. MTP/1 is the Mobitex Transport Protocol and interface, which must be employed by applications developers to access the wireless data services. These are open, license-free protocols but non-standard (except RS-232); there are several terminal manufacturers.

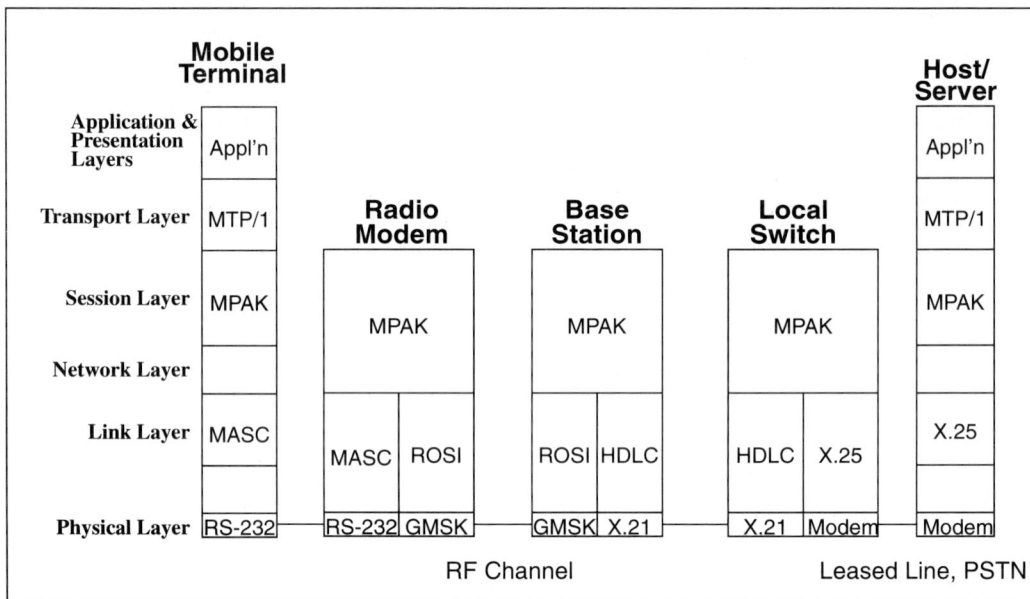

Figure 9.6   Mobitex Communications Architecture

The mobile handles its own radio resource management, like CDPD; received signal strength and data error rates are monitored by the mobile, which also scans the channels of adjacent base stations to determine optimum RF channel selection. Four user priority levels are defined; the highest is strictly for emergency messages. These priorities are used to control the flow of in-bound traffic to the system. The system advertises the lowest priority traffic it is willing to entertain. At coverage borders, mobiles can promote themselves one priority level; this is known as "distance access priority."

Mobility in Mobitex is also similar to CDPD. The mobile terminal notifies the network whenever it has changed base station coverage areas via a ROAM message. The MOX receiving this message in turn notifies other affected network nodes (the last serving MOX, etc.) of the mobile's change in location. Twenty-four-bit addressing supports international roaming.

Other features provided include sleep mode for mobile battery life extension, and store-and-forwarding of email intended for mobiles with message storage notification to the sender. There has been criticism that RAM's primary shortcoming is poor in-building coverage, which RAM is addressing through continued deployment of additional base stations.

No security features are provided, as RAM believes that the complexity of airlink attacks is sufficient to discourage even sophisticated hackers.[18] Each subscriber device and fixed host in a Mobitex network is assigned a unique eight-digit *Mobitex Access Number* (*MAN*), which is stored in non-volatile memory. A unique *Electronic Serial Number* (*ESN*) is permanently stored in the radio modem and is validated by the network with the MAN whenever the mobile registers. A transferable subscription capability allows a user to provide an eight-character password when registering with a different mobile. All identifiers and passwords are transmitted in the clear.

RAM (Mobitex) features are compared with those of CDPD and Ardis in Table 9.4.

Table 9.4   CDPD, RAM and ARDIS Feature Comparison[a]

Feature	CDPD	RAM	ARDIS
Open System Standard	Yes	No	No
Multiple Service Providers	Yes	No	No
Multi-Vendor Infrastructure Equipment	Yes	No	No
Multi-Vendor Subscriber Equipment	Yes	Yes	Yes
Broadcast Service	Yes	?	Yes
Multicast Service	Yes	Yes	Yes
Authentication	Yes	Yes	Yes
Encryption	RC-4 over airlink	End-to-End only	Proprietary over the airlink
	End-to-End		End-to-End
Subscriber Device Power Save Mode	Yes	Yes	Yes
Full/Half Duplex airlink	Full	Half	Half
Network supported Data Compresssion	Yes (V.42bis)	No	No

---

18. RAM Mobile white paper [RAMM95].

Table 9.4   CDPD, RAM and ARDIS Feature Comparison[a]   (Continued)

Feature	CDPD	RAM	ARDIS
Base Sites	10,000 +	1,000 +	1,400 +
Airlink Data Rate	19,200 bps	8000 bps	4800 bps and 19,200 bps

a: Source: P. McConnell [MCCO96]

9.5.3 RadioMail

RadioMail is not a wireless service provider at all, but rather a service providing the backend mailbox solution for wireless services such as RAM and Ardis. In late 1995, fewer than three thousand subscribers were using this service, despite its having received great fanfare in the press. One might conclude from this that relatively few RAM and Ardis applications were horizontal in nature at that time.

9.6 Satellite-Based Systems

Satellite-based systems offer the opportunity for true mobility—the ability to communicate anywhere anytime (as long as you're on Earth). Recent technological advances now make it possible to provide RF coverage to remote locations for small, relatively low power mobile units. Unfortunately, there is a relative dearth of demand for mobile communications services in remote locations. This remains the quandary of satellite-based communications systems.

Early satellite communications services have been provided by high-orbit *geosynchronous* (*GEO*) satellites, which—at altitudes of approximately 35 kilometers—orbit the Earth beyond the outer Van Allen belts. Because of their high altitude, relatively few satellites are required to provide coverage—typically two or three are sufficient, depending on the desired service area.

It's a good thing because GEO satellites are expensive and the systems utilizing these satellites typically suffer from large delays—on the order of 250 milliseconds roundtrip. Because of the distances involved, relatively large dish antenna and relatively high-powered RF transceivers are often required.[19] This might be wireless but it is hardly portable.

Recent advances have popularized so-called *low Earth orbit* or *LEO* satellites. These satellites are not geosynchronous and orbit the Earth at approximately 700 kilometers—below the inner

---

19. This depends on the so-called link power budget and aperture required (to differentiate between two satellites with small angular separation transmitting on a common frequency).

Van Allen belts. Because of their relative proximity, they enable the use of low-power mobile transceivers by subscribers.

Unfortunately, these low altitude satellites each cover a much smaller surface of the Earth, which means that more satellites are required. What's even worse, the low altitude means that the satellites are dragged down by the Earth's upper atmosphere and thus have an operational life of about five years. This adds greatly to the operating cost of such a system.

Despite these drawbacks, visionaries continue to push this application of the Reagan administration's Star Wars defense initiative for commercial purposes. One of the more interesting aspects of the LEO satellite-based communication systems is their reversal of standard cellular systems; in LEO systems, the mobile devices are essentially stationary while the "base station" satellites move at up to 35 degrees per minute (which translates into 7.4 kilometers per second in Earth motion). Because of the smaller coverage areas supported by the LEO satellites, frequency reuse is possible.

LEO systems are classified into one of three groups. The first group is the so-called "Big LEO" group, which will support voice, data, paging, and facsimile services. These systems—which include Iridium, Globalstar, Odyssey, and Inmarsat P—can be characterized as giant cellular systems in the sky, requiring dozens of satellites each. In some cases, *mid-Earth orbit* (*MEO*) altitudes of ten thousand kilometers are used (Table 9.5, Comparison of "Big LEO" Systems).

Table 9.5   Comparison of "Big LEO" Systems[a]

Service	Iridium	Globalstar	Odyssey	Inmarsat P
Proponents	Motorola, others	Loral, QUAL-COMM, others	TRW, Tele-globe, others	Inmarsat P government consortium
Altitude (km)	740 (LEO)	1410 (LEO)	10,500 (MEO)	10,500 (MEO)
Satellites	66	48	12	10 + 2
Ground stations	20	90-200	8	8-12
Access scheme	TDD	CDMA	CDMA	TDMA
Spectrum (service link)	1610 - 1626.5 MHz	1.6 / 2.5 GHz	1.6 / 2.5 GHz	2.0 / 2.2 GHz
Spectrum (feeder link)	20 / 30 GHz	5 / 7 GHz	20 / 30 GHz	5 / 15 GHz
Anticipated cost	$4.0 B	$3.5 B	$2.5 B	$3.0 B

a: Primary source for this table: [RUSC95].

Iridium, a Motorola-led consortium, is the most ambitious of the Big LEOs. It was named for the element whose atomic number matches the originally-planned 77-satellite constellation.[20] Each of the currently-planned 66 satellites is designed to be a self-contained switching center with links to its neighbors for redundancy as well as performance reasons. These small "smart" satellites are intended to be intenetworked together to form an adaptive fault-tolerant network backbone.

Small cellular handset-like mobile devices will communicate directly with a selected Iridium satellite. Terrestrial gateways will interface the satellite network to the PSTN and other terrestrial networks. The service is intended to complement the services provided by less-expensive terrestrial systems.

Globalstar, a consortium led by Loral and QUALCOMM, is slightly less ambitious—it only requires 48 satellites. Each of the satellites will function strictly as a digital repeater in a so-called "bent pipe transponder" mode between the service and feeder links back to Earth locations. Switching and call processing functions are handled by ground stations, which makes satellites less expensive and the system easier to upgrade.

The second group of LEO systems is referred to as the "Little LEOs." This diminutive characterization is only relative to the ambitious "Big LEOs." Little LEO systems are intended to provide narrowband store-and-forward data *a la* two-way paging. These systems are represented by Orbcomm, GE Americom, Starsys, and VITA.

Orbcomm Global LP is a fifty-fifty partnership between Teleglobe, Inc., and Orbital Sciences Corp. At year-end 1995 two satellites were in orbit for beta testing, out of a planned 28-satellite system. This low-cost data service is aimed at applications such as vehicle tracking, pipeline monitoring and low-bandwidth two-way data. It will operate in the VHF band at 137-150 MHz, which permits inexpensive "mobile" equipment.

The third class of LEO systems provides wideband data services. This group of systems is typified by Teledesic, whose bandwidth is much greater than the systems mentioned previously—typically 160 channels at 9.6 kbps (1.5 Mbps) or higher. The idea is to provide broadband bandwidth on demand services analogous to wireless fiber anywhere on Earth. [FREZ95] characterizes this service as "broadband Internet in the Sky."

Teledesic is the brainchild of Craig McCaw, with early funding coming from himself, Bill Gates, and Microsoft. Initially scoffed at because of its 840-satellite requirement, critics are now rethinking their initial reaction to the concept. Teledesic is envisioned as providing two million subscribers basic data rate connections at 16 kbps, for an aggregate 32 gigabits per second bandwidth.

The target Teledesic user is not mobile—fixed location users are assumed. The system will be a highly fault-tolerant geodesic mesh of satellites, with each satellite linked to 8 of its neighbors. Teledesic is envisioned to allow end-users to bypass the local loop upgrade bottleneck for receiving broadband services today.

---

20. The joke inside Motorola was that it was a good thing that 76 satellites were insufficient. The element whose atomic number is 76 is Lead, which somehow lacks the marketing cachet of Iridium. Likewise, the element whose atomic number is equal to the currently-planned number of satellites—66—is dysprosium, which is probably a name better suited for things other than communications services.

Another means of providing high bandwidth services is via *geosynchronous* (*GEO*) satellites. As previously mentioned, these high altitude satellites are expensive and require expensive, high-power "mobile" transceivers. These systems include MOBILSAT (MSAT), a joint effort of American Mobile Satellite Corp. (AMSC) and OmniTracs, Spaceway, and, Cyberstar.

The idea of these GEO services is to provide ubiquitous mobile telephone, facsimile, and data services. "Mobile" devices consist of briefcase-sized transportable units. Because of the extensive coverage provided by high-altitude satellites, only two satellites are required to cover the Earth's landmass. Bandwidths provided for circuit-switched data services will range from 2400 to 4800 bps. X.25 packet-switch data services at up to 3 kbps are also anticipated. As of September, 1995, the FCC had received twelve wideband GEO proposals.

The OmniTracs service provided by QUALCOMM is notable in that it has been fully operational since 1988. This twin GEO satellite-based system supports over 100 thousand mobile devices with data-only services. OmniTracs provides the basis for tracking long-haul truck fleets—strictly a vertical market. It has also provided much of QUALCOMM revenues in the early 1990s.

Some non-"Big Leo" satellite systems are compared in Table 9.6

Table 9.6   Comparison of non-"Big LEO" Systems[a]

Service	Orbcomm	Teledesic	Spaceway	MSAT
Proponents	Teleglobe, Orbital Sciences	Craig McCaw, Bill Gates	Hughes	AMSC & TMI
Altitude (km)	750 (LEO)	700 (LEO)	35,000 (GEO)	35,000 (GEO)
Satellites	2 - 28	840	8	2
Ground stations	4	16	2	2
Access scheme	TDMA	TDMA	TDMA	FDMA
Bandwidth	2.4-4.8 kbps	2M * 16 kbps	1.5 Mbps	1-5 kbps
Service spectrum	137.5 / 150 MHz	20 / 30 GHz	20 / 30 GHz	1.6 / 1.5 GHz
Feeder spectrum	137.5 / 150 MHz	20 / 30 GHz	20 / 30 GHz	13 / 11 GHz
Anticipated cost	$220 M	$9.0 B	$6.2 B	$500 M

a: Primary source for this table: [RUSC95].

In addition to the issues raised previously about satellite-based mobile systems, one should not forget the need for international regulation. Both in terms of orbit and radio frequency in use, these systems are by definition international. The primary authority is the *World Administrative Radio Conference* (*WARC*), organized by the *United Nations International Telecommunications Union* (*ITU*) and held every three years to regulate the use of RF frequencies worldwide. For this and technical reasons (and cost!), satellite systems require extremely long lead times.

9.7 Summary

This chapter has presented a survey of the alternatives to cellular-based systems for mobile data communications. The wide range of technologies and services receiving serious consideration and investment reflects the demand for mobile data capabilities. As technological advances turn dreams into viable commercial opportunities, some of these alternatives will prosper more than others. But none of them appears likely to replace cellular-based systems in the near future. In the next chapter we will discuss the most likely to succeed alternative to CDPD for mobile data networking.

10 *Future Directions in Mobility*

The public telecommunications carriers don't understand the data communications business and couldn't market modems to PC users if their lives depended on it.

—W. Frezza, "Going the Way of Wireless," *Network Computing*, October 1, 1995

The most ubiquitous internetwork is called the Internet. Routing in the Internet is based on the *Internet Protocol* (*IP*). In the late 1970s and early 1980s when the IP was developed, mobility of hosts was never considered. At that time most hosts were simply physically too large to move around.

The explosive growth of the Internet combined with the widespread availability of highly mobile small hosts in the form of laptop and palmtop computers, and personal digital assistants, has created a big demand for the concept of Mobile IP. The current trends point clearly towards further miniaturization and greater mobility. It is not unreasonable to expect many of tomorrow's hosts to be in the form of pagers, cell phones, or even wrist watches. Transparent mobility is a major requirement for the next generation IP (IPv6).

For the Internet to support global transparent mobility, a new set of mobility management protocols that accommodate roaming among different subnetworks and different media types is required. None of the technologies discussed thus far completely addresses this requirement.

However, significant efforts are presently underway to develop a comprehensive solution for transparent mobility in the Internet. In this chapter we discuss two such efforts. First, we survey the so called "Mobile IP" effort that enhances the current Internet Protocol (IPv4) to support mobility. Next, we discuss the next generation of Internet Protocol (IPv6), which is being designed to address the mobility requirement. We then compare and contrast CDPD mobility with Mobile IP. Table 10.1 provides a comparative glossary of CDPD and Mobile IP, which those familiar with CDPD may choose to review prior to reading the chapter.

10.1 Mobility under IPv4

The Mobile IP Working Group of the *Internet Engineering Task Force* (*IETF*) is addressing the requirement of mobility in today's Internet. Mobile IP enables a mobile node to send and receive packets over the Internet using its home address regardless of its point of attachment. In essence, Mobile IP extends the existing Internet Protocol to allow a portable computer to be moved from one network to another without changing its IP address and without losing existing connections.

In this section we will discuss:

- The Mobile IP Standards Process
- A summary of the current Mobile IP specifications
- Existing implementations of Mobile IP

It is important to recognize that Mobile IP is rapidly evolving. By the time that you read this, much of the information provided in this chapter may be somewhat obsolete. Therefore, this entire section should be read with the understanding that it provides only a snapshot as of the time of this writing (June 1996). We intend to maintain current information about various aspects of Mobile IP at the following site:

http://www.neda.com/mobileIpSurvey/html/mobileIP.html

The current base specification for Mobile IP is an "Internet Draft." Internet Drafts are draft documents that may be updated, replaced, or obsoleted by other documents at any time. It is inappropriate to use Internet Drafts as reference material or to cite them other than as "work in progress."

10.1.1 The Mobile IP Standards Process

10.1.1.1 Mobile IP and the IETF

The Mobile IP Working Group of the *Internet Engineering Task Force* (*IETF*) is the culmination of efforts by many individuals interested in the problem of mobile routing of hosts. The first meetings were in the form of *BOF* (*Birds of a Feather*) sessions held at the Atlanta (July, 1991), Santa Fe (November, 1991), and San Diego (March, 1992) IETF meetings. In June, 1992, a proposed charter for a formal Working Group was submitted to the IETF and at the same time a mailing list was set up for conduct of the group's business. Following a revision of the charter, the Working Group was officially formed in June 30, 1992.

10.1.1.2 IETF Mobile IP Working Group Charter, Goals, and Milestones

The IETF *Mobile IP Working Group* (*mobileip WG*) is chartered to develop or adopt architectures and protocols to support mobility within the Internet. In the near-term, protocols for supporting transparent host "roaming" among different subnetworks and different media (e.g., LANs, dial-up links, and wireless communication channels) are to be developed and entered into the Internet standards track. The work is expected to consist mainly of new and/or revised protocols at the (inter)network layer, but may also include proposed modifications to higher-layer protocols (e.g., transport or directory). However, it is a requirement that the proposed solutions allow mobile hosts to interoperate with existing Internet systems.

In the longer term, the group may address, to the extent not covered by the mobile host solutions, other types of internet mobility, such as mobile subnets (e.g., a local network within a vehicle), or mobile clusters of subnets (e.g., a collection of hosts, routers, and subnets within a large vehicle, like a ship or spacecraft, or a collection of wireless, mobile routers that provide a dynamically changing internet topology).

10.1.2 Overview of Draft Version 16 of the IETF IP Mobility Support

In this section we provide an overview of the current base specification for Mobile IP. The terminology is similar to CDPD and is summarized in Table 10.1.

The Mobile IP approach is analogous to postal service delivery: Whenever you move to a new location, you ask your home post office to forward your mail to your new address via the local post office there. Thus, a mobile node first leaves its *home network* and connects to a *foreign network*. An agent on the home network then intercepts packets sent to the mobile node and forwards them to an agent on the foreign agent. This agent then delivers packets locally to the mobile node visiting that network.

10.1.2.1 Mobile IP Entities and Mechanisms

Mobile nodes are supported by two service entities.

- A *home agent* that is the mobile support node on the home network. It keeps track of mobile node location (*mobility binding*) and intercepts and tunnels packets destined for the mobile node.

- A *foreign agent* that is the mobile support node on the foreign network that decapsulates and delivers packets tunneled to the mobile node. Mobile nodes may act as their own foreign agent.

These entities interact in the following ways:

1. Agent Discovery

Home agents and foreign agents may advertise their availability via broadcast on each link for which they provide service. A newly arrived mobile node can likewise broadcast a solicitation on the link to learn if any prospective agents are present. The advertisement is an extension of router advertisement (RFC 1256). It allows a mobile node to determine its point of attachment (moved to a new foreign network or returned to its home network). Advertisements contain:

- Care-of-address (foreign agents only)
- Home agent/foreign agent status bits

2. Registration

When the mobile node is away from home, it registers its *care-of address* with its home agent. Depending on its method of attachment, the mobile node will register either directly with its home agent, or through a foreign agent that forwards the registration to the home agent. Home and foreign agents may reject registration requests; this option is necessary to combat registration attacks by the "bad guys."

Registration attacks can be of at least three types: *Forgery,* whereby bogus mobile node location is sent to the home agent; *Modification*, whereby a valid registration request is altered to send the mobile node's traffic elsewhere; and *Replay* that involves storing a valid registration request for later malicious diversion of mobile node traffic.

To prevent an attacker from changing a mobility binding the following precautions are taken:

- The mobile node and home agent share a security association. This may be a shared secret key or a public/private key pair, or an authentication algorithm such as MD5 (see Chapter 6).
- An authenticator is sent in registration requests and replies. An example is a nonce or timestamp included for replay protection.

3. Tunneling/Encapsulation

Tunneling is used for transportation of mobile node packets from the home network to the foreign network. There are two endpoints: The home agent that encapsulates and transmits; and the care-of address entity that receives and decapsulates. The original packet becomes a payload in the new packet sent to the care-of address.There are various options for implementing this: IP-in-IP (draft), GRE, and Minimal Encapsulation are among the encapsulation options.

10.1.2.2 Mobile IP Operation

The following steps outline the operation of the Mobile IP protocol:

1. Mobility agents (i.e., foreign agents and home agents) advertise their presence via *agent advertisement* messages. A mobile node may optionally solicit an agent advertisement message from any locally attached mobility agents through an *agent solicitation* message.

2. A mobile node receives these agent advertisements and determines whether it is on its home network or a foreign network.

3. When the mobile node determines that it is located on its home network, it operates without mobility services. If it is returning to its home network after being registered elsewhere, the mobile node deregisters with its home agent, by exchanging *registration request* and *registration reply* messages.

4. When a mobile node detects that it has moved to a foreign network, it obtains a care-of address on the foreign network. The care-of address can either be determined from a foreign agent's advertisements (a foreign agent care-of address, see section 10.1.2.2.1), or by some external assignment mechanism such as DHCP (a co-located care-of address, see section 10.1.2.2.1).

5. The mobile node operating away from home then registers its new care-of address with its home agent through exchange of a registration request and registration reply messages, possibly via a foreign agent.

6. Datagrams sent to the mobile node's home address are intercepted by its home agent, tunneled by the home agent to the mobile node's care-of address, received at the tunnel endpoint (either at a foreign agent or at the mobile node itself), and finally delivered to the mobile node

7. In the reverse direction, datagrams sent by the mobile node are generally delivered to their destination using standard IP routing mechanisms, not necessarily passing through the home agent.

10.1.2.2.1. Care-of Addresses

When away from home, Mobile IP uses protocol tunneling to hide a mobile node's home address from intervening routers between its home network and its current location. The tunnel terminates at the mobile node's care-of address. The care-of address must be an address to which datagrams can be delivered via conventional IP routing. At the care-of address, the original datagram is removed from the tunnel and delivered to the mobile node.

Mobile IP provides two alternative modes for the acquisition of a care-of address:

- A *foreign agent care-of address* is a care-of address provided by a foreign agent through its agent advertisement messages. In this case, the care-of address is an IP address of the foreign agent. In this mode, the foreign agent is the endpoint of the tunnel and, upon receiving tunneled datagrams, decapsulates them and delivers the inner datagram to the mobile node. This mode of acquisition is preferred because it allows many mobile nodes to share the same care-of address and therefore does not place unnecessary demands on the already limited IPv4 address space.

- A *co-located care-of address* is a care-of address acquired by the mobile node as a local IP address through some external means, which the mobile node then associates with one of its own network interfaces. The address may be dynamically acquired as a temporary address by the mobile node such as through DHCP, or may be owned by the mobile node as a long-term address for its use only while visiting some foreign network.[1] When using a co-located care-of address, the mobile node serves as the endpoint of the tunnel and itself performs decapsulation of the datagrams tunneled to it.

The mode of using a co-located care-of address has the advantage that it allows a mobile node to function without a foreign agent, for example, in networks that have not yet deployed a foreign agent. It does, however, place additional burden on the IPv4 address space because it requires a pool of addresses within the foreign network to be made available to visiting mobile nodes. It is difficult to efficiently maintain pools of addresses for each subnet that may permit mobile nodes to visit.

It is important to understand the distinction between the care-of address and the foreign agent functions. The care-of address is simply the endpoint of the tunnel. It might indeed be an address of a foreign agent (a foreign agent care-of address), but it might instead be an address temporarily acquired by the mobile node (a co-located care-of address). A foreign agent, on the other hand, is a mobility agent that provides services to mobile nodes.

10.1.2.2.2. Home and Foreign Agents

A home agent must be able to attract and intercept datagrams that are destined to the home address of any of its registered mobile nodes. Using the proxy and gratuitous ARP mechanisms, this requirement can be satisfied if the home agent has a network interface on the link indicated by the mobile node's home address. Other placements of the home agent relative to the mobile node's home location may also be possible using other mechanisms for intercepting datagrams destined to the mobile node's home address.

Similarly, a mobile node and a prospective or current foreign agent must be able to exchange datagrams without relying on standard IP routing mechanisms; that is, those mechanisms that make forwarding decisions based upon the network prefix of the mobile node's destination IP address. This requirement can be satisfied if the foreign agent and the visiting mobile node have an interface on the same link.

In this case, the mobile node and foreign agent simply bypass their normal IP routing mechanism when sending datagrams to each other, addressing the underlying link layer packets to their respective link layer addresses. Other placements of the foreign agent relative to the mobile node may also be possible using other mechanisms to exchange datagrams between these nodes, but such placements are beyond the scope of our discussion.

If a mobile node is using a co-located care-of address, the mobile node must be located on the link identified by the network prefix of this care-of address. Otherwise, datagrams destined to the care-of address would be undeliverable to the mobile node.

---

1. Specific external methods of acquiring a local IP address for use as a co-located care-of address are beyond the scope of this book.

For example, the figures below illustrates the routing of datagrams to and from a *mobile mode* (*MN*) away from home, once the mobile node has registered with its *home agent* (*HA*). In the figures below, the mobile node is using a *foreign agent* (*FA*) care-of address.

In Figure 10.1, a *correspondent node* (*CN*) transmits a packet destined for the mobile node. The packet is routed (1) in the conventional manner to the network specified by the mobile node's home address. At the home network the packet is intercepted by the home agent and tunneled (2) to the foreign agent, which then decapsulates it and forwards (3) the packet to the mobile node by way of a link layer address.

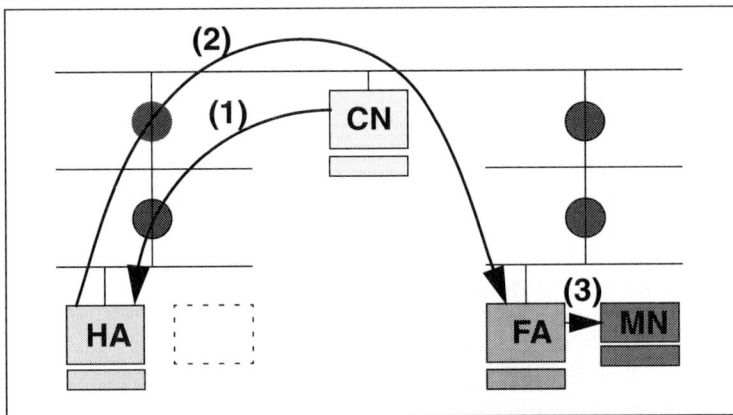

Figure 10.1   Mobile IP Routing to Mobile Node

In Figure 10.2, the visiting mobile node transmits a packet to the correspondent node. Routing of this packet is done in the conventional way, with no need to involve either the home or foreign agent.

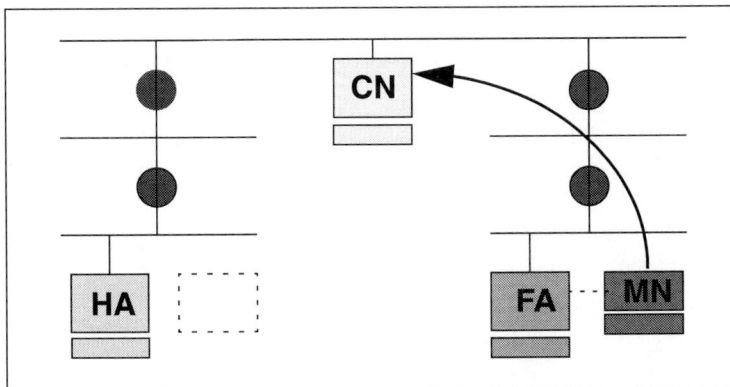

Figure 10.2   Mobile IP Routing to Correspondent Node

10.1.2.3 Mobile IP Protocol Walkthrough

The Mobile IP protocol is outlined in the steps below, under four basic procedural categories. In our discussions MN denotes "Mobile Node," HA denotes "Home Agent," and FA denotes "Foreign Agent".

1. Network Attachment

During this phase, foreign and home agents advertise their presence via agent advertisement messages. The mobile node may also optionally solicit an agent advertisement message from them.

1. MN - attaches to a new foreign network
2. MN - solicits an agent advertisement (if necessary)
3. FA - sends advertisement

2. Registration

Now that the mobile node is on a foreign network, it obtains a care-of address on this network and registers its new care-of address with its home agent, possibly via the foreign agent.

4. MN - requests registration from FA
5. FA - forwards registration request to HA
6. HA - sends registration reply to FA
7. FA - forwards registration reply to MN
8. HA - proxy ARPs for MN

3. Data Transfer to the Mobile Node

Data sent to the mobile node's home address are now intercepted and tunneled by the home agent to the mobile node's care-of address. These are then received at the tunnel endpoint (foreign agent for example) and delivered to the mobile node.

9. HA - intercepts, encapsulates, and forwards packets to FA (arrow 2 in Figure 10.1)
10. FA - decapsulates and forwards to MN (arrow 3 in Figure 10.2)

4. Data Transfer from the Mobile Node

Data from the mobile node are delivered to their destination using standard IP routing mechanisms, not necessarily passing through the home agent.

11. MN - Encapsulates and forwards packets to Destination (Figure 10.2)

10.1.3 Implementations Based on Mobile IP Drafts

A number of implementations of the Mobile IP protocols, both from industry and academe, have been proposed and developed over the years. Some of the more visible ones are discussed in this survey, which takes a snapshot of existing implementations of Mobile IP as of June, 1996. Most of the implementations reflect work in progress, and thus the information presented here has limited time value. Since the specifications of Mobile IP are just Internet draft RFCs, and the specifications can not be considered stable, implementations based on the Mobile-IP draft specifications are likely to evolve.

> **Note:** This section is intended to provide background information only. None of the authors or other real, corporate, or academic entities provide any warranty that the information about any of the implementations is fit for any specific purpose. Furthermore, not all the information included in this section has been independently verified. Inclusion in this section in no way constitutes a recommendation of software implementation.

10.1.3.0.1. Royal Institute of Technology, Sweden (1)

> Package Name: mobile-ip
> Latest Version: 0.6, July 1995
> Base Specification: Mobile-IP draft RFC Version 11
> Developer/Author:Anders Klemets, klemets@it.kth.se
> Availability: ftp://it.kth.se/pub/klemets
> Platform: SunOS 4.1.3

- From: "Package's Announcement"

   This implementation includes all the basic functionality such as the minimal encapsulation protocol; MD5 authentication, and support for other authentication algorithms; mobile-foreign and foreign-home authentication, and nonce based IDs. There is also provision for signaling between the link layer and the mobile IP code.

10.1.3.0.2. Royal Institute of Technology, Sweden (2)

> Package Name: Mobile IP MIB
> Latest Version: January 1996
> Base Specification: Mobile-IP draft RFC Version 14
> Developer/Author:Fredrik Tarberg, d91-fta@it.kth.se, and Fredrik
>   Broman,d91-fbr@it.kth.se
> Availability: http://www.it.kth.se/~d91-fta/exjobb/exjobb.html
> Platforms: MachOS, Solaris

- From: "Package's Announcement"

Building upon the implementation by Klemets, this is an extension of his work to the IETF IP Mobility Support draft version 14 and IP Encapsulation within IP Draft version 1 in January 1996. A Management Information Base for Mobile IP was developed and implemented, and the Mobile IP implementation was ported to MachOS and Solaris. Latency and throughput tests on the protocol were also performed.

10.1.3.0.3. Digital Equipment Corporation

Package Name: RoamAbout
Latest Version: February 1994
Base Specification: Unknown, possibly Mobile-IP draft RFC Version 11
Developer/Author: Digital Equipment Corporation
Availability:
http://www.digital.com/info/Customer-Update/940208042.txt.html.
Platform: MS-DOS 3.3

- From: "Package's Announcement"

RoamAbout Mobile IP mobile client/server networking software enables mobile users with portable computers to connect to their company's network wherever they are working. These portable computers keep their permanent IP network address independently of their physical location, so mobile users have the same environment and level of service both in the workplace and away from it. It supports IP and includes client support for Dynamic Host Configuration Protocol (DHCP) servers.

10.1.3.0.4. FTP Software and Telxon Corporation

Package Name: FTP Software Mobile IP Stack
Latest Version: December 1995
Base Specification: Unknown, possibly Mobile-IP draft RFC Version 12
Developer/Author:FTP Software and Telxon Corporation
Availability: http://www.telxon.com/tch1.htm
Platforms: MS-DOS and MS-Windows

- From: "Package's Announcement"

This integrated mobile Internet Protocol (IP) implementation, first introduced September of 1995, allows mobile workers to take notebook, portable, or pen-based computers anywhere they go in a corporate facility and maintain continuous wireless connections to an enterprise computing network. The initiative extends wired, in-building network environments by supporting a virtual office where mobile computer users can stay in touch with associates and manage business as if they were at their desks. It combines FTP Software's DOS and Windows network software, Aironet's wireless LAN access points and Telxon's portable and pen-based computers to enable the TCP/IP networking protocol to better meet the full needs of mobile users. It allows users to roam across multiple segments of TCP/IP enterprise networks, without disrupting wireless network connections, and access applications and information, send and receive electronic mail, and update and query databases.

10.1.3.0.5. Carnegie Mellon University

Package Name: Mobile IP Daemon
Latest Version: December 1995
Base Specification: Mobile-IP draft RFC Version 12
Developer/Author: John F. Dru, drum@uiuc.edu, and Adam S. Epstein, ase+@cmu.edu
Availability: http://www.ini.cmu.edu/~ae26/mip/
Platform: Linux

- From: "Package's Announcement"

The Mobile IP Daemon implements the three functions of advertisement, solicitation, and registration for the Mobile Node, Home Agent, and the Foreign Agent. Only encapsulation and decapsulation are in the kernel. The Daemon is run on the HA, FA, and MN; listens for registration traffic on UDP port 434; periodically sends out advertisements and solicitations; maintains binding tables; and is configured by command line arguments, and the file /etc/mipd.conf.

10.1.3.0.6. National University of Singapore

> Package Name: mip
> Latest Version: 1.0, December 1995
> Base Specification: Mobile-IP draft RFC Version 13
> Developer/Author: Y.Z. Li, K.C. Chua, and Y.C. Tay,
>   mobileIP@hornbill.ee.nus.sg
> Availability: http://zaphod.ee.nus.sg/mip/mip-doc.html
> Platform: Linux

• From: "Package's Announcement"

This is another Linux implementation. Some modules have not been imple-
mented.The system supplies an interface to user programs through the
existing TCP/IP socket. The source code with the implementation is free software and can be redistributed and modified under the terms of GNU General
Public License.

10.1.3.0.7. SUNY Binghamton

> Package Name: Linux-MobileIP
> Latest Version: 1.0, May 1996
> Base Specification: Mobile-IP draft RFC Version 16
> Developer/Author: Vipul Gupta, Abhijit Dixit, and Ben Lancki,
>   mobileip@anchor.cs.binghamton.edu
> Availability: http://anchor.cs.binghamton.edu/~mobileip/
> Platform: Linux

• From: "Package's Announcement"

This is so far the latest implementation, based on draft version 16 of the IP
Mobility Support. Linux Mobile-IP is an implementation of Mobile-IP for the Linux
operating system. Among other features, this release supports operation of a
mobile host on a foreign network even in the absence of foreign agents, e.g. one
is able to remove a portable computer from an ethernet LAN in a Lab, drive
home (several miles away), and reattach to the Internet using PPP without
disturbing any existing TCP connections. To the best of the authors' knowledge, it
is the first IETF compliant Mobile-IP implementation for Linux with such support.

10.2 Mobility under IPv6

A new version of the Internet Protocol, IPv6, is being developed with 128-bit addresses. IPv6 remedies perceived flaws in the existing version of IP (that is, IPv4). Mobile computers are likely to account for a substantial fraction of the population of the Internet during the lifetime of IPv6.

The development of IPv6 presents a rare opportunity, in that there is no existing installed base of IPv6 hosts or routers with which compatibility must be maintained. All IPv6 nodes may be assumed to perform the few operations needed to support Internet-wide mobility. The most important function needed to support mobility is the reliable and timely notification of a mobile node's current location to those other nodes that need it. The home agent needs this location information in order to redirect packets from the home network to the mobile node. Correspondent nodes need this information in order to send their own packets directly to the mobile node.

10.2.1 The IPv6 Standards Process

It is important to recognize that IPv6 is rapidly evolving. The current base specification for IPv6 is an "Internet Draft." Internet Drafts are draft documents that may be updated, replaced, or obsoleted by other documents at any time. It is inappropriate to use Internet Drafts as reference material or to cite them other than as "work in progress." Therefore, this entire section should be read with the understanding that it provides only a snapshot as of June, 1996.

10.2.2 Overview of Mobility Support in IPv6

From the model of operation enabling mobile networking for IPv4, the authors of the Mobile IPv6 draft [PERK96] borrow the concepts of home network, home address, home agent, care-of address, and binding. Mobile computers are assigned (at least) two IPv6 addresses whenever they are roaming away from their home network. One (the home address) is permanent; the other (the IPv6 link-local address) is used temporarily. In addition, the mobile node will typically autoconfigure a globally routable address at each new point of attachment. Every IPv6 router supports encapsulation, so every router is capable of serving as a home agent on the network(s) to which it is attached.

Using IPv4 terminology, the basic model of operation in IPv6 assumes that mobile node can always be reached by sending packets to its home (permanent) address. Whenever the mobile node is not present on its home network, packets arriving for it there will be intercepted by the home agent and tunneled to a care-of address.

Care-of addresses can be constructed by the mobile node using the methods of automatic address configuration. If the mobile node receives router advertisements, it must use automatic address configuration to construct a globally unique, routable address. This routable address can be used by the mobile node as its care-of address.

After determining its care-of address, a mobile node must send a binding update containing that care-of address to the home agent (and any other correspondent nodes that may have out-of-date bindings in their binding cache). By default, correspondent nodes send packets to mobile nodes by using routing headers instead of encapsulation. As detailed in the next section, correspondent nodes are usually expected to deliver packets directly to the mobile node's care-of address, so that the home agent is rarely involved with packet transmission to the mobile node.

It is essential for scalability and minimizing network load that correspondent nodes be able to learn the care-of address for a mobile node and to be able to cache this information for use in sending future packets to the mobile node's care-of address. By caching the care-of address of a mobile node, optimal routing of packets can be achieved between the correspondent node and the mobile node. Routing packets directly to the mobile node's care-of address also eliminates congestion at the home agent and thus contributes significantly to the overall health of the Internet.

Moreover, many communication events between mobile nodes and correspondent nodes can be carried out with no assistance from the home agent. Thus, the impact of failure at the home agent can be drastically reduced; this is important because many administrative domains will have a single home agent to serve a particular home network, and thus a single point of failure for communications to nodes using that home agent.

Communications between the home agent and a mobile node may depend on a number of intervening networks. Thus, there are many more ways that packets can fail to reach a mobile node when the home agent is required as an intermediate node. This would be particularly relevant on, say, trans-oceanic links between home agent and mobile node. Caching the binding of a mobile node at the correspondent node enables communication with the mobile nodes even if the home agent fails or is difficult to contact over the Internet.

In the typical case, when a mobile node has configured its care-of address at one of its own interfaces, transferring data to the mobile node means no more work for routers on the link at its current point of attachment, than transferring data to any other node on that link. This improves performance further.

10.3 Comparison of Mobile IP and CDPD

How do Mobile IP and CDPD compare? We can compare these mobile data systems from a variety of perspectives including:

- Objectives, goals and design assumptions
- Technical architecture and design
- Model and terminology
- Operational assumptions

- Standardization process
- Potential

The final topic in our comparison is a prediction and a discussion of issues surrounding coexistence and convergence between these standards.

Obviously, the goal is to objectively compare Mobile IP and CDPD. In particular,

- For the most part we limit ourselves to a comparative analysis of the CDPD specifications and current Mobile IP specifications. In other words we do not compare existing or future implementations of mobile devices or networks.
- We limit the comparative analysis to the mobility dimension of CDPD. This limitation is necessary for a meaningful comparison. In addition to mobility support, the CDPD specifications cover the airlink protocols, network management, network administration, accounting, and conformance testing. Thus, we limit ourselves to Part 500 (Mobility Management), Part 501 (Mobile Network Location Protocol), Part 507 (Mobile Network Registration Protocol), and Part 406 (Airlink Security) in our analysis of CDPD.

10.3.1 Objectives, Goals and Assumptions

Both CDPD and Mobile IP require mobile hosts to be able to communicate with other systems that do not implement mobility functions. No changes or enhancements are required for systems that do not support mobility, to be able to communicate with mobile hosts.

10.3.1.1 Underlying Data Link Layer

Mobile IP makes no assumption about any particular link layer technology. One of the driving requirements for design of Mobile IP was that it should be completely independent of the data link.

In the case of CDPD, there were no external requirements for support of data links other than the CDPD airlink (an overlay on AMPS). From the onset the CDPD architects recognized that mobility for CDPD could be independent of CDPD's airlink. To this end, CDPD was designed under a self-imposed requirement for CDPD mobility to be independent of the airlink.

10.3.1.2 Link Layer Efficiency

CDPD treats the airlink as a precious resource and minimizes the number of bytes transferred over the air. Trade-offs made between layering integrity (Layer 3 vs. Layer 2) and airlink efficiency in CDPD favor airlink efficiency.

Mobile IP is contained strictly within Layer 3. Mobile IP recognizes that the link by which a mobile node is attached to the Internet may often be a precious wireless link, which should be optimized where possible by the Layer 3 protocol (in this case Mobile IP).

10.3.1.3 Network Layer Support

CDPD was designed to not only support IP, but also to be a multi-protocol mobility solution. Mobile IP is a pure IP solution. Both CDPD and Mobile IP require that mobility be supported without the mobile system needing to change its IP address. This is a departure from existing IP networks.

10.3.1.4 Network Administration and Management

CDPD assumes that the network is centrally administered, managed and operated by cooperating cellular Service Providers. Mobile IP assumes no additional constraints beyond the existing mode of operation of the Internet. This is probably the most fundamental difference between CDPD and Mobile IP and has serious ramifications on address assignment and security.

10.3.2 Technical Architecture and Design

CDPD is based on early Mobile IP work, and thus resembles but does not exactly match Mobile IP. In particular, the triangular routing mobility approach is essentially the same in both CDPD and Mobile IP.

The following enumerates major areas of design differences between the two approaches:

- The user's IP address must be assigned by the CDPD service provider. Mobile IP makes no such assumptions.
- Mobile IP allows for co-location of mobile node and the foreign agent. Combining the M-ES and the Serving MD-IS was not considered and is not practical in CDPD.
- CDPD's mobility tunnel is based on CLNP. Mobile IP's mobility tunnel is IP-based.
- Mobile IP is a pure IP design. CDPD is a multiprotocol design.
- Mobile IP operates completely above the data link layer. CDPD mobility is mostly above the data link layer.
- Since the infrastructure of the CDPD network is closed there are less security considerations for CDPD.

10.3.3 Model and Terminology

The terminologies of CDPD and Mobile IP are different. CDPD is following the OSI reference model terminology. Mobile IP adheres to conventional IP terminology with some extensions. Table 10.1 maps the key concepts of Mobile IP to their corresponding terms in CDPD.

Table 10.1   Comparative Glossary

Mobile IP		CDPD	
Name	**Definition**	**Name**	**Definition**
Correspondent Node	A peer with which a mobile node is communicating. A correspondent node may be either mobile or stationary.	End System (ES)	Any computer, not considered to be performing routing or bridging functions. ESs are the actual physical and logical nodes that exchange information.
Router	Any computer performing routing or bridging functions.	Intermediate System (IS)	A router that relays data packets toward their intended destinations, without knowledge of CDPD and Mobile End-System mobility issues. Such systems are the backbone of the CDPD network and are often standard, commercial, off-the-shelf routers.
Node	A host or a router.	System (S)	Any computer, not considered to be performing routing or bridging functions
Mobile Node	A host or router that changes its point of attachment from one network or subnetwork to another. A mobile node may change its location without changing its IP address and may continue to communicate with other Internet nodes at any location using its (constant) IP address.	Mobile End System (M-ES)	An End System that accesses the CDPD Network through the Airlink Interface. The remote computer that uses cellular channels to access the CDPD network over the wireless interface.
Stationary Host (SH)	A computer that is not considered to be mobile.	Fixed End-System (F-ES)	A non-mobile End System. A host system that supports or provides access to data and applications. The F-ES connects to the CDPD network via a router.

Table 10.1 Comparative Glossary (Continued)

Mobile IP		CDPD	
Name	**Definition**	**Name**	**Definition**
Home Agent (HA)	A router on a mobile node's network that tunnels datagrams for delivery to the mobile node when it is away from home and maintains current location information for the mobile node.	Home MD-IS	Each Mobile End System (M-ES) is permanently associated with a Mobile Data Intermediate System (MD-IS) referred to as its home MD-IS. The Home MD-IS acts as an anchor for a particular set of M-ESs as they travel, by maintaining a database of locations of all of its M-ESs.
Foreign Agent (FA)	A router on a mobile node's visited network that provides routing services to the mobile node while registered. The FA detunnels and delivers datagrams to the mobile node that were tunneled by the mobile node's home agent. For datagrams sent by the mobile node, the FA may serve as a default router for registered mobile nodes.	Serving MD-IS	When a Mobile End System travels out of its home area, the mobile Data Intermediate System in this new location is known as the serving MD-IS. The serving MD-IS notifies the home MD-IS of the M-ES's new location.

10.3.4 Operational Assumptions

Mobile IP uses the Internet as an operational model. Operational assumptions for Mobile IP are the same as those for the Internet, which can best be described as "managed chaos."

On the other hand CDPD assumes a clearly defined network with well defined boundaries of authority and responsibility. The CDPD internetwork is a collection of CDPD service provider networks. Based on bilateral agreements, each Home MD-IS interoperates with various serving MD-ISs, which may be administered by various CDPD service providers.

The infrastructure of the CDPD network is a closed network. This implies that some level of trust, order, and accountability can be expected. "Control and Order" expresses the general flavor of CDPD's operational assumptions.

These operational assumptions had a direct impact on many of CDPD's protocol design decisions, particularly in the areas of security, manageability, and scalability.

Because the mobility tunnel begins and ends within the CDPD networks, to some extent it does not require the level of security that is necessary between the home agent and the foreign agent in Mobile IP.

Even though securing the network layer of the CDPD network is not required in the CDPD specifications, the CDPD specification team recognized that providing data confidentiality and authentication for the mobility tunnel was important. *Network Layer Security Protocol (NLSP)*, which can be considered an adjunct to CLNP, provides comprehensive security services. Unfortunately, it is a lot more theoretical than real.

10.3.5 Standardization Process

Mobile IP specifications are the product of one of IETF's Working Groups. The standardization process is completely open and based on volunteers' effort. This process is also complex and dynamic. "Rough Consensus and Running Code" best expresses the general flavor of Mobile IP's standardization process.

Sometimes, IETF Working Groups are highly efficient and produce high quality specifications in short time frames. That has not been the case with the Mobile IP Working Group.

The CDPD specification effort was funded by a group of cellular service providers. The specification was developed by a small team of paid consultants under the direction of cellular service provider representatives. There was significant schedule pressure in the CDPD specification development process. The CDPD Release 1.0 specification was developed in less than a year, and the following Release 1.1 was developed in about one year.

10.3.6 Potential

The value of coupling mobility with Internet access is significant. Any solution that provides mobile connectivity to the Internet is likely to be in high demand and heavily used. From this perspective, the opportunity for widespread deployment of both CDPD and Mobile IP technologies is immense.

However, in some ways these technologies are in competition with one other. Unless CDPD services are widely deployed soon and unless the subnetwork-independent characteristic of CDPD mobility is further developed and adopted by users of other than cellular-based media, it is unlikely that CDPD mobility will become the mainstream solution to Internet mobility.

The Mobile IP standardization process has been quite slow and the base specification for Mobile IP has not yet reached RFC status as of this writing. However, Mobile IP enjoys certain characteristics that seem to ensure its survival until it becomes widely adopted. These characteristics include complete openness, subnetwork independence, user orientation, and proven correct specifications.

Another key factor in the widespread deployment of any network is the fitness of the network operators and equipment manufacturers for the job at hand. CDPD network operators are cellular service providers and CDPD equipment manufacturers are typically *tele*-communication equipment suppliers. Mobile IP network operators are likely to be Internet Service Providers and Mobile IP equipment manufacturers are typically *data*-communication equipment suppliers. We note that the entire Internet phenomenon was essentially independent of the public telecommunications providers.

It is important to recognize that even though CDPD mobility has the potential to become a generalized mobility solution and compete with Mobile IP, it was not designed as such. Since CDPD's mobility management scheme is similar to that of Mobile IP, either could be adapted to interoperate with the other. Depending on the degree of integration desired, this could be a relatively easy or a significant job.

Finally, CDPD devices are native IP hosts that can communicate with Mobile IP hosts without any modifications. The whole point of the Internet is that the local subnetwork connection is largely irrelevant to communications with the rest of the IP-based world. This is the foundation and the benefit of layered communications protocols. It is the communication itself and not the protocol used that is important.

Bibliography

[BERT92] D. Bertsekas and R. Gallager, *Data Networks*, Prentice Hall, 1992.

[BLAC96] U. D. Black, *Physical Layer Interfaces and Protocols*, IEEE Computer Society Press, 1996.

[BRAD96] S. O. Bradner and A. Mankin, *IPng, Internet Protocol Next Generation*, Addison-Wesley, 1996.

[BROD94] I. Brodsky, "Cellular's Multi-pronged Data Strategy," *Wireless for the Corporate User*, Vol. 3, No. 4, 1994.

[BROD96] I. Brodsky, "Countdown to mobile blast-off," *Network World*, February 19, 1996, p. 44.

[BRUN96] L. Bruno, "Internet Security: How Much is Enough?," *Data Communications*, April, 1996, pp. 60-72.

[BRYA96] J. Bryant, "The Standards Status," *Wireless Business and Technology*, Vol. 2, No. 4, May, 1996, pp. 26-32.

[BURS93] T. P. Bursh, K. K. Y. Ho, F. F. Kunzinger, L. N. Roberts, W. L. Shanks, L. A. Tantillo, "Digital Radio for Mobile Applications," *AT&T Tech. Journal*, July/August 1993, Vol. 72, No. 4, p. 19.

[CALH88] G. Calhoun, *Digital Cellular Radio*, Artech House, 1988.

[CDPD93] CDPD System Specification Release 1.0, July 19, 1993.

[CDPD95] CDPD System Specification and Implementors Guide, January 19, 1995.

[CHAN96] D. Chan, "Packet Data Services over TDMA," contribution to TDMA Forum by AT&T Wireless Services, January, 1996.

[CORR93] O. C. Corr, "Money from Thin Air - The McCaw Fortune," *The Seattle Times*, April 4, 1993.

[DANI95] D. Daniel, "Review of Dedicated Packet Systems," Wireless Data Communications: Technologies, Products and Systems Conference, Vancouver, BC, January 26-27, 1995.

[DERO94] J. F. DeRose, *The Wireless Data Handbook*, Quantum Publishing, 1994.

[DIFF76] W. Diffie and M. E. Hellman, "New Directions in Cryptography," *IEEE Transactions on Information Theory*, Vol. 22, No. 6, 1976, pp. 644-654.

[DRYD94] P. Dryden, "Roaming Enhancements Extend Nets," *Communications Week*, October 31, 1994, pp. 19-21.

[DZIA95] M. Dziatkiewicz, "Cracking the Code of Cellular's MINs and ESNs," *America's Network*, August 1, 1995, p. 8.

[EMCI95] "MTA-EMCI Study, "U.S. Wireless Data Market Surpasses One Million Subscribers," Economic and Management Consultants International, Inc., August, 1995.

[FALC95] D. D. Falconer, F. Adachi, B. Gudmundson, "Time Division Multiple Access Methods for Wireless Personal Communications," *IEEE Communications*, January, 1995, Vol. 33, No. 1, pp. 50-57.

[FRAN95] Y. Frankel, A. Herzberg, P. A. Karger, H. Krawczyk, C. A. Kunzinger, M. Yung, "Security Issues in a CDPD Wireless Network", *IEEE Personal Communications*, Vol. 2, No. 4, August, 1995, pp. 16-27.

[FREE95] R. L. Freeman, *Practical Data Communications*, John Wiley and Sons, Inc., 1995.

[FREZ95a] W. Frezza, "Satellite Data / On Top of the World," *Network Computing*, November 15, 1995, p. 33.

[FREZ95b] W. Frezza, "Going the Way of Wireless," *Network Computing*, October 1, 1995, p. 86.

[GAGL91] R. M. Gagliardi, *Satellite Communications*, Second Edition, Van Nostrand Reinhold, 1991.

[GARE94] R. Gareiss, "X.25 Packet-Switching Goes Mobile," *Data Communications*, September 21, 1994, pp. 41-42.

[GARE94b] R. Gareiss, "PCS: Making Sense of the New Services," *Data Communications*, October, 1994, pp. 49-52.

[GILL96] I. Gillott, "Wireless nets come of age," *Network World*, February 19, 1996, p. 50.

[GROB94] M. Grob and F. Quick, "White Paper on Mobility Management for Packet Data Services," TIA, TR 45.5.1.5/94.07.21.06.

[HAYM94] W. Haymond, "Comparison [of CDPD] with Other Networks," CDPD Software Developer's Conference, October 6, 1994.

[HIRS95] E. Hirshfield, "The Globalstar System," *Applied Microwave and Wireless*, Summer, 1995, pp. 26-41.

[HODG90] M. R. L. Hodges, "The GSM Radio Interface," *British Telecom. Tech. Journal*, Vol. 8, No. 1, January, 1990, pp. 31-43.

[HORW95] E. Horwith, "What's Wrong with Wireless?," *Network World*, November 13, 1995, pp. 64-72.

[IELL94] A. Iellinio, "Few Winners in Cellular Modem Race," *Network World*, September 5, 1994.

[IOAN93] J. Ioannidis, "Protocols for Mobile Internetworking," PhD Thesis, Columbia University, 1993.

[JABB95] B. Jabbari, G. Colombo, A. Nakajima, J. Kulkarni, "Network Issues for Wireless Communications," *IEEE Communications*, January 1995, Vol. 33, No. 1, pp 88-98.

[JIRA95] D. A. Jiraud, "LEO Satellite Channels for Packet Communications," *Applied Microwave and Wireless*, Summer, 1995, pp. 42-55.

[KAUF95] C. Kaufman, R. Perlman, M. Speciner, *Network Security: Private Communication in a Public World*, Prentice Hall, 1995.

[KLEI75] L. Kleinrock, *Queueing Systems, Volume I, Theory*, John Wiley, 1975.

[KLEI76] L. Kleinrock, *Queueing Systems, Volume II, Computer Systems*, John Wiley, 1976.

[KOHN95] R. Kohno, R. Meidan, L. B. Milstein, "Spread Spectrum Access Methods for Wireless Communications," *IEEE Communications*, January 1995, Vol. 33, No. 1, pp 58-67.

[KRAM95] M. Kramer, "Going Beyond the Beep," *PC Week*, December 11, 1995, p. 115.

[KRAU93] J. A. Krauss, "FCC Creates New Wireless Business Opportunities," *Applied Microwave and Wireless*, Fall 1993, pp. 13-29.

[KRIS95a] P. Krishna, et. al., "A Cluster-based Approach to Routing in Ad-Hoc Networks", USENIX Symposium on Location Independent and Mobile Computing, April, 1995.

[KRIS95b] P. Krishna, et. al., "Efficient Location Management in Mobile Wireless Networks", Technical Report #95-011, Dept. of Computer Science, Texas A&M University, College Station, TX, 1995.

[KUNZ95] C. A. Kunzinger, "Network Layer Mobility: Comparison of CDPD and Mobile-IP," IBM Document Number TR 29.2003, available via WWW at http://www.raleigh.ibm.com/nethome.html.

[LAND95] "AT&T Wins Measure of Support for Narrowband PCS Protocol," *Land Mobile Radio News*, Phillips Publishing, November 6, 1995.

[LEE-89] W. C. Y. Lee, *Mobile Cellular Telecommunications Systems*, McGraw-Hill, 1989.

[LEE-93] W. C. Y. Lee, *Mobile Communications Design Fundamentals*, John Wiley and Sons, 1993.

[LEOP93] R. J. Leopold, A. Miller, J. L. Grubb, "The Iridium System: A New Paradigm in Personal Communications," *Applied Microwave and Wireless*, Fall, 1993, pp. 68-78.

[LIN-83] S. Lin and D. J. Costello, *Error Control Coding*, Prentice-Hall, 1983.

[MCCO96] P. McConnell, *A Comparison of CDPD, Ardis and RAM Wireless Data Communications Systems*, Sierra Wireless, Inc., white paper, 1996.

[METR94] Metricom marketing brochures, Metricom, Inc., 1994.

[MILL94] K. Miller, "Why the Carriers Love CDPD," *Data Communications*, December 1994, pp. 17-18.

[MOBI89] Mobitex Terminal Specification, Ram Mobile Data, Inc., 1989.

[MOBI92] "Update of Ram Mobile Data's Packet Data Radio Service," Ram Mobile Data,Inc., 1992.

[MOBI94] Mobile Data Report, August, 1994.

[MOUL95] M. Mouly, M. Pautet, "Current Evolution of the GSM System," *IEEE Personal Communications*, October, 1995, Vol 2., No. 5, pp 9-19.

[PADG95] J. E. Padgett, C. G. Gunther, T. Hattori, "Overview of Wireless Personal Communications," *IEEE Communications*, January 1995, Vol. 33, No. 1, pp. 23-41.

[PAHL94] K. Pahlavan and A. Levesque, "Wireless Data Communications," *Proc. of IEEE*, Vol. 82, No. 9, September 1994.

[PAHL95] K. Pahlavan and A. H. Levesque, *Wireless Information Networks*, John Wiley and Sons, Inc., 1995.

[PATE95a] K. Pate, "Paging Evolves into Messaging with Technological Innovations," *Radio Communications Report*, May 22, 1995.

[PATE95b] K. Pate, "AT&T Unveils Messaging Standard to Rival FLEX," *Radio Communications Report*, Vol. 14, No. 21, Nov. 6, 1995.

[PEDE95] A. Pedersen, "MSAT (Mobile Satellite) Wide Area Mobile Data Applications," *WDC*, January 26-7, 1995.

[PERL92] R. Perlman, *Interconnections: Bridges and Routers*, Addison-Wesley, 1992.

[PETE96] L. L. Peterson and B. S. Davie, *Computer Networks: A Systems Approach*, Morgan Kaufman Publishers, Inc., 1996.

[PHIL96] B. Phillips, "Wireless LANs - Not of This World," *OEM Magazine*, Vol. 4, No. 24, February 1996, p. 78.

[PIRN95] T. Pirner, "OmniTRACS and Other Satellite Technologies," *WDC*, January 26-27, 1995.

[RACO94] Racotek marketing literature, 1994.

[RADI96] RadioMail marketing literature, 1996.

[RAHN93] M. Rahnema, "Overview of the GSM System and Protocol Architecture," *IEEE Communications*, April 1993, pp. 92-100.

[RAMM95] *The Inherent Security of Data over MOBITEX Wireless Packet Data Networks*, A RAM Mobile Data white paper, October 1995.

[RDLA92] Radio Data Link Access Procedure, Motorola, March 30, 1992.

[RICH95] "IP Innovation Fosters Mobility without Address Headaches," *Network World*, February 6, 1995, p. 41.

[RSA-92] RSA Data Security, Inc., "The RC4 Encryption Algorithm," March 12, 1992.

[RUSC95] R. Rusch, "The Market and Proposed Systems for Satellite Communications," *Applied Microwave and Wireless*, Fall 1995, p. 10.

[SANT94] R. Santelesa, "Metricom--Forging a New Wireless World," *Digital Media*, April 25, 1994.

[SESH93] N. Seshradii, C. W. Sundberg, V. Weeradrody, "Advanced Techniques for Modulation, Error Correction, Channel Equalization and Diversity," *AT&T Tech. Journal*, July/August 1993, Vol. 72, No. 4, pp. 48-63.

[SLEK90] A. G. Slekys, "Exploring the Digital Wave," *Cellular Business*, February 1990, pp. 72-94.

[SPAN95] O. Spaniol, A. Fasbender, S. Hoff, J. Kaltwasser, J. Kassubek, "Impacts of Mobility on Telecommunications and Data Communication Networks," *IEEE Personal Communications*, October 1995, pp. 20-33.

[SPAN96] O. Spaniol, A. Fasbender, S. Hoff, J. Kaltwasser, J. Kassubek, "Challenges for Wireless Networks and OSI," *Applied Microwave and Wireless*, Winter, 1996, Vol. 8, No. 1, pp. 50-76.

[STAL93] W. Stallings, *Networking Standards*, Addison-Wesley, 1993.

[STEE95] R. Steele, J. Whitehead, W. S. Wong, "System Aspects of Cellular Radio," *IEEE Communications*, January 1995, Vol. 33, No. 1, pp. 80-87.

[STEN95] M. E. Steenstrup, ed., *Routing in Communications Networks*, Prentice-Hall, 1995.

[STEV94] W. R. Stevens, *TCP/IP Illustrated, Volume 1, The Protocols*, Addison-Wesley, 1994.

[STEV95] W. R. Stevens, *TCP/IP Illustrated, Volume 2, The Implementations*, Addison-Wesley, 1995.

[STEV96] W. R. Stevens, *TCP/IP Illustrated, Volume 3, TCP for Transactions, HTTP, NNTP and the Unix Domain Protocols*, Addison-Wesley, 1996.

[SULL94] M. Sullivan, "Wireless LANs, Status and Future," *Applied Microwave and Wireless*, Fall 1994.

[SWEE95] D. Sweeney, "Everything You Need to Know About Wireless Data," *Mobile Office*, October 1995, Vol. 6, No. 10, p. 56.

[TANN95] A. Tannenbaum, *Computer Networks*, Prentice-Hall, 1995.

[TAYL94] K. M. Taylor, "Big Bandwidth, Small Cities," *Data Communications*, August 1994, pp. 95-97.

[TAYL95] K. M. Taylor, "Going Wireless: Cellular Phone Melded with Modem," *Data Communications*, September 1995, pp. 37-8.

[TOMS95] N. Toms, "The Evolution of Wireless Data," WDC95 - Wireless Data Communications: Technologies, Products and Systems Conference Proceedings, Vancouver, BC, January 26-27, 1995.

[VANJ90] V. Jacobson, "Compressing TCP/IP Headers for Low-Speed Serial Links," RFC 1144, DDN Network Information Center, SRI International, February 1990.

[VITE95] A. Viterbi, PIMRC '95 Keynote Presentation, Toronto, September 26, 1995.

[WHIP95] D. P. Whipple, "The CDMA Standard," *Applied Microwave and Wireless*, 1995.

[WHIT93] J. F. White, "What is CDMA?," *Applied Microwave and Wireless*, Fall 1993, pp. 5-8.

[WILL95] M. Williams, D. Ong, "PCS and RF Components," *Applied Microwave and Wreless*, Spring 1995, pp. 10-22.

[WONG95] P. Wong and D. Britland, *Mobile Data Communications Systems*, Artech House, 1995.

GLOSSARY

A

A-Interface The network (air) interface between a Mobile End System (M-ES) and the Cellular Digital Packet Data (CDPD)-based wireless packet data service provider network.

access control A network function that determines whether a particular mobile device is permitted to access the network.

accounting A network function that tallies the usage of various network resources.

accounting collector Responsible for the storage and processing of accounting information received from accounting distributors.

accounting distributor Responsible for receiving information from accounting meters or other distributors, and distributing that information to accounting collectors or other distributors.

accounting meter Performs measurements and aggregates the results of those measurements (i.e., into an accounting traffic matrix).

accounting traffic matrix A traffic matrix is a collection of information, gathered over a period of time, containing statistics on Mobile End System (M-ES) registration, de-registration, and Network Protocol Data Unit (NPDU) traffic.

acquisition The process by which a Mobile End System (M-ES) locates a Radio Frequency (RF) channel carrying a channel stream, synchronizes to the data transmissions on that channel stream, and determines whether the channel stream is acceptable to the M-ES for network access.

adaptive retransmission algorithms Used by self-adjusting timers to determine and dynamically set timers to effectively adjust data traffic in the event the link is slower than usual due to congestion or other network conditions.

adjacent cell Two cells are adjacent if it is possible for a Mobile End System (M-ES) to maintain continuous service while switching from one cell to the other.

adjacent MD-IS Two Mobile Data Intermediate Systems (MD-ISs) are adjacent if each MD-IS controls one of a pair of adjacent cells.

Administrative Domain The subscriber administration, billing administration, and network management functions over which each network service provider has control and responsibilities.

Advanced Mobile Phone System (AMPS) The North American analog cellular phone system. The spectrum allocated to AMPS is shared by two cellular phone companies in each area or region (geographic market). This system was deployed during the 1980s and today it and its variants represent nearly 85% of the cellular voice systems installed throughout the world.

airlink The physical layer radio frequency channel pair used for communication between the Mobile End System (M-ES) and the Mobile Data Base Station (MDBS).

airlink interface The Cellular Digital Packet Data (CDPD)-based wireless packet data service provider's interface for providing services over the airlink to mobile subscribers.

allocated channel A Radio Frequency (RF) channel that is configured to allow use by Cellular Digital Packet Data (CDPD) transmissions.

AMPS See Advanced Mobile Phone System.

analog signal A continuously variable waveform (such as a sound wave) that can represent an infinite number of values; wireline telephone systems use analog signals to provide voice communication. The term "analog" is used to refer to telephone transmission and/or switching that is not digital. Analog signals are amplified rather than regenerated.

ANSI American National Standards Institute. A group that certifies organizations developing US standards for the information processing industry. ANSI accredited groups participate in defining network protocol standards.

API Application Program Interface.

Application Entity An Application Entity provides the service desired for communication. An Application Entity may exist in an M-ES (Mobile End System) (i.e., mobile application entity) or an F-ES (Fixed End System). An Application Entity is named with an application entity title.

Application Layer Layer 7 in the Open Systems Interconnect (OSI) 7-Layer Network Layer Reference Model. Provides protocols and services required by particular user-designed application processes. Functions pertaining to particular user requirements and application service elements that can be used by more than one application are contained in this layer.

application program interface (API) The interface between the subscriber unit and the multiple application subsystem. Generally consists of simple commands such as "open a connection." These commands are translated by the enabling layer into commands that either control the network connection or communicate data across the network.

application services Telecommunications services that provide value-added features not related to the provision of communications facilities.

ARDIS A wireless packet-switched network for public data communications, jointly owned by Motorola and IBM, that allows people carrying handheld devices to send and receive short data messages.

Area Color Code A color code that is shared by all cells controlled through a single Mobile Data Intermediate System (MD-IS). The value of the Area Color Code must be different between any two adjacent cells controlled by adjacent MD-ISs. Refer to *color code*.

ARN Authentication Random Number.

ARP Address Resolution Protocol. An Internet protocol that runs on Ethernet and all IEEE 802.X Local Area Networks (LANs), and maps Internet addresses to Medium Access Control (MAC) addresses.

ARQ Automatic Repeat reQuest.

AS Autonomous System. A collection of gateways (routers) under a single administrative authority using a common interior gateway protocol for routing packets.

ASCII American Standard Code for Information Interchange.

ASN Authentication Sequence Number.

ASN.1 Abstract Syntax Notation One. A specification language used to define interoperable interfaces, based on standard application layer protocols such as Message Handling System (MHS) or Common Management Information Protocol (CMIP).

asynchronous Literally, not synchronous. A method of data transmission that allows characters to be sent at irregular intervals by preceding each character with a start bit, and following it with a stop bit.

Asynchronous Transfer Mode (ATM)   ATM is the technology selected by the Consultative Committee on International Telephone & Telegraph (CCITT) international standards organization in 1988 for creating a Broadband Integrated Services Digital Network (B-ISDN). It is a fast, cell-switched technology based on a fixed-length 53-byte cell.

AT Command Set   Also known as the Hayes standard AT command set. A language that enables PC communications software to control an asynchronous and "Hayes-compatible modem." Called "AT" because all the commands begin with "AT," which is short for ATtention.

authentication   The process by which a network validates that the user or address is legitimate. It is also the process whereby users of an information source prove they are who they claim to be.

authentication credentials   Information submitted by a network element to allow validation by its peer entity. In the CDPD network, authentication credentials for each NEI consists of an Authentication Sequence Number and an Authentication Random Number.

Authentication Random Number   A random value used in authentication procedures.

Authentication Sequence Number   A sequence count that is incremented for each change of Authentication Random Number (ARN).

available channel   In the CDPD system, a Radio Frequency (RF) channel is available if it is an allocated channel that is not currently in use for either Cellular Digital Packet Data (CDPD) or non-CDPD-based wireless packet data service.

B

backbone   The backbone is the part of the communications network that interconnects Local Area Networks (LANs) together inside a building or across a city or country. LANs are connected to the backbone via bridges and/or routers and the backbone serves as a communications highway for LAN-to-LAN traffic. A backbone can be a LAN, a Wide Area Network (WAN), or a combination of both dedicated to providing connectivity between subnetworks in an Enterprise-wide network.

bandwidth   The bandwidth determines the rate at which information can be sent through a channel: the greater the bandwidth, the more information can be sent in a given amount of time.

base stations   Refer to *Mobile Data Base Station (MDBS)*.

Base-Controlled Hand-off   Cell transfers managed by and initiated from the network, typical of Advanced Mobile Phone Systems (AMPS).

BCHO   Base-Controlled Hand-Off.

BIS   Border Intermediate System.

bit stream   A continuous stream of data bits transmitted over a communications line with no breaks or separators between the characters.

bit time   The time period for the transmission of one bit by the physical layer. For the 19,200 bps CDPD airlink data channel, this is equal to 52.08333 microseconds.

blank and burst   On the AMPS telephone network, certain administrative messages are sent on the voice channel by blocking the voice signal (blanking) and sending a short high speed data message (burst). The blank and burst technique is one that causes a momentary dropout of the audio connection (and sometimes disconnection of cellular modem connections) when a power level message is transmitted to the cellular phone.

BLER   Block Error Rate.

block   In Cellular Digital Packet Data (CDPD), a block is a Reed-Solomon code block, consisting of 63 6-bit symbols, 47 of which are data symbols and 16 of which are forward error correcting parity symbols.

Block Error Rate (BLER)   An averaged estimate of the ratio of transmitted blocks that contain an uncorrectable number of symbol errors to the blocks received successfully.

bps (bits per second)   A measure of data transmission speed.

broadband personal communications standards (PCS)   Consists of 120 MHz of new spectrum available for new cellular networks. Also known as wideband PCS.

broadcast   A transmission in one or more channel streams that is intended to be processed by all Mobile End Systems (M-ES) using the channel stream.

burst   Generally refers to the reverse channel transmissions by the Mobile End System (M-ES). Each transmission is a reverse channel transmission "burst." Can also refer to a "burst error," in which several consecutive symbols are corrupted.

busy state A channel stream is in a busy state if the Mobile Data Base Station (MDBS) signals in the busy/idle flag that a Mobile End System (M-ES) is currently transmitting on the channel.

busy/idle flag An indicator that is transmitted by the Mobile Data Base Station (MDBS) periodically to indicate whether the reverse channel is currently in the busy state or the idle state.

C

CCITT Consultative Committee for International Telegraph and Telephone. Now known as the International Telecommunications Union— Telecommunications Systems (ITU-TS).

CDMA Code Division Multiple Access. Defines how a single channel can be allocated to support multiple users simultaneously.

CDPD Cellular Digital Packet Data.

CDPD cell boundary The locus of points at which a Mobile End System (M-ES) should no longer access service by using the transmissions of a particular cell.

CDPD Forum An industry trade association supporting the development of the Cellular Digital Packet Data (CDPD) commercial marketplace.

CDPD SNDCP Cellular Digital Packet Data (CDPD) SubNetwork Dependent Convergence Protocol.

Cell The geographic region in which Radio Frequency (RF) transmission from one fixed transmission site can be received at acceptable levels of signal strength using an omnidirectional or a directional antenna. In a cellular network, a cell represents a geographic area within which a particular bandwidth of radio frequency channels can be received at adequate signal strength.

Cell Group Color Code A color code assigned to a set of cells. Each member of the set is adjacent to at least one other member of the set and no two members of the set are allocated the same Radio Frequency (RF) channel for Cellular Digital Packet Data (CDPD) use. Each cell is assigned exactly one Cell Group Color Code.

cell site The physical building that houses the cellular telephone base station or the CDPD Mobile Data Base Station (MDBS).

cell transfer The procedure of changing the channel stream in use to a channel stream originating at a different cell.

Cellular Digital Packet Data (CDPD) A wide-area, wireless data networking technology. CDPD is an open standard for using existing cellular networks for wireless data transmission. Packets of data are sent along channels of the cellular network.

cellular modems A device that combines data modem and cellular telephone transceiver technologies in a single unit. This allows a user to transfer data on the cellular network without the use of a separate cellular telephone.

CGSA Cellular Geographic Service Area.

channel A 30 kHz cellular voice channel. A voice-grade transmission facility with defined frequency response, gain, and bandwidth. Also, a path of communication, either electrical or electromagnetic, between two or more points. Also, channel is used to describe the distribution path into the market for value-added resellers.

channel bandwidth The frequency range of a Radio Frequency (RF) channel—in Cellular Digital Packet Data (CDPD), 30 kHz.

channel hopping The process in CDPD of changing the Radio Frequency (RF) channel supporting a CDPD channel stream to a different RF channel on the same cell. This is typically used to avoid collisions with voice traffic use of the RF channel.

channel stream A shared digital communications channel between a Mobile Data Base Station (MDBS) and a set of Mobile End Systems (M-ESs) considered as a logical concept, separate from the frequency of the Radio Frequency (RF) channel used to implement the channel at any given time.

circuit The physical connection (or path) of channels, conductors and equipment between two given points through which an electric current may be established. Includes both sending and receiving capabilities.

circuit switched The process of setting up and keeping a circuit open between two or more users, such that the users have exclusive and full use of the circuit until the connection is released.

CLNP Connectionless Network Protocol.

CLNS Connectionless Network Service.

clone A mobile device, typically a cellular telephone, that claims to possess the same address identifier as another mobile device.

CMIP Common Management Information Protocol [CCITT-X.711].

CMIS Common Management Information Service [CCITT-X.710].

CMISE Common Management Information Service Element.

co-channel interference Interference between signals transmitted in a given Radio Frequency (RF) channel in a particular cell and signals transmitted on the same RF channel in a different cell. A receiver that is in a position to receive from both cannot filter out the undesired signal, and consequently the noise level at the receiver increases.

code division multiple access (CDMA) Defines how a single channel can be allocated to support multiple users simultaneously so that all mobile users transmit on the same frequency with different pseudo-random signals. Originally developed to support voice. One of two digital cellular standards in the US.

code word When used in the context of the Reed-Solomon encoding, it refers to the 63 6-bit symbols (378 bits) resulting from the encoding of 47 6-bit (282 bits) information symbols. This is done by appending 16 6-bit parity symbols.

color code A code that is assigned to the members of a set, under some definition of adjacency, in such a way that each member of the set is assigned a value for the color code that is different from those assigned to all adjacent members of the set.

Comite Consultatif International Telegraphique et Telephonique (CCITT) Consultative Committee for International Telegraph and Telephone. A standards organization that devises and proposes recommendations for international communications. Refer also to *American National Standards Institute (ANSI)*.

compression The removal of redundant or unnecessary information from a set of data.

confidentiality A security process that ensures that the content of a transmitted message cannot be determined except by the possessor of a key associated with the message, even if the transmitted bits are observed.

connectionless network protocol (CLNP) The standard OSI connectionless network protocol.

connectionless network service (CLNS) An International Standards Organization (ISO) internetwork service.

control channel   Within the cellular telephone system, several of the channels are assigned as 'control' channels. Instead of supporting voice communications, these channels allow the base station to broadcast information to the cellular phones in its area. Cellular phones continuously monitor this broadcast information, selecting the base station that provides the best signal.

control flag   A 6-bit flag transmitted in the forward channel data stream, comprised of a 5-bit busy/idle flag and one bit of the 5-bit decode status flag.

correctable error   An error in a transmitted block that can be corrected by application of the Reed-Solomon decoding process.

COTS   Connection-Oriented Transport Service.

CRC   Cyclic Redundancy Check. These are used for the purposes of error detection.

credentials   Refer to Authentication Credentials.

CSI   Channel Stream Identifier.

CSMA/CD   Carrier Sense Multiple Access with Carrier Detection.

cyclic redundancy check (CRC)   A computational means to detect errors in frames transmitted between devices. The mathematical function is computed at the originating device before a frame is transmitted. Its numerical value is computed based on the content of the frame. This value is compared with a recomputed value of the function at the destination device. Refer also to *Frame Check Sequence (FCS)*.

D

data compression   Reducing the size of a file of data by eliminating unnecessary information, such as blanks and redundant data.

data encryption   The processing of data under a secret key so that the original data can only be determined by a recipient in possession of the secret key.

Data Link Layer   Layer 2 in the Open Systems Interconnect (OSI) 7-Layer Network Layer Reference Model. Provides communication among two or more systems. The Data Link Layer performs error checking, addressing, and other functions that are required to ensure accurate data transmission between adjacent systems.

database   A collection of data structured and organized in a disciplined to provide quick access to information of interest.

datagram   A finite-length packet with sufficient information to be independently routed from source to destination.

dB   Decibels.

de-encapsulation   The process of extracting a data packet from the user data field of the encapsulating data packet.

decibel   A unit of measurement for relative signal strength. The value is expressed as 10 times the logarithm of the value taken base 10.

Decode Status Flag   A 5-bit flag used by the CDPD Mobile Data Base Station (MDBS) in the forward channel transmission to indicate the decoding status of Reed-Solomon blocks received on the reverse channel from the CDPD Mobile End System (M-ES).

decompression   The restoration of redundant data that was removed through compression.

decryption   The processing of received data by the possessor of a secret key in such a way that the intended contents of the data are restored.

decryption key   The secret key required to decrypt received data.

dedicated channel   A Radio Frequency (RF) channel that is allocated solely for the use of Cellular Digital Packet Data (CDPD).

default route   A routing table entry that is used to direct any data addressed to any network numbers not explicitly listed in the routing table.

demultiplexing   The process of distributing data received in a shared data stream to the several entities that share the data stream. Demultiplexing can occur at several layers of a protocol stack. Refer to *Multiplexing*.

deregistration   In the CDPD network, the process of dissociating an Network Entity Identifier (NEI) from the CDPD network.

DES   Data Encryption Standard. An encryption/decryption algorithm defined in FIPS Publication 46.

destination address   An address attached to the information of a message that imparts the intended destination of the message.

Diffie-Hellman EKE   A procedure to exchange electronic keys between communicating devices. Used in CDPD.

digital cellular technology Refers to the cellular telephony standards that involve digitizing a voice signal, then transmitting the data serially.

Digital Sense Multiple Access With Collision Detection (DSMA/CD) A technique used by Cellular Digital Packet Data (CDPD) to arbitrate access to the reverse channel stream by more than one Mobile End System (M-ES).

Directory Service A Directory Service is like a white pages service in which the user supplies the name of an entity, and receives information about that entity such as address, title and description. The user can also search on a particular characteristic and receive one or more directory entries (entity names) that match that search. A directory user can request the address of another entity in order to establish communication. Addresses for real-time communication are Presentation, Session, Transport or Network Addresses for Application Entities in a Mobile End System or Fixed End System. Addresses for message exchange are Distinguished Names which are presented to a Message Handling Service along with a message body.

Directory System Agent (DSA) Directory Information is distributed over Directory System Agents. Each DSA holds a fragment of the Directory Information Base (DIB). The DSA fills the requests that it can (e.g., from Directory User Agents), and refers requests that it cannot fill to other DSAs using the Directory System Protocol.

Directory System Protocol (DSP) The protocol used between the various Directory System Agents that make up a global Directory Service.

Directory User Agent (DUA) A process, sometimes incorporating a user interface, that is used to gain access to a Directory Service. The DUA uses the Directory Access Protocol over an OSI stack to access the Directory Service. Typically, some application process acting as a DUA would access Directory Services to obtain network addresses for entities with which it wants to communicate.

distribution frequency The number of times in which a message of a particular type is transmitted per unit time, particularly for messages related to radio resource management.

DNS Domain Name System.

Domain Naming System (DNS) A mechanism used in the Internet for translating names of host computers into addresses. It is a network database system that provides translation between host names and addresses.

dotting sequence An alternating series of 38 bits used for the purposes of symbol (bit) timing recovery at the CDPD Mobile Data Base Station (MDBS) for reverse channel transmissions by the CDPD Mobile End System (M-ES).

DS0 Data Switching class 0—a 56 Kbps data channel.

DSA Directory System Agent. Directory Information is distributed over Directory System Agents. Each DSA holds a fragment of the Directory Information Base (DIB). The DSA fills the requests that it can (e.g., from Directory User Agents), and refers requests that it cannot fill to other DSAs using the Directory System Protocol.

DSMA/CD Digital Sense Multiple Access with Collision Detection.

DSP Directory System Protocol.

DTE Data Terminal Equipment.

DUA Directory User Agent.

duty cycle In Cellular Digital Packet Data (CDPD), the amount of time that a Mobile Data Base Station (MDBS) or Mobile End System (M-ES) can access the channel. For an MDBS, the duty cycle is continuous. For an M-ES, it is intermittent and is controlled through the DSMA/CD protocol.

E

E-Interface The network interface between the Cellular Digital Packet Data (CDPD) networks and other external networks.

EID Equipment Identifier.

EIRP Equivalent Isotropic Radiated Power.

EKE Electronic key exchange.

Easter Egg Would we really hide our names in the specifications? Well ... the devices need to be tested for conformance ... especially that Reed-Solomon coding ...

electronic key exchange A security procedure by which two entities establish secret keys used to encrypt and decrypt data exchanged between them. The procedure used in CDPD is based on a form of public key cryptography developed by Diffie and Hellman.

encapsulation   (1) The addition of control information to a body of data, either preceding the data, following the data, or both. CDPD uses encapsulation of end-users' packets in ConnectionLess Network Protocol (CLNP) Protocol Data Units (PDUs) for redirection between home and serving MD-ISs (Mobile Data Intermediate Systems).

encryption   The processing of data under a secret key in such a way that the original data can only be determined by a recipient in possession of the secret key. The process reduces the possibility of eavesdropping.

encryption key   The secret key used to perform the encryption process.

end system (ES)   Any computer not considered to be performing routing or bridging functions. In Internet terminology, an ES is a host; ESs are the actual physical and logical end nodes that exchange information.

end-to-end communications   Data delivered between a source and destination endpoint.

end-to-end connection   Connections between the source system and the destination system.

end-to-end data confidentiality   The provision of data confidentiality between the sender and receiver of a communication.

enhanced specialized mobile radio (ESMR)   A recent enhancement to Specialized Mobile Radio (SMR). ESMR is a national network of dispatch radio systems featuring both voice and data communications. It is a circuit-switched network that replaces SMR systems with all new digital cellular technology. Based on Motorola Integrated Radio System (MIRS) technology, ESMR consolidates many smaller SMR systems into a larger network. Voice quality is inferior to current cellular networks, and data is limited to 4800 bps circuit-switched connections with gateways into the Public Switched Telephone Network (PSTN).

enhanced throughput cellular (ETC)   AT&T technology in which cellular-specific modems manage the challenges of cellular connections.

entity   An abstract representation of a device or process implementing a defined set of functions, particularly functions related to the execution of a protocol.

equalization   The process of reducing signal distortion over transmission paths by putting in compensating devices. The telephone network is equalized by the spacing and operation of amplifiers along the way.

equipment identifier (EID)   A unique electronic serial number for the CDPD subscriber device.

ERP   Effective Radiated Power.

error correction   Refer to *V.42 error correction.*

error rate   In data transmission, the ratio of the number of incorrect elements received to the total number of elements received.

ES   End System.

ESB   End System Bye packet. Part of CDPD Mobile End System (M-ES) registration procedures.

ESH   End System Hello packet. Part of CDPD Mobile End System (M-ES) registration sequence.

ESMR   Enhanced Specialized Mobile Radio.

ESN   Electronic Serial Number. A unique number assigned to a cellular telephone or cellular modem by the manufacturer. This number is required by the cellular carrier when applying for cellular service.

ESQ   End System Query packet. Part of CDPD Mobile End System (M-ES) registration procedures.

Ethernet   A network standard for the hardware and data link levels. .

external F-ES   A Fixed End System (F-ES) connected to the CDPD network outside the administrative domain of the service provider.

external interface   The Cellular Digital Packet Data (CDPD)-based wireless packet data service provider's interface to existing external networks. The external application service providers communicate with CDPD subscribers through this external interface.

F

F-ES   Fixed End System.

fade   A temporary reduction in received signal strength.

FCC   Federal Communications Commission.

FCS   Frame Check Sequence.

FEC   Forward Error Correction.

Fascicle A collection of documents (or a bundle of hay.) Used in CCITT standards. We needed a new name for the collections of CDPD specification Parts. The discussion went:
"What shall we call these collections?" ... "I've always wanted to write a Fascicle! Let's call them Fascicles!" ... "Done!"

file transfer protocol (FTP) Common Internet file transfer program that uses Transmission Control Protocol/Internet Protocol (TCP/IP)

firewall A security router that filters traffic based on addresses.

Fixed End System (F-ES) A non-mobile end system. A host system that supports or provides access to data and applications.

flow control A procedure that allows an entity to cause a remote entity to suspend or resume the transmission of data.

FM capture In extreme cases of co-channel interference, a receiver may experience what is referred to as "FM capture," which is a co-channel interference condition where the good signal is treated as noise and the interferer is selected. Cellular users often experience FM capture as a momentary burst of someone else's conversation.

fonts Subject of much debate at specification meetings. Why did we end up with New Century Schoolbook anyway?!!

forced hop A channel hop made by the Mobile Data Base Station (MDBS) because non-Cellular Digital Packet Data (CDPD) activity is detected on the channel that is currently in use.

forward channel The transmission channel for data from the MDBS to the M-ES.

forward error correction The addition of parity information to transmitted data that allows a receiver to correct errors that may occur during the course of transmission.

frame A Link Protocol Data Unit.

frame check sequence (FCS) The standard 16-bit cyclic redundancy check used for High-level Data Link Control (HDLC) and frame relay frames. The Frame Check Sequence (FCS) detects bit errors occurring in the bits of the frame between the opening flag and the FCS, and is only effective in detecting errors in frames no larger than 4096 octets. Refer to *Cyclic Redundancy Check (CRC)*.

frame flag sequence   The unique bit pattern "01111110" used as the opening and closing delimiter for the link layer frames.

frame header   Address information required for transmission of a packet across a communications link.

frame relay   A packet-oriented Wide Area Network (WAN) connection that offers high performance. Often called a fast-packet switching network because tasks such as error checking, packet sequencing, and packet acknowledgment are handled by the end systems involved in the transmission rather than by the network itself.

frame relay access device   Required for connection into a frame relay network.

frequency modulation   A modulation technique in which the carrier frequency is shifted by an amount proportional to the value of the modulating signal. The amplitude of the carrier signals remains constant. The deviation of the carrier frequency determines the signal content of the message.

frequency-shift keying   A modulation scheme that uses different frequencies to denote a one or a zero.

FTP   File Transfer Protocol.

full-duplex   Capability of simultaneously transmitting and receiving.

G

gateway   A protocol conversion facility allowing connection of dissimilar communication systems.

Gaussian minimum shift keying (GMSK)   A member of the class of constant-envelope continuous-phase modulations with a Gaussian filtered phase response. Used in the airlink physical layer in Cellular Digital Packet Data (CDPD) and GSM.

GHz   GigaHertz, Hz x 10^9 (One million cycles per second).

Global Positioning System (GPS)   A system of satellites orbiting the earth used for navigation and location. Position on earth is determined by referencing multiple satellites in the system whose orbits are precisely known and thus provide a reference frame for measuring distances.

Global Standard For Mobile Communications (GSM)   A digital cellular standard used primarily in Europe and some other countries. Primarily a Time Division Multiple Access (TDMA) cellular voice service, though data services are offered over GSM. Formerly called Groupe Speciale Mobile.

GMSK	Gaussian Minimum Shift Keying.
GSM	Global Standard for Mobile communication.

H

half-duplex	Capability of transmitting or receiving, but not both simultaneously.
half-duplex M-ES	A Mobile End System (M-ES) that can either transmit or receive, but cannot do both simultaneously, for example, an M-ES that has a single transceiver (radio).
handoff	The process of passing a Radio Frequency (RF) connection to another available channel either at the originating cell site, a neighboring cell site, or in another service provider's coverage area. As the subscriber moves from one location to another, the connection is continually handed off from channel to channel and from cell site to cell site.
Hayes AT command interface	Traditional method to control a modem and begin and end data transmissions.
Hayes-compatible AT command set	Used to control a modem and to initiate a connection to the network.
HDLC	High-level Data Link Control.
header	The initial portion of a Protocol Data Unit (PDU) containing control information. Also referred to as the Protocol Control Information (PCI)
high-level data link control (HDLC)	A link-level communications protocol developed by the International Standards Organization (ISO). HDLC manages synchronous, code-transparent, serial information transfer over a link connection.
Home MD-IS	The CDPD network component that performs the Mobile Home Function.
hop	A change of Radio Frequency (RF) channel used to carry the Cellular Digital Packet Data (CDPD) data for a channel stream.
hop channel	A Radio Frequency (RF) channel that has been declared a candidate for carrying a Cellular Digital Packet Data (CDPD) channel stream after a channel hop.
host	The computer providing file transfer and communications services to client computers.

hybrid CDPD   Circuit-switched CDPD (Cellular Digital Packet Data), a technology known as hybrid CDPD, is the system architecture developed by the CDPD Forum for interconnecting circuit-switched data, including cellular and land-line links, with the CDPD network.

hysteresis   Mechanism to reduce unnecessary continual cell change.

I - J

I-interface   The network interfaces between CDPD service provider networks.

ICMP   Internet Control Message Protocol.

idle state   A channel stream is in an idle state if the Mobile Data Base Station (MDBS) signals in the busy/idle flag that no Mobile End System (M-ES) is currently transmitting on the channel.

IEEE   Institute for Electrical and Electronics Engineers.

IETF   Internet Engineering Task Force. The IETF is a large open community of network designers, operators, vendors, and researchers whose purpose is to coordinate the operation, management, and evolution of the Internet, and to resolve short- and mid-range protocol and architectural issues. It is a major source of proposed protocol standards which are submitted to the Internet Activities Board for final approval.

in-band control   Control information that is provided in the same channel as data.

Integrated Services Digital Network (ISDN)   A network interface that integrates voice, data, and video signals into a single digital telephone line. The worldwide telephony standard for digital telecommunications.

Inter-Area Cell Transfer   A cell transfer between two cells that are controlled by different serving Mobile Data Intermediate Systems (MD-ISs).

Inter-Service Provider Interface   Cellular Digital Packet Data (CDPD)-based wireless packet data service provider's interface to cooperating CDPD-based wireless packet data service provider networks.

intermediate system (IS)   A node that is connected to more than one subnetwork with a primary role of forwarding data from one subnetwork to another. In Internet terminology, ISs are known as routers that relay data packets from ESs to their intended destinations.

internal F-ES   A Fixed End System within the administrative domain of theCDPD service provider. Typically provides value-added support services such as network management, accounting, directory, and authentication services.

International Standards Organization (ISO)   Organization that determines standards for international and national data communications. The US representative to the ISO is the American National Standards Institute (ANSI).

Internet   A set of networks using a set of network-independent protocols for communication that have been defined under the aegis of the Defense Advanced Research Projects Agency.

Internet (Internetwork)   (1) The global collection of interconnected local, mid-level, and wide area networks that use Internet Protocol (IP) as the network layer protocol. (2) Any connection of two or more local or wide area networks.

Internet address   An assigned number that identifies a host in an Internet. It has two or three parts: network number, optional subnet number, and host number.

Internet Protocol (IP)   A connectionless protocol that requires no prior call setup between the source and destination systems.

Intra-Area Cell Transfer   A cell transfer between two cells that are controlled by the same serving Mobile Data Intermediate System (MD-IS).

IP   Internet Protocol.

IP address   Internet Protocol address.

IS   Intermediate System.

IS-95   The CDMA (Code Division Multiple Access) standard.

ISC   Mobile Data Intermediate System Confirm packet. Part of Mobile End System (M-ES) registration procedures.

ISO   International Standards Organization.

K

Kbps   Kilobits per second.

key   A quantity required for the execution of security algorithms that is intended to be used only by legitimate entities.

key exchange   A procedure by which the value of a key is shared between two or more parties.

key generation   The process of creating a key.

key management   The rules and procedures governing the creation, distribution, and replacement of keys.

key sequence number An identifier associated with a key that allows one value of a key to be distinguished from an older or newer value of the key.

kHz kiloHertz, Hz x 10^3.

km kilometer.

L

LAN Local Area Network. A network that takes advantage of the proximity of computers to offer relatively efficient, higher speed communications than long-haul or wide-area networks. Electronic mail, messaging, file sharing, and database access are common LAN applications.

landline Fixed connection that uses wires, not radio transmission.

LAPD Link Access Protocol for the D Channel. It is a Link Layer protocol defined in Consultative Committee for International Telegraph and Telephone (CCITT) specifications Q.920 and Q.921 and forming the basis of the Cellular Digital Packet Data (CDPD) Link Layer's Mobile Data Link Protocol (MDLP).

latency The slight delay in data delivery through a network.

Layer Entity An entity performing the functions required for a layer of protocol.

Layer Management Entity Identifier An identifier used to select an entity concerned with a particular set of layer management functions.

Layer Service A term that applies to the layers of the OSI Reference Model. A Layer Service represents a set of functions offered to a network user by a Layer Service Provider. A Layer Service consists of one or more primitives which are invoked by either the user or the provider.

Layer Service Provider Each layer of the OSI Reference Model is a Layer Service Provider. Examples of layers are Presentation, Session, Transport, Network, and Link. The Layer Service is made available through Service Access Points.

LD Location Directory.

legacy system Refers to older equipment and systems that are doing an important job for a company, but which would not be implemented on the same platform if deployed today. Legacy systems were often developed by people other than those who are responsible for them now.

Link Access Procedure for Modems (LAPM)   LAPM is the V.42 standard determined by a consultative committee of the International Telecommunications Union-Telecommunications Systems (ITU-TS) and specifies the use of LAPM as an error-control protocol. LAPM provides somewhat better performance than Microcom Networking Protocol (MNP) 4, including improved setup and better performance over poor lines.

Link Access Protocol on the D-channel (LAPD)   A protocol that operates at the data link layer (layer 2) of the OSI architecture. LAPD is used to convey information between layer 3 entities across the frame relay network. The D-channel carries signaling information for circuit switching.

Link Layer   That layer of a distributed communications system concerned with the operation of a data link between two or more entities. Provides services such as data encryption, data compression, and flow control.

Link Protocol Data Unit (LPDU)   The Protocol Data Unit (PDU) exchanged between Link Layer entities. Also known as a frame.

LMEI   Layer Management Entity Identifier.

Location Directory (LD)   The repository of information specifying the current Forwarding Address of a collection of mobile hosts to be accessed by the redirectors. For Cellular Digital Packet Data (CDPD), refer to *Mobile Network Location Protocol* And *Home Mobile Data Intermediate System.*

LPDU   Refer to *Link Protocol Data Unit.*

LSDU   Link Layer Service Data Unit.

M

M-ES   Mobile End System. An M-ES is a wireless communications device that conforms to Cellular Digital Packet Data (CDPD) standards. The end system that provides remote access to theCDPD network via the airlink. In the majority of cases, the M-ES is a laptop equipped with a Radio Frequency (RF) modem. In the CDPD network, the M-ES is a unique network node and has a unique network address.

MAC   Medium Access Control.

MAC Layer   That layer of a distributed communications system concerned with the control of access to a medium that is shared between two or more entities.

MAC protocol	The procedures used to control access to a medium that is shared between two or more entities.
management	Protocols and procedures concerned with configuration, administration, and similar functions.
management entity	An entity concerned with supporting management.
management information base (MIB)	The database used by network management systems and contains technical information about each device on the network.
market	A geographical area of demand and responsibility for cellular service.
MAS	Mobile Application Subsystem. An MAS is application software that is independent of the Cellular Digital Packet Data (CDPD) Network.
maximum power level	Maximum power output limit for Mobile End System (M-ES).
MCHO	Mobile Controlled Hand-off.
MD-IS	Mobile Data Intermediate System.
MD-IS serving area	The set of cells controlled by a single serving Mobile Data Intermediate System (MD-IS).
MDBS	Mobile Data Base Station.
MDLP	Mobile Data Link Protocol. The Link Layer protocol defined in CDPD networks.
medium access control (MAC)	The function of controlling access to a medium that is shared between two or more entities.
Medium Access Control (MAC) Layer	Refer to *Medium Access Control*.
message	A meaningful unit of information. A Protocol Data Unit (PDU) of defined format and purpose. Refers to the basic unit of data being transmitted.
Message Handling System (MHS)	A supplementary service that implements Message Store and Forward Message Handling. MHS is used within the Cellular Digital Packet Data (CDPD) network. MHS provides for distribution lists, return receipts and allows for gateways to proprietary message systems, including alternative delivery mechanisms such as telex or fax.
Message Store (MS)	Acts as a mailbox for storing messages coming from a Message Transfer Agent and destined for a User Agent.

message transfer agent (MTA)	Performs Message Routing (e.g., to other MTAs) and message delivery to User Agents and Message Stores.
messaging API (MAPI)	An application protocol.
MHF	Mobile Home Function.
MHS	Message Handling System.
MHz	MegaHertz (Hz x 10^6).
MIB	Management Information Database.
microslot	The time between two consecutive busy/idle flags (60 bits, or 3.125 milliseconds at 19.2 kbps). It is used in CDPD only.
middleware	Software that isolates applications from the protocol requirements, hardware, and actual operations of a particular network. May perform protocol conversions between disparate systems. Refers to any software that resides between a client program and a server program. Middleware includes protocol stacks, network operating systems, and messaging systems.
MME	Mobility Management Entity.
MNLP	Mobile Network Location Protocol.
MNP-10	Microcom Networking Protocol Ten. MNP-10 provides a proprietary error-correcting and data compression protocol for dial-up modems from 2.4 to 14.4 Kbps. MNP-10 consists of Adverse Channel Enhancements that optimize performance in environments with poor or varying line quality, such as cellular telephones, international telephone calls, and rural telephone service.
MNRP	Mobile Network Registration Protocol.
Mobile Application Subsystem (MAS)	That portion of a Mobile End System (M-ES) concerned with the provision of application services. The MAS contains the application software that is independent of the CDPD network. In most cases, this includes network software.
Mobile Data Base Station (MDBS)	Component of the CDPD network that provides data link relay functions for a set of radio channels serving a cell. An MDBS is located in each cell site, and its primary role is to relay data between Mobile End System (M-ES) and the Mobile Data Intermediate System (MD-IS). It is the stationary network component responsible for managing interactions across the airlink interface.

Mobile Data Intermediate System (MD-IS)   The CDPD network element that performs routing functions based on knowledge of the current location of the M-ES. Responsible for CDPD mobility management. It operates a Cellular Digital Packet Data (CDPD)-specific Mobile Network Location Protocol (MNLP) to exchange location information.

Mobile Data Link Protocol (MDLP)   The Link Layer protocol used in Cellular Digital Packet Data (CDPD). Provides Temporary Equipment Identifier (TEI) management, multiple frame operation, unitdata transfers, exception condition detection with selective reject recovery, etc.

Mobile End System (M-ES)   An end system that accesses the CDPD network through the airlink interface. The device that allows mobile users to work in an untethered fashion while remaining connected to a data network. The system's physical position may change during data transmission.

mobile home function   A Mobile Data Intermediate System (MD-IS) mobility function that (1) maintains an information database of the current serving area of each of its homed Mobile End Systems (M-ESs), and (2) operates a packet forwarding service for its homed M-ESs.

Mobile Identification Number   When the "SEND" key is pressed, a cellular phone transmits an origination message to the base station. This message includes the dialed digits and the identity of the calling cellular phone. The calling cellular phone is identified by its Mobile Identification Number (MIN), which is usually the same as its ten-digit phone number.

Mobile Network Location Protocol (MNLP)   In the CDPD network, protocol used between the Home Mobile Data Intermediate System (MD-IS) and the Serving MD-IS to keep the Home MD-IS updated on the location of a Mobile End System (M-ES).

Mobile Network Registration Protocol (MNRP)   In the CDPD network, protocol used between the Mobile End System (M-ES) and the Serving Mobile Data Intermediate System (MD-IS) to announce the M-ES's Network Entity Identifier (NEI) and to confirm the service provider's willingness to provide service.

Mobile Serving Function (MSF)   A Mobile Data Intermediate System (MD-IS) function that (1) maintains an information database of the Mobile End Systems (M-ES) currently registered in the serving area, and (2) de-encapsulates forwarded packets from the MHF and routes them to the correct channel stream in a cell where the destined M-ES is located. Refer to *Serving Mobile Data Intermediate System*.

mobile switching center (MSC)   The location of the Digital Access and Cross-connect System (DACS) in a cellular telephone network.

mobile-controlled handoff	The decision to initiate a transfer or handoff from one cell to another cell is under the control of the mobile device. Used in CDPD.
mobility management	A service provided by the Network Layer. Mobility is primarily a routing issue in that Network Protocol Data Units (NPDUs) that are destined for a Mobile End System (M-ES) must be routed toward that Mobile End System. In the CDPD network, the home Mobile Data Intermediate System (MD-IS) forwards NPDUs to the serving Mobile Data Intermediate System for a Mobile End System.
Mobitex Asynchronous Communications Protocol (MASC)	The layer that communicates with the Mobitex radio modem. Used in the RAM mobile data network.
Mobitex Packet (MPAK)	The RAM Mobile Data Network Layer protocol.
Mobitex Transport Protocol (MTP1)	The RAM Mobile Data Transport Layer protocol.
modem	MOdulator-DEModulator. A device that translates computer information for transmission on both cellular and regular telephone lines.
modem pool	A device that provides the equivalent of multiple data modems. Typically deployed by cellular carriers to provide circuit switched data services.
modulation	The analog waveform of a transmitted digital signal.
Motorola Integrated Radio System (MIRS)	Technology developed by Motorola. ESMR is based on this technology. Nextel is the largest company deploying ESMR. (Now called iDEN).
MS	Message Store or More Segments.
MSC	Mobile Switching Center.
MSF	Mobile Serving Function.
MTA	Message Transfer Agent.
MTS	Message Transfer System.
multicast	A one-way point to multi-point routing and relaying service that allows a message to be addressed and delivered to all members of a group, regardless of their current location.

multipath fading The singal degradation that occurs when multiple copies of the same radio signal arrives at the receiver through different reflected paths. The interference of these signals, each having traveled a different distance, result in phase and amplitude variations. The radio signal processing in both the base station and mobile units have to be designed to tolerate a certain level of multipath fading.

multiplexing The process of mixing data originating from several entities into a single shared data stream. Multiplexing can occur at several layers of a protocol stack.

N

N=7 frequency plan The feature of the cellular system that distinguishes it from earlier technology is the allocation of channels within geographic areas called cells. By using only a fraction of the total allocation of channels in each cell, and coordinating the frequency assignments in neighboring cells, the set of available channels can be reused in non-adjacent cells. The complete set of available channels is divided into seven groups. This frequency plan is known as the "N=7" frequency plan.

NAM Number Assignment Module. Cellular phones are configured with NAM parameters, which include the Mobile Identification Number (MIN) and various other data about radio channels. To use any cellular phone over a cellular network the NAM must be configured correctly. The MIN is usually the same as the phone number and is assigned by the cellular carrier. The other parameters in the MIN ensure that the cellular phone will be able to access the cellular system correctly, and are usually provided by the carrier or dealer. To verify the user's identity, the cellular phone also transmits an Electronic Serial Number (ESN) when it communicates with the MTSO. This ESN is permanently assigned to the phone, and is entered by the carrier in the MTSO database when a user signs up for service.

Narrowband Personal Communications Standards (PCS) Refers to a new spectrum available for paging services, including two-way paging. Unlicensed Personal Communications Services (PCS) refers to spectrum from 1910 MHz to 1930 MHz available for cellular PBXs and cellular LANs. Broadband (or wideband) PCS is the service of most interest to wide area cellular data users. Broadband PCS consists of 120 MHz of new spectrum available for cellular networks.

NDIS Network Driver Interface Specification.

NEI   Network Entity Identifier.

network   A collection of computers or other similar devices linked for communication.

Network Driver Interface Specification (NDIS)   Application programming interface standard for attaching to data communications devices.

Network Entity Identifier (NEI)   An Internet protocol address, or ConnectionLess Networking Protocol (CLNP) address, or any other protocol addressing utilized by the provider in transmission and receipt of Cellular Digital Packet Data (CDPD) services. The address that identifies that a user is authorized to use the service.

Network Information Center (NIC)   Any organization that is responsible for providing network users with information about services provided by any network.

Network Layer   Layer 3 in the Open Systems Interconnect (OSI) 7-Layer Network Layer Reference Model. Internet Protocol (IP) and ConnectionLess Network Protocol (CLNP) reside at this layer. Provides packet routing and relaying between end systems on the same network or on interconnected networks and is independent of the transport protocol used.

Network Layer Protocol Identifier (NLPI)   An identifier allowing entities providing different Network Layer protocols to be distinguished from each other.

network management   The process of managing the various functions of the network.

network management agent   Each device connected to the network runs a corresponding network management agent. The agent collects information about the network device and sends the information to the Management Information Database (MIB) to be recorded. Provides the network management system with a device's status.

Network Management System (NMS)   A system concerned with performing management functions.

network number   The part of an Internet address that designates the network to which the addressed node belongs.

Network Protocol Data Unit (NPDU)   Network Layer Protocol Data Unit. The NPDU comprises the Network Layer Service Data Unit and the Network Layer Protocol Control Information.

Network Service Access Point (NSAP)	The NSAP is an abstraction of a point where the Network Layer service user and the Network Layer service provider meet. Each Network Entity may be accessed through one or more NSAPs by its users. Each NSAP has one or more NSAP-Addresses.
NIC	Network Information Center. An organization that provides network users with information about services provided by the network.
NLPI	Network Layer Protocol Identifier.
NMF	Network Management Forum.
NMS	Network Management System.
node	A node is an entity that participates in network communication. Examples of nodes are End Systems and Intermediate Systems.
noise	Noise is the addition of interference, making it harder to identify the signal that was transmitted. Noise is introduced by various processes in the telephone system including relays and crosstalk. In the cellular environment, noise is introduced by radio interference.
non-persistent	A property of a Medium Access Control (MAC) protocol by which a MAC entity shall sample the state of the medium at random intervals and shall only attempt to access the medium if the medium is in an idle state at the time of sampling. If the medium is in a busy state, it will revisit the medium after a random time period.
NPDU	Network Protocol Data Unit.
NSAP	Network Service Access Point.
NSAP-Address	The NSAP-Address uniquely identifies a Network Service Access Point (NSAP).
NSAP-Selector	A component of an Network Service Access Point (NSAP)-Address used to select the Network Layer service user. The NSAP-Selector is sometimes referred to as a Transport-Selector; however, a user of the Network Layer need not be a transport service.
Number Assignment Module (NAM)	Cellular phones are configured with NAM parameters, which include the Mobile Identification Number (MIN) and various other data about radio channels

O

octet	Eight consecutive bits.
open system	A system with publicly known protocols or architectures, one that requires no special protocols and is simple to implement.

Open Systems Interconnection (OSI) 7-Layer Network Layer Reference Model	An international standardization program facilitated by International Standards Organization (ISO) and Consultative Committee for International Telegraph and Telephone (CCITT) to develop standards for data networking that facilitate multivendor equipment interoperability. OSI includes the following seven layers: Physical Layer, Data Link Layer, Network Layer, Transport Layer, Session Layer, Presentation Layer, and Application Layer.
OSI	Open Systems Interconnection. A set of protocols designed to be an international standard method for connecting different types of computers and networks. Europe has done most of the work developing OSI.
OSI reference model	An "outline" of OSI that defines the seven layers of the model and their functions. Sometimes used to help describe other networks. Refer to *Open Systems Interconnection (OSI) 7-Layer Network Layer Reference Model*.
OSPF	Open Shortest-Path First. Interior Gateway Protocol; a proposed replacement for Routing Interchange Protocol (RIP).
Otto	Playful (and big) four-legged friend of the specification team that appeared as a glossary item and as an Easter Egg entry in the spec. Happy hunting!

P

packet	Network Protocol Data Unit
packet switching	Sending data in packets through a network to some remote location. Each packet contains enough addressing information to allow proper routing (whether connection oriented or connectionless). Packetization allow sharing of the data link between multiple peer communications.
packet-switched data network	Networks that use packet switching technology for delivery of data units. Examples include Cellular Digital Packet Data (CDPD), RAM Mobile Data, ARDIS, and Metricom's Ricochet.
PCCA AT command set	The new PCCA AT command set for wireless modems contains well-defined commands for obtaining link status information. Refer to *AT command set*.
PCI	Protocol Control Information.
PCMCIA	Personal Computer Memory Card International Association. The standardizaton organization for credit-card size packages for memory and I/O (modems, LAN cards, etc.) for computers, laptops, etc.

PCS	Personal Communications Services. A wireless technology being developed in the US. *Narrowband PCS* refers to a new spectrum available for paging services. The digital signals of PCS are a series of rapid pulses, unlike analog's steady flow.
PDA	Personal Digital Assistant.
PDU	Protocol Data Unit.
peer network entities	The origin and destination of all data transmissions.
peer-to-peer communications	Communications between two entities that operate within the same protocol layer of a system.
peer-to-peer protocols	Describes the relationship between a telephone system and the external computer. Refer to *peer-to-peer communications*.
Personal Communications Services (PCS)	Refers to the next generation of cellular systems. Will include data services.
Personal Digital Assistant (PDA)	A hand-held or custom-built Mobile End System (M-ES).
PhPDU	Physical Layer Protocol Data Unit (PDU)—a bit.
PhSAP	Physical Service Access Point.
PhSDU	Physical Service Data Unit.
Physical Layer	Layer 1 in the Open Systems Interconnect (OSI) 7-Layer Network Layer Reference Model. That layer of a distributed communications system concerned with the actual transmission of data across a physical medium. The physical layer provides a physical connection for transmission of data between two data link entities.
PIN	Personal Identification Number.
ping	An ICMP message that is sent out to a known IP address. If the signal arrives at the known address, it returns to its point of origin, confirming connectivity.
point of presence	An entry point for connection into the network.
Point-to-Point Protocol (PPP)	An Internet protocol that provides a method for transmitting datagrams over serial point-to-point links.
point-to-multipoint delivery	Delivery of data from a single source to several destinations.

point-to-point delivery   Delivery of data from a single source to a single destination.

power product   A configurable parameter broadcast by the Mobile Data Base Station (MDBS), defining the desired relationship between received signal strength and transmitted power level at any single point.

PPP   Point to Point Protocol,

Presentation Address   The network name of an Application Entity within a Data Service. The Presentation Address takes the form of: optional Presentation Selector (SSAP-Selector) + Session Selector (TSAP-Selector) + Transport Selector (NSAP-Selector) + a required NET. Presentation Addresses are stored in the Directory Service. Application Entity Titles are used to retrieve the Presentation Address from the Directory Service.

primitive   An abstraction representing the communication between layer entities operating at different layers or between a layer entity and the management entity controlling it. There are four types of primitives in the OSI (Open Systems Interconnection) model)—request, indication, response, and confirm.

protocol   A set of procedures for exchanging information between peer entities. A formal description of message formats and the rules two computers must follow to exchange those messages. Protocols can describe low-level details of machine-to-machine interfaces, such as the order in which bits are sent across wire, or high level exchanges between allocation programs, such as the manner in which two programs transfer files across the Internet.

Protocol Control Information (PCI)   The part of the Protocol Data Unit that contains addressing, control, flags, and optional information needed by peer Layer Service Providers to provide the service. Refer to *protocol data unit* and *service data unit*.

Protocol Data Unit (PDU)   The unit of information that is exchanged by peer Layer Service Providers to implement the protocol that offers the service. The PDU consists of a Protocol Control Information and Service Data Unit.

PSTN   Public Switched Telephone Network. Actual telephone wires.

public switched telephone network (PSTN)   Public telephone network.

PVC   Permanent Virtual Circuit.

Q

QOS   Quality of service.

R

radio channel   Refer to *channel*.

radio frequency (RF)   The frequency in Hertz (cycles per second) of the carrier frequency being transmitted or received.

radio resource management   The set of management functions concerned with the determination of Radio Frequency (RF) channels to be used for Cellular Digital Packet Data (CDPD) by the Mobile Data Base Station (MDBS), the location and acquisition of those channels by the Mobile End System (M-ES), channel hopping and cell transfer, and the proper determination of power levels by the M-ES.

radio resource management entity   A management entity or subentity concerned with the operation of the radio resource management protocol.

rampdown   The process of reducing transmission power from the nominal power level to a level below a defined threshold.

rampup   The process of increasing transmission power from a level below a defined threshold to the nominal power level.

raw bit rate   The data channel bit rate that includes all protocol overhead and system overhead data bits.

Rayleigh fading   Multipath fading, arising from an ensemble of reflected signals arriving at the receiver antenna and creating standing waves.

RBOC   Regional Bell Operating Company.

RC-4   An encryption/decryption algorithm supported in Cellular Digital Packet Data (CDPD).

RDC   Redirect Confirm packet. Used in Cellular Digital Packet Data (CDPD) mobility management.

RDE   Redirect Expiry packet. Used in Cellular Digital Packet Data (CDPD) mobility management.

RDF   Redirect Flush packet. Used in Cellular Digital Packet Data (CDPD) mobility management.

RDQ   Redirect Query packet. Used in Cellular Digital Packet Data (CDPD) mobility management.

RDR   Redirect Request packet. Used in Cellular Digital Packet Data (CDPD) mobility management.

RDS   Redirection Server.

readdressing   The process whereby the serving Mobile Data Intermediate System (MD-IS) receives the encapsulated packets, de-encapsulates them, then locates the Mobile End System (M-ES) to determine the cell and channel stream associated with the M-ES. The function is also performed by the Foreign Agent in Mobile IP.

Readdressing Service (RS)   Function performed by a serving Mobile Data Intermediate System (MD-IS). A specialized router that accepts data packets from the redirector and then delivers the de-encapsulated packet to the intended Mobile End System (M-ES).

reassembly   The process of combining a number of the Link Layer Service Data Unit (LSDU) into an SN-Data Protocol Data Unit (PDU) or SN-Unitdata PDU.

received signal strength indication   The measured power of a received signal.

redirection and forwarding   The process whereby the home Mobile Data Intermediate System (MD-IS), upon the receipt of packets, encapsulates the packets with the address of the serving MD-IS and forwards them on to the serving MD-IS.

Reed-Solomon code   A forward error correcting code used in Cellular Digital Packet Data (CDPD).

Reed-Solomon forward error correction   Refer to *Reed-Solomon code*.

reference channel   Continuously keyed forward-transmission Radio Frequency (RF) channel, used for signal quality assessment.

registration   The process whereby a Mobile End System (M-ES) identifies its NEI to the CDPD network through exchange of MNRP messages with the serving MD-IS.

Registration Sequence Count   An 8-bit counter maintained by the Mobile End System (M-ES) and incremented on each successful establishment of a data link connection with a serving Mobile Data Intermediate System (MD-IS). Used to prevent registration errors due to varying network transit delays between serving MD-IS and home MD-IS.

registration timer values   Time values passed from Mobile Data Intermediate System (MD-IS) to a Mobile End System (M-ES) to inform the M-ES of the period of registration. The M-ES must register again prior to expiration of the registration timer.

reliable sequenced delivery   The delivery of a set of Protocol Data Units (PDUs) from a source to a destination with no errors in any PDU, in the order transmitted, and without gaps or duplicates.

reverse channel   The airlink channel between the Mobile End System (M-ES) and the CDPD network. On the reverse channel, information moves from the Mobile End System to the CDPD network. Refer to *Forward Channel*.

RF   Radio Frequency.

RF channel   A portion of the electromagnetic spectrum defined by a central frequency and a channel bandwidth.

RF channel number   An identifier assigned to a Radio Frequency (RF) channel to distinguish it from other RF channels.

RF channel pair   Two associated Radio Frequency (RF) channels, one forward and one reverse. The former is used to support forward transmissions from the Mobile Data Base Station (MDBS) to the Mobile End System (M-ES). The reverse channel carries data information from an M-ES to an MDBS, and is a Contention Based communication channel.

RFC   The internet's Request for Comments documents series. The RFCs are working notes of the Internet research and development community. A document in this series may be on any topic related to computer communication, and may be anything from a meeting report to the specification of a standard.

RIP   Routing Interchange Protocol. A protocol which may be used on internets to pass routing information between gateways. It is used on many Local Area Networks (LANs) and on some of the NSFNET intermediate level networks.

RLP   Radio Link Protocol.

RNR   Receive Not Ready.

roam   Traveling outside of a local cellular coverage area.

router   A special-purpose dedicated computer that attaches to two or more networks and examines received packets from one network. Based on the destination address of the packet, forwards it to the most appropriate next network.

routing area subdomain	The combined geographic area of all Mobile Data Base Stations (MDBSs) controlled by a single Mobile Data Intermediate System (MD-IS).
RR	Receive Ready.
RRM	Radio Resource Management.
RRME	Radio Resource Management Entity.
RRMP	Radio Resource Management Protocol.
RS	(1) Readdress Service. (2) Reed-Solomon.
RSSI	Received Signal Strength Indication.

S

SABME	Set Asynchronous Balanced Mode Extended.
SAP	Service Access Point.
SAP-address	Service Access Point Address.
SNDCF	Subnetwork Dependent Convergence Function.
SDU	Service Data Unit.
secret key	A key whose value is not disclosed to unauthorized entities.
sector	A cell controlled through a directional transmitting antenna.
security	The set of functions concerned with ensuring that only authorized users of the network can use the network, and only in authorized ways.
Security Management Entity	A management entity or subentity concerned with the operation of the security management protocol.
security policy	Determines who has access to what resources, and from what types of threats the application should be protected.
security threat—communications compromise	Threats associated with message communication, such as eavesdropping on messages transmitted over the airlink.
segmentation	The process of fragmenting an SN-Data Protocol Data Unit (PDU) or SN-Unitdata PDU into a number of Link Service Data Units (LSDUs).
Serial Line Internet Protocol (SLIP)	A protocol used between a host and the service provider to transmit IP datagrams through a serial port.

Service Access Point (SAP)   An abstraction of a point where a Layer Service User and the Layer Service Provider meet. Each Layer Service may be accessed through one or more SAPs by its users. Each SAP has one or more SAP-Addresses.

Service Data Unit (SDU)   When a user of a layer service requests the Layer Service Provider to transfer data to a remote service user, the user data is termed a Service Data Unit. The Layer Service Provider attaches a small header, called the Protocol Control Information, to the user data. The combination of the Protocol Control Information and SDU is called a Protocol Data Unit.

service provider   The operator of an network, responsible for the quality of the services it provides via the network and for administration of its subscribers and users (e.g., assignment of IDs, passwords, and capabilities).

Service Provider Identifier (SPI)   The unique identifier for a licensed facilities-based cellular Service Provider furnishing Cellular Digital Packet Data (CDPD) Services.

Service Provider Network Identifier (SPNI)   An identifier for the service provider operating a particular CDPD network.

Serving Mobile Data Intermediate System (serving MD-IS)   The CDPD network entity that operates the Mobile Serving Function. The serving MD-IS communicates with and is the peer endpoint for the MDLP connection to the M-ES.

Session Layer   Layer 5 in the Open Systems Interconnect (OSI) 7-Layer Network Layer Reference Model. Allows cooperating application entities to organize and synchronize information exchange and to manage data exchange.

SIM   Subscriber Identity Module.

sleep mode   A mode of operation in which a CDPD Mobile End System (M-ES) with at least one active Network Entity Identifier (NEI) conserves power by periodically turning off its receiver. The CDPD network infrastructure provides cooperating procedures to ensure continuous communications.

SLIP   Serial Line Internet Protocol.

slotted   A Medium Access Control (MAC) protocol is slotted if attempts to transmit can only be made at times that are synchronized between contending devices.

SME   Security Management Entity.

SMR   Specialized Mobile Radio.

SMTP   Simple Mail Transfer Protocol.

SN-data PDU   A Protocol Data Unit (PDU) of the Subnetwork Convergence Layer that is transmitted using *reliable sequenced delivery*.

SNDCF   Subnetwork Dependent Convergence Function.

SNDCP   Subnetwork Dependent Convergence Protocol. A Network Layer protocol that supports subnetwork convergence.

sniffer   A device used by the Mobile Data Base Station (MDBS) to monitor the transmission output of a non-Cellular Digital Packet Data (CDPD) base station in order to determine whether a Radio Frequency (RF) channel is available for CDPD use.

SNMP   Simple Network Management Protocol. The Simple Network Management Protocol is the Internet's standard for remote monitoring and management of hosts, routers and other nodes and devices on a network.

SNMP agent   An agent in a SNMP system. The SNMP agent operates to collect management information on network devices and to execute operations commanded from the SNMP manager.

SNPA   Subnetwork Point of Attachment.

SNSDU   Subnetwork Service Data Unit.

Sockets Interface   The Sockets Interface, introduced in the early 1980s with the release of Berkeley UNIX, was the first consistent and well-defined application programming interface (API). It is used at the transport layer between Transmission Control Protocol (TCP) or User Datagram Protocol (UDP) and the applications on a system. Since 1980, Sockets has been implemented on virtually every platform.

specialized mobile radio (SMR)   (1) A wireless data service that operates in the 806 to 821 MHz and 851 to 866 MHz bands. (2) Analog trunked radio systems primarily used for dispatch applications. (3) Dispatch radio systems combined into the national ESMR network.

spectrum   A continuous range of frequencies, usually wide in extent, within which waves have specific common characteristics.

SPI   Service Provider Identifier.

SPNI	Service Provider Network Identifier.
SREJ	Selective Reject.
store-and-forward	Description for networks that keeps temporary copies of transmitted data for later delivery to its intended recipient.
SU	Subscriber Unit. A radio frequency modem used to acquire the airlink.
subnet	A portion of a network, which may be a physically independent network, that shares a network address with other portions of the network and is distinguished by a subnet number. A subnet is to a network what a network is to an Internet.
subnet number	The portion of an Internet address that designates a subnet. It is ignored for the purposes of Internet routing, but is used for intranet routing.
Subnetwork Dependent Convergence Protocol (SNDCP)	The sublayer "glue" that reconciles the difference between the services requested by the Network Layer protocol and the services available from the Data Link Layer protocol. For example, in the CDPD network, the Network Layer protocol requires support for NPDUs of up to 2048 octets while the data link layer only supports data link frames of 130 octets maximum. The SNDCP provides the segmentation and assembly service to bridge that gap.
Subscriber Identity Module (SIM)	A subsystem defined within the CDPD M-ES. The SIM holds the NEI and its associated authentication credentials. The separation of this function as a separate module allows the possibility of removable modules.
Subscriber Unit (SU)	The Radio Frequency (RF) modem used to acquire the airlink; can be an integral part of the Mobile End System (M-ES) or a separate component.
Supervisory Audio Tone (SAT)	Within the cellular telephone system, to verify that the connection between the base station and cellular phone is functioning properly, the base station transmits a SAT, which is inaudible. The cellular phone, on receiving the SAT, retransmits this tone back to the base station. The SAT tone is used by the base station and the cellular phone to decide if there is interference. If temporary interference is detected, the audio connection is muted briefly, and the listener hears a dropout. If interference is prolonged, the call will be dropped.
support services	Services that are necessary for the provision of other services.
sushi tolerance	Primary requirement/qualification to becoming a member of the specification team. ;-) Kudos to Claude for enduring our prodding and bravely swallowing that oyster!

Switched Virtual Circuit (SVC)   A network connection that provides a fixed circuit only for the duration of a session.

symbol   (1) Six consecutive bits of a Reed-Solomon block forming an element of a Galois field. (2) The instantaneous frequency of a Gaussian Minimum Shift Keying (GMSK) waveform that defines a single bit.

synchronization   The process of achieving a common interpretation of a transmitted bit stream between more than one entity at the same point in the bit stream. Synchronization may be required at each layer of a protocol stack.

synchronization word   A distinctive bit sequence inserted into a data stream to provide a reference marker in a bit stream.

synchronous   The communications method where characters are spaced by time, not by start and stop bits. Synchronous transmission of a message requires fewer bits and less time than asynchronous transmission. Refer to *asynchronous*.

T

T1   (1) A term for a digital carrier facility used to transmit a DS-1 formatted digital signal at 1.544 megabits per second. (2) Transmission rate of 1.544 Mbps on T1 communications lines. Also referred to as digital signal level 1 (DS-1).

TCP   Transmission Control Protocol. A transport layer protocol for the Internet. A connection oriented stream protocol.

TCP/IP   Transmission Control Protocol/Internet Protocol. A set of protocols developed to link computers and data communications equipment across many kinds of networks.

TDMA   Time Division Multiple Access.

TEI   Temporary Equipment Identifier.

Telecommunications Industry Association (TIA)   Standards organization.

telemetry   A communications system for the transmission of short digital or analog data that monitors status information for a remote process, function or device.

Telnet The virtual terminal access protocol used by the Internet. It allows a user at one site to interact with a remote timesharing system at another site as if the user's terminal was connected directly to the remote computer.

Temporary Equipment Identifier (TEI) A temporary identifier assigned to a data link to distinguish it from other data links in a Mobile Data Intermediate System (MD-IS) serving area.

threshold The minimum value of a signal that can be detected by the system or sensor under consideration.

throughput The actual amount of useful and non-redundant information that is transmitted or processed. Throughput is the end result of a data call. Throughput is a measure of the efficiency of a communications link.

TIA Telecommunications Industries Association.

Time Division Multiple Access (TDMA) A medium access control scheme where each member of a device population is assigned transmission slots separated in time.

time-out value Round trip timer value. Determines when a sending system should retransmit data following an extended period of time in which an acknowledgment has not been received.

Tojo Source of inspiration to specification team. We all worked for dinner at Tojo's! Easily selected by the specification team as the best Japanese restaurant in North America. (If you need directions, just ask one of us.)

token ring A type of Local Area Network (LAN). Examples are IEEE 802.5, ProNET-10/80 and FDDI. The term "token ring" is often used to denote IEEE 802.5.

TP4 International Standards Organization (ISO) Transport Protocol class 4.

training Modems include a variety of mechanisms that are intended to reduce errors. Modem protocols, especially those that operate at higher bit rates, include training and equalization functions in their handshake sequences. The purpose of the training sequences is twofold: to allow the modems to negotiate a common method of modulation, and to allow them to equalize their receiving circuitry for variations in signal levels and other parameters.

transmission attempt In the case of the Mobile End System (M-ES) Medium Access Control (MAC) layer entity, it refers to the act of attempting to transmit by sensing the state of the channel.

transmission burst   The sequence of bits transmitted by a Mobile End System (M-ES) in a single access to the reverse channel.

Transmission Control Protocol (TCP)   A connection-oriented protocol that provides reliable end-to-end service. Responsible for ensuring data integrity end-to-end, given that Internet Protocol (IP) is a connectionless protocol.

transport connection   A point-to-point association between two endpoint entities providing reliable sequenced delivery independent of the network or networks used to connect the devices.

Transport Layer   Layer 4 in the Open Systems Interconnect (OSI) 7-Layer Network Layer Reference Model. Transpor Protocol 4 (TP4), Transmission Control Protocol (TCP) and User Datagram Protocol (UDP) reside at this layer. Connection-oriented service provides reliable and transparent transfer of data between cooperating session entities.

Transport Protocol 4 (TP4)   International Standards Organization (ISO) connection-oriented transport protocol class 4.

tunneling   Temporarily changing the destination of a packet in order to traverse one or more routers that are incapable of routing to the real destination. For example, to route through a backbone whose internal routers don't contain entries for external destinations, the entry border router must "tunnel" to the exit border router.

U

UA   User Agent. Also Unnumbered Acknowledgment.

UDP   User Datagram Protocol.

uncorrectable error   An error occurring in a block which has more symbols in error than can be corrected by the Reed-Solomon code.

User Agent (UA)   Related to the messaging supplementary service. A user agent is an application entity that acts on behalf of a user and interfaces to a local message transfer agent. A user agent provides submission and delivery services and other message handling operations such as composing, forwarding/distributing, replying, examining.

User Datagram Protocol (UDP)   A connectionless protocol that provides end-to-end communication with fewer capabilities than Transmission Control Protocol (TCP). Each UDP datagram is handled independently. UDP does not guarantee delivery of data.

V

V.42 bis data compression   Consultative Committee for International Telegraph and Telephone (CCITT) data compression standard. Compresses data on the fly at up to a theoretical maximum ratio of 4:1.

V.42 error correction   Consultative Committee for International Telegraph and Telephone (CCITT) error-correction standard specifying both Microcom Networking Protocol (MNP) 4 and Link Access Procedure for Modems (LAPM). Applies only to full duplex devices.

vertical market   Refer to *vertical market application*.

vertical market application   An application that is industry-specific and typically very task-specific. Including systems for on-line reservations, point-of-sale, utility monitoring, or dispatch services. Such applications have been customized to meet the needs of a specific industry and its particular customers.

vertical market application environment   The environment provided by a Mobile Application Subsystem (MAS) that supports a particular application that is specified in advance and may be customized.

visiting M-ES   A Mobile End System (M-ES) that is capable of supporting service in areas beyond its home area.

W

WAN   Wide Area Network. A network that links a wide geographical area.

wide-area service identifier (WASI)   Unique identifier for a business grouping of licensed facilities-based cellular service providers of Cellular Digital Packet Data (CDPD). It is used within CDPD for access control decisions.

wide-area-network (WAN)   A network that links a wide geographical area.

window segment size   A parameter used to control the flow of data across a connection.

wireless   Communication by means of electromagnetic radiation, particular in the Radio Frequency (RF) portion of the spectrum. Can refer to various technologies for transmitting data, including those used by ARDIS, RAM, or Cellular Digital Packet Data (CDPD).

wireless data network   A radio-based network for data transmission. Cellular Digital Packet Data (CDPD) is an example.

X

X.25   A network-level interface protocol and the underlying Link Layer protocols for connecting to a packet-switching network. Routes packets of data through a network to destination nodes. Used to connect remote terminals to host systems; provides any-to-any connections for simultaneous users.

INDEX

A

Abstract Syntax Notation (ASN.1), 17
Access control, 134, 226
Accessing the mobile network, *See* Mobile
    network access
Accounting:
    CDPD, 120-21
    usage, 247-52
Accounting meters, 250-51
Accounting model, CDPD, 249-51
Acknowledgment, 2
Active threats, 218
Address, destination, 14
Address-Pair Index, 189-90
Adjacent channel interference, 68
Administrative domain, 49-50
Administrative Redirection approach, to mobility,
    29-31
Advanced Mobile Phone System (AMPS), 59,
    69-76, 125
    and CDPD, 98
    cellular operation, 72
    channels, 70-71
    data transmission via, 76-78
    mobile call origination, 73
    mobile call termination, 73-74
    mobility management, 75-76
    Radio Resource Management (RRM), 74
    roaming, 71
Agent, 245
Agent advertisement message, 306
Agent solicitation message, 306
A-Interface (airlink), 108-9, 161-62

Airlink data link protocol, 178-84
    addition of Zap, 181-82
    removal of CRC, 181
    selective reject mechanism, 180-81
    sleep mode, 182-84
Airlink MAC parameters, 175-76
    Max_blocks parameter, 176
    Min_count and Max_count parameters,
      75-76
    Min_Idle_Time parameter, 175
Airlink MAC sublayer, 168-72
    Busy/Idle indicator, 170-71
    Decode Status flag, 171
    Reed-Solomon blocks, 169-71, 177, 181
Airlink physical layer, 162-63
    definition of, 161
    See also Mobile network access
Air True (Air Communications, Inc.), 77
Aloha scheme, 166-67
American Mobile Satellite Corp. (AMSC), 301
American National Standards Institute
    (ANSI), 226
Ameritech, 94, 95
AMPS, *See* Advanced Mobile Phone System
    (AMPS)
Application Awareness approach, to mobility,
    24-26
Application layer, 18
Application program interfaces (APIs), 18, 54,
    102, 291
Applications-enabling protocols, 271-76
    Limited Size Remote Operation Service
      (LSROS), 271

Intelligent network (IN) telephony standard, 83
Interactive Mail Access Protocol (IMAP), 265-66
Inter-area mobility, CDPD, 143-45
Intermediate Systems Confirm (ISC), 138-39
Intermediate systems (ISs), 14
Internal connection handoffs, 83
Internal F-ESs, 116
Internet Drafts, 315
Internet Engineering Task Force (IETF), and
    Mobile IP, 304
Internet protocol (IP), 16, 130, 303, *See* also
    Mobile IP
Internetwork, 34
Interpersonal Message (IPM) UA, 255
Intersystem communications directory, 258
Intra-area mobility, CDPD, 141-43
IP, *See* Internet protocol (IP)
IPM-UA, 255
Iridium, 300
IS-41, 75
ISM band, 51, 280
Isochronous communication, 4

J

Japan, cellular systems in, 83-84
Joint Technical Committee (JTC), 91
JTACS/NTACS, 69

K

Key, 221
Key management, 225-26
Keystream, 234

L

LAPD, 130, 178, 180-81
LAPDm, 82
LEO satellites, 298-99
Limited Size Messaging (LSM), 266-70
    definition of, 267
    how LSM works, 268
    LSM Access Unit, 269
    LSM Message Server, 269

messaging communication stacks, 270
protocols, 269-70
requirements/objectives, 267
Limited Size Remote Operation Service
    (LSROS), 271
Link Access Protocol--D (LAPD), 130, 178,
    180-81
Link-by-link confidentiality, 225
Link protocol data units (LPDUs), 13, 19
Linus Mobile-IP, 314
"Little LEOs," 300
LLC, *See* Logical link control (LLC)
Load Control Transponders (LCTs), 282
Local area network (LAN), 11
Local area network (LAN) shared channel of
    operation, 164
Location areas, 72
Location Directory, 136, 140, 152-53, 155, 157
Logical link control (LLC), 178, 181, 295, 297
Low Earth orbit (LEO) satellites, 298-300
    comparison of, 299
LPDUs, *See* Link protocol data units (LPDUs)
LSM, *See* Limited Size Messaging (LSM)
LSROS, *See* Limited Size Remote Operation
    Service (LSROS)

M

McCaw Cellular Communications, Inc., 93-94
MAHO, *See* Mobile-assisted handoff (MAHO)
Mailbox Service approach, to mobility, 28-29
Major Trading Areas (MTAs), 90, 286
Managed Object Ensemble, 246
Managed objects, 242
Management communication protocols, 242-43
Management Entity (MME), 229
Masquerades, 220, 236
Max_blocks parameter, 176
MCHO, *See* Mobile-controlled handoff (MCHO)
MCI, 77
MDBS, *See* Mobile Data Base Station (MDBS)
MD-IS, *See* Mobile Data Intermediate System
    (MD-IS)
MD-IS Confirm (ISC), 138, 231

(CAC), 252
Home Accounting Collector (HAC), 252
Home Accounting Distributor (HAD), 252
    management, 244
    Serving Accounting Distributor (SAD), 251
User Agents (UAs), 253, 255
User Datagram Protocol (UDP), 17
User-friendly naming, 256
US West, 94

V

V.42bis data compression, 103, 191
Vertical applications, 262, 263-65
    field service applications, 263
    government, 264
    mobile professional applications, 263
    point-of-sale applications, 264
    telemetry, 264
    transportation applications, 263-64
Visiting locations registers (VLRs), 63, 75- 76, 293
    purpose of, 75

W

Wide area networks (WANs), 15
    mobility management in, 123-60
Windowing, 6-7
Window size, 7
Wireless host, 50
Wireless LANs/metropolitan networks, 217-83
    infrared systems, 280
    Metricom Ricochet, 281-83
    narrowband RF systems, 280
    spread spectrum systems, 280-81
Wirelessness, 50-52
    definition of, 23fn
World Administrative Radio Conference
(WARC), 302

X

X.25, 15-16, 83
X.400 (message transport), 102
X.500, 117

X.700, 246
X.700 (CMIP), 102
Xstream Air Network (MCI), 77

Z

Zap frame, 181-82